# COMPARATIVE POLITICS.

SIX LECTURES READ BEFORE THE ROYAL INSTITUTION
IN JANUARY AND FEBRUARY, 1873.

WITH

# THE UNITY OF HISTORY.

THE REDE LECTURE READ BEFORE THE UNIVERSITY OF CAMBRIDGE,
MAY 29, 1872.

BY

EDWARD A. FREEMAN, M.A., HON. D.C.L.,
LATE FELLOW OF TRINITY COLLEGE, OXFORD.

"Facies non omnibus una,
Nec diversa tamen, qualem decet esse sororum."
OVID, *Met.* ii. 13.

LONDON:
PRINTED BY WILLIAM CLOWES AND SONS,
STAMFORD STREET AND CHARING CROSS.

# PREFACE.

THE six Lectures read before the Royal Institution are an attempt to make something like a systematic application of a line of argument which has been often made use of in particular cases both by myself and by other writers. They are an attempt to claim for political institutions a right to a scientific treatment of exactly the same kind as that which has been so successfully applied to language, to mythology, and to the progress of culture. But of course they do not themselves attempt to do more than make a beginning, by applying the Comparative method to some of the most prominent institutions of those among the Aryan nations whose history was best known to myself and was likely to be best known to my hearers. Nothing more than this could well be done in a course of Lectures, even if my own knowledge had enabled me to carry my illustrations over a much wider range. But I trust that others whose studies have lain in other branches of history may be led to take up the subject and to carry it on farther. What I have done may perhaps be enough to show that Greeks, Italians, and Teutons have a large common stock of institutions, institutions whose likeness cannot be otherwise accounted for than by the supposition of their common primitive origin. It remains now to show how much of this common stock is common to the whole Aryan family, how much of the common Aryan stock may be common to the Aryan and Semitic families, how much of the possible common Aryan and Semitic stock may be common to the races of the Eastern hemisphere or to the whole of mankind. On none of these points have I even attempted to enlarge; I have merely pointed them out as questions to which my own inquiries naturally lead up, and which I hope may be thoroughly worked out by some of those scholars who are qualified to take them in hand.

Even within the range of the three branches of the Aryan family which I chose for special examination, the limits and nature of a course of lectures did not allow of anything more than to choose some of the more prominent instances illustrating the positions laid down, and even among these it was of course impossible to follow out any matter in all its bearings. The really practical object of a lecture is, after all, not so much direct teaching as the suggestion of points for thought and study. With this view I have, since the lectures were delivered, added a considerable number of notes and references, in which I have gone somewhat further into several points than I could do in the lectures themselves. These may, I hope, set some of my readers on further inquiries; I can hardly expect that in their necessarily desultory shape they can do much more.

I have no doubt that both in the lectures and in the notes many things will be found which have been already said both by myself and by other writers. Probably many things will be found which both myself and other writers may find occasion to say again, as often as it may be needful to put forth correct views of matters about which popular errors and confusions are afloat. There is a large class of people who pay little heed to a thing that is said only once, but on whom, when it is said several times and put in several shapes, it at last has an effect. I believe that this class is more numerous—its needs are certainly better worth attending to—than those fastidious persons who are disgusted if they are ever called upon to hear the same thing twice. Besides this, the same fact constantly has to be looked at from different points of view, to be used to illustrate several general propositions, to be set before several classes of readers or hearers. I find also that the best and most successful writers are always those who have least scruple in putting forth the truths which they have to enforce over and over again. And I believe that their so doing is one element of their success.

To the six lectures read before the Royal Institution this year I have added the Rede Lecture which I had the great pleasure of being called on to give before the University of Cambridge last year. It was of course written before the Royal Institution Lectures were either written or designed. Without forming part of the same course, it deals with a kindred subject. Both are meant as contributions to the same object, to the breaking down of the unnatural barrier between what are called "ancient" and "modern" subjects in language, history, and everything else. If I should ever see the establishment of a real School of History and a real School of Language in the University of Oxford, I shall feel, not only that the principles for which I have been fighting for years have been put into a practical shape but also that a step has been taken towards the advancement of really sound learning greater than any that has been taken since the sixteenth century.

Since these lectures were written I have fallen in with the work of M. de Coulanges called *La Cité*

# ERRATA.

Page 40, heading, read "Rise and Fall of."
„ 43, *l.* 7, *dele* comma after "own."
„ 65, *l.* 9 from bottom, for "These" read "This."
„ 78, *l.* 10 from bottom, for "any member" read "all its members."
„ 89, *l.* 6, *dele* comma after "done."
„ 95, *l.* 3 from bottom, for "true-city life" read "true city-life."
„ 117, *l.* 6, *dele* comma after "community."
„ 118, *l.* 6, for "must have been" read "was."
„ 162, *l.* 14, for "yet" read "as yet."
„ 191, *l.* 7 from bottom, for "do" read "did."
„ 194, *l.* 5, *dele* comma after "rights:"
„ 202, *l.* 9, for "blood" read "birth."
„ 214, *l.* 3, for "body," read "body of men."
„ 287, *l.* 12, for "extent also," read "extent, also."
„ 311, *l.* 7, for "the" read "an."
„ 334 *l.* 4, for "dare" read "dare to."
„ 352, *l.* 10 from bottom, for "*apostolicum* orbis" read "apostolicum *orbis*."
„ 362, *l.* 6, for "men" read "man."

*Antique*, at least in the English form into which it has been thrown by Mr. T. C. Barker in his book called 'Aryan Civilization.' It deals of course with many of the subjects with which I have dealt, and those which it does deal with, are of course dealt with far more fully than I have done. But the book, notwithstanding its general title, is almost wholly confined to Greek and Roman matters, and deals hardly at all with the kindred Teutonic institutions. Nor can I at all pledge myself to the author's views on all matters, as he seems too anxious to account for everything by reference to a single principle, that of religion. How much I have learned from the writings of Professor Max Müller, Mr. E. B. Tylor, and Sir Henry Maine, may be seen throughout the book. Among foreign writers it will be seen that I have drawn most largely on the great *Deutsche Verfassungsgeschichte* of G. H. Waitz. It should be a matter of rejoicing among scholars that we shall soon have a companion work for our own History from the hands of Professor Stubbs.

SOMERLEAZE, WELLS,
*September* 26*th*, 1873.

# CONTENTS.

# COMPARATIVE POLITICS.

## LECTURE I.

### THE RANGE OF THE COMPARATIVE SCIENCES.

THE establishment of the Comparative Method of study has been the greatest intellectual achievement of our time. It has carried light and order into whole branches of human knowledge which before were shrouded in darkness and confusion. It has brought a line of argument which reaches moral certainty into a region which before was given over to random guess-work. Into matters which are for the most part incapable of strictly external proof it has brought a form of strictly internal proof which is more convincing, more unerring. In one department, the first, perhaps the greatest, to which it has been applied, the victory of the Comparative Method may now be said to be assured. The Science of Language has been placed on a firm basis, from which it is impossible to believe that it can ever be dislodged. Here and there we come across facts which show us that there are two classes of men on whom its truths have as yet been thrown away. There are men whom we cannot exactly call scholars, far less philologers, but who often have a purely literary knowledge of several languages, who seem really never to have heard of the discoveries of modern science, and who go on guessing and dogmatizing as if Comparative Philology had never been heard of. And there are others, a more hopeless but, I believe, a smaller class, who really know what the objects and results of the scientific method are, but who cast them away as delusion, who look on the sure truths of science as dreams and on their own fancies as the only realities. The former class, whom the light has not yet reached, may possibly some day learn; at all events they will some day die out. The latter class, whom the light has reached but who count the light for darkness, will certainly never learn, and most likely they will never die out. Such men are to be found in all branches of study. There are those who have heard all that natural science has to say for itself, but who still believe that the earth is flat or that the moon does not go round on its axis. But the numbers and importance of such men are daily lessening. Some years back there were men whose attainments in some branches of linguistic study were of real importance, but who sneered at the scientific doctrine of the relations of languages as the "Aryan heresy." Such men are most likely no longer to be found. The disbelievers in Comparative Philology, as distinguished from those who never heard of it, seem now to be confined to that class of harmless lunatics who put forth elaborate theories about "Man's first word," or who still believe that the Irish language is derived from the Phœnician. With regard to Comparative Philology the battle is won. No man who has any right to be listened to on such a subject doubts that the doctrine of the relations of language has passed out of the stage of controversies and questions into the stage of admitted truths. There is, of course, still room for difference of opinion as to points of minuter detail; as to the main principle and its leading applications there is none.

Comparative Philology then is fully established as a science. And, as far as this country is concerned, we may fairly say that it was on the spot where I now stand that its claims to rank as a science were established. Other applications of the Comparative Method are later in date, and they have not yet won the same strong and unassailable position. One reason, of course, is that they are later in date, that they have not had so long a time to work their way into men's minds. But this is not the only cause why Comparative Mythology and other applications of the Comparative Method have not won the same complete acceptance from every one qualified to judge which Comparative Philology certainly has won. In no other case—so at least it strikes me—can the application of the Comparative Method be so clear and simple, so utterly beyond doubt or cavil, as it is in the case of language. In the case of language the method is self-convincing. It is hard to conceive that the doctrine of the relations of language, if once clearly stated to a mind of ordinary intelligence, can fail to be received at once. When it is not so received, it can only be because of the difficulty which we all more or less feel when we are called on, not only to learn but to unlearn. The opposition to the scientific treatment of language or of any other subject always comes from teachers who find it hard to cast aside an old method and to adopt a new. It never comes from learners to whom all methods are alike new, and who find the scientific method by far the easiest. That Comparative Philology is sometimes misunderstood, even by those who profess to accept its teaching, is shown by the fact that there are a good number of people who believe that the great result of the scientific study of language is to show that Greek and English are both of them derived from Sanscrit. But this kind of thing will die out of itself. No one who has from the beginning been taught according to the scientific method, and who has never heard of any other, will ever fall into confusions of this kind. And it seems impossible that, with any one whose mind is able to give a fair field and no favour, Comparative Philology can fail to be accepted at once. To many it will come, not as something new, but as the fuller revelation of something towards which they have been feeling their way of their own heads. Every one who has learned any two cognate languages otherwise than as a parrot, must have found out detached pieces of Grimm's Law for himself. When a man has got thus far, and when the complete doctrine and its consequences are set before him, they carry their own conviction with them. We see what kind of words the various Aryan languages have in common, and what kind of words each language or group of languages has peculiar to itself. The inference as to the affinity of those languages to one another, and as to the condition of those who spoke them at the various stages of the great Aryan migration, is one which it is impossible to withstand. Comparative Philology has in truth revealed to us several stages of the præ-historic growth of man for which we have no recorded evidence, but which it makes far more certain than much which professes to rest on recorded evidence. It teaches us facts about which no external proof can be had, but for which the internal proof, when once stated, is absolutely irresistible.

With Comparative Mythology, on the other hand, the case seems to be different. The mere statement of the doctrine does not in the same way carry conviction with it. The phænomena presented by Comparative Philology cannot reasonably be explained in any other way than that in which Comparative Philology professes to explain them. We find, for instance, the word *mill*, or some word evidently the same, used in the same sense in a number of different languages, between some of which the process of borrowing from one another is historically impossible (1). Even in the case of a single word, it would be hard to believe that the likeness was the result of accident. It would be hard to believe that, by sheer chance, without any connexion of any kind with each other, a large number of isolated nations separately made up their minds to call a mill a mill. But when we find the same phænomena, not in one or two words, but in many, the notion of accidental likeness becomes impossible. With such facts before us, there is no withstanding the inference that all those languages were once one language, that the nations which speak those languages were once one nation, and that those nations did not part asunder till they were so far civilized as to have found out the use of mills, and of all other objects the names of which are common to the whole group of languages. But when we find a legend, or several legends, which seem to be common to several distant ages and nations, the doctrine of a common derivation from a common stock is not in the same way the only possible explanation. It may be shown by argument to be the right explanation in each particular case; but the mere statement of the doctrine does not of itself convince us that it must be the right ex planation in any case. The alleged points of likeness between legend and legend will not seem so indisputable to every mind as the identity between two cognate words. Some minds may refuse to see the likeness at all; others may see the likeness, but may hold that it can be accounted for by some other means than that of referring both to a common source. To fall back on our former illustration, the art of grinding corn may have been invented over and over again by any number of independent nations. The point on which the Comparative Philologer takes his stand is that it is inconceivable that, in such a case, they should all have called the instrument of grinding a mill. In the same way some of the simple stories, the obvious characters, the easily imagined situations, which form the staple of the legendary lore of most nations, may have been invented over and over again in distant times and places. There is at least nothing obviously absurd in thinking so; there is no absolute need to account for the likeness by the theory that all must have come from one common source. Comparative Mythology begins to be really convincing only when it can call Comparative Philology to its help. When a name in a Greek legend cannot be reasonably explained by the Greek language, but can be explained by the Sanscrit, the probability that the Greek and the Indian story really do come from the same source comes very near to moral certainty. Yet even here there is room for difference of opinion in a way in which there is not in the case of Philology proper. We are told, for instance, that the *Charites,* the Graces, in the Greek mythology are the same as the *Harits*, the horses of the Sun, in the Indian mythology. The philological connexion of the two names is beyond all doubt; the Greek and the Sanscrit word both obviously come from a common root, from the primitive meaning of which both have wandered very far indeed. But it does not seem to follow that there must be any nearer connexion between the *Charites* and the *Harits* than the general connexion which exists between any two words which come from a common root. Some minds may refuse to see any likeness between the solar horses of the Indian legend and the graceful female forms of the Greek legend. They may be inclined to think that the singular *Charis* of the Iliad, the plural *Charites* of the Odyssey, may be independent creations of the Greek mind, wrought out after the separation of the Greeks and their immediate kindred from the common family. They may deem that *Charis* and the *Charites* are as directly impersonations as *Atê* and the *Litai*; they may deem that they took their name from the noun χάρις, in the later and ordinary sense of the word, after that later and ordinary sense had parted off from the original root. Such a view is at least not obviously absurd, nor is it at all inconsistent with the acceptance of the general doctrine of Comparative Mythology (2). In the case of language, any particular language may develope any number of new words from the old roots; it may adopt any number of new words from foreign tongues. But the invention of a new root in any particular language is a thing which we cannot conceive. As to mythology the case is different. We may allow that there is a great stock of legend common to the whole

Aryan family, or common to all mankind, and yet we may hold that many particular legends, Hellenic, Teutonic, or any other, are due to the independent play of fancy after Hellênes, Teutons, or any other branch of the common stock, had become a distinct people with a distinct language. For my own part, I firmly believe that Comparative Mythology really has brought to light a vast common stock of legend, the groundwork of which is to be found in the physical phænomena of nature. But I must decline to believe that the whole mythology of the Aryan nations, as we find it in Greek and Teutonic literature, has this origin and no other. I believe that a large part of Greek and Teutonic mythology has its source in solar legends. But I must decline to believe that every hero of Greek or Teutonic legend must needs be the sun, save only that small minority who are not the sun but the wind (3).

The difference then between Comparative Philology and Comparative Mythology would seem to be this. Comparative Philology is, within its own range, the absolutely universal solvent: Comparative Mythology must be content to be only one most important solvent among others. To admit this implies no kind of undervaluing of the Comparative Method as applied to mythological subjects. It is still by that method that the mythology of any people must be tested. That method is still the safeguard against all unscientific treatment of the subject—against running, for instance, to Egypt, Phœnicia, or Palestine, for the explanation of particular Greek legends. The scientific method is first to find out what there is in the Indian, Greek, Teutonic and other Aryan mythologies which can be fairly set down as springing from one common stock. When this is clearly made out, we are then in a position to determine what part of the mythology of each people is due to independent invention since the dispersion, what part, if any, is due to importation from non-Aryan sources, Semitic or any other.

Besides Comparative Philology and Comparative Mythology, there is a third branch of knowledge to which the Comparative Method has lately been applied with much success. In truth, as in the case of Comparative Philology itself, this Institution has been one chief means of bringing what may be fairly called a new science into general notice. I mean the scientific inquiry into manners and customs, and the grouping together of the wonderful analogies which they set before us in times and places the most remote from one another. This is an inquiry which follows easily, and almost necessarily, upon Comparative Philology itself. We have seen that, by Comparative Philology alone, without any external evidence of any kind, we can find out a great deal as to the social, political, and religious state of the various branches of the Aryan stock at various stages of their dispersion. We can see that some of the most important steps in the march of human culture were taken while the Aryan nations were still a single people. We can see that other steps were taken independently by different branches of the common stock, after they had parted off from one another. Sometimes we can go so far as to see that some invention or discovery was made by a particular branch, after it had parted off from the common centre, but before it had parted off again into the particular nations which meet us in written history. The evidence of language alone thus gives us a general notion of the amount of advance which had been made by the Aryans before the dispersion. It gives us also the means of tracing in some degree the further advance made by the Eastern and the Western Aryans after the Eastern and Western branches had parted, but while the forefathers of Greeks, Italians, and Teutons still kept together. We can see that further steps were taken by the common forefathers of Greeks and Italians, after they had parted company with the Teutons, but before Greeks and Italians were parted asunder by the Hadriatic. But in this line of inquiry it is to language alone that the Comparative Method is directly applied. The knowledge which it brings to light as to the growth of human culture is most important in itself, and it is established by the most certain of proofs; still it is only an incidental result of an inquiry which has another immediate object. But in the third branch of inquiry of which I am speaking, the Comparative Method is directly applied to the growth of culture itself. The immediate object of research is no longer language, it is no longer legend as legend; it is the customs, the social institutions, the religious ceremonies, of the different nations of the earth into the nature and origin of which the inquirer is now searching. Such a research could hardly be carried on except by one to whom the studies of Comparative Philology and Comparative Mythology were already familiar: linguistic science gives the inquirer help at every step; legendary lore gives him help more precious still; but his immediate object is different from either. He deals with customs and ceremonies, even with legends as they either spring out of or give birth to customs and ceremonies, much as his fellow-inquirers deal with language and with legend looked at for its own sake. He traces the religious rite, the social or domestic order, up to its root, just as his brethren do with words and with legends. He finds perhaps that the custom, civil or religious, has shrunk up into a mere superstition or prejudice, which at first sight seems purely arbitrary and meaningless. It seems arbitrary and meaningless, just as many a word, many a legend, whose history is full of life and meaning to the scientific inquirer, seems arbitrary and meaningless to those who stand without the gate. But, by comparing together the analogous customs of various, often most remote, ages and countries, the scientific inquirer is led up to the root; he is led up to the original idea of which particular customs, ceremonies, and beliefs, are but the offshoots. And in all these cases, as the inquiry can be carried upwards, so it can be carried downwards. Here comes in the doctrine of Survivals (4). It is a fascinating process by which we learn to trace out the way in which a belief, a word, a legend, we might add a grammatical form, survives in this or that phrase or custom, whose origin has long been forgotten, and which, without a knowledge of that origin, seems utterly meaningless. As the Comparative Philologer shows that inflexions and terminations which seem to be purely arbitrary were once whole and living words, having as true a meaning as the root which they now simply serve to modify—as he can trace out a long history of language and of much beside language in the single letter, the mere *Yes'r* and *Yes'm*, to which a short and careless utterance has cut down the once sounding titles of *Senior* and *mea Domina* (5)—as the Comparative Mythologer groups together the utterances of primæval thought on the great mysteries of nature, as he traces them on, through legends of Gods and heroes, down to some feeble echo in the tales of the nursery or the cottage fire-side—so their fellow-worker, the votary of our third science which yet lacks a name, traces out the embodiments of primæval thought in ancient rites and customs; he follows the ancient belief and its utterances down to some faint and forgotten shadow lingering on in some proverbial saying, in some familiar gesture, it may be even in some common article of dress, in some faint relic of any of these kinds which we see or hear or wear or practise every day of our lives, without a thought of the primæval source from which it sprang, or of the long pages of history of which it is the memorial. For this science, I say, the offspring doubtless of the two earlier sciences, but which has fully established its right to rank side by side with either of them, we need a name. Let us hope that a name may be found for it, if not—what may perhaps be hopeless—within the stores of our own mother-tongue, yet at least within the range of the foreign words which have been already coined. It would be a pity if a line of inquiry which has brought to light so much, and from which so much more may be looked for, should end by cumbering the dictionary with some fresh word of new and barbarous formation (6).

This third, as yet nameless, science follows the Comparative Method no less strictly than it is followed by Comparative Philology and Comparative Mythology. But it is still less safe in this case than in the case of Comparative Mythology to argue that every instance of likeness in times and places far away from one another necessarily proves that they are strictly sprung from a common source. When we find either a legend or a custom repeated in this way in distant times and places, we may be sure that there is a connexion between the several instances; but we need not infer that there is the same kind of direct connexion which we infer when we find the Greek, the Teuton, and the Hindoo using the same words and grammatical forms. If we find the same custom, as we often do, at opposite ends of the earth or in ages far away from one another, we need not infer that that custom must have been handed down from a time when the forefathers of the two nations which are found using it formed one people. It may be so; doubtless it often is so. But it may also happen that the custom is in each case an independent invention, the fruit of like circumstances leading to like results. Or it may be that the custom, without being itself in strictness a common possession, may be in each case the offspring of a common idea, an idea common to all mankind or to some one of the great divisions of mankind. Or again it is quite possible that a custom may have been simply borrowed by one nation from another, either while its meaning was still remembered or after it had been forgotten. But, notwithstanding all these chances, the method employed in this form of research, just as much as in the other two, is strictly Comparative. The customs are dealt with in the same way in which the words and the legends are dealt with in the other cases. And all three forms of inquiry stand in a close relation to one another. Comparative Mythology could not get on at all without Comparative Philology; and the science of customs, ceremonies, and survivals bears on both Philology and Mythology at every step. And the three may be ranged in a certain order. Comparative Philology is the purest science of the three: its evidence is the most strictly internal; it makes the least use of any facts beyond its own range; its argument is that which most distinctly carries its own conviction with it. Comparative

Mythology does all this in a less degree; the third nameless science does so in a less degree still. Each depends more on facts which do not come immediately within its own range than Comparative Philology does. Still all three hang together; all are branches of one inquiry; all are applications of one method, of that method the introduction of which marks the nineteenth century, like the fifteenth, as one of the great stages in the developement of the mind of man.

My beginnings have thus far, I fear, been dry and abstract. But I have been anxious to fix the exact relations between the chief subjects to which the Comparative method of research has as yet been applied. It was important for my purpose to do this, as my object in this course of Lectures is to attempt the application of the same method to another subject. Or, to speak more accurately, I should perhaps not so much say another subject as a special and most important branch of that third class of subjects of which I have already spoken. I wish that what I have to say may be looked on as an attempt to follow in the same path as two inquirers both of whom are well known in this place, Professor Max Müller and Mr. E. B. Tylor. With Mr. Tylor's subject I wish specially to connect my own: I should indeed wish that mine may be looked on as a part of his. But, as for the whole, so for the part, it is not easy to find a name. My own subject I wish to speak of as *Comparative Politics;* but I feel that that is a form of words which is not a little liable to be misunderstood. But I may perhaps be allowed to make use of it, after I have explained the sense which I wish the words to bear. In the phrase of *Comparative Politics* I wish the word *Politics* to be taken in the sense which it bears in the name of the great work of Aristotle. By Comparative Politics I mean the comparative study of political institutions, of forms of government. And, under the name of Comparative Politics, I wish to point out and bring together the many analogies which are to be seen between the political institutions of times and countries most remote from one another. In this sense my subject is the more minute treatment of a part of Mr. Tylor's subject, namely those customs, ceremonies, formulæ, and the like, which have to do with the political institutions of different ages and nations. The analogies which may be marked between the most remote ages and countries as to their forms of government, their political divisions, the partition of power among different bodies or magistrates, are far more and far more striking than would come into any one's mind who has not given special attention to the inquiry. In some cases the likeness is seen at the first glance; in others it lies perhaps somewhat below the surface: but it needs only a little thought, backed by a little practice in researches of the kind, in order easily to see the real likeness which often lurks under superficial unlikeness. As in Comparative Philology a small amount of practice teaches the learner to mark connexions between words at which the unlearned are certain to mock, so it is with this study also. The most profitable analogies, the most striking cases of direct derivation, are not those which are most obvious at first sight.

But another warning must be given. In tracing out an analogy or parallel of any kind, points of unlikeness are as carefully to be studied as points of likeness; it is in truth the points of superficial unlikeness which often give us the surest proofs of essential likeness. When we stop to compare, when we mark this and that point of difference in detail, it is the surest proof of a real likeness between the two things which we are comparing. When we stop to comment on the small differences between one human face and another, it is because we recognize all alike as human faces, because we see in all of them that essential likeness which alone enables us to see the points of unlikeness. So it is with the subject of our present inquiry. We are concerned with the essential likeness of institutions, and we must never allow incidental points of unlikeness to keep us from seeing that essential likeness. And this caution is the more needed, because points of likeness and unlikeness which, in their practical results, in their bearings on later history, are of the very first importance, may, in our way of looking at the matter, be purely incidental. I will illustrate my meaning by an example. The English Parliament consists of two Houses: the Assemblies of most other mediæval European states consisted of three or more. The practical importance of this difference has been almost boundless in its effects both on the history of England and on the history of the many kingdoms and commonwealths which have copied the political institutions of England. The peculiar relation of the two Houses of Parliament to one another depends on there being two Houses and not more. The whole doctrine of two branches in a legislature, the *bicameral* system as it is called, the endless attempts, successful and unsuccessful, to set up artificially in other lands what has come to us ready-made through the facts of our history, all go on the principle that there shall be two Houses and no more. Now, if we look to the history of our own constitution, we shall find that this particular number of two, as the number of the Houses of our Parliament, is not owing to any conviction that two Houses would work better than either one or three, but was a matter of sheer accident. The Estates of the Realm are, in England no less than elsewhere, three—Nobles, Clergy, and Commons (7). In France, we all know, the Clergy remained a distinct member of the States-General as long as the States-General lasted. In England the Clergy could never be got permanently to act as a regular parliamentary Estate (8). The causes of this difference belong to the particular history of England; the effects of it are that the Parliament of England remained a Parliament of two Houses only, and that a crowd of constitutions, European and American, have followed the English model. The accident then has, in its consequences, been one of the great facts of later political history; but, in our point of view, it is a mere accident with which we are in no way concerned. How these Estates grew up in nearly every European country is essentially a part of our Comparative inquiry; how it happened that, in one particular country, one of these Estates failed to keep its distinct political being is a matter of ordinary constitutional history. Still less have we anything to do with the questions whether the effect of the accident, that is the particular form of the English Parliament, has been good or bad, or whether the attempts to reproduce the same model in other countries have been wise or foolish. For our present purpose we must throw ourselves into a state of mind to which political constitutions seem as absolutely colourless as grammatical forms,—a state of mind to which the change from monarchy to democracy or from democracy to monarchy seems as little a matter of moral praise or blame as the process by which the Latin language changed into the French or the process by which the High-German parted off from the Low.

For the purposes then of the study of Comparative Politics, a political constitution is a specimen to be studied, classified, and labelled, as a building or an animal is studied, classified, and labelled by those to whom buildings or animals are objects of study. We have to note the likenesses, striking and unexpected as those likenesses often are, between the political constitutions of remote times and places; and we have, as far as we can, to classify our specimens according to the probable causes of those likenesses. For, though the genuine Comparative Method may be as strictly applied to this inquiry as to any of the others, yet in this inquiry it is further off than in any of the others from being the one universal solvent. It is still less safe than in the case of Comparative Mythology to infer that every case of likeness between two political institutions is necessarily to be explained by supposing that both of the two are vestiges of one common stock. There are at least three causes to which likenesses of this kind may be owing, and we must consider to which of the three any particular case of likeness ought to be referred. And, as always happens in such cases, the three classes which we may thus form will be found to some extent to run into one another, and there will be cases about which it may be matter of doubt to which of our classes we ought to refer them.

Thus the likeness between any two institutions, identity of name, identity of nature, or any other point of likeness, may be the result of direct transmission from one to another. And this transmission may take several forms. It may be in the strictest sense a direct handing on from one state of things to another: or it may be simple imitation, in all the various shades which simple imitation may take. Thus it constantly happens that the institutions of a ruling city or country will appear again in its dependencies. They are adopted by or forced upon its subject provinces; they are reproduced as a matter of course in the colonies which it plants with its own citizens. Take for instance, what so long was the greatest dependency of England,—a conquered province if we look to one class of its inhabitants, a colonial settlement if we look to another class,—the so long separate but dependent kingdom of Ireland. In Ireland, as an English colony, the whole machinery of English Government, central and local, was reproduced as a matter of course. The Houses of Parliament, the Courts of Law and their Judges, the Ecclesiastical establishment in all its branches, the local administration under Lords Lieutenant, Sheriffs, Justices of the Peace, and the like, were all simply, as a matter of course, modelled according to the English pattern. Some differences may be found: thus the functions of an Irish Grand Jury are not exactly the same as those of the English body of the same name. But differences of this kind, mere matters of the minutest detail which have grown up in comparatively recent times, in no way affect the general reproduction of the institutions of the mother country in the colony. The English carried their whole system into Ireland; so did the Crusaders carry their whole system into their conquests in the East: the most perfect system of feudal law is to be found in the Assizes of the Christian Kingdom of Jerusalem (9). These cases, which are the types of countless others, are cases of direct handing on of names and institutions from one country to another. It is a process which can hardly be called imitation; it is not so much the framing of something after the model of something else; it is rather the actual translation of the thing itself to another soil. There was most likely no thought about the matter: men who settled in a new land carried with them their own institutions and the names of those institutions as a matter of course. Cases of imitation properly so called are something different. In them men, after thought and debate, choose one model to follow, when they might have chosen another. The imitative work, however closely it may reproduce the likeness of the original, is not the original: it is not even the transplanted original; it is something which has a distinct being and which starts from a beginning of its own. Such are the cases which I have already spoken of, in which the constitution of the English Parliament, a constitution which in England came about as the mere result of circumstances, has been deliberately imitated in other countries. Most of the legislative Assemblies of Europe have followed the English model more or less closely. But the reproduction of English forms in this way is quite another process from their reproduction in Ireland. The difference may be likened to the difference between the real kindred which springs from natural parentage and the artificial kindred which springs from the legal fiction of adoption. And again, wide differences may be marked between different cases of simple imitation. Let me take an instance from the mere use of a borrowed name. There is a *Capitol* at Washington and there is a *Capitol* at Toulouse. In both cases alike the name is used in mere imitation of the Capitol at Rome. I say mere imitation, because it is hardly likely that, even at Toulouse, the name *Capitolium* and the magistracy of the *Octoviri Capitolini* were strictly handed on by direct transmission from Roman days (10). Yet we feel that the name Capitol is in its place at Toulouse in a way in which it is not in its place at Washington. In the second birth of municipal freedom it was natural that the citizens of Toulouse, cleaving to the memories of Rome, her laws and her language, should give to their institutions names borrowed from the old stock. At Washington the name of Capitol was mere imitation, it was the mere calling up of a name which had been dead for ages and with which those who made the new use of it had no direct connexion of any kind. At Toulouse, though I believe the use of the name to be imitation and not direct transmission, yet it is imitation of a kind which differs as little as may be from direct transmission. So again, to take another illustration from the same region, the city of Alby kept its Consuls down to the great French

Revolution (11), and, before many years had passed from that Revolution, Consuls were ruling, not only over Alby but over all France. Both, no doubt, were cases of imitation, yet we feel that for the commonwealth of Alby to give to its magistrates the name of Consuls, in days when the memory of the Roman consulship was still a living thing, was something different from that mere dead imitation of times and things which had utterly passed away which gave the name of Consuls to the elder Buonaparte and his colleagues. We may thus distinguish imitation from direct transmission, and we may see wide differences between different cases of imitation. But, in the whole class with which we are dealing, the names and institutions of one time and place are consciously transferred to some other time and place. A thing which already exists is moved from an old home to a new one; the thing is done openly; there is no mystery about it; the process needs not to be searched out by inference or analogy; it takes its place among the facts of recorded history. The political institutions of one people have been handed on to another people, or they have been purposely imitated by another people. We find analogous cases within the range of the other kindred sciences. Religious beliefs and sacred legends have been spread in the same way. The creed of a conquering people has been spread over its subjects and neighbours, or a people have of their own free will adopted a creed which arose in some distant age and country. Christianity and Islam alike have been spread in both of these ways, by the swords of conquerors as well as by the preaching of missionaries. Open and undoubted connexions of this kind between the religious beliefs of different nations have nothing in common with those subtler connexions which are revealed to us by Comparative Mythology. So too with language itself: a conquered or neighbouring people adopts the language of a more powerful people. Thus the tongues of Greece, Rome, Persia, and Arabia, to say nothing of the tongues of modern Europe, have been spread over vast regions whose nations have adopted the speech of their conquerors or civilizers. Or again, a people, without necessity or compulsion, may adopt, if not the whole language, yet a large part of the vocabulary, of another nation, just as they may adopt the whole or part of its institutions. In this way the purity of our own tongue has given way to a jargon drawn from every quarter of the world, and even our High-Dutch kinsfolk seem to be too ready to follow us in the same evil path (12). Processes like these, which have their place among the recorded facts of history, stand distinct from the no less certain though unrecorded facts which are taught us by Comparative research.

It is for the most part not very hard to know when a case of likeness between political institutions ought to be referred to this first class. The connexion in such cases is for the most part a matter of recorded history or of immediate inference from recorded history. With regard to our second and third classes our course is not so clear: we no longer have recorded history to help us, and it may often be a question to which of the two classes any particular instance belongs. When we find a likeness between the institutions of any two nations, which likeness we cannot reasonably attribute to conscious transmission or imitation during historical times, there are two possible ways in which the likeness may be explained. It may well be that there is no direct connexion whatever, conscious or unconscious, between the two. The likeness may be real and beyond doubt, but there may be no reason to believe either that one people has borrowed from the other, or that both have inherited from a common source. The cause of the likeness may simply be that like causes have, at however great a distance of time and place, led to like results. The institutions of a people are the natural growth of the circumstances under which it finds itself; if two nations, however far removed they may be from one another both in time and in place, find themselves under like circumstances, the chances are that the effect of this likeness of circumstances will show itself in the likeness of their institutions. The same evils will suggest the same remedies; the same needs will suggest the same means of supplying them. There can be little doubt that many of the most essential inventions of civilized life have been invented over and over again in distant times and countries, as different nations have reached those particular points of social advancement when those inventions were first needed. Thus printing has been independently invented in China and in mediæval Europe; and it is well known that a process essentially the same was in use for various purposes in ancient Rome, though no one took the great step of applying to the reproduction of books the process which was familiarly used for various meaner purposes (13). What happened with printing we may believe also to have happened with writing, and we may take another illustration from an art of quite another kind. There can be no doubt, from comparing the remains of the earliest buildings in Egypt, Greece, Italy, the British Islands, and the ruined cities of Central America, that the great inventions of the arch and the dome have been made more than once in the history of human art. And moreover, much as in the case of printing, we can see in many places strivings after them, and near approaches made to them, which still never reached complete success (14). Nor need we doubt that many of the simplest and most essential arts of civilized life,—the use of the mill, the use of the bow, the taming of the horse, the hollowing out of the canoe,—have been found out over and over again in distant times and places. It is only when we find the unmistakeable witness of language, or some other sign of historical connexion, that we have any right to infer that the common possession of inventions of this kind is any sign of common derivation from one primitive source. So it is with political institutions also. The same institutions constantly appear very far from one another, simply because the circumstances which called for them have arisen in times and places very far from one another. The whole system of historical analogies rests on this doctrine. We see the same political phænomena repeating themselves over and over again in various times and places, not because of any borrowing or imitation, conscious or unconscious, but because the like circumstances have led to the like results. To master analogies of this kind, to grasp the laws which regulate the essential likeness and not to be led away by points either of likeness or unlikeness which are merely incidental, is the true philosophy of history. Of the way in which political circumstances and institutions repeat themselves, where no kind of borrowing or imitation can be thought of, many instances will occur to any one who thinks at all upon the matter. Let me take a most striking case from very modern history. It is shown beyond doubt in the writings of the founders of the Constitution of the United States that they had no knowledge of the real nature of the Federal Constitution of the Achaian League (15). But two sets of commonwealths, widely removed from one another in time and place, found themselves in circumstances essentially the same. The later Federal union was therefore cast in a shape which in several points presents a likeness to the elder one, a likeness which is all the more striking and instructive because it was most certainly undesigned. Washington and Hamilton had very faint notions that they were doing the same work which had been done twenty ages before them by Markos of Keryneia and Aratos of Sikyôn; but they did the work all the same. But, on the other hand, the Federal Constitution of Switzerland is a conscious reproduction of the Federal Constitution of America, with such changes as were called for by the different circumstances of the two commonwealths (16). A better illustration can hardly be found of the difference between likenesses which are owing to direct transmission or imitation and likenesses which are simply owing to the law that like causes produce like effects.

We have thus seen that class of likenesses which come of direct and conscious reproduction or imitation, and we have seen the class where the likeness is simply the natural result of like circumstances. But beyond these two lies the third class, the class which forms the more immediate subject of our inquiry, the class of likenesses where there is, on the one hand, no reproduction, no imitation, but, where, on the other hand, the connexion is something closer than that of mere analogy. These are the cases where there is every reason to believe that the likeness really is owing to derivation from a common source. Where nations have been wholly cut off from one another during the historic times, and where there is no affinity of language to make us believe that they are scattered colonies of a common stock, this explanation is not to be thought of. But when we see nations which have been, during the historic times, more or less widely parted off from one another, but which are proved by the evidence of language really to be such colonies of a common stock—when, among nations like these, we find in their political institutions the same kind of likenesses which we find in their languages and their mythology—the obvious inference is that the likeness in all these cases is due to the same cause. That is to say, the obvious inference is that there was a time when these now parted nations formed one nation, and that, before they parted asunder, the common forefathers of both had made certain advances in political life, had developed certain common political institutions, traces or developements of which are still to be seen in the political institutions of the now isolated nations. At the time of the dispersion each band of settlers took with it a common tongue, a common mythology, a common store of the arts of social life. So it also took with it certain principles and traditions of political life, principles and traditions common to the whole family, but which grew up, in the several new homes of the scattered nations, into settled political constitutions, each of which has characteristic features of its own, but all of which keep enough of likeness to show that they are all offshoots from one common stock. To trace out likenesses of this kind, to distinguish those likenesses which really mark the offshoots of a common stock from those which are better referred to either of the other classes which I have distinguished, is the object of the inquiry which I have ventured to call Comparative Politics. Having thus, in this Introductory Lecture, tried to establish the possibility of such an inquiry, its proper objects and its proper limits, I wish to go on, in the Lectures which are to follow, to illustrate the subject in some detail from those political institutions which were common to the races which hold the highest place in the history of mankind. My matter hitherto has perhaps been uninviting: it has certainly been of a kind which carries with it a certain strain on the mind, and which does not allow of any lively treatment. The matter which I have in store for the rest of the course will, I trust, be found of a more attractive kind; and I shall hope that those who have followed me thus far will not refuse to follow me in tracing out the signs of original unity which are to be found in the primitive institutions of the Aryan nations, above all, in the three most illustrious branches of the common stock—the Greek, the Roman, and the Teuton.

## LECTURE II.

# GREEK, ROMAN, AND TEUTON.

We are now fairly embarked on our subject. We are now in a position to trace out all that the Comparative method of inquiry has to tell us of the earliest political state of that branch of mankind to which we ourselves belong. We are now ready to stand face to face with our own immediate forefathers and kinsmen. And, along with them, we are ready to look, with fresh interest and reverence, on those other branches of the common stock — kinsmen themselves, though kinsmen less nearly allied — who went before our own race in holding the first place among the nations of the earth. In the pages of history truly so called — in the records which set man before us in his highest form—the records which do not simply burthen the memory with the names of barbarian Kings, but which teach the mind and the heart by the deeds and words of the heroes of our common nature — the records which set before us, not the physical bigness of Eastern kingdoms but the moral greatness of Western commonwealths—in that long history of civilized man which stretches on in one unbroken tale from the union of the towns of Attica to the last measure of progress in England or in Germany—in this long procession of deeds wrought long ago but whose effects still abide among us, of men whose very memories have often been forgotten, but whose works still live in lands which they never heard of—in this mighty drama of European and Aryan history, three lands, three races, stand forth before all others, as those to whom, each in its own day, the mission has been given to be the rulers and the teachers of the world. The names of those three races were the last words of my first lecture, and the political institutions of those three races, and the relations of those institutions to one another, will be the main subject of my whole course. Their history has ever been the main subject of my own studies; their history I may reasonably suppose to be better known than any other to most of my hearers in this or in any other audience. As the Aryan family of nations, as a whole, stands out above the other families of the world, so the Greek, the Roman, and the Teuton, each in his own turn, stands out above the other nations of the Aryan family. Each in his turn has reached the highest stage alike of power and civilization that was to be had in his own age, and each has handed on his own store to be further enriched by successors who were at once conquerors and disciples. We get our glimpses of all three in times when the light of authentic history is but beginning feebly to struggle through the mists of legend. Yet, even in those earliest glimpses, we see a people who have already risen far above the state of savages, a people who already enjoy the most essential inventions of civilized being, who have already grasped the first principles of domestic and religious life, who have already taken the first steps in the growth of social order, of military discipline, and of civil government. Our first glimpses of history, in its highest and truest sense, show us the land which is at once the border land of Europe and Asia and the most European of all European lands—the land which, above all others, is the land of hills and valleys, of islands and peninsulas, of harbours and inland seas—the land formed by the hand of Nature to be the home of those countless independent commonwealths which were the earliest and the most brilliant, if not the most lasting, of all the forms of man's political life (1). There, in the mother-land of Hellas, the native land of art and song and wisdom, and more glorious still as the native land of law and freedom, we see the Aryan man in the first form in which European history or legend shows him, already possessed of all the needful arts of life, already gathered into organized civil communities, already taught to obey the voice of the elders of his people; but already knowing how, by the shout of applause or by yet more emphatic silence, to teach the elders of his people what the will of the people itself deems good. He has already Kings, but he has also already Assemblies; he has already courts where the man who has suffered wrong may come and seek for right at the judges' hand. Out of the common stock of the common race he has already brought to perfection the noblest forms of the common speech and of the common store of legend; he speaks the tongue of Homer, and bows before the Gods of whom Homer sang. We see him, in these his earliest days, brought face to face alike with kindred tribes and with the worthiest rival of any alien stock; we see him spreading the name and arts of Hellas over all the Ægæan and Ionian coasts (2); here winning island after island from the grasp of the men of Tyre and Sidon (3); here raising his laggard kinsmen of Asia, of Sicily, and of Epeiros, to the level of the brethren who had so far outstripped them in the race (4). We see him, as time rolls on, planting his colonies, each colony a centre of civilized life and political freedom, on all the coasts from the Iberian to the Tauric peninsula (5). We see him in his own land rearing to the service of the Gods or of the State the first buildings, the first painted and sculptured forms, that really deserved the name of art (6). We see him bring to perfection, as in a moment, the living strains of the tragic and the comic muse, and we see him hand down to all who shall come after him the first-fruits of man's political wisdom, the great possession for all time (7). Another act of the drama shows us that a day so bright as this was in truth a day too bright to last; we see the political independence of the nation, both in its own land and in its plantations on foreign shores, die out step by step till its very name has passed away. But it shows us too how, in the well-known phrase, the captive land led captive her conquerors; how the Macedonian who dealt the first blow to her political freedom became the armed apostle of her culture; how he carried her tongue, her art, and her wisdom into lands which the colonists of her days of freedom had never reached (8). And, yet more, we see how the power which was to take her place in the world's annals became her scholar in the act of becoming her conqueror—how, under the Roman sway, Greek became more than ever the common speech of civilized man—how at last the throne of Rome was fixed in a Grecian city—how Greek and Roman came to be words of the same meaning (9)—how the Greek speech and the Greek creed kept its hold on one half of the divided Empire—and how, even under the sway of the Barbarian, that speech and creed have lived on to our own day.

From Greece we change the scene to Italy. Of the three great peninsular lands of Southern Europe, the central one, as compared with the group of islands and promontories to the east of it, forms a solid and compact land, which nature seems to have marked out for a single dominion. And, placed in the midst of that great inland sea whose shores formed the whole civilized world of early times, no other land seems so clearly marked out as the destined home of universal Empire. And so it was: a single city of central Italy made its way, step by step, to the dominion of Italy, and from the dominion of Italy to the dominion of the Mediterranean world. Step by step, the ruling city called in her allies and subjects to share in her own citizenship. A day at last came when York and Antioch not only obeyed a single ruler, but were as truly formed into a single state as were the village of Romulus and the village of Tatius in the first days of Roman legend (10). Greece had won the intellectual dominion of the world by her arts and her philosophy.

Rome won the political dominion of the world by her arms, and kept her hold of it by her abiding Law. For the song of Homer and the lore of Aristotle she had the sword of Sulla and Cæsar, the dooms of Servius and Justinian. Her tongue and her law she has handed on to every later age, and with them she handed on another gift, not, like them her own, by birth, but which she had made no less her own by adoption. The old creeds which had grown and stiffened out of the traditions which were the common heritage of the whole Aryan folk gave way to a creed which arose in a distant corner of Rome's dominion, among a despised people of alien blood and speech. If the Aryan world of Europe has learned its arts and its law from its own elder brethren, it is from the Semitic stranger that it has learned its faith. But before a Semitic faith could become the faith of Rome and of Europe, its dogmas had to be defined by the subtlety of Grecian intellect, the constitution of its organized society had to be wrought into shape by the undying genius of Roman rule. This Semitic faith, banished from its Semitic home, became the badge of Rome's dominion: the sway of Christ and Cæsar became words of the same meaning (11). It was with a true feeling of the doom which was in store for her, that the men of those ages which a shallow view of history looks on as the ages of Rome's decline dared to give the name of Eternal to the city which was then in the childhood of her second life, preparing for a new and mightier dominion over the minds of men (12). Eternal indeed Rome has shown herself in her tongue, in her laws, and in the borrowed faith which, by her own law of adoption, she made her own. But she became eternal by still working out the same law which had been the law of her greatness from her earliest days. Rome became mistress of the world by doing what Athens and Sparta and Carthage had never done, by gathering those whom she had conquered into her own bosom. And she has remained the mistress of the world, because she knew how to carry on the same law in what seemed to be the days of her overthrow and bondage. The spell which she once threw over those whom she conquered she now knew how to throw over those who conquered her: she won the Goth to restore her material fabrics (13), and the Frank to restore her political dominion. The local Rome has fallen from her high estate, but she is the Eternal City none the less. Wherever men speak her tongue, wherever men revere her law, wherever men profess the faith which Europe and European colonies have learned of her, there Rome is still.

We have now come to the third race, to the race of which we ourselves are members, to the predominance of the Teutonic nations, alike on either side of the German Ocean and on either side of the Atlantic. Of that race we may, for the purposes of the present inquiry, boast ourselves as the truest representatives. The boast may be a startling one, but, for the purposes of the present inquiry, it is a true one. In purity of language indeed, our tongue, with the strong Romance infusion which has crept into its vocabulary, cannot compare for a moment with the speech either of our High-German or of our Scandinavian kinsfolk. And, if we would see the ancient Teutonic institutions still abiding in their ancient form, it is not in the Teutonic island but on the Teutonic mainland that we must seek for them. But those well nigh unchanged relics of the earliest times linger on only in a few Alpine valleys. The Landesgemeinden of Uri and Unterwalden are the truest representatives on earth alike of the Germans of Tacitus and of the Achaians of Homer; but they are the Assemblies only of districts, not of nations, hardly even of tribes (14). Among the great nations of modern Europe, our own is, beyond all doubt, the one which can claim for its political institutions the most unbroken descent from the primitive Teutonic stock. The very fact which for so many ages gave Germany the highest place among nations at the same time cut her off from all claim to be the truest representative of the oldest Teutonic days. The Teutonic Kingdom, whose King was also Roman Emperor, was the foremost example of that fusion which has made the modern world; it was the foremost example alike of Roman influence on the Teuton and of Teutonic influence on the Roman. But, for that very reason, it could not be the foremost example of a state whose modern institutions have grown of themselves, step by step, out of the oldest institutions of the common stock. The Scandinavian nations have been even more out of the way of direct Roman influences than ourselves; still they too cannot lay claim to the same unbroken political descent. All honour, all success, to the new-born freedom of those three noble realms; still it is but a new-born freedom, a freedom which has come into being within the memory of living men, a freedom whose foundations could be laid only by sweeping away the encroachments of despotism and oligarchy (15). But, widely as our present constitution differs from the rude traditions and customs of the followers of Hengest and Cerdic, there still is no break between them: all is growth within the same body; there has never been any moment when the old was swept away and the new was put in its stead. Alone among the political assemblies of the greater states of Europe, the Parliament of England can trace its unbroken descent from the Teutonic institutions of the earliest times (16). There is absolutely no gap between the meeting of the Witan of Wessex which confirmed the laws of Ælfred (17), or that far earlier meeting which changed Cerdic from an Ealdorman into a King (18), and the meeting of the Great Council of the Nation which will come together in a few days within the precincts of the home of the Confessor. There are many points in which other lands have kept far greater traces in detail of ancient institutions than we have done; but no other nation, as a nation, can show the same unbroken continuity of political being. In this way we may claim to have preserved more faithfully than any of our kinsfolk the common heritage of our common fathers.

This boast we may truly make; but the very causes which enable us to make it shut us out from any claim to represent the general march of the Teutonic element in European affairs. Britain, like Scandinavia, was a world of its own (19): it was not, like the rest of Western Europe, a Roman land overrun by Teutonic settlers who grew as it were from colonists into conquerors. It is a land which had ceased to be Roman before its Teutonic conquerors set foot in it. Hence we have no true Roman element in us; we have nothing which has lived on uninterruptedly from the days when Severus and

Constantine reigned at York, and when London had for a moment changed its name for that of the Roman Augusta (20). Whatever Roman element we have in us we owe, not to direct transmission from the elder Empire, but to our conversion by Roman missionaries, to our conquest at once by Romance-speaking warriors and by Romance-speaking lawyers, to the spirit of imitation which decked the lords of the island world with titles borrowed from the Cæsars of the mainland (21). In the three homes of our folk, in the oldest England by the Eider and the Slei, in the newer England which we made for ourselves in the island world of Britain, in that newest England of all which is spread over the islands and continents of the Ocean, we have of a truth had our mission, but it has been a mission apart from the mission of our kinsfolk in the general course of European history. On the European mainland the Teutonic conquerors of Rome appear, like the Roman conquerors of Greece, in a character made up of that of conquerors and of disciples. The process was indeed different in the two cases. No Roman ever forgot the name or the speech of Rome, or merged his national being in that of his Greek subjects. But the Teutonic conquerors of the Roman provinces were proud to continue her dominion in their own persons; they were proud to bear the titles of her ancient rule, and step by step to adopt her speech and to forget the land and the race from which they sprang. Never were the three races which have been foremost in European history brought more closely together—never did the magic power of Rome stand forth more clearly—never did she show herself more proudly as the historic centre, binding together the times before her and the times after her—than in the days when Greek and German, Byzantion and Aachen, disputed the heritage and the titles of the dominion which the local Rome had lost, but which was Roman still, into whatever hands it fell (22). Out of the union of Roman and Teutonic elements arose the modern world of Europe. The other races of Europe play but a secondary or a hidden part alongside of them. In Eastern Europe the Slave has played over again, with less brilliancy, the same part which the Teuton played in the West: he too has been half conqueror, half disciple. Bulgaria, Servia, Russia, are to the Eastern Empire and the Eastern Church what the kingdoms of Western Europe are to the Western Empire and the Western Church. The day of greatness of the Slavonic nations is perhaps yet to come. Their early advance was checked, and their progress was thrown back for ages, by a crowd of the most opposite enemies (23); and their revival in later times has placed them high among the rulers of the world, but has hardly placed them among its enlighteners. The other great European race, the race which came before the Teuton as the Slave came after him, the great Celtic race which formed the vanguard of the Aryan march to the West, still lives, still flourishes, still plays a foremost part in the history of the world; but he plays that part under a borrowed guise. The Celt in his own person, speaking his own tongue, lingers only in corners here and there, one degree only more visible than the Iberian whom he dislodged. To fit himself to play a foremost part in the history of Europe, the Celt has had to borrow the garb of two successive conquerors. The Celt of Gaul has wrought many a brilliant page in the history of Europe; but he has wrought it only as one who has taken to himself the name of a German tribe, and who speaks one of the many dialects of the undying tongue of Rome.

Thus much written history would teach us, that these three races, the Greek, the Roman, the Teuton, have played, each in his own day, the foremost part in European history, foremost alike in the arts of war and peace, foremost in literature and philosophy, foremost in the twofold rule over the bodies and the souls of men. But written history by itself could never have told us in what relation those three races stood to one another. That there was something in common between the men of the two great peninsulas, that Greece and Italy were not foreign to one another in the way in which Egypt and Carthage were foreign, could not but force itself on men's minds. But for ages there were no better means of explaining their undoubted likeness than by dreams of primæval and heroic colonists passing from the Eastern peninsula to the Western. Hêraklês, Evandros, Odysseus, passed from Greece to leave their mark on Italy, and the Sabine Numa learned of the Samian Pythagoras the sacred lore with which his infant city was to worship the common Gods of Greece and Italy (24). But that Greece and Italy had aught in common with the Goth, the Frank, and the Saxon, perhaps never came into men's minds, unless indeed we may see some shadows of the great truth in those wild tales which spoke of Hêraklês and Odysseus as leaving traces of their presence by the banks of the Rhine and the Danube, as well as by those of the Tiber and the Arno (25). It is to the Comparative method of research that we owe that greatest discovery of modern science which puts all these facts in their true order and their true relation to each other. From that method we have learned that the three ruling races were but tribes of one greater race, branches of one common stock, detachments of one vast army, some of which reached their destined quarters earlier than their comrades. We see and know the relation in which the three ruling races stand to each other; we see also the relation in which they stand to other members of the great family whose place in the world's history has been less brilliant. It may be that the Celt came too soon, that the Slave came too late, to have any direct share in the work of their brethren; but they are brethren none the less. We can now see the great family in its primæval home, already risen far above the state of savages, furnished already with the ruling thoughts and the main inventions of civilized life. We see men among whom the family life, the social life, has already taken the first and greatest steps, who have already developed the great conceptions of government and religion, who have already learned to build—let us rather say to *timber*—houses, to *ear* the ground, to tame the horse and the hound as their helpers in warfare, either with men of other stocks or with the wild deer of their own woods and wastes, with the bull whose horns have been taught to sound the song of freedom, with the lion whose backward path modern science has mapped out from the caves of

Mendip to the banks of the Strymôn (26). We see the many kindred streams flow off from the common source; one branch has already passed off into the far East, again to meet in far-off ages with their severed brethren, to give worthy foes to Miltiadês and Alexander, to Julian and Heraclius (27), and to give foes, subjects, teachers, and learners, to the founders and rulers of our own realm in the far-off Aryan land. They passed to the land of morning; others took another line of march, as if to follow the great light whose daily course held so deep a sway over their thoughts to his home or his tomb beyond the stream of Ocean (28). And in that great company marched together, not yet parted off into people, nations, and languages, the forefathers of Camillus and of Brennus, of Cæsar and of Vercingetorix. There marched, as yet brethren of one house and speech, the forefathers of Thêseus and Achilleus, the forefathers of Theodoric and Charles, the forefathers of Hengest and Cerdic. And there, carrying as it were the brightest destinies of the world within them, marched the men of whose stock should come the great champions of right and freedom, the forefathers, as yet one in speech and brotherhood, of Kleisthenês the son of Megaklês, of Caius Licinius, and of Simon of Montfort. But after a while they part company. One band leads the van of the westward march, to bear the brunt of the strife against the older tenants of the land, themselves as it were to take their place, to live on in distant islands and peninsulas as isolated fragments of a once wide-spread and unbroken people (29). While the Celtic vanguard presses to the Ocean, two other swarms press towards the shores of the two great inland seas to whose presence it is owing that Europe has not been as Africa, or even as Asia. The Northern swarm lags behind for a while, husbanding its strength for the days when its scattered tribes should gather themselves into the nations of Germany, of Scandinavia, and of England—for the days when offshoots from those main stems should grow into the commonwealths which have guarded the source and the mouth of the great Teutonic stream (30), which have planted a root of freedom even on the dreary shores of Iceland, and which have called into being the mightiest commonwealth of all in the new English land beyond the Ocean. But our own day was not to come till our kinsmen who pressed on, as it might then seem, with a happier lot, to the brighter shores of the southern sea had done their work and had made the way ready for us. Leaving the common centre as an united band, but parting off into two companies at the head of the great Hadriatic Gulf, the forefathers of the Hellênes and the forefathers of the Italians spread themselves over the two peninsular lands where the written history of Aryan man was to begin. They played their part, each branch in its turn; the Western branch entered into the heritage of the Eastern, till the time came when our own race was to enter upon the heritage of both, to become the direct inheritors of Rome, and, through Rome, the indirect inheritors of Greece.

These then are the three great historic races, the races which have played the foremost part among mankind, the races whose history really makes up the political history of man. But striking and instructive as the history of each of them is in itself, it becomes more striking and instructive still when we look on those three races as brethren of one common stock, parted kinsmen who shared a common heritage which they knew not of. And there are moments in the history of the world when not only these three races, but all the European branches of the great family seem as it were gathered together, sometimes to do battle against a common enemy, sometimes, as it were, to meet at the hearth of that abiding power which might well pass for the common centre of them all. We read a casual notice that Frankish and English ambassadors found their way to the court of Justinian, and the utmost that we feel is a kind of languid curiosity, awakened by one of the very few times when the name of our nation in its earliest days is to be found in the pages of writers who still spoke the tongue of Greece (31). But when we think that those Frankish and English ambassadors represented the two great branches of the Teutonic race, that they brought with them, if not the homage, at least the awe and wonder, of the conquered Celtic lands of Gaul and Britain—when we think that the prince to whose court they went was himself a kind of triple-bodied Gêryôn, a Roman Cæsar of Slavonic birth, reigning in a Greek city over all lands from the Ocean to the Euphrates (32)—it would seem as if representatives of every European branch of the common stock had been gathered together beneath the roof of the man who gave the world the abiding gift of the Imperial Law. Or take another instance, not this time from a peaceful gathering, but from the field of battle. On the field of Châlons every European branch of the Aryan family seemed to have sent its contingent to the host which was to drive back the Turanian invader. Side by side, equal in might and dignity, emblems of the world that was passing away and of the world that was coming in its stead, marched Aëtius and Theodoric, the Roman and the Goth. But the Roman came from the Illyrian land by the Danube; the Goth ruled over Celt and Iberian on either side of the Pyrenees (33). And around their banners gathered the Frank and the Saxon, representatives of the two great branches of the Teutonic race, along with the Celt from his Armorican peninsula and the Sarmatian from the furthest European home of the common family (34). One name alone is wanting. Greece and Macedonia sent no help against a foe in whose presence they might well have remembered that Xerxes and Darius were their kinsmen. All that the eldest brethren of the house could give was the Hellenic-sounding name borne by the Patrician who led the hosts of Rome to their last victory.

Those days were the true Middle Ages, the days when the Roman and Teutonic elements of modern European life stood side by side, not as yet wrought together into the whole which was to come of their fusion. And the history of those wonderful ages gains a fresh life if we remember that when Alaric led his host from the walls of Athens to the walls of Rome (35), he was marching through the lands of men of the same primæval blood and speech as his own. And now what had those scattered brethren in common? What, above all, had the three great races in common, the Greek, the Roman, the Teuton? For those three must, as I have already said, form the main subject of our inquiry. Their own importance is higher than that of any other race: I who have taken the matter in hand am better able to deal with them; you who hear me will most likely be better able to judge of what I say, if I keep myself for the more part within the limits of the races which hold the foremost place in European history. For the more part, I say, not exclusively. While keeping our main attention fixed on these three races, I shall still freely, as occasion may serve and as my own knowledge may allow me, draw illustrations from other branches of the Aryan family, and even from nations which stand outside the Aryan pale. In an inquiry of this kind, which as yet is purely tentative, it is well to draw our illustrations from as wide a range as may be. The points of likeness between the primitive political institutions of the various Aryan nations are beyond doubt, but we meet with striking likenesses also among nations which are not Aryan. These facts suggest that we should very carefully examine every case of likeness, that we should see as well as we can to which of the three causes of likeness which I traced out in my former lecture it may most safely be referred. One of those three causes,—that of direct transmission, whether taking the form of conscious imitation or not,—may be pretty well laid aside while dealing with the primitive institutions of any nation. Men who are in the state in which any of the Aryan nations were at the time when we get our first glimpses of them are not likely to borrow institutions from any foreign source, except when they come in contact with nations in a state of civilization out of all comparison with their own. The Celt of Gaul was not likely to adopt the manners or institutions of the Iberian, nor was the Iberian likely to adopt the manners and institutions of the Celt. But both stood ready to be moulded by the manners and institutions of the Greek colonists of Massalia or of the Roman colonists of Aquæ Sextiæ (36). It is absolutely certain that the primitive Greek, the primitive Teuton, and the primitive Italian did not borrow from one another. We may even be certain that the different tribes of the three races did not borrow from one another—that the Ionian did not borrow from the Dorian, the Latin from the Oscan, or the Frank from the Saxon. But, setting actual borrowing of any kind aside, it requires close examination in each particular case to say whether the likeness between the institutions of any two given tribes or nations is due to the actual sharing of a common heritage or to the like working of like circumstances in different times and places. Even between two

Aryan races, even between two tribes of the same Aryan race, it is not always safe hastily to decide that the likeness must be due to one or other of these causes. Greater caution still is needed when we come to likenesses between Aryan nations and nations of another stock. We shall presently see that the Old Testament, to go no further, furnishes us with several cases of striking likeness between Hellenic or Teutonic institutions and the institutions of the primitive Semitic tribes. Is such a likeness as this, not indeed accidental but incidental? Is it due simply to the working of like circumstances bringing about like results? Or are we to suppose that, beyond the common heritage of the Aryan nations, there is a wider common heritage in which Aryan and Semitic nations share alike (37), or even a wider heritage still, common to all mankind? I will not venture to decide dogmatically in favour of any of these alternatives. I do not think that the time has come in which it is safe to decide dogmatically in favour of any of them. In an inquiry which is still only in its infancy, it is safer to mark such cases for further examination, but to leave their full explanation till the inquiry itself shall have reached a further stage. With our present amount of knowledge, the wisest course is to collect instances from all quarters, to classify them so far as we have the means of doing so, but not to be hasty in such classification, not to be disheartened if there are many instances which we have to leave unclassified altogether.

In carrying out our inquiry as to the connexion between Primitive institutions, we may apply nearly the same rules as those which have been suggested in the case of Comparative Mythology. It is not safe to set down any instance of likeness as being necessarily a case of an inheritance from the common stock, unless we have some corroborative evidence besides the likeness itself. We have the highest degree of such corroborative evidence whenever Comparative Philology steps in to help us. If two distinct nations of the Aryan family—or, by the same argument, if two distinct nations of any other family—have a common institution called by a common name, and if the likeness is plainly not a case of imitation or borrowing from one another, such an institution may be set down without any kind of doubt as being a clear case of common inheritance from a common stock. But the negative argument the other way is by no means equally strong. The caprice of language is so great, words drop out of use in one tongue and are kept in use in another in such a singular way, that the mere fact that cognate institutions are not called by cognate names is not of itself proof that they are not part of a common heritage. We must weigh all the circumstances and all the different forms of evidence. Of all the forms of corroborative evidence, the philological form is doubtless the highest, but it is not the only one. If two nations are shown by other evidence, especially by philological evidence applied to other subjects, to be kindred nations, holding in common a large share of the primitive common stock—if the nature of their political institutions, no less than of their language, their mythology, their customs of other kinds, naturally suggests the thought of a common derivation—the mere fact that their institutions do not bear cognate names is not enough to disprove, or even to throw doubt upon, the common derivation of those institutions. In many, perhaps in most, cases we shall find that the kindred institutions bear names which are not philologically cognate, but which translate one another, sometimes in a very remarkable way. The institutions are the same; the names are not the same; they may not even come from a common root; but they are the names which most closely answer to one another in meaning in a later stage of the two languages. This is in truth exactly what we might look for. The common stock of language which the undivided Aryan family possessed in common—even the stock which its European branches possessed in common after their separation from the Eastern branch — was, in the nature of things, a vocabulary of the simplest kind, a vocabulary consisting mainly of nouns expressing the most familiar objects and verbs expressing the most familiar actions. Words expressing objects or processes which are at all complicated or abstract belong to a later stage. Those each nation has formed for itself; it has formed them out of the old common roots, but it has formed them each for itself, and after its own fashion. Now this argument specially applies to the names of political institutions. We may believe that the primitive Aryans, before their separation, had already taken the first steps in political life; that they had already developed a simple form of government, traces of which are still to be found among the scattered members of the common family. That such is the case, or is likely to be the case, is the ground-work of the whole of the present inquiry. But, though we may believe that the Aryans before the dispersion had worked out for themselves something which we may fairly call common political institutions, we cannot believe that they had worked out for themselves any refined or exact political vocabulary. The political stock which the scattered brethren carried off with them at the dispersion must have consisted of a few acknowledged customs, a few acknowledged simple principles; but their dictionary of political terms must have been short. They may have had—I firmly believe that they had—among them the germs of monarchy, of aristocracy, and of democracy, but they certainly had not names for those abstract ideas. It was each nation working for itself after the dispersion, which worked for itself, out of the common stock of principles and customs, such more elaborate political forms as suited its own circumstances. And for those forms it devised names out of its own vocabulary as it stood at the time. In this way, while we fully believe that there is a common political heritage belonging to the whole family, yet it is in no way wonderful, it is rather what we should in every way expect to happen, that each nation should have a political vocabulary of its own. That is to say, most of the names of particular officers and the like in each particular nation were independently given by each nation in the particular language into which the common speech had by that time grown among them.

And now let us illustrate all this by examples taken from the political history and political nomenclature of the three great races of which we have mainly to speak. In future lectures I hope to draw out more fully in detail how, as far as we can go back, by the help of history or legend, into Hellenic, Italian, or Teutonic antiquity, we find in all alike the germs alike of the monarchic, the aristocratic, and the democratic principles of government. That union of the three which Tacitus thought, if possible, could not be lasting, seems in truth to have been a common Aryan heritage—possibly a heritage of all mankind (38). In later times conscious attempts have been made, or, without any conscious attempt, men have been led by the circumstances in which they found themselves, to devise forms of government after this model. In so doing, as in so many other cases, they have often, wittingly or unwittingly, fallen back upon the earliest models that were to be found. There is one form of government which, under various modifications, is set before us in the earliest glimpses which we get of the political life of at least all the European members of the Aryan family. There is that of the single King or chief, first ruler in peace, first captain in war, but ruling, not by his own arbitrary will, but with the advice of a council of chiefs eminent for age or birth or personal exploits, and further bringing all matters of special moment for the final approval of the general Assembly of the whole people. I am far from saying that this form of government is peculiar to the Aryan nations; but I wish to deal with it first of all as something which seems to be common to all the Aryan races, and which is undoubtedly common to the three great races with which we are chiefly concerned. It is the form of government which we see painted in our first picture of European life in the songs of Homer; it is found alike in the realm of the King of Men at Mykênê and in the realm of the King of Gods and Men on Olympos. It is the form of government which tradition sets before us as the earliest form of that ancient Latin constitution out of which grew, first the Commonwealth and then the Empire of Rome. It is no less the form of government which we see in the first picture of our own race drawn for us by the hand of Tacitus (39), and in the glimpses given us by our own native annals of the first days of our own branch of that race when they made their way into this island in which we dwell. Differences of detail may easily be marked in the different forms of the common constitution, as it appears in each of the three great races and even at different times and among different tribes of the same race. The titles of the chief ruler, the manner of his appointment, the range of his powers, differ in different cases. With these differences of detail I shall have to deal in my next Lecture. I have now only to speak of the common element in all. And in all, I think, we shall see the same general system of the single head of the state, the smaller Council, and the final authority of all, the general Assembly of the whole people. And, when the likeness is so close between the three branches of this great family which cannot possibly have borrowed their institutions from one another in later times, but which remained together as one people till a late stage of the general dispersion of the Aryan nations, the presumption surely is in favour of the belief that political institutions which are so strikingly alike are in truth a common heritage, a primæva form of government under which the forefathers o Greeks, Italians, and Teutons lived together, before Greeks, Italians, and Teutons had parted off into separate nations. This presumption may be met by the objection at which I have already hinted, namely, that the several powers of the State, analogous as their form and powers may be, are not, as a rule, called by cognate names in the three languages, Greek, Latin, and Teutonic. But, if I have suggested the objection, I think I have also answered it beforehand. I think that the diversities of name are exactly what we ought to expect. Each race carried away certain general principles of government from the common stock; but the details of each particular constitution, still more the details of its political vocabulary, were worked out by each nation for itself, or rather by each tribe of each nation for itself, in times long after the dispersion. At all events, the points of likeness and unlikeness between the early political vocabulary of the three races form a part of our subject, and it is with some inquiry into them that I purpose to fill up the rest of the space which is left me to-day. We shall find few or no cases in which the actual names of any office are akin in the three languages; but we shall find that most of them can be traced up to common roots, and that there are several cases in which names, though they are not cognate with one another, yet most certainly translate one another.

Let us begin with the familiar names of the chief of the State in the three languages. It is plain at first sight that the words *βασιλεύς*, *Rex*, and *King* are not words of common origin. Nor is the matter mended if, instead of those three familiar names, we use older or less usual names in each of the three languages, if we take the older or poetic Greek title *ἄναξ* (40), or if for the comparatively modern title of *King* we take the older *Thiudans* or *Drihten.* But the fact that *Cyning, King,* in all its forms, is a comparatively modern title, is an important point in the argument. It shows how offices which were substantially the same were called by different names at different times, or by different branches of the same race. The Gothic *Thiudans* and the English *Cyning* must have expressed an office substantially the same, because the Latin *Rex* and the Greek *βασιλεύς* translate both of them. The names are in no way kindred in origin, but they are closely kindred in meaning: *Cyning* from *cyn* and *Thiudans* from *thiuda*, each called after the *kin* or people, pretty well translate one another (41). We thus find two nations so nearly allied in speech, though so widely cut off in history, as the English and the Goths, nations about which we can hardly doubt that their institutions came from a common source, calling the head of the people by names which in both cases meant the head of the people but which are in no way philologically akin. There is, then, no need to be surprised if, among branches of the Aryan family which are less nearly akin, we do not always find cognate offices called by cognate names. We shall rather be surprised to find in how many cases the names are cognate. The Latin *Rex* and the Teutonic *Cyning* have nothing in common in their names; but, if we go one step beyond the titles borne by the men themselves, we shall find that the *regnum* of the one is the same thing as the *rice* of the other; if we say of the one that he *rexit*, we say of the other that he *rixode* (42). We may go further East and

West, and find the same name in the Celtic both of Wales and Ireland, and in the far-off Sanscrit (43). We then see that both the idea of government and this particular root to express government had borne fruit in the Aryan mind, not only before the Latin had parted off from the Teuton, not only before the Celt had parted off from both, but before the great separation had happened between the European and the Asiatic branches of the great family. It is therefore owing merely to one of the accidents of language that, while Latin and English had a cognate noun and a cognate verb to express the kingly office, Latin had, and English had not, a cognate noun to express the King himself. And if the comparatively modern forms, both of English and of High-German, give us no cognate name for *Rex*, we have in the older Gothic the form *Reiks*, which, if it does not strictly translate *Rex* and *Cyning*, is not very far removed from them in meaning (44). If then we find these traces of common origin in Latin, Teutonic, Celtic, and Sanscrit, we may be sure that the absence of any such analogies, at all events of any such palpable analogies, between races so much more closely allied as the Greek and the Latin, must be a mere caprice of language, though a strange one indeed. I say no such palpable analogies, because I leave it to stronger philologers than myself to say whether any kindred may lurk between ἄρχειν and *regere*. However this may be, it is at least plain that the most obvious words, ἄναξ and βασιλεύς, are in no way akin either to *Rex* or to *Cyning*. But, whatever may be the origin of those names, there is nothing wonderful in each tribe calling its particular officers by names of later formation in its own language. That the words *Rex* and βασιλεύς should be quite distinct is no more wonderful than that the names given by different Italian and different Greek tribes to other closely allied officers should be wholly distinct also. Latium has its *Prætors* and *Dictators*, Samnium has its *Imperators*, while Rome has *Prætors*, *Dictators*, and *Imperators* all at once. The only difference—a difference of no importance for our purpose, though of great importance in a strictly philological view—is that *Prætor*, *Dictator*, and *Imperator* are all words of easy formation in Latin, while βασιλεύς has plenty of Greek derivatives, but, as far as we can see, no Greek cognates. So the Assembly is in old time the ἀγορή; at Athens it is the ἐκκλησία; at Sparta it is the ἁλία. But the Spartan name appears again at Athens as the name, if not of the popular Assembly, yet of the popular court of justice (45), and, by that cycle which in so many ways binds together the last and the first days of independent Greece, the ἀγορή which we have seen among the Achaians of Homer appears again among the Achaians of Polybios (46). The Greek γένη and the Latin *gentes* are palpably the same in name as well as in substance; but the φρατρίαι and φράτορες of Athens have in their political use no Latin cognates, though we see in them the missing Greek cognates of the names of kindred, *brother* and *frater* (47). So the Athenian βουλή answers to the Spartan γερουσία; but now mark that the Spartan γερουσία translates the Latin *Senatus*. Mark too, that the aristocratic order at Athens and at Rome are respectively the ἱππεῖς and the *Equites*, words which have a philological connexion in the far-off kindred of ἵππος and *equus*, but which in their actual shapes are distinct and comparatively late formations (48). A whole flood of analogies now pours in upon us. The γερουσία and the Senate are kindred institutions, institutions which, one can hardly doubt, are really part of the common heritage. But the analogy of the names is simply a case of that kind of analogy which springs from like causes producing like effects. In an early state of society, age implies rule and rule implies age; this is taught us by a whole crowd of words in all languages. From the Elders of Midian and the δημογέροντες of Ilios, we have not only Spartan and Roman Senators, but πρέσβεις, ambassadors, whose name of age has passed into a name of office: we have Christian *Presbyters* and

English *Ealdormen*; we have the long string of names which spring from the mediæval use of *Senior* (49), *Monseigneur, Monsieur, Sire, Sir,* and endless others. And, to end as we have begun, beyond the Aryan fold, we have the *Sheikhs* of the Arab, and among them the most famous of his class, the Old Man of the Mountain (50). So again the ἱππήλαται of Homer, the ἱππεῖς of Athens, the *Equites* of Rome, appear again in the *Caballeros,* the *Cavalieri,* the *Chevaliers,* of Romance Europe, and in the *Ritterschaft* of the Teutonic mainland. Here again the names are simply analogous. Wherever, as always will be in an early state of society, there is no professional army, but an armed nation serves without pay, if such an army uses horsemen as part of its force (51), that force is sure to be made up of the noble and wealthy: *cavalry* and *chivalry* will be the same. In the later days of Rome the *Equites* ceased to be a military body; but in after ages, when the same state of things came again, new words were made, no longer from the now obsolete *equus,* but from the word *caballus* which had taken its place. In Germany again the same causes again called forth the word *Ritter,* and its English equivalent comes into use in the later years of our national Chronicle, when King William dubs his son Henry to *rider* (52). No such title is heard of in the earlier days of England. The Thegn, the Ealdorman, the King himself, alike fought on foot; the horse might bear him to the field, but when the fighting itself came, he stood on his native earth to receive the onslaught of her enemies (53).

All these are instances of the way in which, especially in so young a form of research as this, we must ever walk warily, and most carefully distinguish cases of likeness which there is every reason to believe are really owing to inheritance from a common stock, and cases where the likeness is simply the likeness of analogy, the effect of like results springing from like causes. We have seen how much is proved by the presence of cognate names of offices, how little is proved by its absence. Our preliminary work is now over. We have defined the nature of our method; we have traced out the limits within which it will for the present be wise commonly to confine its application. In the following lectures I shall try to grapple with the leading analogies to be found in the great institutions of the three races with whom we have mainly to deal. In my next lecture I purpose to deal with the State itself, with the primitive conception of the commonwealth, as we see it in our first glimpses of Greek, Roman, and Teutonic political life. I shall thence go on to the head of the State, the King, and to its body, the Assembly. And the course may well be wound up with some instances of special analogies in the institutions of the three races, all helping to show, on the one hand, how truly human nature is one; how, without regard to races and times, men are by like circumstances moulded to like forms; and, on the other hand, to show how great is the common heritage which the tribes of the common family bore away from their primæval home, how many are the signs of ancient brotherhood, which, notwithstanding distance of place and time, notwithstanding mutual ignorance and mutual hatred, may still be traced among them.

LECTURE III.

## THE STATE.

In my two former lectures we have, I trust, seen somewhat of the general nature of that common political heritage a share in which probably belongs to every member of the great Aryan family, and most certainly belongs to each of its three most illustrious branches. Our earliest glimpses of the life of our forefathers and kinsfolk set them before us as already gathered together in organized societies, as having already developed the first principles of political government, and, what is more, as already showing the germs of the three great forms of political government,—as showing the germs of monarchy, of aristocracy, and of democracy. Wherever we find, in however rude a shape, the King or other chief, the Council of elders or nobles, and the general Assembly of the people, the substance of all three is there. Nor must we in this matter be led away by mere names. The first element, that of the King or other chief, may remain after the kingship in the ordinary sense has been abolished, just as the forms and titles of kingship may remain after the real kingly power has passed away. The aristocratic element again, the Council, may or may not take the form of an hereditary body. Aristocracy, I need hardly say, in its strict sense, is the rule of the best: indeed aristocracy would be the rule of the ideally best, those who are really wisest, bravest, and most upright. Any other standard, be it that of age, of birth, or of wealth, is simply a substitute which is accepted because, in an imperfect world, the rule of the ideally best is something which may be talked about, but which will never be found in actual being (1). In the most conservative society of men that ever was, the community which never wholly abolished any one of its ancient institutions, in the Commonwealth of Rome, we see how both the kingly and the aristocratic elements of the State, in the common sense of those words, might be swept away without at all sweeping away the substance of either the kingly or the aristocratic power. Personal kingship was swept away, but the kingly power was not swept away: it was simply put into commission, entrusted to two men for a year, instead of to one man for life (2). Afterwards, as the needs of the State called for such a change, it was further divided among various magistrates of various ranks, but to all of whom some portion of kingly dignity still clave (3). So again, when, as the monarchy had changed into a commonwealth, so the commonwealth changed into a monarchy, the change was not made by abolishing old offices, or by creating new ones, but by gathering all the offices of state into the hand of a single man. As the separation of the various duties of the King created the various magistracies of the Commonwealth, so in turn the union of the various magistracies of the Commonwealth created the Emperor (4). So with regard to the aristocratic branch, the object of all popular movements at Rome was, not to abolish the Senate, not even greatly to lessen the powers of the Senate (5), but to break down the distinction of old and new citizens, and to throw the Great Council of the Commonwealth open to any member. In this way the three powers went on, though the hands which held them might be changed. The kingly power went on, though there was no longer a personal King; the aristocratic power went on, though it was no longer confined to a particular order of the Commonwealth; and thereby for two glorious centuries Rome came nearer to being aristocratic, in the literal sense, than any other government that the world ever saw. If the rule of the best was ever reached in any political community upon earth, it surely was in the commonwealth which strove against Hannibal and overthrew him. If there ever was a time when the ideal picture of the poet was to be found on earth, the time when

> "None was for a party,
> When all were for the state,
> When the rich man helped the poor,
> And the poor man loved the great,"

that time was surely to be found in those brightest days of the Roman Commonwealth, when the elder distinctions of patrician and plebeian had passed away, and when the later distinctions of rich and poor had not begun to show themselves (6). The great idea of the State, the City, the Commonwealth, the great whole in and for which each of its members lived and worked and fought and died, had never reached to greater sway over the minds of men than in the long struggle between the first of cities and the first of men. Thus it was shown that the very greatest of men, in the single strength of the wisest head, the stoutest heart, and the strongest arm, was, after all, a power less mighty than the enduring strength of an united people (7). To show how the idea of the State—that is, in those days, the idea of the City—could rule men's heads and guide their actions, I might find examples equally to the purpose in the history of other commonwealths, in democratic Athens or in oligarchic Venice. But

Rome stands out above all, because in no other commonwealth did the three primitive elements of government live on so long side by side, with changed forms indeed, but with the strength of all three undiminished. Among the ranks of her own citizens, Rome had in those days no elements of weakness: every citizen had his place, and knew his place, and did his work in his place. Her one element of weakness lay without her walls, in that she was a city ruling over other cities (8). But here, as in all history, and as pre-eminently in Roman history, the good and the bad, the strong and the weak sides, spring from the same source, and can hardly be separated from one another. The noblest and the vilest deeds of the true Roman went hand in hand. To Rome, to the State, to the whole of which he was but an unit, he was ready at any moment to sacrifice himself and all that he had; and to the State, to which he was ready to sacrifice himself, he was no less ready to sacrifice all that came in the way of the greatness of the Roman Commonwealth. To Rome he would sacrifice the laws of eternal justice, the rights of other nations and commonwealths, the very faith of treaties, and what we should deem the truth and honour of Rome herself.

The State then, in what is in some sort the highest conception of it, is a City; and it can hardly fail to be a City bearing rule over other cities. Now the conception of the State as a City is far from being the earliest conception of the State; still it is one which has much in common with the earliest conception of the State as opposed to the conception of it which now prevails in modern Europe. The modern conception of the State is a Nation. It is perhaps not very easy to define a Nation; still the word conveys an idea which, if not always very accurate in point of philosophy, is at least practically intelligible. Whatever else a nation may be or may not be, the word suggests to us a considerable continuous part of the earth's surface inhabited by men who at once speak the same tongue and are united under the same government. Anything differing from this strikes us as exceptional. Thus Switzerland and Scotland give us examples of nations, which we feel to be nations, but which are formed by the artificial union, through the circumstances of their history, of parts of three adjoining nations which have parted off from their natural brethren and have found adoptive brethren among strangers. On the other hand, in North America we see, in the United States and the adjoining dominions of the British Crown, a continuous territory inhabited by men speaking the same language, but who, being separated from one another by the circumstances of their history, no longer feel themselves to be members of the same nation. By a process analogous to the Roman law of adoption, that law by which a man might artificially become a member of a family to which he did not belong by birth, those parts of the German, Burgundian, and Italian nations, which have joined together to form the modern Swiss nation, and those parts of the Irish, English, and British nations which have joined together to form the modern Scottish nation, have cast away their original nationality and have made for themselves a new one (9). But the Publius Cornelius Scipio who finally overthrew Carthage was, Æmilius as he was by birth, as good a Scipio as the elder Publius who had given Carthage her death-blow at Zama. And so the artificial Scots, the artificial Switzers, have formed a nation as real and true as if it had been a nation strictly answering to some linguistic or ethnological division. And, in the other case, the events which have caused the English settlers north and south of the great American lakes to part off into two distinct nations have the character of a family quarrel, which, because it is a family quarrel, is harder to heal than a quarrel between strangers. But we feel that all cases of this kind either way are exceptional cases, accounted for by exceptional causes; the normal nation is one where the continuous speakers of a single tongue are united under a single government; such a nation forms the ideal of a State, whether kingdom or commonwealth, which forms the ground of all modern political speculation.

Now this fact that we expect, as a rule, the nation to form a single government—the fact that political unity enters into our general idea of a nation—shows how greatly we have changed in this matter from the political ideas of earlier times. Take Greece for example. There was in the Greek mind a distinct idea of a Greek nation, united by a common origin, speech, religion, and civilization. Every Greek was a brother to every other Greek, as contrasted with the outside Barbarian (10). But that the whole Greek nation, or so much of it as formed a continuous or nearly continuous territory, could be united into one political community, never came into the mind of any Greek statesman or Greek philosopher. The independence of each city was the one cardinal principle from which all Greek political life started. The State, the Commonwealth, was in Greek eyes a City, an organized society of men dwelling in a walled town as the hearth and home of the political society, and with a surrounding territory not too large to allow all its free inhabitants habitually to assemble within its walls to discharge the duties of citizens. During the most brilliant times of the Greek Commonwealths, the City, and nothing higher or lower, was the one acknowledged political unit. A scattered tribe was not enough, an unwalled village was not enough; while, on the other hand, no Greek of those days willingly merged his city in any greater aggregate (11). And the higher was the civilization, the fuller was the political developement, of any branch of the Greek nation, the stronger was the feeling with which it clave to the full political independence of every separate city. The feelings which we bear towards the Nation, the Greeks bore towards the City (12). We have heard in modern times of "oppressed nationalities"—a form of words which, I suppose, means much the same as oppressed nations. That form of words implies that such nations are wronged by being put under a government which is not of their own nation. With exactly the same feelings did the old Greeks look upon those cases in their own political world when it was not nation that was subject to nation, but city that was subject to city. For one city to bear rule over another was common enough, when one city was stronger and another weaker; but such a relation was always deemed to be unjust, at all events in the eyes of the weaker city. And in such cases it was always, in the strictest sense, city bearing rule over city; the subject city still kept on its being as an organized political community, and it therefore felt only the more keenly the loss of its full political independence (13). The theory of the independence of each city, the universal doctrine of Greece, was, though as we shall presently see in a very modified form, the political doctrine of ancient Italy also. The feeling has affected language in a way which makes it hard to represent some familiar Greek and Latin expressions in any modern speech. Πατρίς, *patria*, may often be well enough translated by *country*, *patrie*, *Vaterland*; but the true *patria* of the Greek or the Roman was not a country in our sense: it was not Greece but Athens, it was not Italy but Rome, which was the *patria* of the Athenian or the Roman (14). Scipio at Liternum was held to be in exile as much as if he had banished himself to Spain or Syria. And when Tiberius removed his dwelling from Rome to Capreæ, men wondered that a Roman citizen, a Roman prince, could so long "carere patria;" a phrase which, if we translate it "to be without a country," sounds strange indeed when applied to one who had simply moved his dwelling from Rome to an island off the coast of Campania (15).

But the idea of the City, on the face of it, marks in truth a very advanced state in the political developement of any people. If we look at the history of

Greece only, we shall find abundant signs that that political life of the city which comes out with such brilliancy in the days of the Persian and Peloponnesian wars, and which was already fully established in the days of Homer, was far from being the earliest social condition of the Greek people. The thing in fact hardly needs proof: it needs no evidence to show that a wandering tribe cannot build cities, nor is it likely that men should gather themselves together in political societies within walled towns till they have been long accustomed to the practice of agriculture and of life in settled dwellings. As the settled village is an advance on the wandering tribe, so the walled city is an advance on the unwalled village; its origin is often to be found in the hill-fort which formed the rude citadel of the village, the primæval fortress where men and cattle might seek shelter in case of a sudden inroad of their enemies. The hill-fort might itself grow into the city, as so many ancient Gaulish hill-forts have grown into ancient Roman and modern French cities (16), or as the greater Athens of later times gathered round the holy rock of Athênê, once itself the city, but now its venerable Akropolis (17). Or again, as population grows and civilization advances, the hill-fort may be wholly forsaken for some more tempting site in the plain; as when the lofty Dardaniê made way for holy Ilios, the city of articulate-speaking men (18). Greek city life could not have existed as long as the forefathers of the Hellênes were slowly making their way from the head of the Hadriatic gulf down to the peninsula of Attica and the great island of Pelops (19). The point is that even the first rudiments of Greek city life could hardly have come into being till the Hellênes had long been in possession of the peninsular land between Mount Olympos and Cape Malea. The Homeric poems contain passages which seem to contrast the social state of the Achaian princes and people with other races, at least not wholly alien, which were still on a lower social level (20). It is worth noticing too that the familiar word δῆμος, the people, seems to have first of all meant the ground, and thence to have been transferred to the inhabitants or tillers of the ground (21). This change of meaning could hardly have taken place after city life was fully established. And side by side with the greatest developement of the later meaning of the word, side by side with the Athenian Dêmos himself, we see the local divisions of the land, which still bore the same name, witnesses of the time when Dêmos had meant the land itself, and not those who dwelt upon it (22). But other proofs show that the state of society which we see in the Homeric poems succeeded, no doubt by gradual stages, to one far less advanced, which still left traces of itself in historic times. In historical times the cities are everything; treaties and leagues were, in the more advanced regions of Greece, made only between city and city. But the most ancient of common Greek institutions, the great religious union of the Amphiktyons, was not an union of cities. Athens and Sparta, as Athens and Sparta, had no part or lot in it. The Amphiktyonic body was an union of races, races some of which had risen to greatness in other parts of Greece, while others remained in their ancient obscurity in their old seats by Thermopylai. In that great religious convocation, the Dorian and the Ionian race had each its equal vote alongside of Malians and Phthiôtic Achaians. Athens and Sparta, as severally the greatest Ionic and the greatest Dorian city, might practically command the Ionian and the Dorian vote; but, as the cities of Athens and Sparta, they had no formal place in the Council. This feature in the Amphiktyonic body, a feature which could not possibly have been introduced at any moment in the recorded history of Greece, at once shows the vast antiquity of the Amphiktyonic union, and it also shows that the system of cities with which we are so familiar in Grecian history grew out of an earlier system of tribes (23). So again, even in the historic times of

Greece, we find that there were large districts, Ætolia, Akarnania, some parts of Arkadia, in which city life was very imperfectly developed, where walled towns at special points were not unknown, but where the city had not wholly swallowed up the tribe and the village, in the way in which it had done, in the lands of Athens, Corinth, or Bœotia (24). We find also in the historic times more than one instance in which a Greek city—Elis for example, and Megalopolis in after times—was formed by the union of several villages, or of towns so small that they hardly deserved the name of cities (25). And we see too, in the case of Mantineia and of Sparta itself, a tradition so strong that it can hardly have been groundless, which told that those cities had themselves been formed in a like sort, in days which must have been older than the Homeric catalogue (26). So again, in those neighbouring nations which were not strictly Greek, but to whom the true Hellênes seem to have stood in the relation of members of the same family who had outstripped their brethren, among Epeirots and Macedonians, we find much the same state of things as in the ruder parts of Greece itself: the city is not unknown, but the tribe and the village still remain the leading features of national life (27). We might have inferred without historical evidence, from the very nature of the case, that the Greek system of cities grew out of an earlier system of tribes and villages, but there is in truth quite enough of strictly historical evidence to prove the point.

The system of cities was thus, even in Greece, far from being a thing which had been from the beginning. But it became, as we all know, the great characteristic of Grecian politics, the feature to which Greece owes at once the brilliance and the shortness of its history. For the city, according at least to Greek political ideas, kept on one feature of the life of the tribe, even more strictly than it was kept on by the tribe itself. The City, the State, the commonwealth, was an assemblage of γένη, of *gentes*, of natural or artificial families. Citizenship was thus a matter of hereditary descent: mere residence, even to the ninth and tenth generation, could never confer the civic franchise (28). Once or twice in the history of a city, when the original citizens had shrunk up into a narrow oligarchy, a large admission of the unenfranchised classes to the rights of citizenship might change the commonwealth from an oligarchy into a democracy (29). Now and then too citizenship might be bestowed by special decree on a stranger, whether a resident on the spot or a distant prince who had deserved well of the commonwealth (30). But there was no way by which the necessary extinction of citizen families could be, as a matter of ordinary course, supplied by new blood. A Greek city might hold other cities in bondage; she might have other cities united to her on terms of either equal or dependent alliance; but the breaking down of the citizen barrier, the admission of allies or subjects to a common franchise, was, we may say, unknown in the historical times of Greece. It had been done once before history began, when all the Attic towns were either persuaded or constrained to merge their political being in that of the one city of Athens (31). It was tried once in historical times, in a feeble and unsuccessful way, when the commonwealths of Argos and Corinth were for a moment thrown into one (32). But, as a rule, through the most brilliant days of Greece, each city clave to its separate political being. The higher the political developement, the higher the material and social civilization of any Grecian city, the more fervently, the more obstinately, it clave to its distinct and independent being as a sovereign commonwealth. It might be a ruling city, and it never dreamed of granting its citizenship to its subjects; it might be a dependent city, and it dreamed perhaps of throwing off the yoke of its too powerful neighbour, but never of asking for its franchise.

From this cause sprang two results. Greece never

became, in any political sense, a nation. And those parts of Greece which, in her latest days of independence, came nearest to becoming a nation were not those parts which had filled the foremost places in her earlier and more brilliant days. In the last, the Federal, age of Greece the parts of Greece which showed the fullest national life were precisely those more backward districts where Greek city life had never developed itself in its fulness. Ætolia, Akarnania, even the hellenized Epeiros, now show a truer national life than Athens. But in those later days one great step in political progress was taken. The Federal principle had hitherto lurked in Greece only in the parts where either city life was hardly developed at all, or where the cities were small and of little account in Grecian politics. It had long bound together the fierce tribes of Ætolia and the respectable but insignificant towns of the original Achaia (33). It now became the leading principle of Greek politics. The greater part of Greece was mapped out among Federal commonwealths. But the greatest cities of the olden time kept aloof from a system which so greatly trenched on the separate independence of each particular city. Athens never joined the Achaian League; Sparta was enrolled in it against her will (34). In these last days of independent Greece a new form of political life arose. But it was simply a developement or modification of her old system of independent cities. The cities gave up so much of their independent political being as to group themselves into Confederations, to let several cities form a single State in their dealings with other States. But the Confederation was still a Confederation of cities. The internal constitutions of the cities remained untouched. Each still remained a distinct and sovereign commonwealth in all its domestic affairs. The form of a Federal Commonwealth, a *Bundesstaat* (35), and that a Federal Commonwealth formed, not of tribes or cantons but of cities, was the nearest approach to national unity to which the most advanced parts of Hellas in the days of her independence ever reached.

Here then is one idea of the State: that in which the State, the Commonwealth, the body in which a man enjoys political rights and discharges political duties, the body round which all his patriotic feelings centre, is not a nation, not a country in our sense, but a single city. There is no doubt that such a system as this calls forth the powers of man to their very highest point; there has never been another political society in the world in which the average of the individual citizen stood so high as it did under the Athenian Democracy in the days of its greatness. The weak point of such a system is that it is too brilliant to last; the high-strung enthusiasm to which it owes its being, and without which it cannct be kept up at the same level, is not likely to last for many generations (36). Again, such a system can last only as long as it forms the whole of its own civilized world. Where the strength of a country is cut up among a number of absolutely independent cities, indifferent or even hostile to one another, they must give way as soon as an united power of equal strength and equal intelligence is brought to bear upon them. Greece drew increased strength, and even increased union, from the attacks made upon her by the brute force of Persia: she could not bear up against the single power of Macedonia, schooled in her own arts and discipline. The lesson did its work in the revival of Greek independence in the Federal period. But even then the degree of union that was reached was simply Federal, and even that degree of union was never extended over the whole land. Greece never became a nation: a people whose idea of political life does not go beyond the separate and independent city never can become a nation; it never can endure when the forces of a nation are brought against it. But it none the less shows the powers of man in a higher form than they can reach under any other system; and, although the system itself is one which cannot last in its full force and glory through more than a few generations of men, its history is none the less rich in abiding lessons for all time.

From the idea of the State as the single independent city, the idea which gave all its brilliance to the peninsula east of the Hadriatic, we turn to another idea of the State, or rather to a modification of the same idea, which was worked out in the political history of the other great Mediterranean land. Italy, no less than Greece, was from the earliest times parted out into small commonwealths, or rather it was occupied by distinct settlements, clans, or tribes, which grew into distinct commonwealths. The idea of the independent city may be said to have been the leading political idea of ancient Italy, no less than of ancient Greece, but it was never carried out in the same completeness. We must set aside that part of Southern Italy which was in after times directly colonized from Greece, and the history of whose Greek cities is simply a part of the history of the Greek cities elsewhere. In that much larger part of Italy which was untouched by Greek colonization, though the walled city seems to have been everywhere the ideal political unit, yet true-city life, according to Greek notions, never reached the same complete predominance. From the beginning the towns were smaller, and they were more ready to join themselves together by a Federal tie. There never could have been more than a very few Italian cities, and those scattered at distances as great as that which separated Rome from Capua, which could have had any claim to rank alongside of the great cities which in Greece lay as near together as Thebes, Athens, Corinth, Sikyôn, and Argos (37). Hence the history of ancient Italy is a history of confederations, far more than a history of single cities; and the Italian confederations had from the beginning a closer union and a nearer approach to national unity than the later and more brilliant confederations of Greece. Latium, Samnium, and the rest, had more in common with Ætolia and Akarnania than with the more strictly civic confederation of the Achaian League. The real elements of old Italian life are the *gens* or clan and the tribe. The city is rather the fortress, the place of meeting, the place of shelter, of the tribe or collection of tribes, than the actual home and dwelling-place which it was in Greek ideas (38). At the same time it was in Italy that the idea of the city, the single independent city—the ruling city—was carried out on a scale in which it never was before or after. A group of Latin villages grew together to form a border fortress of Latium on the Etruscan march (39). That border fortress grew step by step to be the head of Latium, the head of Italy, the head of the Mediterranean world. The idea of the city—the ruling city—gathering around it the various classes of citizens, half-citizens, allies, and subjects (40), all looking to the local city as the common centre, whether of freedom to be exercised or dominion to be endured, all this finds its greatest and mightiest developement in the Latin city of Rome. Rome alone among cities can rightly call herself eternal; but she won her eternity by casting off, more than any other city ever did, the trammels which narrowed the greatness and shortened the life of the other ruling cities of the world. The course by which Rome rose to her dominion was set forth by one of her own Cæsars in her own Senate; it was by granting, step by step, equal rights with her own alike to faithful allies and to conquered enemies. Claudius argued, with thorough insight into the history of the state over which he ruled, that the dominion of Athens and Sparta had been short, because they had failed to grant their citizenship to their allies and subjects; that the dominion of Rome had been lasting, because the allies and subjects of Rome had been freely allowed to become Romans. The plebeian, the Latin, the Italian, each in his turn, had been admitted to the rights and honours of the conquering city. From Italy, so Claudius argued, the same process should go on to Gaul and Spain;

and so it did go on till, when the franchise of the Roman city had become nothing worth, all the free inhabitants of the Roman world were admitted to it (41). But mark that it was to the franchise of the Roman city, to the local burghership of a single town, that Latium, Italy, and the world, were gradually admitted. They were admitted to a body of exactly the same nature as the hereditary burghers of an old Greek or a mediæval Italian city, to a body essentially the same as the freemen of a modern English borough. We may, in a sense, say that a city grew into a nation, or into more than a nation, when its citizenship was thus extended to the whole of the then civilized world. Still it was the local franchise of a city; it was a franchise which, as long as it remained any real franchise at all, could be exercised nowhere except in that city (42). The result was that, long before the world had become Roman, even before all Italy had become Roman, the municipal government of the Roman city had been tried and found wanting as the government of so large a part of the world. The constitution which, for its own proper use, had been one of the best that the world ever saw—a constitution all the better because it grew up bit by bit as it was wanted—broke down when it was put to an use for which it was utterly unfitted. The burghers of a single Italian city could not govern the whole world; they could not even govern Italy. They could not even administer the affairs of their own city, when they themselves were numbered by hundreds of thousands. The despotism of the Cæsars was the stern remedy for an incurable disease. As regards the city itself, if, as Mæcenas thought, life even in torments is better than death (43), the disease was a smaller evil than the remedy. As regards the subject lands, they gained by getting one master instead of many. The moral of Grecian history is that a system of independent cities cannot bear up against an united kingdom or commonwealth. The moral of Roman history is that, if a single city aspires to universal dominion, it may indeed become the seat of a power which deserves to be called eternal, but it can become mistress of the world only by the sacrifice of its own freedom. The distinction between citizen and subject may be swept away; but it will be swept away, not by raising the subject to the level of the citizen, but by bringing down the citizen to the level of the subject.

We thus see that, though Greece and Italy alike took the independent city as their leading political idea, the results which were worked out were widely different in the two cases. The earlier and fuller establishment of the Federal principle in

Italy, the greater readiness in communicating the franchise to allies and subjects, both worked to the same end. And I suspect that both of these were different results of the same cause, and that that cause was that the clan feeling, the tribe feeling, had by no means so wholly given way to the city feeling as it did in Greece. The truth is that, if we read history as chronology requires us to read it, beginning with Greece, thence going on to the Roman conquerors of Greece, and thence to the Teutonic conquerors of Rome, we are, for many purposes of this inquiry, reading history backwards. We find the primitive conception of the State in an earlier form among the Italians than we find it among the Greeks, at all events than we find it in those Greek states of which we have most knowledge. And we find it in a still earlier form amongst the Teutonic nations than we find it among the Italians. The notion of the State as a city is, as we have seen and as it must be in the nature of things, a later notion than the notion of the State as a tribe. We have seen that, even in some parts of Greece, the notion of the city—the ruling idea of fully developed Greek political life—grew but slowly, and never bore the same fruits which it bore in the great Greek city commonwealths. Among the Teutonic nations we may fairly say that the city commonwealth never became an essential element of political life at all. The conception of the absolutely sovereign city commonwealth is not a strictly Teutonic conception; it has never been the ruling political idea of any Teutonic people. The Greeks reached the city stage so early, they carried out its leading idea to such perfection, that they never reached the national stage. The Teutons passed from the tribal stage into the national stage without ever going through the city stage at all. The Italians followed an intermediate course; they reached the city stage, but they never carried it to the same perfection to which it was carried in Greece. The older ideas of the clan and the tribe kept far more power; down to the latest days of Rome's freedom they exercised an influence which they lost at a far earlier stage of Athenian political history.

To trace out the difference in this respect between the history of the three chief races which we are comparing, we must go back to the very beginnings of political life. The Greek philosophers themselves saw that the original element of the State—of the City—was to be found in the family. But they perhaps did not attach its full importance to the stage which comes between the family in the narrower sense and the political commonwealth (44). The great practical element in all early political societies is the family, but it is the family, not in the narrower sense of the mere household, the father and his immediate children, but in the form which the family takes when it has swelled into the clan. The clan may take many forms: it may long keep up the wild independence, the predatory life, the attachment to the hereditary chief of the race, which distinguishes the Celtic clans and septs both in Britain and in Ireland (45). In a higher stage it may take the shape of the agricultural village community, such as we see it in forms common to the Aryan races both in East and West (46). The two things in short, the clan and the village community, are the same thing, influenced only by those circumstances, geographical or otherwise, which allow one clan or company to adopt a more settled life, while another is driven to linger in, or even to fall back upon, a ruder state of things. The γένος of Athens, the *gens* of Rome, the *mark* or *gemeinde* of the Teutonic nations, the village community of the East, and, as I have said, the Irish clan, are all essentially the same thing. All are parts of the common heritage; all mark a stage in progress which is essentially the same, although the further developements of each have branched off into such widely different shapes. In each case, the community thus formed is the lowest political unit—it is the association next above that of the mere household. It does not stand immediately below the tribe, as we find between them the intermediate association of the *hundred* or *curia*. Still, the tribe on the one side, the clan or *gens* on the other, stand out in such a much more marked way than the intermediate group that we may venture to say that, as the commonwealth, whether city or nation, is formed by an union of tribes, so the tribe is formed by an union of *gentes*.

The names γένος and *gens* at once proclaim that community of blood is the idea which lies at the root of the association so called. We have no English name which exactly expresses the same idea (47); but the local nomenclature of our own land makes it plain that this lowest political unit was at first, here as elsewhere, formed of men bound together by a tie of kindred, in its first estate natural, in a later stage either of kindred natural or artificial. A large proportion of the parishes of England bear names which come directly from old Teutonic patronymics. Uffington, Gillingham, a crowd of others—the same name not uncommonly repeating itself in distant parts of the country—point beyond all doubt to the Uffingas, the Gillingas, and so forth, as their original Teutonic settlers (48). These names answer exactly to those borne by the *gentes* of Athens and Rome, to the Alkmaiônidai and the

Julii, and to those borne by the clans and septs of the Scot both in his own island and in Britain (49). In all these cases the name is strictly a patronymic; the race is called after a supposed forefather. But in none of these cases are we bound to look for actual kindred among all the members of the body (50). Still it is none the less true that the idea of the family runs through all. The family is the starting-point: the common patriarch, divine or human, real or mythical, Alkmaiôn, Julus, Offa, Donald, is the tie which binds together all the members of his house, whether really sprung of his blood or not. The adopted son, the freedman, the client, the favoured stranger, might be received in their several degrees within the pale of the house, so that real purity of blood would become a mere name, a simple legal fiction (51); still it was into the house, the *gens*, the clan—that is, into the family, to its name, its rights, its sacred ceremonies and traditions (52)—that he was admitted. Both at Rome and at Athens the *gentes* were joined together into a higher union, that of the *curia* or the φρατρία—that is, the brotherhood, the name which still so strangely preserves the common Aryan word which the Greek tongue has lost in its older and nearer meaning (53). The gathering of *curiæ* or φρατρίαι again forms the tribe; the gathering of tribes forms the State. But alike at

Rome and at Athens, tribes formed of *curiæ* and *gentes* lost their political significance, and gave way as political institutions to tribes of later origin founded on another principle. In the later stages of both commonwealths, the elements of which the commonwealth was made up were no longer the primitive genealogical tribes, but tribes which were essentially local. But the smaller groups of which the tribes were immediately made up, the *gentes* and the groups intermediate between the *gentes* and the tribes, still lived on, though, by one of those accidents which are to be found in all these histories of political growth, it happened that the element which kept most of its importance differed in the two cases. In the later stages of the Athenian commonwealth we hear far more of the φρατρία than we do of the γένος. At Rome the *curiæ* sank into a mere name at a comparatively early stage, while the *gentes* remained and flourished, and had the most abiding influence on the national character and the national history.

At Rome then the influence of the family community was far stronger, far more lasting, than it was at Athens. One cause of this difference may seem a small one. There can be little doubt that the fact that the *gentes* of Rome survived longer and played a greater part in history than the Greek and Teutonic unions which answer to them is largely owing to an accident of Roman nomenclature, though we cannot doubt that the apparent accident had itself some determining cause. Megaklês the Alkmaionid, or Godric the Uffing, remembered and boasted of the name of his real or mythical forefather, but he did not bear it about with him as part of himself, as his *nomen* to which his own personal name was only a *prænomen*, in the way in which the names of the patriarchs of their house were borne by Titus Quinctius or Caius Julius (54). But other causes were doubtless also at work. There can be little doubt that the genealogical associations at Rome drew much of strength and permanency from the fact that they were, more largely than at Athens, local associations also. No fact in what we may call mythical history seems better established than the tradition that the city of Rome grew out of the union of two or more village communities. So, as we have seen, did many Grecian cities, Sparta itself among them (55). But at Sparta the origin of the ὠβαί—the Spartan *curiæ*—and tribes is not to be looked for in the old Lacedæmonian local divisions, but in the divisions which the Dorian conquerors brought with them and which they established in all the Dorian cities of Peloponnêsos. These tribes, common to the Dorians everywhere, together with the ὠβαί of which they were formed, lived on as divisions of the ruling Spartan people, alongside of the local divisions earlier than the conquest, just as, both at Athens and Rome, we find the local tribes either supplanting or existing alongside of the tribes which were purely genealogical (56). At Athens, if the city was formed by the geographical union of earlier villages—a process which must not be confounded with the political union of the towns of Attica—it must have been at a time so early as to have left no trace of itself either in legend or in tradition. A prying eye may perhaps find out some slight and doubtful traces of inhabitants of the soil earlier than the historic Athenians, but they will hardly find traces of the fusing together of neighbouring and kindred villages (57). We find at Athens the four Ionic tribes, common probably to the Ionians everywhere; but we have no such local memories as those which connect the Ramnes with the village of Romulus and the Titienses with the village of Titus Tatius (58). Add to this the feeling of which I shall have to speak in another lecture, the strong conservative feeling which runs through the political revolutions of Rome in a far higher degree than through those of Athens. It thus came about that the old Ionic tribes at Athens were swept away as political bodies, and that the φρατρίαι and *gentes* lived on only as family brotherhoods and religious associations, no longer as component members of the commonwealth. The ancient genealogical tribes gave way to the later tribes of the constitution of Kleisthenês, tribes which were mere artificial divisions, and which had no real tie either of descent or of locality. The Ten Tribes were indeed made up of *δῆμοι*, and the *δῆμοι* were doubtless, in the strictest sense, village communities; but care was specially taken that the *δῆμοι* which made up a tribe should not lie geographically together (59). For such a change there were good reasons in the political experience of the time; but the substitution of a new local division for one purely genealogical marks a great revolution in men's ideas, and shows how far real statesmanship could prevail over mere traditional memories (60). The Dêmos often bore the name of the Gens (61). Still in the later political arrangements of Athens the Gens had passed utterly away, and the Dêmos was not itself a political unit, but a mere local division of a new local tribe.

At Rome, on the other hand, the commonwealth, both in its earlier and its later form, was made up of tribes which were essentially local. Such, we can hardly doubt, were the old Patrician tribes which represented the original communities of which the city itself in its first estate was made up. The settlement of Romulus and the settlement of Tatius, that is the tribes of the Ramnes and the Titienses, occupied two distinct hills among the famous seven (62). It is more certain that the new Roman people, the *Plebs*, was made up from the beginning of strictly local tribes; it is certain that, as the State grew, it grew by the addition of fresh local tribes. When a new town or district was enfranchised, its territory formed a new tribe; and of the thirty-five tribes of the later commonwealth the local city of Rome contained four only (63). And the local tribe too, like the Attic δῆμος, was often closely connected with the clan (64). And though the δῆμος, as an element of the State, was essentially a local division, yet, as the δῆμοι were in their origin *gentes* or village communities, it was quite possible that, at the time when the δῆμοι were mapped out, the δῆμος might nearly answer to some *gens* and its following. And in the like sort, though the δῆμοι and the new tribes were local in their origin, yet, when once established, they became genealogical. So it was with the local Roman tribes also. Their names show that they too were often connected with a *gens*, and the connexion is marked in a special way in one case which has been preserved to us either by history or by tradition. When Attus Clausus and his following moved to Rome, they formed the Claudian tribe as well as the Claudian *gens*. But the Claudian tribe had not, like an Attic Dêmos, sunk to be a mere local division ; it was a component part of the Roman commonwealth, with its independent vote in the Assembly of the Roman tribes. Through all these causes, the ideas which were at the root of every commonwealth—the ideas of the clan and the tribe—lived on at Rome with far greater strength, and with a far closer connexion with the political life of the commonwealth, than they kept at Athens. But, because the ideas of the clan and the tribe remained more lively, the idea of the city was less perfect. The Roman commonwealth was a city commonwealth, because the city of Rome was the one heart and home of the State. But, in this like Athens, though unlike every other Greek city, the life of the commonwealth was not shut up within the walls of the city. Rome was a city commonwealth; we cannot call it a mere city commonwealth, when the City itself had little more than a ninth part of the voting power of the State—four votes only out of thirty-five. In all these ways the conception of the city was less perfect at Rome, less perfect in Italy generally, than it was in Greece. For that very reason the political system of Rome was more long-lived than that of Greece. Rome never, in strictness, became a nation; but it came far nearer to becoming a nation than either Greece as a whole or any particular Greek commonwealth.

We now come to the institutions of our own forefathers and kinsmen—to the primitive conceptions of the State as held by the nations of the Teutonic race. Our own early history is the true key to the early history of Greece and Italy. Among the ancient Germans and Scandinavians, and not least among the Teutonic settlers in our own island, we see many things face to face which in Greece and Italy we see but darkly; we see many things for certain which in Greece and Italy we can only guess at; we see many things still keeping their full life and meaning, of which in Greece and Italy we can at most spy out traces and survivals. It is among the men of our own blood that we can best trace out how, as in Greece and Italy, the family grew into the clan—how, as in Greece and Italy, the clan grew into the tribe—and how at that stage the developement of the two kindred races parted company—how among Teutons, on either side of the sea, the tribe has grown, not into the city but into the nation. But, before I try to work out this comparison and contrast in any detail, I would first speak of two facts which strongly illustrate the different political and social ideas of those two great branches of the Aryan family, the Greek and the

Italian on one side, our own forefathers on the other. I choose two facts, two formulæ, two fashions of speech, standing out on the surface of those transitional ages when the Roman and the Teutonic system stood side by side. They will show how utterly unlike from one point of view, close as is their likeness from another, are the political ideas and manner of speech of those in whose minds the city is everything, and of those with whom the city is unknown or secondary, with whom the tribe grew at once into the nation. Both examples come from early ecclesiastical history. When Christianity gradually became the religion alike of the Roman Empire and of the conquerors who embraced its civilization, those who obstinately clave to the old idolatry were called, both in Latin and in Teutonic speech, by names which in themselves expressed, not error in religion, but inferiority of social state. The worshipper of Jupiter or of Woden was called in Latin mouths a *pagan*, in Teutonic mouths a *heathen*. The two names well set forth the two distinct standards of civilization which were held by those who spoke the two languages. The *paganus* was the man of the country, as opposed to the man of the city. The Gospel was first preached in the towns, and the towns became Christian while the open country around them still clave to the old Gods. Hence the name of the *pagan*, the rustic, the man who stood outside the higher social life of the city, came to mean the man who stood outside the pale of the purer faith of the Church (65). But in the England of the sixth century, in the eastern Germany of the eighth, no such distinction could be drawn. If all who dwelled without the walls of a city had remained without the pale of the Church, the Church would have had few votaries indeed among the independent Teutons. In their ideas the opposition between the higher and the lower stage was not the opposition between the man of the city and the man of the country; it was the opposition between the man of the occupied and cultivated land and the wild man of the wilderness. The cities, where there were any, and the villages and settled land generally, became Christian, while the rude men of the heath still served Woden and Thunder. The worshippers of Woden and Thunder were therefore called *heathens* (66). *Pagan* and *Heathen* alike mark the misbeliever as belonging to a lower social stage than the Christian. But the standard of social superiority which is assumed differs in the two cases. The one is the standard of a people with whom the city is the centre of the whole social life; the other is the standard of a people among whom the city, if it was to be found at all, was simply the incidental dwelling-place of a part of the nation which was in no way privileged over those who dwelled beyond its bounds.

The other instance from the same period is this. In the organization of the Christian Church the ecclesiastical divisions always followed the civil divisions of the time; a fact which, as they commonly outlived those divisions, makes the boundaries of ecclesiastical provinces and dioceses of such primary importance in historical geography. But in Roman and in Celtic or Teutonic Europe—for in this matter we may class Celt and Teuton, Scot and Englishman, together—the ecclesiastical divisions represent civil divisions of quite different kinds. In Italy, Gaul, or Spain, the Bishop was placed in the city; the city was his hearth and home, the chief seat of his spiritual labours; it was from the city that he drew his title, and the limits of his spiritual jurisdiction were marked by the limits of the civil jurisdiction of the city. In Britain and Ireland, on the other hand, either there were no cities at all, or, where there were any, they were not, as under the Roman system, the centres of all political and social life. Hence the Bishop was not the Bishop of the city, but the Bishop of the tribe or nation: the limits of his diocese were fixed by the limits of the principality; his see, his *bishop-stool*, was not necessarily fixed in the most populous spot in his diocese, and the title of the Bishop, like the title of the King, was more commonly taken from the people than from any place in their territory (67). Titles like Meath, Ossory, Argyll, and Galloway are vestiges of the days when men spoke also of an Archbishop of the English and a Bishop of the South-Saxons (68). And all bear witness to a state of things when the tribe and not the city, the people and not the territory, was the source and limit alike of temporal and of ecclesiastical rule.

That our own forefathers and kinsmen, in the picture which Tacitus gives us of their earliest state, lagged behind their kinsfolk in the two southern peninsulas, as we see them in the Homeric poems and in the earliest traditions of Rome, is a matter neither of shame nor of regret. Our political developement has been slower, but it has also been surer. By never reaching to the highest civilization of one age, we have been able to reach to a yet higher civilization in another age. By never passing through the exclusive city stage, we have been better able to reach the national stage. In a word, when we compare Teutonic history with the history of ancient Greece and Italy, we see that what we have lost in brilliancy we have gained in permanence. The commonwealths of Greece shone with a meteoric brightness too glorious to be lasting. Her isolated cities were not—they could not be—wrought together into a single nation. Rome founded, not indeed a lasting nation, but a lasting power, by bringing the whole of the then civilized world under the dominion of a single ruling city. But the nations of the Teutonic race, alike in Germany, in Britain, and Scandinavia, grew from tribes into nations without ever going through the Greek stage of a system of isolated cities. The first glimpse which Tacitus gives us of the men of our own race sets them before us as being still in a distinctly lower stage of society than the Homeric Achaians. Their state answers rather to the state of those races on which it is plain that the Homeric Achaian looked down as being in a social state inferior to his own. They had risen far above the mere hunting and fishing stage, far above the pastoral stage; they have not reached the stage of the city, but they have reached the stage of the village community. The lowest unit in the political system is that which still exists under various names, as the *mark*, the *gemeinde*, the *commune*, or the *parish* (69). This, as we have seen, is one of the many forms of the *gens* or clan, that in which it is no longer a wandering or a merely predatory body, but when, on the other hand, it has not joined with others to form one component element of a city commonwealth. In this stage the *gens* takes the form of an agricultural body, holding its common lands—the germ of the *ager publicus* of Rome and of the *folkland* of England (70). This is the *markgenossenschaft*, the village community, of the West. This lowest political unit, this gathering of real or artificial kinsmen, is made up of families, each living under the rule, the *mund*, of its own father, that *patria potestas* which survived at Rome to form so marked and lasting a feature of Roman law (71). As the union of families forms the *gens*, and as the *gens* in its territorial aspect forms the *markgenossenschaft*, so the union of several such village communities and their *marks* or common lands forms the next higher political union, the *hundred*, a name to be found in one shape or another in most lands into which the Teutonic race has spread itself. As an intermediate union between the *gens* and the tribe, the hundred would seem to answer to the Roman *curia*, the Athenian φρατρία, the Lacedæmonian ὠβά. But there is one Roman division, standing alongside, as it were, of the *curiæ*, whose name, as in so many other cases, exactly translates the Teutonic name of which we are speaking. It seems almost impossible but that the Teutonic *hundred* and the Latin *century*, in the earliest usage of each, must have answered to one another. Both names, in their actual historic use, are mere survivals. Neither the hundred nor the century, as we know them, answer to a real hundred of anything; but every name must have had a real meaning when it was first given, and there must have been a time when the hundred or century must have been a real hundred or century of something, whether of houses, or families, or fighting men (72). Above the hundred comes the *pagus*, the *gau*, the Danish *syssel*, the English *shire*, that is, the tribe looked at as occupying a certain territory (73). And each of these divisions, greater and smaller, has its chief. In a primitive society, where patriarchal ideas still live on, age implies rule and rule implies age, and the Teutonic chiefs, great and small, bore a name of that large class of which we have already spoken, as showing how, in early times, length of days was looked on as the natural source of dominion. In England, at least, the chief, greater or smaller, bore the common title of *ealdor*; in the mere family the father is at once the *ealdor*, without further election or appointment from above or from below. We have the *hundredes-ealdor*, the *curio*; but the name in its special meaning belongs to the common father, the common chief, of the whole tribe. He bears, in his peaceful character, the long-abiding title of *Ealdorman*, which in war time he exchanges for that of

*Heretoga*, in later form the *Herzog*, the *Dux*, the leader of the army (74). He is the highest chief, the community over which he bears rule is the highest political unit, which we see in our earliest glimpses of Teutonic polity. For the whole history of our land and our race will be read backwards, if we fail always to bear in mind that the lower unit is not a division of the greater, but that the greater is an aggregate of the smaller. The hundred is made up of villages, marks, *gemeinden*, whatever we call the lowest unit; the *shire*, the *gau*, the *pagus*, is made up of hundreds; and in the same sort the *pagus* is not a division of the kingdom, but the kingdom is an aggregate of *pagi*.

Of the kingdom and its growth I shall have to speak more fully in my next lecture. We are now speaking of the state of things in which the tribe, the *gau*, the union of marks and of hundreds, is the highest strictly political conception. In the days with which we have now to deal, the tribe was the State, the *gau* was the territory of the State. The tie of kindred between various tribes of the same stock might be strongly felt, they might be capable on occasion of common action, their common origin and its claims might be kept in memory by the recognition of a common name; still the several tribes had not been fused into the higher political unit, the nation. Each tribe was a distinct commonwealth;

its union with other tribes was temporary, or at the most federal; each had its own chief, its own *Ealdorman* or *Heretoga*, whose rule in ordinary times did not extend beyond his own tribe, though in times of danger a common *Heretoga*—the germ of the future King—might be chosen to lead the common forces of all the tribes which acknowledged any common tie (75). A more lasting union of several tribes of this kind formed the nation, the highest conception of the State or commonwealth in Teutonic political language, from whence it has become the ruling idea in the political ideas and language of modern Europe. The *Gens*, the *Curia*, the tribe, of Greece or Italy, each has its close Teutonic parallel; but here the lines diverge, the parallelism ceases. In Greece and Italy the union of tribes formed only the city; among all the branches of the Teutonic stock the union of tribes formed the nation.

I shall show in my next lecture how, as the *Ealdorman* or *Heretoga* was the chief of the tribe, so the King was the chief of the nation. And the process of the joining together of tribes into nations may be best traced out by marking how the rule of independent Ealdormen gave way to that of a common national King. In some lands the old system lingered on longer than others. Among the Continental Saxons it lingered longer than it did anywhere else on so large a scale. The Old-Saxons, the long-abiding foes of the Frankish power, the men who clave so stoutly to their old freedom and their old Gods, never coalesced so closely as to have a common King. Yet we may say that they learned to become a nation by another process. They contrived a form of national unity which dispensed with a personal head. It was theirs to form an union which, rude as it may seem beside the more finished constitutions either of earlier or of later days, may fairly claim the name of the earliest Teutonic confederation (76). In other lands too, on the northern moorland or among the southern mountains, by the mouths of the Elbe and the Eider or by the sources of the Rhine and the Reuss, smaller portions of the Teutonic race either kept or won back again the old freedom, the old political system, of the earliest times. In Frisian Ditmarsen the old system of the *mark* and the *gau* lived on from the days of Cæsar and Tacitus to be overthrown by the Danish Kings of the House of Oldenburg (77). In the Three Lands of the Alemannian mountains, in the valleys of the young Rhine and the young Rhone, it was won back to live on to our own days (78). Elsewhere tribes grew into nations, Ealdormen grew into Kings, and, in some cases, nations and their kings have grown into dominions and rulers greater still.

This old Teutonic constitution, the constitution once common to the whole race, but which lived on longest among those Continental branches of the race which were most closely akin to ourselves, was brought into the Isle of Britain by its Teutonic conquerors. Our forefathers, the Angles and Saxons, brought over with them the divisions, the institutions, the titles, of their old land into the land which became their new home. This is one of the distinctive features of our island history, one which we share with a small part only of the Teutonic lands on the mainland. The change between the Germany of Tacitus and the Germany which, less than a hundred years later, began to send forth Franks and Saxons, Burgundians and Lombards, must have been a change indeed. The tribes had been gathered into nations (79). But the swarms which parted off from the central hive carried their own institutions with them into every land where the Roman influence was not too strong for them. Wherever they found or made a land empty of inhabitants, wherever they really became the people of the land and not merely a conquering class among their Roman subjects, all the old divisions and the old institutions sprang up again on the new soil (80). In our own island above all, settled as it was bit by bit by small parties of Teutonic invaders, before whom, in all those parts of the island where they really did settle, everything British and everything Roman was utterly swept away, the process had to begin again from the beginning. In all that was strictly England things started utterly afresh: marks grew into hundreds, hundreds into shires, shires into kingdoms, separate kingdoms into one united kingdom, on the soil of England itself. In Britain therefore we can actually look upon the process, while in Germany we can see only the results. The ancient system was doubtless modified by the circumstances of men who found themselves in a land where they had to win and hold every inch of ground with the sword's point. The *mark* and the *gau* show themselves again, but they do not show themselves by the same names. The village community with its common land, the joint possession of a clan reverencing a supposed common ancestor of the *Basingas* or the *Wellingas*, is as clearly to be marked in England as in Germany. But, as in later times the *mark* has been almost stifled between the ecclesiastical parish and the feudal manor (81), so we may suspect that from the beginning it showed some points of difference from the same institution on the Continent. We may suspect that the tie of kindred, everywhere to some extent artificial, was more largely artificial in England than it was on the mainland. And we may be sure that small settlements planted in a hostile land would from the beginning show a special tendency to unite into larger wholes. Marks and hundreds planted in Kent or Sussex by the followers of Hengest and Ælle could never have been wholly independent; they must from the beginning have acknowledged the supremacy of the common *Heretoga* under whom their settlers had made their way into the land. In England therefore the system must from the beginning have been touched with some shadow of the coming kingship. Still the same elements were there, and in England, as in Germany, the larger bodies were formed by the union of the smaller. By a strange chance, the group answering to the German *gau*, the English *shire,* bears a name which expresses the exactly opposite idea to that of union. But there is reason to believe that both the name and its meaning are due to events in English history some centuries later than the first settlement. The later English *pagi,* to use the name by which they appear in Latin writers, were strictly *shires,* divisions shorn off from a large whole. But they were formed in imitation of those earlier English *pagi* which were formed by the process of union. The oldest *pagi* of England do not, in ancient usage at least, admit the name of *shire.* They bear strictly tribal names, whether, like the East-Saxons, the *pagus* itself has become the kingdom, or whether, as with the Sumorsætas and Dorsætas, several *pagi* joined to form one larger kingdom of the West-Saxons (82). The aggregate of tribes was thus able to form, what the aggregate of cities never could form, a nation in the highest sense.

I might go on almost for ever on the fascinating, but still somewhat obscure, subject of the old Teutonic polity, whether in Germany, Britain, or Scandinavia. But my main business now is only to insist on the one great difference between Teutonic and Hellenic politics; the presence of the city as the leading political idea in the one system and its absence in the other. We see how closely the primitive elements correspond; so closely that we cannot doubt for a moment as to their being portions of a common Aryan inheritance. But we see also how they were modified by the one great distinction between village and city life. The Greek commonwealth grew, flourished, and decayed as a city, amazing the world perhaps alike by the splendour of the days of its greatness and by the long wretchedness of the days of its decay. Meanwhile among the despised Barbarians, scorned by kinsfolk who had forgotten their kindred, slowly and obscurely, shires were melting together into kingdoms and tribes into nations. Thus were formed those nations of Teutonic blood which settled within the Continental provinces of the Empire, and foremost among them the nation to whom, in course of time, the Empire itself was to come as part of their inheritance—the mighty people of the Franks (83). So too in our own island we can see the steps by which the English nation in Britain, and that greater English whole of which the English in Britain are now but a part, grew out of those endless Teutonic settlements on the British coast, of which the keels of Hengest and Horsa brought the earliest. We can see, though somewhat dimly, a crowd of petty States under their separate chiefs, whether bearing the title of King or Ealdorman, gathered together into the great kingdoms of Northumberland, Mercia, and East-Anglia. We can see more clearly the confederated West-Saxon principalities fused together into the one West-Saxon kingdom, and we can see the West-Saxon kingdom grow into the Kingdom of England and into all that the Kingdom of England has added to it in later times (84). All the events of our history, election, commendation, conquest, all help in the work of fusion; till, instead of a system of isolated cities, instead of a single city bearing rule over subject cities and provinces, we have a political work more lasting than the other, more just and free than the other, the nation which knows no distinctions among its members, and which gives equal rights to the dwellers in every corner of its territory.

In this way we see that the Teutonic history is in some sort the key to the history of the two southern peninsulas. We see the institutions of the Teutonic people, domestic, social and strictly political, at an earlier stage than we see those of the Greeks and Italians. While therefore we see the general likeness, the evident common origin of all, we see also something of the different steps by which these two great divisions of the Aryan family shaped their several institutions out of the common stock. Among the Germans of Tacitus we see a state of things in which the elements common to all have been less changed than in any other picture that we have of any European people. In the Homeric Achaians we see a stage somewhat more advanced in itself, and still further modified, even then, by the tendency of the Greeks to centre all their political life within the walls of a city. Out of the state of Homeric Greece the state of historical Greece grows by pure and natural developement. Out of the old Teutonic state of things the institutions of modern Europe have also grown, but not by the same unmixed course of developement. Everywhere the original Teutonic stock has been more or less modified by an infusion of Roman elements. I speak of Western Europe in general, of the Romance-speaking no less than of the Teutonic-speaking lands, for I am not now speaking of language but of political institutions. In the languages of Southern Europe Latin is, of course, the main stock; the Teutonic element which all of them have in a greater or less degree is a mere infusion, just as, in the languages of Northern Europe, the Teutonic is the main stock and the greater or less Romance element is a mere infusion (85). But with regard to political institutions, we may, even in Southern Europe, look upon all that came from a Roman source as an infusion into a Teutonic body. One spot alone in Western Europe—if it has any right to be reckoned as part of Western Europe—the island commonwealth of Venice, never acknowledged a Teutonic master, and kept on its unbroken connexion with the elder state of things (86). Everywhere else Teutonic kingdoms were founded; and, though their institutions were largely modified by the laws and institutions of their Latin-speaking subjects, yet, even in Gaul, Spain, and Italy, we must look on the rule of Gothic, Frankish, Burgundian, Lombard, and Norman Kings as a rule essentially Teutonic, though largely modified by the Roman traditions of the several countries. And, on the other hand, there is no Teutonic country, not the Scandinavian kingdoms themselves, which has, even in its political institutions, kept wholly clear of the influence of Rome. Throughout Western Europe we may set down the strictly political institutions as Teutonic, but as everywhere modified, in some countries very slightly, in others very largely, by the traditions of Roman times, and by the influence of that undying Roman Law which has been the foundation of the later jurisprudence of every European nation but our own.

And, besides this general influence of the elder state of things on the political institutions of the Teutonic kingdoms of modern Europe, there has been one case at least in which the direct continuity of Roman institutions, strengthened by that other source of likeness which brings like events out of like causes, went far to bring about a revival of an elder state of things. These causes made mediæval Italy, with its system of city commonwealths, a living revival of the political story of ancient Greece. On the points of likeness and unlikeness between the two I will not here enlarge, as it is a subject which I have done my best to deal with in detail in another shape (87). I will only say here that, though the Teutonic political system did not, like that of Greece, assume the city as the necessary starting point of political life, yet it showed itself quite able to take in the city, even the virtually independent city, as one important element among others in its political system. In all lands but our own the Roman cities lived through the storm of Teutonic invasion; and presently, both in our own land and in the lands where the Roman had never dwelled, cities of purely Teutonic birth began to arise (88). In our own land, the strong feeling of national unity, the strong central authority of the Crown, the work which was begun by the great West-Saxon Kings and which was carried to its full perfection by the Norman Conqueror, hindered English municipalities from ever growing into sovereign commonwealths. Yet it is a thought worth bearing in mind, how near the Five Boroughs of Danish England once were to forming an independent confederation of city commonwealths, how near Exeter once was to being, like Thebes or Sparta, a city ruling over neighbouring and weaker cities (89). Here, as in every other part of Western Europe, a new element, unknown to the ancient Teutonic institutions, gradually arose—the element of cities which everywhere enjoyed a certain measure of self-government and local independence, a measure which, wherever the central government was weak, came in practice very near to absolute freedom. In Italy it reached its highest point, and Florence was for some ages as truly an independent democracy as Athens. In the Teutonic lands themselves the developement of the independent cities seems less brilliant; but it perhaps seems less brilliant only because the Italian cities have a special charm of their own. They have that combined charm of classical, of mediæval, and of modern associations, which appeals to a wider range of sympathies than aught that attaches to the cities on the Rhine or the Danube, to the Teutonic Rome girded by the Aar or to the Teutonic Carthage girded by the Trave (90). Yet the German cities have their history too, their history artistic, social, mercantile, religious, as well as strictly political. And, in their strictly political aspect, the history of the League of the Northern Hansa and of the Old League of Upper Germany (91) is as rich in political teaching as the history of the Italian cities themselves. We may learn more from the Bern of Berchthold and the Erlachs, where no King or Tyrant ever dwelled, than we can learn from the Bern of Theodoric and Can' Grande (92). The internal histories of the Teutonic cities, their internal disputes and revolutions, the origin of their exclusively patrician governments, the more rare aspirings of their democracies, teach us better to understand the history of Rome and Athens themselves. But between the cities of the elder Greek and Italian world and the cities of mediæval Europe one great point of difference must always be borne in mind. In ancient Greece the cities were everything; their territory took in the whole land, they acknowledged no superiority, even of the most formal kind, in any earthly power. But in Germany the free cities and their dominions were always mere oases in a land of princely rule; and even in Italy the city commonwealths never wholly covered the whole surface of the land, and never wholly threw off the formal superiority of the King of Italy and Emperor of the Romans.

In all these inquiries the question is ever suggesting itself, how far we are to see in the analogies between ancient and mediæval city-commonwealths merely the working of the law that like causes should produce like effects, and how far we are to see any tradition, any imitation, of Roman institutions in the municipalities of the purely Teutonic parts of Europe. This is a question far too wide for discussion here. In England, in this as in other matters, there was no room, no opportunity, for direct Roman influences. Many of our

English towns are simply Teutonic village communities which grew and prospered so as to outstrip their neighbours. But where an English town arose—even after an interval of desolation—on the site, often even within the walls, of a fallen Roman city, there was at least the memory of the past to influence the history of the restored erection. Yet it is certain that nothing in the institutions of any English city can really be traced to a Roman source; there is nothing Roman in the municipal institutions of Bath or Chester or even Exeter, any more than there is on such purely English sites as Reading or Northampton (93). In Italy and Southern Gaul, on the other hand, whether there be any direct transmission or not, there is, as we have already seen, not a little of that natural and inevitable imitation which closely borders on direct transmission. In Germany, on the other hand, in such cases as the common use of the name *Patrician* for the ruling families, we see imitation of another kind. It is not such a dead imitation as the consulship of Buonaparte, because there is a real analogy between the patricians of Rome and the patricians of Bern or Nürnberg; but it is not the same kind of natural imitation as the consulship at Milan or Alby. We may be satisfied with saying that in the mediæval city-commonwealths there is a Roman element clearly shown—even we in

England have what we may call the element of suggestion—but that its nature and degree varies widely in different lands and times. But it is the likeness from analogy between the ancient and the mediæval cities which gives the comparison of the two its real historic interest and value. What amount of likeness between them may be due to direct transmission is little more than a matter of antiquarian research in each particular place.

We have thus traced the origin and history of the two great ideas of the State, the conception of the State as a city and the conception of the State as a nation. We have seen how the common elements developed up to a certain point side by side among the southern and northern branches of the European Aryans, and how, after reaching a certain point in common, the developement of the Greek and Italian nations and that of the Teutonic nations branched off in different directions. We have traced the course of the *family*, the *gens*, the *hundred*, and the *tribe*, till they grow into the Greek or Italian city and into the Teutonic nation. The causes of the divergence hardly belong to our present subject. Those causes are many and various, and not least among them are those geographical causes which made the Mediterranean lands take the lead in

European civilization and which made Greece take the lead among Mediterranean lands. In those lands a political growth, quicker, more brilliant, but less lasting, led them to the developement of the city; our growth, slower, obscurer, but steadier and more lasting, led us to the developement of the nation. And in this developement we, the great Teutonic colony in this once Celtic island, have assuredly played no mean part among our brethren and kinsfolk of the common stock. It is, as I have already said, in our land that the old Teutonic institutions have really had the freest play, that they have grown and developed with the most unbroken continuity down to our own day. Nowhere else have both liberty and national unity received so few checks. The Scandinavian nations have drawn even less than ourselves directly from Roman sources; their national life has been more unbroken than our own, but their political life has been far less so. Germany has split asunder and is being welded together again before our eyes. So has Italy. In both cases perhaps the nation has split asunder because the real power of the local kingdom was crushed between the weight of the Imperial dignity which was joined to it (94). We have had no such breaks: the causes of the difference belong to quite other branches of historical research; but the fact is in its place here. The stages by which the Teutonic tribe, by admitting tribe after tribe to equal fellowship, grew into the modern European nation—a process at once the parallel and the contrast to that by which a single Italian city came to embrace whole kingdoms and nations within the pale of its municipal franchise—can nowhere be so well studied as in the history of our own land.

## LECTURE IV.

## THE KING.

FROM the State itself we come to its head, to its chief, above all to the chief in his most clearly defined and fully developed form, when he holds the rank of a King. Now, what is a King? The question is far more easily asked than answered. We commonly know a King when we see him; but it is quite another matter to say offhand in what his kingship consists. Some Kings are hereditary; others are elective. Some Kings reign with absolute power; the power of others is narrowly limited by Law. Some Kings acknowledge no superior on earth; others admit a greater or less superiority in a feudal or federal chief. In some kingdoms the kingly office, like most other offices, is confined to the male sex; in others it is open to both sexes alike. Some Kings go through an ecclesiastical ceremony of consecration; some dispense with any such rite. Yet, amidst all this unlikeness, it is plain that there is a common idea of kingship, which is at once recognized, however hard it may be to define it. This is shown, among other things, by the fact that no difficulty is ever felt as to translating the word *King* and the words which answer to it in other languages. Between any Romance and any Teutonic language, *Rex* and its derivatives, *Cyning* and its cognates, are felt to answer to one another. No man ever doubts as to using *Rex* or *Roi* to translate *King* or *König*, in any of the possible changes which may be rung on the two sets of words. If we go on into Greek, we find that, in those stages of the language with which most of us are chiefly familiar, in its classical and in its modern stage, βασιλεύς answers to *Rex* and *King* as exactly as they answer to one another. For some ages indeed βασιλεύς bore the special sense of *Emperor*; and, to express the lowlier rank of *King*, the word ῥήξ was imported bodily from the Latin (1). But this was a change of meaning which rose out of distinct and known historical causes, and, when these historical causes came to end, the usage of the Greek language fell back upon what it had been before they began. Even now that the constitutions of most European kingdoms are so constantly verging towards a common model, there is still a good deal of difference between one King and another; and within our own memories, indeed within a very few years, there was a greater difference still. Yet no one doubts as to who is a King and who is not. Or, if any such doubt is raised, the question is always as to the claim of this or that particular person to be a King, not as to his right to be called a King if he can make his claim good. Till 1806 the rank of Emperor of the Romans, King of Germany and Jerusalem, was in theory open to every baptized man (2). Till 1795 the rank of King of Poland was, not only in theory but in practice, open to all men of princely birth in other lands and to the whole nobility of the Polish Kingdom. The Polish King often rose from a private station and his children often went back to a private station. His powers within his own kingdom were narrowly limited, perhaps beyond those of any other single ruler that ever bore the kingly title. Yet no one ever doubted that a King of Poland was a King, that he was entitled to the rank and style and other privileges of a King, as much as if his kingship had been at once hereditary and absolute. In short, wide as have been the differences between one King and another in different times and places, there is still a common idea which runs through all the various types of kingship, and which stamps all Kings everywhere as members of the same class. In modern Europe, taken alone, the definition of kingship would perhaps not be very hard to make. As a rule, we may set it down that the King is the head of a nation, accepting the rough definition of a nation which I have tried to give in a former lecture. The chief exception to this definition is found in those German princes who within the present century have taken the kingly title. I think that we all must feel that they are an exception. We somehow cannot help feeling that a King of Bavaria or Saxony is hardly, in the Homeric phrase, so much of a King (3) as a King of Spain or Sweden. In the case of Württemberg this is felt still more strongly; for Saxony and Bavaria answer, in name at least, though not in boundaries, to divisions of the German nation so great and ancient that they might almost pass for nations themselves (4). In Italy, on the other hand, if there was any incongruity in the separate kingdoms of Sardinia and the Two Sicilies, that incongruity has come to an end (5). On the whole, speaking roughly—and it is only very roughly that we can speak on the whole matter—it certainly seems that we expect a King to be the chief of a nation. It seems also to belong to the idea of a King that he should be, both in rank and in power, the first person in that nation. That he must be the first in rank need hardly be argued, and I think we may say, that, however narrowly the power of a King may be limited by law, he still remains first in power.

Even where the royal authority had sunk to the lowest ebb, as in Poland and at one time in Sweden, though the power of the King was less than that of some other powers in the State, yet he had no personal superior or equal. Then again, it seems implied in the idea of a King that he should hold his office for life, as distinguished from the President or other republican magistrate who is appointed only for a fixed term (6). And I think it also belongs to the idea of kingship that the office should be permanent; that is, that the King should be succeeded by another King, whether the law of succession be hereditary, elective, or of any other kind. Sulla and Cæsar, as Perpetual Dictators, held more than royal authority for life; but, as the office was a special creation for their own lives, they were not Kings, as we very clearly see by Cæsar's longing to be a King (7). Again, in modern conception, the King, whether his power be great or little, is irresponsible. The royal command is no excuse for an illegal act done by another, but there is no legal way of punishing an illegal act done by the King himself. History indeed will show that this last is a very modern conception (8); still it does seem now to be part of the idea of a King which is as fully recognized as any other. On the whole, we should perhaps not be far wrong if we define a King as a chief of a nation, first in rank and power in that nation, holding a permanent office for life, and, in modern conception at least, personally irresponsible for his actions. To this we must, till very lately, have added that he must be admitted to his office with ecclesiastical rites. I am not sure that it is not here that the true mystery and dignity of kingship really lay. The crowned and anointed King was something different from any other mortal, however high in rank and power. A divinity hedged him in which did not hedge in either the republican magistrate or the hereditary prince of less than kingly rank. The ecclesiastical consecration of the King is the expression in a Christian shape of the same feeling which, among most heathen nations, has made it essential that the King should be the child of the Gods (9). In either case the king is sacred in a way in which other rulers are not. But this religious sanction of kingship, which was its very essence a few centuries back, seems to be gradually dying out in Europe. Two causes have brought this about. One is the separation between ecclesiastical and temporal matters which prevails in many countries, and the general unwillingness in all countries to acknowledge any ecclesiastical influence in temporal things. The other cause is of quite another kind. When lawyers ruled that the King never died, that the throne never could be vacant, that the new King was King as soon as the breath was out of the last King's body, they took away all the force and meaning of the ancient crowning rite. Whatever a coronation is now, it is no longer the actual admission to the kingly office. No wonder then that in several kingdoms of Europe the rite has been dispensed with altogether.

The modern or lawyers' theory of the Crown as the fountain of honour, the fountain of justice, the original grantor of all property in land, the source from which the Assembly of the Nation itself derives its being, is, I need hardly say, simply a lawyers' theory. History has nothing to do with it, except, as was done long ago by the strong hand of John Allen, to trace the steps by which it grew up (10). The primæval kingship, whether Greek, Latin, or Teutonic, was something of quite another kind. The King was not the lord of the soil, but the chieftain of the people. The origin of modern kingship can easily be traced up, as Allen has traced it, to the gradual infusion of doctrines borrowed from Imperial Rome—indirectly therefore from the monarchies of the East—into the simple political creed of our forefathers (11). And it is among our forefathers and kinsmen, both in our own island and on the Teutonic mainland, that we can best trace the growth of kingship, the chieftainship of the nation, out of the chieftainship of the smaller elements out of which the nation was formed. We have seen that both in Greece and in Italy the growth of strictly national life was checked by the early growth of the city life. The same cause equally hindered the growth of kingship, according to our conception of it. In Greece and Italy, when we get our first glimpses of those lands, we see a fuller developement of kingly government than we see among the Teutonic nations at the time when we get our first glimpses of them. But the same causes which led to this speedy growth of kingship in Greece and Italy also brought it more speedily to an end. In Greece, above all, as we see it in the Homeric picture, every settlement has its own King. But then, at least in the more advanced parts of Greece, every settlement is a city, and kingship in a single city is not a form of government which is likely to last. The Greek King is a King in the fullest sense of the word; he is, in truth, far more of a King than either his Italian or his Teutonic parallel. His claim to his throne might satisfy a Court divine of the reign of Charles the First. He is no mere chief, no mere magistrate, either chosen by the people or responsible to the people; the mortal King on earth is the living image of the immortal King on Olympos. He is at once his child and his representative among men.

The Homeric King is Zeus-born and Zeus-nourished; he comes of the divine stock, and he rules by the divine commission. The sceptre which he wields is the gift of the God from whom alone he holds his right to wield it. That sceptre passes on from father to son by a right as strictly hereditary as the sceptre of David or of Hugh Capet (12). The succession may be disturbed by foreign conquest or, more rarely, by domestic revolution; but no *Comitia*, no *Gemót*, was ever held in any Hellenic city, to decide, by an ordinary process of the law, who should be placed by the will of the people upon a vacant throne (13). The divine origin, the divine authority, of the Kings of heroic Greece, stand out in strange contrast with the narrow extent of their territory, with the narrow range of their powers, and with the unpretending simplicity of their manner of life. The King, Zeus-born and Zeus-nourished as he is, does not rule by his own will. We are dealing with a state of things too early to speak of law and constitution, but the King can rule only according to the customs and traditions of his people (14). He can rule only by the help of his Council of Elders and with the good will of the general Assembly of his whole folk. Nothing of the pomp and circumstance either of modern or of Eastern kingship surrounds him. His house is accessible to all; his personal life is spent in the same way, at once simple and public, as the life of any other member of the Commonwealth. Divine as he is, no wide barrier parts him off from the other chiefs of his people. He is perhaps only one among many bearers of the kingly title. Even within the narrow bounds of Ithakê, there were many Kings besides the divine Odysseus (15). We have the picture of this form of government only in a legendary and poetical shape; but of the reality of the state of things described in the Homeric poems, and among them of the real existence of the heroic kingship, I at least have never entertained a doubt.

From Greece we will turn to Italy. We have there no Homer to set before us a living picture of the earliest civilized times of the country, but we have the universal tradition of all time that there had been Kings both in Rome and in other Italian cities, although, in the historical days of Rome, kingly rule had, both at Rome and in other Italian cities, become a thing of the past. And here I will bring in another argument, in case any sceptic should be found daring enough to hint that the existence of Kings, whether at Rome or at Athens, rests so wholly on the evidence of poetry and legend that it cannot be made a matter of serious political argument or comparison. To discuss the value of the sources either of old Greek or of old Italian history would carry me too far away from my subject; but the existence both of the early Hellenic and the early Italian kingship can be proved by a line of argument almost stronger than contemporary evidence itself. The existence of the early kingship can be proved by the argument from survivals, from the traces which it left behind among the institutions of later times. Had Rome never had Kings, the names *Interrex* and *Interregnum* could never have been found among her republican institutions down to the last days of the Commonwealth. No one would ever have given the name of *Interregnum* to the time which sometimes came between two consulships—no one would ever have given the name of *Interrex* to the magistrate who held the chief power during such an occasional vacancy—unless there had been a time when the *Interregnum* had been the time, not between the terms of office of two Consuls, but between the reigns of two Kings, unless there had been a time when the *Interrex* really was, as his name implies, the magistrate who was to preside at the election, not of Consuls, but of a King (16). These names would of themselves be enough, in the absence of history or tradition, to prove that Rome once had Kings. And we may add that they prove, not only that

Rome once had Kings, but that those Kings were elective and not hereditary. So again, the fact that the title of King still remained at Rome as the style of one of the priests of the national religion proves that there once had been Kings who more truly deserved the name. There could never have been a *Rex sacrificulus* unless he had been a survival of a real *Rex* (17). No one would have given the kingly name to a petty priestly functionary, unless the received legend had been true. That title shows of itself there once had been Kings who were judges and rulers and generals, as well as priests. It shows that their civil and military functions had been transferred to others, while some religious motive made it needful that there should still be one who bore the title of King, in order to do those priestly acts which a King alone could do. We may be sure that, however meaningless a name may become, it is never meaningless in its first use, and that the words *Interregnum*, *Interrex*, and *Rex sacrificulus*, could never have been found except in a state which had once been governed by Kings. These survivals of kingship under the Commonwealth prove that there had been an earlier time of real kingship, just as the phantom Consuls and Tribunes under the Empire would of themselves be enough to prove that Consuls and Tribunes had once been active powers in the State (18). Had we no record of the deeds of either Cæsar, the Fasti alone would teach us that the Empire had grown out of an earlier commonwealth. So in Greece, the Spartan Kings were something more than survivals; they held the kingly office itself, greatly shorn of its ancient powers, but keeping up all its ancient religious sanctity (19). Still they are survivals so far as this. It is inconceivable that the Spartan kingship, as we see it in the historic times, could ever have been devised as a new thing; the existence of Kings with such small powers shows of itself that there had once been Kings with greater powers. But besides the Kings of Sparta, there was a King at Argos as late as the Persian War. We know nothing as to the exact extent of his powers, and we may suspect that his kingship had been greatly cut down from the kingship of Diomêdês and Têmenos. Still, as he is put on a level with the Spartan Kings, it may seem that he still retained the functions of general (20). And at Athens we have in the King Archôn, the *βασιλεύς* of the days of the democracy, the exact parallel to the *Rex sacrificulus* at Rome (21). No people would have given the title of King to a magistrate appointed by lot for a single year, if it had not once been ruled by real Kings—if there had not been functions which, it was held, could be rightly done by no one but a King, and which the nominal King of later times was appointed in order to discharge.

The existence of kingship then in the early days both of Greece and of Italy may be set down as an undoubted fact. But such light as we have sets before us the old Italian kingship as something widely differing from the kingship of the heroic days of Greece. The difference is, no doubt, partly owing to the difference in the character of the two nations, partly to the different nature of the evidence from which we have to learn anything about their early polity. And again, the difference in the nature of our evidence is, in some degree at least, owing to the difference in the character of the two nations. In Italy we have no Homer; we have not even such approaches to a Homer as we have among our own forefathers and kinsfolk; but it is doubtless owing to the difference between the Greek and Italian character that we have no Italian Homer. It is no wonder then if an old Achaian King comes before us surrounded by a poetic halo, while the Roman King seems a person almost as prosaic and matter-of-fact as the Consul who follows after him. A desperate attempt to transfer Greek ideas into Latium may call Romulus the son of a God and Numa the husband of a Goddess (22); but the constitution-making of Ancus and of Servius is as much a matter of everyday life, of everyday truth and falsehood, as the constitution-making of Licinius or of Sulla (23). But on one point tradition cannot well have gone astray, and on that point we have seen that the unerring argument from survivals steps in to confirm the tradition. The Greek kingship was hereditary; the Italian, at all events the Roman, kingship was elective. The Roman kingship was not confined to any divine race; it was not even confined to the citizens of the Commonwealth; it was open to the stranger, to the captive, perhaps even to the slave (24). Such a system might in practice give Rome much better Kings, but it swept away all the mystery and divinity of kingship. A Roman King might be the worshipper, the favourite, of Jupiter Optimus Maximus; but he was not his child. Ancus and Servius might be Jove-nourished, as well as Agamemnôn and Achilleus; but they were not Jove-born. It may be that we see the Roman kingship only in a later form. It may be that an earlier hereditary kingship had gone before it, and that the elective kingship of our traditions was only a step in that course the next step in which exchanged elective Kings for Consuls. But it is just as likely that the two modes of succession, the hereditary and the elective, stood, each alone in its purity, in the old Achaian and in the old Italian polity, while in the old Teutonic polity we find the mingling together of the two. At all events, it is a thing to be noted that, in a Commonwealth like Rome, where family traditions, family influences, and family character play so great a part, there should have been no one among the proudest patricians who dared to claim a descent from the first founder of the city (25).

Now the great distinction between the history of kingship in ancient Greece and Italy and its history among the Teutonic nations lies in this: the Teutonic kingship went on and flourished, and grew into the kingship of modern Europe, while the Greek and Italian kingship for the most part died out, and left only survivals such as those which I have just been speaking of. This, it seems to me, was the necessary fate of kingship, when the kingdom was confined to a single city. The tendencies of a city community are essentially republican. They may be aristocratic or they may be democratic, but in either case they are opposed to the government of a single person for life. The awe and mystery of kingship are out of place when a King goes in and out before the eyes of all his subjects, as the King of a single city must do. At Rome, where the King had less divinity about him, the change from Kings to Consuls was a mere constitutional change; it was hardly so great a change as when the exclusive patrician government was broken down, and the consulship was thrown open to plebeians. If it was thought that the State would be better governed by placing at its head two Consuls chosen for a year, rather than a King chosen for life, there was no reason why the change should not be made. In Greece, where the King had a greater share of divinity about him, the change was probably harder; it was certainly more gradual. In Sparta, the most conservative of Greek States, kingship always went on. The power of the King might be lessened; he might cease to be the real head of the state; he might be provided with a colleague, and might be made responsible to other powers in the Commonwealth; but the kingship of the sons of Hêraklês was something too holy to be utterly swept away. Small as might be his real powers, the King, living or dead, was the object of a reverence which was shared by no mere elective magistrate; and bitter was the taunt when the deposed King, who had sunk to the discharge of some lowlier function, was asked by his former colleague how it felt to be a magistrate after being a King (26). Thus the Herakleid kingship lived on, and, living on, it was able in the last days of Sparta to win back its ancient powers, and the last Kleomenês could stand forth in the eyes of Hellas as a King indeed (27). Even in the less conservative Athens kingship died out but slowly, and it is to be remarked that the cause which tradition gives for the abolition of kingship at Athens is exactly the opposite to that which tradition gives as the cause for its abolition at Rome. The Athenians decreed that they would have no more Kings because Kodros was so good; the Romans decreed that they would have no more Kings because Tarquinius was so evil (28). In the former reason, whether it be historical or not, we can see a sign of that religious reverence which belonged to kingship in Greece, but which did not belong to it at Rome. The Athenian tradition went on to say that the first change still left the supreme power held for life by a member of the ancient kingly family. But the Archon was now responsible; he was doubtless also elective; he was chosen, like our own ancient Kings, from a single royal family. Next, the post was held for ten years only, but it was still confined to members of the same house (29). It was not till the rule of a single person was abolished, till a board of nine Archons took the place of one, that other families were allowed to share the supreme dignity with the house of Kodros. And, when we remember that one of these nine elective magistrates still held a nominal kingship, we may believe that the title of βασιλεύς had all along gone on, in some secondary way, alongside of the vaguer name of ἄρχων (30). The rest of Athenian history consists in a series of changes by which the powers of the Archons were gradually transferred to other bodies in the State, to the popular assembly, to the popular courts of justice, to the magistracy of the Ten Generals (31). The Archonship, the vestige of ancient kingship, might be cut down to a shadow; but it was too holy a thing to be altogether swept away. It lived on through all changes, till at last, when it was a shadow indeed, it was again for a moment united with more than kingly power. There came a time when Hadrian, Imperator and Augustus of Rome and of the world, did not deem it beneath him to be also, for a single year, the Archon by whose name that year was marked in the annals of the democracy of Athens (32).

The Roman kingship fared otherwise. The revolution which swept away the thing itself swept it away far more thoroughly. There were no such gradual stages to break the fall of the elective kingship of Rome as broke the fall of the hereditary kingship of Athens. It is a mere conjecture that a special right to a share in the chief magistracy was for a moment reserved to the house of the fallen King (33). At all events, Rome had nothing answering to the archonship for life or for ten years. Into the place of the King chosen for life there at once stepped the two Consuls, or rather Prætors, chosen for a single year. But the point is that the Consuls did step into the place of the King, and that they kept it. Where kingship had nothing specially divine about it, where kingly government was put an end to, not because of the virtues, but because of the crimes of the King, there was no need to deal very tenderly with the kingly house or with the kingly office. But, on the other hand, there was not at Rome any such wish as there was at Athens to do away with the kingly power. At Athens the archonship went on, but its duties were gradually cut down to a routine of religious and lesser judicial functions. The Archons neither commanded the armies of the State nor presided in its Assemblies. The Polemarch, with his warlike title, became as mere a survival as the *βασιλεύς* with his kingly title (34). But at Rome the kingly power remained; it was indeed put into commission, but nothing was taken away from its authority, and not much from its dignity. On great emergencies, the single kingship rose again for a six months' space in the person of the Dictator; Prætors, Censors, Curule Ædiles, arose by the side of the Consuls: as all shared somewhat of kingly power, so all shared somewhat of kingly worship. Magistrates who still bore about them such badges of dignity as

"The purple gown,
The axes and the curule chair, the car and laurel crown;"

magistrates who presided in the assemblies of Senate and People (35), and who commanded the armies of the commonwealth with all the authority of the ancient Kings, point to a far different state of feeling from that which was ever lessening the power of the Athenian Archons. Athens and Rome alike abolished the kingly title and office, but at Athens the kingly power was abolished as well as the kingly office; at Rome the kingly power went on, held for short terms, and divided among many holders, but still never wholly swept away. And mark the consequence. In Greece the kingly power, and more than the kingly power, came back again in many of her cities under the form of the tyranny. But the tyranny was ever unlawful; the definition of the Tyrant is that he held kingly power in a Commonwealth where there was no King by law. But just as at Sparta the lingering on of a nominal kingship made Kleomenês able to change the shadow into a reality, so at Rome it was found that the great powers with which the magistrates of the commonwealth were clothed opened the way for bringing back the rule of one under another form. Had the same man at Athens been at once Archon, General, and Prytanis, he would still have been far from being

King or Tyrant; but at Rome, when all the great powers of the State were gathered together in the hands of a single man, it was found that their union made an Emperor.

The heroic kingship then died out in Greece, and in Italy too, if it ever existed there in its strictly heroic form. But it is well to mark that it went on in those kindred and neighbouring lands which had so much in common with Greece, but in which the fully-developed system of Greek city life was never established. The Macedonians, and the people of the land vaguely called Epeiros, the Molossians, Chaonians, and Thesprotians, are best looked on as undeveloped Hellênes, as Greeks among whom the tribe never altogether gave way to the city. Among them then the ancient kingship went on in the historic times. But we may see how, as they came more and more within the range of directly Hellenic influences, they gradually approached to Hellenic political life. This might have happened in Macedonia, if her great Kings had thought it enough to become the pupils of Greece, instead of becoming at once her pupils and her conquerors. In Epeiros it did happen. By the time of the Peloponnesian war, kingship had been done away with both in Chaonia and in Thesprôtia. Chaonia indeed was passing through a stage through which Athens and other

Greek states had passed. She chose two annual chief magistrates; but she chose them out of a single ruling house (36). Among the Molossians kingship lived on, but it lived on to supply, in the Epeirote Alexander and the more famous Pyrrhos, Hellenic champions against the Barbarians of the West. But in the end kingship was swept away there also, and in the latest days of Grecian freedom, Epeiros, now fully acknowledged as a Greek State, holds an honourable place among the Federal Commonwealths of Hellas (37). Such a national promotion was well deserved by a nation among whom King and people met face to face, where the King swore to obey the laws, and where the people swore to preserve the kingdom to him as long as he obeyed them. In Macedonia itself, the kingly power was kept within bounds, if not by so well-balanced a constitution as this, yet at least by the frequent gathering, whether at set times or only when occasion called for them, of armed assemblies of the Macedonian people (38). But a Macedonian republic was unheard of, till it suited the crooked policy of Rome to part out the conquered kingdom into four dependent Commonwealths (39). But long before that time, Macedonian Kings in other lands had set themselves free from the fetters of Macedonian kingship, and indeed from most of the restraints of European life. In the Macedonian kingdoms of Asia and Egypt we see the old limited kingship of the house of Têmenos strangely changed into the full despotism of the East, and yet more strangely allied with the full intellectual culture of Greece, though, save here and there in an outlying colony (40), without any trace of her political freedom. But, before Ptolemies and Seleukids had founded their lesser thrones, an union of functions no less incongruous had been seen in the person of him of whose dominion they were glad to part out the fragments. Strange indeed was the mixture of powers which Alexander held when he was at once King of Kings on the throne of Cyrus, lawful King of the free people of Macedonia, and elective chief of the Hellenic confederacy by the vote of the Corinthian Synod (41).

Another union of functions no less strange arose in after times, which leads us, in this enquiry into the forms of early Aryan kingship, from one main branch of our subject to another. The partition of the ancient powers of the Roman Kings had formed the various magistracies of the Roman Commonwealth. They formed a strong and dignified Executive, alongside of which Senate and People alike could hold their fitting place. In after days, when Senate and People alike had shown themselves unworthy to rule, the union of the various powers of the State in a single hand again brought back a monarchy, though a monarchy now no longer constitutional, but despotic. Cæsar, Father of his Country, High Pontiff of the Gods, Consul of the Commonwealth, Prince of the Senate, Imperator of the Army, and himself wielding also that Tribunitian power which was meant to be the check on all the other powers, was, in truth, master of Rome and of the world (42). By his side the old magistracies went on as shadows, and the Imperial Consul himself deigned to take one of his own subjects as his colleague in that temporary dignity (43). That dignity lingered on, till at last it was again by chance united with something of real power and honour; and the consulships of Theodoric (44), of Boëtius (45), of Belisarius (46), may at least count for more than the Athenian archonship of Hadrian and the Athenian generalship of Constantine (47). And the master of Rome and of the world could still say, like Julius himself, "I am Cæsar, not King" (48). He might be βασιλεύς in the tongue of his Greek subjects (49); he might clothe himself with the robes and diadem of Eastern kingship (50); even in his own city his dominion might be *regnum* (51), his house might be *regia* (52), his wife might be *regina* (53), but he himself never dared to call himself, no flatterer ever dared to call him, by the forbidden and dreaded title of *Rex* (54).

Since the *Regifugium* of the Tarquins, Rome never had a King, till a King came to her from quite another stock and in quite another guise. Step by step, she took Kings of Teutonic race within the pale of her honours; she had Alaric to her general (55); she had Chlodwig to her Consul; she had Pippin to her Patrician (56); till at last the spell of spells was broken, and she had Charles to her Cæsar and Augustus. The Imperial style of Rome and the kingly style of Germany were joined in the hands of the Emperor of the Romans, the King of the Franks and Lombards. Still Rome herself had not yet a King; it was a later stage still which joined into one style the powers which were yet distinct in the same hands, and which gave the world that long line of *Reges Romanorum* which reaches from Henry of Franconia to Joseph of Austria, and which there may still be some living who remember (57). The Empire of Rome and the Kingship of Germany were now fairly merged in one; we have traced the one to its ending; we must now trace the other from its beginning.

Nothing can be plainer, both from the description given by Tacitus and from the narrative in our own English Chronicles, that kingship, in the distinctive sense, was not universal, and therefore we may safely infer not immemorial, among the Teutonic nations. He distinguishes those tribes which had Kings from those which had none, and he distinctly marks one most important difference between Kings and lesser chieftains: the Kings were chosen for their nobility, the lesser chieftains, the *duces* or *principes*, for their personal merit (58). We here see plainly enough the practice as to the appointment of Kings which was universal among all the Teutonic, and, as far as I know, among the Slavonic nations also, and which seems the most natural in an early state of society. On the one hand there is no strict law of hereditary succession; on the other hand the kingly office is not put up to indiscriminate competition among the whole nation. As at Rome, the people have a voice in choosing their ruler, but as in Greece, the King must come of a special and a divine stock; the ruler of men must be the child of the ruler of the Gods; the patriarch to whom he traces up his pedigree must be no other than Woden himself (59). Thus far our fathers felt with the Achaians of the days of Homer. But they felt too with the practical mind of the Roman, that the rule of men could not be safe. trusted to the chances of mere hereditary succession; the sentiment of kingly descent was satisfied if the King came of the divine stock, while some degree of fitness for his office was secured by a free choice among those in whose veins the sacred blood of Woden flowed. The King was the noblest among the noble; he was, as his name speaks, the embodiment of the *kin*; he was the leader of the nation, the choice of the nation, the nation, as it were, itself incarnate in the person of a single man. Kingship was an office; it was an office which, like any other office, the nation gave and the nation could take away (60). But it was something more than an office; it was the privilege of the chosen house which extended itself beyond the actual holder of the office to all the members of the *cynecyn*, the stock of stocks, the stock from which alone Kings could be chosen, and of which every member was in some sort kingly (61). A kingship which was hedged in by such divinity as this might seem as if it must have been in the strictest sense immemorial, as if it would be wholly impossible to fix the time or the cause of its beginning; and yet, as I just before said, it is certain that the Teutonic kingship, as a form of government, was not immemorial. In the days of Tacitus, kingship was still the exception among the German nations, and it is quite certain that among one great division of the German people kingship remained unknown till national independence came to an end. The Old-Saxons never had Kings till they had to acknowledge one who was King of the

Franks and Lombards also (62). And among the Saxons who crossed over the sea to Britain, as well as among their Anglian and Jutish fellows, kingship was unknown till after they were firmly established on British ground (63). Mighty and worshipful as was the Teutonic King, clothed as he was with the mysterious holiness of a child of the Gods, he and his office were still, in some sort, novelties. There had been a time when kingship had been unknown; there were branches of the race in which it always remained unknown. In fact there can be little doubt that, wherever a Teutonic King is found, his kingship had displaced an earlier government of chiefs who bore the lowlier, but more ancient, titles of *Ealdormen* or *Heretogan.*

The key to this seeming contradiction would seem to be found in this, that the King represents the national as distinguished from the tribal stage of political developement. The lowlier chiefs, Ealdormen or Dukes, were the chiefs of separate tribes; as the union of tribes grew into a nation, the nation chose a King as the chief of all. They chose him perhaps because he was in some sort a King already. Some faint signs may be seen in our glimpses of the days of our earliest fathers which look as if there were kingly houses before there was such a thing as kingly government. It would seem that the kingly house, the *cynecyn*, the noblest among the noble, the house which most truly embodied the whole being of the race, was called, when the nation felt the need of a common chief, to take its place at the head of all. The house which was already kingly in point of descent became kingly in point of political power. That is to say, kingship is the rule of the noblest, the rule of those who spring from the *cynecyn*, the rule of the *cyn* itself embodied in its highest members. In this way we may say that the King became a King because he was a King already. He became *Rex*, because he was, before all men, *generosus*; he became the ruler of men, because he was already the highest among them. In the far-off Sanscrit a kindred line of thought has produced a cognate title, and we see in the distant *Ganaka* a closer approach in name to our own *King* than in the nearer *Rex* and βασιλεύς (64). The Teutonic King reigned—*rixode*—over his *rice*, his *regnum*; but he took his title, not from his office, but from his dignity. He was not the mere *Rex*, the mere ruler; he was the *King*, the chief of the kin on earth, the man who could boast of kindred with the powers of Heaven.

With the introduction of Christianity, the King's claim to reverence as the child of the Gods came to an end. The pedigree of the kingly house was still traced up to Woden; but, as the Cretans showed the tomb of Zeus, so it was now found out that Woden had been only a mortal man, the descendant of Noah and Adam in such and such a degree (65). But the King must still have a sacred character of some kind about him. The Hebrew rite of anointing had come into use as the inauguration ceremony of the Emperors, and from them it was extended to Kings of lower degree. The King's commission was still divine; but its divinity no longer consisted in descent from the false God of the heathen; it was divine, because it was bestowed with ecclesiastical rites by the highest ministers of the Church within his kingdom. Now, how far did this change affect the real nature and extent of the kingly power? It swept away one form of mystery and sanctity, but it put another form in its stead. We might perhaps say that it swept away the sanctity of the race, while it increased the sanctity of the person. Of all doctrines the most opposed to any kind of Christian teaching is that which sees any exclusive virtue, which acknowledges any exclusive privilege, in particular races or families. In a Christian commonwealth, the law may decree hereditary succession, whether to the Crown or to anything else; but the law decrees it simply because such hereditary succession is deemed to work for the common good, not because there is any inherent excellence in this or that particular line. Christianity has had to struggle with exclusive prejudices of this kind, just as it has had to struggle with the world-wide sin of slavery, itself only another outgrowth of the same exclusive feeling. Under Christian influences, the sentiment of birth may remain as a sentiment; it may remain in the form of political institutions, whether we deem them good or bad; but its inherent sanctity passes away. When Æthelberht plunged beneath the waters of baptism, his special privileges, his special sanctity, as a son of Woden were washed away for ever. The sanctity of the Christian King, the Anointed of the Lord, was of another kind; it was a sanctity of person and office, not of descent. The King was admitted to share somewhat of the official holiness of the priest and the Bishop. But that holiness was purely official; it was a holiness bestowed and measured according to an acknowledged law; it was bestowed by a competent authority, and by a competent authority it might be taken away. The change from the son of Woden to the Anointed of the Lord clothed the King with even higher personal worship than he had held before. But it brought out more strongly the notion that the King held an office, a trust, bestowed on him for the common good of his people. Christianity therefore made it easier to choose freely within the royal house; it made it easier, in case of need, to choose beyond the bounds of the royal house; it made it easier, in case of need, to remove by legal form a King who had shown himself unworthy of the trust which the law had bestowed on him. It was by a later change again that the King gradually changed from the chief of the people into the lord of the land, that the notion of office began again to be lost in the notion of possession, and that the kingdom began to be looked on as a personal estate, which must, like any other estate, pass on from father to son, according to some rule of hereditary succession strictly laid down beforehand. A strict law of hereditary succession, if it be inconsistent with the theory of popular election of the King, is no less inconsistent with the theory of his ecclesiastical consecration. The object of the crowning and anointing is to make a man full King who up to that moment is at most only King-elect. But according to the strict doctrine of hereditary right, the King is full King already, and his crowning and anointing sinks into a mere pageant, empty or edifying, as men choose to look upon it.

The kingship which went through these stages, heathen and Christian, came in, as I have already said, gradually. In some lands, the *Heretogan* or

*Ealdormen*, the *Duces*, *Principes*, *Judices*, *Satrapæ*, and so forth, of the Latin writers, long held their ground. Even the smallest kingdom was probably formed by the union of several small states of this kind. For this process we may find parallels far beyond the range of the Teutonic race and even of the Aryan family. The Old Testament history sets before us the many Kings of Canaan, reigning each one in his own city, much like the Kings of heroic Greece. But it also sets before us, in the case of Gibeon, at least one city which, though not ruled by a King, was a great city, as one of the royal cities (66). It tells us how there were Dukes of Edom before there were Kings (67); and the history of Israel itself shows, perhaps more clearly than any other, how a confederacy of kindred tribes might pass into an united nation, and how the Judges of the Hebrews, like the Judges of the West-Goths, might pass away before the power of a single King over the whole folk. And not only were there Dukes, Ealdormen, and Judges before there were Kings, but, in some cases, nations which had already tried kingly government, fell back upon the earlier rule of Dukes, Ealdormen, or Judges. I leave Ægyptologers to say what amount of historical truth there may be in the tale told us by Herodotus, how the single kingdom of

Egypt was once split up among twelve confederate Kings. But be the tale true or false, the state of things which it describes is one that has several parallels in undoubted history. The Lombards, after experience of kingly government through several reigns, fell back upon the government of separate Dukes, and, according to one account, the same thing happened among ourselves in the West-Saxon kingdom (68). This process must be distinguished from another, which has something in common with it, and which may be looked on as a sort of transition between the government of separate Dukes or Ealdormen and the fully established monarchy of later times. In the view which we have taken of the origin and nature of kingship, it is plain that kingship does not imply *monarchy* in the literal sense. Indeed it should be remembered that, in days when the meaning of words was strictly cared for, the words "monarch" and "monarchy" were never applied to the rule of ordinary Kings, but were reserved for the universal dominion of the Emperor (69). Long after an union of tribes had reached a feeling of national unity so strong that it bore a common name and was capable of something like common action—a feeling strong enough to lead them to forsake the rule of mere Dukes or Judges for that of Kings—it still did not follow that there should be only one King in the nation. It was an easy result from the original nature of Teutonic kingship, that, where the whole house was kingly, where the kingliness of the house was the source of its claim to rule, it should be held that every member of it had a right to be kingly in office as well as in birth. Hence came the constant subdivision of a kingdom among a King's sons, either at his death or during his lifetime—a process which fills up nearly the whole history of Frankish kingship under Merwings and Karlings alike. Hence too the constitution of the West-Saxon kingdom among ourselves, the confederate principalities each ruled by an Under-king of the kingly house, all of them admitting the superiority of the head King of the whole people. The notion of a Heptarchy in England has long been cast to the winds, but, had men chosen to talk of a Pentarchy in Wessex, there would have been something to say for the name (70). So again, in the Scandinavian North, in almost every great expedition we find mention of several Kings and of several Earls—the Earls of course answering to English Ealdormen or Heretogan—joined together as leaders of a confederate host. And mark that, among the invaders who fell in the great slaughter of Brunanburh, among the seven Earls and the five

Kings who stayed to feed the wolves and ravens of Northumberland, we are told that the Kings were young; we hear nothing of the age of the Earls. Surely this is another form of the distinction drawn long before by Tacitus. The Kings were chosen for their birth, for their kingliness; they might therefore well be young. The Earls, we may well believe, were still chosen for their personal strength and valour; they therefore might well be δημογέροντες, *seniores*, Ealdormen, in the literal sense of the words.

In all this, in the crowd of petty Kings who were displaced to make room for the great kingdoms of later times, be it in the very beginning of English kingship under Ida in Northumberland or in its later Northern stage under the fair-haired Harold of Norway (71), we see the living image of the same state of things as we see in the many Kings within the little isle of Ithakê, or in that other royal crowd whom Odysseus dealt with so tenderly in the hour of trial before Ilios (72). But, while Greek kingship died out in Greece itself, while even in Macedonia it lived on only to be swallowed up in the dominion of Rome, the kindred Teutonic kingship has gone on and flourished down to our own times. It has gone on and flourished in modern Europe, while it died out in old Greece, mainly because tribes could be gathered into nations, while cities could not. But its fate in different European lands has been widely different. In all, kingship itself has been more or less affected by the influences which I have already spoken of as working a change in its original Teutonic character. In all it has been affected by the ecclesiastical ideas which gather round the ecclesiastical rite of consecration; in all it has been affected by ideas borrowed from the Roman Civil Law; in all it has been affected by feudal and territorial notions which taught men to look on kingship as a property rather than an office; in all it has been affected by the developement of those ideas which grew out of the union of the Teutonic *comitatus* with the Roman tenure of lands by military service (73). The sacred character which the King received from the new religion was perhaps only a fair exchange for the sacred character which he lost by the abolition of the old. But the Teutonic King was neither a despot nor a constitutional abstraction; he was not a lord of the soil, nor was he a mere head of an ascending series of feudal chiefs. In different ages and countries he has become all these things. In one age he became an absolute master, by dint of clothing the hereditary King with those attributes with which, in the theory of the Civil Law, the Roman people, at each election of an Emperor, clothed its

Imperial Tribune (74). In another age the personal relation of lord and man swallowed up the relation in which each member of the commonwealth stands to its head. But in all the King changed from the chief of a people, wherever that people might be found, into the ruler of a certain portion of the earth's surface, by whomsoever that portion of the earth's surface might be inhabited. New-fangled territorial titles—King of England, King of France, and the like—displaced those ancient titles of national chieftainship which were borne alike by the King of the Macedonians and the King of the Medes and Persians, by the Emperor of the Romans and the King of the West-Goths, by the King of the English and the Duke of the Normans (75). And as kingship changed from the chieftainship of the people to the lordship of the soil—as it changed from an office to a property—as the territorial kingdom came to be looked on as a vast estate—so men began to think that it was not enough that the King should have about him the sentiment which clave to the descendant of former Kings, that it was not enough that he should be chosen out of the one kingly house; lawyers and courtiers began to dream that the territorial property into which they had changed the kingly office ought to pass, like any other territorial property, according to some fixed law of hereditary succession. They devised for us all those lawyers' subtleties of primogeniture, representation, and the like, which gave our Crown for a season to Edward of Caernarvon and Richard of Bourdeaux, but which would have bidden Ælfred to stand aside, and to forbear from touching the inheritance of his brother's child. All these various influences have affected kingship in every European kingdom; but it has been affected by these several influences in very different degrees in different lands. And, if the nature of kingship itself has thus come to differ under different circumstances, the degree of power attached to the kingly title has differed no less. Kingship has come, in different lands, to wear all the different forms with a sketch of which I began the present lecture. There is still one European land where, as in the days of the old Cæsars, what seems good to the Prince has the force of law (76). There are other lands in which the law still clothes the sovereign with vast, though strictly defined, powers, but where some of those powers are exercised only through advisers in whose choice the sovereign has hardly a personal voice, while there are other powers which neither sovereign nor minister would for a moment dream of exercising at all. If we look to the history of our own land, we find in this matter of the developement of kingship, as in most others, a stronger historical continuity than elsewhere. At no stage of the process which changed the Ealdorman or Heretoga of a corner of Hampshire into the King of the English and Lord of the Isle of Britain did he ever wholly lose the old character of the chief of the people (77). Every change which in other lands affected the primitive nature of Teutonic kingship was slower in reaching us, and had less effect when it did reach us, than it had elsewhere. The coming of the Norman handed over the English Crown to Kings of foreign speech; but it did not wholly break the continuity of English political traditions. Nay rather, it was the firm hand of the great William which put the last stroke to the work of Ecgberht and Æthelstan, and which made England for ever a realm which, since his day, no man has thought of parting asunder. And the Conqueror, who claimed the Crown by English Law, who professed to rule according to English Law, handed down the tradition of English Law to all those who came after him. The King has been mighty, but the Law has ever been mightier. The Laws of King Eadward grew into the Great Charter; the Great Charter grew into the Petition of Right; the Petition of Right grew into that fuller establishment of our liberties which marked the great day when Englishmen for the last time chose themselves a King (78).

If we look through all the stages of our history, we shall, I think, see that of all European nations we have fallen away the least from the old heritage of our fathers, and that, when we have fallen away from it, we have in many cases only come back to it in other forms. We have never wholly cast aside either the hereditary or the elective principle; our sovereign is still crowned and anointed with the same rites as Eadward, Harold, and William, and is still clothed with those powers, ecclesiastical as well as temporal, which William knew how to defend against Hildebrand himself (79). Even in so small a matter as the descent of the Crown among members of the old kingly house, no other land can show a succession of Kings so nearly unbroken. Nowhere else, even by help of female succession, can any royal house trace up its descent to the chiefs who, fourteen hundred years back, led the nation into the land in which they still dwell. Under Cerdic and Cynric the people of the West-Saxons made their first settlement in the Celtic land. And ever since—save when for a moment the old stock gave way, twice to foreign conquest, once to popular election—the children of Cerdic and Cynric have ruled over the people of the West-Saxons and over all into which the realm of the West-Saxons has grown. Every sovereign of Wessex or of England, before and since the age of Cnut, of Harold, and of William, has been, at least on the female side, the offspring of the first founder of the nation (80).

Among our kinsmen on the mainland kingship has run another course. Nowhere but in our own island had the old Teutonic kingship, like other old Teutonic institutions, the same chance of growing and improving, of modifying themselves by a purely native growth, on a soil where the utter sweeping away of an earlier state of things had made as fully their own as the land from which they set forth to win it. In our island—a world of its own—the Teutonic State and the Teutonic kingship could grow up undisturbed by Roman influences, till Roman influences came to show themselves in their later forms, ecclesiastical and feudal. Elsewhere, wherever the Teutonic nation and its King established themselves on the conquered Roman soil, they stepped at once within the magic circle of Roman influences. Some of the Teutonic kingdoms which were thus founded on Roman soil fell back again, like those of the Vandals in Africa and the Goths in Italy, within the grasp of the reviving Roman power. The Goth in Spain, himself for a while cut short by the Roman revival (81), lived on to fall beneath the yoke of invaders foreign alike to Aryan speech and to Christian faith. Others were absorbed one by one into the dominion of a kindred people mightier than themselves. Step by step, a single Teutonic nation rose to the first place, and united under the Frankish sceptre the ancestral land of Germany and the conquered land of Gaul. But, in so doing, the Frankish kingship lost the power which the English kingship still kept, of handing on the unmixed Teutonic traditions of earlier times. The fact that the Frankish power never became wholly Gaulish, that the Teutonic lands of the Eastern Franks and of the dependent Allemani and Bavarians still formed part of the Frankish dominion, saved that dominion from becoming wholly Roman: it saved the Frank, even on Gaulish soil, from wholly casting away the speech and traditions of his fathers. Still the great territorial conquest won by the Franks on Roman ground did not fail to do its work. When the nation, King, nobles, freemen, sat down in the new homes which they had won among a conquered people whose civilization was higher than their own, they could not keep their old simple social state, their old simple political traditions, free from all foreign intermixture. Mere increase of dominion cannot fail to add to the kingly power (82), and it adds to it still more when increase of dominion takes the form of foreign conquest. The King who rules according to his own will over the greater numbers of the conquered strangers will insensibly take to himself a greater share of power than of old, even over his own countrymen. Add to this that, in the Gaulish land, the Franks found an elaborate system of law, ecclesiastical and civil, fully established; and the Frankish King lent no unwilling ear to the Roman priest or the Roman lawyer who taught him that he need not look on his power as bounded by the restraints put upon it by the customs of his own people. The Lord of Gaul, the Advocate of the Orthodox Church, might claim to himself all the powers which had been exercised by Constantine and Theodosius, which were still exercised before his eyes by Justinian or Heraclius. At last, under a new and mightier dynasty, the two natures of Roman and Teutonic rule were joined in one: the Frankish King became the Roman Cæsar. But, step by step, the kingship of Germany was crushed in pieces beneath the weight of the Imperial dignity, and the Lord of the World (83) came, as Lord of the World, to have less of real power than the lords of very small portions of its surface. Between domestic weakness and foreign aggression, the once united German Kingdom broke up into a lax Confederation, and out of that lax Confederation the kingdom of Henry of Saxony and Rudolf of Habsburg has again sprung to life before our eyes (84). Meanwhile the

Western part of the old Frankish realm fell away from the common centre, and a small principality by the Seine, peopled by a fragment of the old Celtic race, grew, under the borrowed name of France, into one of the foremost powers of the European world. While in the Eastern (85), the German, realm, the Crown first became purely elective and then practically hereditary under elective forms (86), the Crown of the Western France became more purely hereditary than that of any other kingdom, because there never was lacking a male heir of the first patriarch to claim it. But, perhaps partly for that very reason, when the magic spell of that long succession was once broken, it has been found harder than in any other land to find a stable government of any kind to take the place of the unbroken kingship of eight hundred years. In Germany, as I have said, the royal power came to nothing, because the kingdom split asunder into states which were virtually independent. In France the same thing happened at an earlier time; but the Crown contrived to annex the separate principalities one by one, and so to establish, step by step, a despotism over the whole land. England, after its final union, never split asunder. The policy of William secured that, though the Crown might be weaker than the united nation, yet each single man in the nation, the very highest not excepted, should be weaker than the Crown (87).

In the constitutional monarchies of modern times, the Crown is the Executive power; but its free action as such is more or less hampered by the conventional necessity of acting by the advice of Ministers who are approved by a majority of the Legislature. Kingship has lost nothing of its dignity; it has lost little of its legal powers; what modern practice does is to provide the Sovereign with a Mayor of the Palace whom the Legislature can practically remove at pleasure. I mention this now, because it is of some importance to distinguish between kingly dignity and kingly power. We have seen how, in the Roman Commonwealth, the ancient powers of the Kings were not so much taken away as put into commission in the hands of the Consuls and other magistrates. Something of the same kind has happened in some republican states in later times. It is worth noticing how, in popular talk, the notion of a Republic seems naturally to suggest the notion of a President. That is to say, it is taken for granted that the State must have a personal head, even though that personal head may be chosen for a definite term, and may be subject to legal punishment in the case of proved crime. That such a way of speaking leaves out of sight most of the great Commonwealths of history, that it leaves out of sight the most successful Commonwealth of modern times, is a slight matter. It is an established maxim among political talkers that the one state in Europe where republican institutions are immemorial, the one state where they have been fairly tried and have thoroughly succeeded, should be left out of sight in all such inquiries. People who would be ashamed not to know all about the political condition of every other European nation, would deem it beneath them to stop and think whether the Swiss Confederation or any of its Cantons is governed by King, President, or Council (88). History shows that the tendency of republican states in general is against vesting the Executive power in any single person. There has indeed commonly been a chief magistrate, under some title or other; but he has been only the chief of the Executive; he has not been himself the whole of it. He has been, like the Swiss President, a mere Chairman of a Council, not, like the American President, an independent power in the State. The notion that a republic must have a President at its head is simply a shadow of kingship. Men have been so accustomed to kingly government, to a personal head of the State, that it seems natural, even in getting rid of kingship, to keep the personal head, and simply to make him elective instead of hereditary, appointed for a fixed time instead of for life. The American President, in the original conception of his office, is a four years' King; and the early Presidents ruled with far more of personal kingly power than the King of any kingdom where the modern theory of constitutional government is fully established. The cause is obvious: hereditary succession gives no guaranty for any personal qualifications in the King. His power is therefore not only limited by law, but it is held that, even in the exercise of his legal powers, he is bound to follow the advice of Ministers who are practically appointed and removed by the popular branch of the Legislature. But the President, it might be thought, need be bound by no such fetters. He is chosen for a fixed time: he is chosen, it might be hoped, on account of his personal fitness to rule. It might therefore seem to follow that, while his office lasts, his personal power ought to be greater than that of a constitutional King; it might seem to follow that such authority as the law gives him he may use purely according to his personal discretion, and that his Ministers should be his servants, and not his masters. But it is clear that there is a tendency at work to hamper the personal freedom of action of the

Presidents of the United States, in nearly the same way, so far as the different forms of the Constitution allow, in which the personal freedom of action of the constitutional Kings of Europe is hampered. That is to say, though the President is not a King, though his position has nothing of kingly dignity, of kingly mystery, or of kingly duration, yet his powers are in themselves so essentially kingly that it seems an obvious thing to treat him as a King, and to give him, like a King, Ministers who shall control rather than obey him. The Executive Council, such as we see in the Swiss Confederation, alone avoids every tendency of the kind. To a body of seven men, chosen by the Legislature for the term of its own being, no scrap or rag of kingship can cleave (89).

There is one feature in which it might seem that the modern conception, I will not say of kingship, but of royalty, has gone back to the ideas of the very earliest times. In fully developed constitutional States, the notion of kingship, either strictly as an office or strictly as a possession, has well nigh died out. But the notion of royalty as a dignity belonging to royal personages, as something which cleaves, not only to Kings themselves, but to all their kindred and belongings—the notion that such kindred and belongings form a separate class or order apart from other men—is stronger now than it ever was since men reverenced in their Kings the son of Zeus or of Woden. In no time or place was kingship, as an office or possession, more highly magnified than in the days of Elizabeth and her father. But the notion of royalty in the modern sense could have no place where the sovereign was the child of an English mother, and could trace back her descent to ancient Kings through a long succession of uncrowned ancestors (90). We have seen that the notion of the kingliness of the race is probably older than kingship, either as an office or as a possession. It would seem also to be more lasting. The feeling which binds all the royal houses of Europe together, as members of one class, would hardly have been understood by the followers of Thomas of Lancaster or Henry of Richmond. It would perhaps have been more intelligible to those who, when a number of tribes were welded together into a nation, placed, as a matter of course, a son of Woden at its head. It would have been least of all intelligible in the days when personal rule was at its highest in point of real power, at its lowest in point of outward dignity. Men marched off into a distant banishment, or opened their veins to die without a thought of resistance, at the mere bidding of a Cæsar who, in outward form, was simply the first magistrate of the Commonwealth. The successors of that Cæsar, Lords of the World, waited on by Kings and sovereign Dukes, commanded no such obedience. The notion of mere rank and dignity and the notion of real power are in themselves distinct. There are times when the two are joined together; there are other times when they would seem to be not only distinct, but actually hostile.

I have now dealt with the general notions of the State itself in its two great forms: as the city and as the tribe growing into the nation. I have dealt with its chief, in his various forms, sometimes the King sinking into the republican magistrate, sometimes the republican magistrate growing into the King. The next time I come before you I shall have to deal no longer with the head of the State, but with its body, with the Assembly of the city or nation in all its forms, from the *Agorê* of the Homeric Achaians to the Parliament of the United Kingdom.

## LECTURE V.

# THE ASSEMBLY.

WE have now dealt with the general idea of the State, whether as a tribe growing into a nation or as shut up within the walls of a single city. From that general idea we have passed to the head of the State, to the King. We have seen in old Greece the power of the Kings of particular cities vanish away, as those cities changed into commonwealths, first aristocratic and then democratic. We have seen the powers of the Roman Kings put, as it were, into commission among the great magistrates of the Republic, and then gathered together again, in far more than their old strength, in the hands of the Emperors. We have traced the origin and growth of Teutonic kingship; we have seen how, as the tribe grew into a nation, its chief grew into a King; we have seen how the various forms of modern European royalty started off from this primitive source, and how strangely the greatest among them became for ages allied, or rather identified, with the still abiding dignity of the Roman Augustus. We have now to turn from the head of the State to its body, from the King to the Assembly of the People. The body follows the same law as its head. Where the city is the commonwealth and the commonwealth never stretches beyond its walls, the Assembly may shrink up into, or it may never develope itself beyond, the gathering of a mere oligarchic body. As the highest franchise of the city may be shared by all the citizens, or may be confined to the members of an exclusive order, so the sovereign Assembly of the commonwealth may be less or greater in its numbers. The sovereign body is the Assembly of all those citizens who hold the highest franchise, whether they form the narrowest oligarchy or the most open democracy. In either case, each member of the ruling body discharges his own duty in the Assembly in his own person, and not through a representative. In a city commonwealth the idea of representation, of choosing certain citizens to act on behalf of the whole body, is not likely to come into any man's head. Where all the citizens in a democracy, or all the citizens of the ruling order in an oligarchy, can habitually come together in their own persons, as in a city commonwealth they can, it is not likely that they will willingly give up their highest right to a few members of their own body. They may entrust greater or less powers to smaller Councils and to individual magistrates; and the Councils and magistrates of an oligarchy will commonly be entrusted with far larger and more independent powers than the Councils and magistrates of a democracy. But in either case the Assembly of the whole people, or of the whole privileged class of the people, remains the sovereign power of the commonwealth. And, as the Assembly of the city is not likely to change itself into a representative body within its own walls, so it is not likely to merge its own being as a sovereign and independent Assembly in any body beyond its own walls. If the city be connected with other cities by a Federal tie, it may give up to the general Assembly of the whole Confederation the right of deciding on the relations of the Confederation to foreign powers, and all other such matters as naturally come within the range of Federal authority. But the Assemblies of the several cities did not in such a case cease to exist; they do not cease to be sovereign and independent within the range of all powers which they do not expressly give up to the Federal body (1). And, stranger still to our notions, among the Confederations of Greece even the Federal body itself did not assume a representative character; as every citizen of the individual city had his place in the sovereign Assembly of that city, so each citizen of the Confederation had his place in the sovereign Assembly of the Confederation (2). Wherever the independent city is the leading political idea, whether the city remain absolutely independent for all purposes or it is content to yield part of its sovereign rights to a Federal authority—whether it strictly confines its citizenship to the dwellers in its own walls or freely grants it out to all the inhabitants of a large country—in either case alike each citizen keeps his personal right to attend and vote in the sovereign Assembly of the State of which he is a member. It seems to be a law of its being that the primary Assembly of the city should never grow into or merge itself in the representative Assembly of a nation.

Where, on the other hand, the tribe and not the city is the leading political idea, the case is widely different. We have seen how tribes grew into nations, how, from being independent political bodies, they sank into mere divisions of a greater body. In this process the Assemblies of the State follow the same law as the State itself. The tribe and the city start from the same point, for in truth the city is only a tribe, or more than one tribe, surrounded by a wall. In the Assembly of the tribe, no less than in the Assembly of the city, every man who enjoys the full franchise, every freeman of the tribe, has the right to appear in person. But, as the tribe merges itself in a greater whole far more easily than the city, so the Assembly of the tribe shares a like fate. As the tribe ceases to be the State, and becomes a mere division of the State—as the chief of the tribe becomes a mere subordinate deputy of the King who is the chief of the nation (3)—so in the like sort the sovereign Assembly of the tribe merges itself in the sovereign Assembly of the nation. It may cease to exist altogether, or it may go on as a purely local body; but if so, it has ceased to be sovereign; it is merely the Assembly of a certain division of the State or of its territory; it does not, like the several members of a Confederation, retain its independent sovereignty within its own range. It is only under the most exceptional of circumstances that the tribal Assembly can live on through all changes, and, after having sunk into the Assembly of a mere corner of a vast kingdom, can come forth again as the sovereign assembly of an independent state. In one lucky corner of the world things have taken this exceptional course. We cannot see the Dêmos of Athens on his Pnyx; we cannot see the Comitia of Rome in the Forum or on the field of Mars; but any man who chooses may, on the first Sunday of next May, see the Germans of Tacitus with his own eyes (4).

It must be constantly borne in mind that the true difference between an aristocratic and a democratic government, as those words were understood in the politics of old Greece, lies in this. In the democracy all citizens, all who enjoy civil rights, enjoy also political rights. In the aristocracy political rights belong to only a part of those who enjoy civil rights. But, in either case, the highest authority of the State is the general Assembly of the whole ruling body, whether that ruling body be the whole people or only a part of it. Two great examples of the aristocratic Assembly went on into modern times, the Great Council of Venice and those great and tumultuous *comitia* of the whole nobility of Poland which came together for the election of a King. This aristocratic Assembly, when it came together, was far more truly to be called a mob than the Assembly of democratic Athens. But it might be argued in return that, if the Polish Assembly was an oligarchy as opposed to the excluded classes of the nation, the Athenian Assembly was also an oligarchy, as opposed to the excluded classes of slaves and strangers. It is certain that, in Athens or in any other democratic commonwealth, those who enjoyed the political franchise were far fewer in number than those who were shut out from it. But, according to Greek ideas, this in no way interfered with the democratic character of the commonweath and its Assembly. The shutting out of slaves and strangers was as much a matter of course, according to Greek ideas, as the shutting out of women and children is according to the ideas of nearly every state in the world. The constitution of the city community, whether aristocratic or democratic, rests wholly on the principle of hereditary burghership. The slave of course has no rights; that is involved in the very nature of slavery (5); neither has the resident stranger who has not been adopted into the burghership, even though he and his forefathers for generations may have lived and been born in the land. The answer to any claim on his part would have been that he had his own hereditary burghership somewhere else—let him go and enjoy his civil and political rights there. The slaves and strangers who were shut out at Athens were, according to Greek ideas, no Athenians; but every Athenian had his place in the sovereign assembly of Athens, while every Corinthian had not his place in the sovereign assembly of Corinth. But the aristocratic and the democratic commonwealth both agreed in placing the final authority of the State in the general Assembly of all who enjoy the highest franchise. From this point all the political assemblies of the world, all at least of that part of the world with which we are concerned, take their start, and the democratic model is the older and purer of the two (6). The ways in which distinctions arise between different classes in the same state are various, and of some of them I shall have to speak in my last lecture. But it is plain that, whether we take the city or the tribe for our starting point, the oldest and purest model is that in which the sovereign assembly takes in all who are members of the State. That it shuts out those who from any cause are not members of the State must be taken for granted. We must not bring in modern ideas, which belong wholly to a state of things in which nations have taken the form of territorial kingdoms. With us every one born in the land is of right a British subject, and the rights of a British subject may be obtained with very little trouble by those who are not born in the land. The like is the case in most other modern kingdoms and commonwealths. This is because they have all become territorial, because they have learned to put birth within the land in the place of descent from the original stock. In a tribe, as long as it retains the feelings of a tribe, in a city, as long as it retains the principle of hereditary burghership, naturalization must always remain a matter of special favour. No length of residence, not even birth in the land of other than citizen parents, can ever give it of right.

I have wandered to some extent from the subject of Assemblies, but it was not foreign to my subject to clear away one or two difficulties which might arise from the seemingly twofold character of some commonwealths, and of their sovereign Assemblies. In the primitive conception, the Assembly is the gathering of the whole people, the gathering of all the men of the tribe, of all the citizens of the city. Now in all primitive societies the distinction between soldier and civilian is unknown. To fight when called on is not the special profession of any particular class; it is the duty of all men alike who are able to bear arms. And we may add that, in some states of society, fighting is not merely every man's duty when called on; it is something very like the chief business of life. From this it follows that, in all early states of society, the army is the Assembly, and the Assembly is the army (7). The same body of men, if called together for a peaceful purpose, form the political Assembly; if called together for a warlike purpose, they form the army. But the men are the same in either case, and it is not till political refinement has made great advances that any distinction is drawn between the members of the State in their civil and in their military character. It is plain that such a distinction was likely to be first drawn among the greater civilization and more complicated relations of city life. As long as the tribe remains the ruling idea, nay, even long after the tribe has grown into, or merged itself in, the nation, the nation is still the army and the army is the nation. The Assembly meets in arms, ready to act as an army, if need should so demand; and the army, whether under Agamemnôn beneath the walls of Ilios (8), under Alexander far away in Bactria (9), or under our Eadward on the shores of Kent (10), can, in the like case of need, discharge the duties of the Assembly. But in the city commonwealth it is gradually found that, though every citizen is bound to serve in arms when called on, yet there is no need for every citizen to be called on to serve at the same moment (11). An army, though only a temporary army, is thus formed, distinct from the whole body of the people. Those citizens who are in arms give up for a while their full rights as citizens; the authority of the General without the city rises far above the restraints which fetter the authority of the Magistrate within the city; and the citizens who form the army are content to receive orders from the citizens who remain at home and can go through the accustomed forms of a peaceful Assembly (12). And in the case of a city commonwealth another element comes in. In the city everything is local; the Assembly must be held in the accustomed place, perhaps within the precincts of some revered temple; if it were held elsewhere, it would lose all its virtue, and its acts might seem to be of no force. Hence, while in other states of society the military Assembly is common, among the settled city commonwealths of Greece it is rare, and under the stern discipline of a Roman army it was unknown. Alexander brought his traitors before the assembly of his soldiers, but Titus Manlius struck off his son's head by the sole authority of the Consul and father. In Athenian history the military Assembly is heard of only in cases of some desperate emergency, when the Mede holds the soil of Athens but when Athens herself is in her ships by Salamis (13), or when, in the days of the Four Hundred, the fleet at Samos, cleaving to the old laws and freedom, declares that the city has revolted from them (14). In the Federal period we hear more commonly, though still rarely, of military assemblies, of the nation in arms on foreign service exercising, under the walls of a besieged city, the authority which, under common circumstances, it would have exercised in the regular place of Federal meeting (15). The cause of the difference is obvious. The citizens of a Confederation were used to exercise political powers at a distance from their own homes; the place of Federal meeting at Megalopolis or Aigion could never become surrounded with the same sacred and exclusive associations which to the mind of the Athenian gathered round the holy rock of Athênê. To discharge the rights of citizens on an unusual spot, or under unusual circumstances, was a slighter shock to a body of men gathered together from several confederate commonwealths than it was to men whose every political idea centred within the walls of a single city.

But we must go back to earlier times, to the very first glimpses which we get of the political life of those three branches of the Aryan family with which we are now specially concerned. If there is anything which we can fairly look upon as a common political heritage, as something handed on from the days when Greek, Latin, and Teuton were still one people, it is surely to be seen in the great elements of political life which are common to all three, in the general Assembly of the people presided over by the King or other chief, and guided rather than restrained in its deliberations by the working of the smaller Council, whether of hereditary nobles, of elders serving for life, or of magistrates or senators clothed with a temporary authority by the Assembly itself. The exact constitution, the exact limits of the authority, of the three great political elements vary from time to time and from place to place, but the three elements themselves are always there. It may be that the Achaian King in Homer exercises a greater control over the course of things in the Assembly than the German King in Tacitus. Differences of this kind will be found everywhere, but the essential elements remain the same under all varieties of detail. Everywhere alike we find the general Assembly, the smaller Council, and the King himself. In those states in which kingship has either not yet arisen or has given way to magistrates periodically renewed, we find his forerunner or his successor. In every page of the Homeric poems, in every gathering which they set before us, political, military, festive, or religious, the three elements come before us with more or less distinctness, according to the circumstances of the case. The Zeus-born and Zeus-nurtured King is ever surrounded by the chiefs, the elders, the lesser Kings, who form the nearest circle round him. And these again are surrounded by the wider circle of the whole body of the tribe, the city, or the army. We see them, not only in the mortal world of Hellas, but in the lands called into being by the play of Hellenic fancy, in the mythic isle of the Phaiakians and among the Gods themselves on Olympos. To the mind of the Greek the Gods whom he worshipped were beings who shared the nature and the passions of man. They were in truth men: they were mightier indeed and happier than the mortal men on earth, free from the toils and pains and cares of earthly life, and with no doom of coming death before their eyes (16). But they were still Gods after the likeness of men, Gods who shared the loves, the hates, the counsels, of their worshippers, who had spots which they loved on earth, and of whose blood the Kings and heroes of mortal blood were sprung. The immortal people on Olympos, like the mortal people in Ithakê or like the confederate host before Ilios, had their supreme King, their smaller Council, their general Assembly of the whole divine race. The will of Zeus in heaven, like the will of Agamemnôn on earth, may be a will which it is dangerous to disobey, but it is not the will of a despot who is obeyed without dispute or criticism. The great Gods and Goddesses who form the inner Council, the Senate, the Gerousia, the Areiopagos of Heaven, at least speak their minds freely before the Father of Gods and Men. And, when need calls for such a gathering, once in the course of the Homeric tale, the summons goes forth which gathers the Agorê, the Comitia, the *Mickle Gemót* of the immortal nation, to come together to share the counsels of the Lord of that triple world. From that great *Himmelsgemeinde*, if I may coin a word in the one modern speech on which the inheritance of old Hellas has fallen, which came together at the summons of Themis, none stay away; the river-Gods come, and the nymphs from the groves and fountains and grassy meadows, to sit in council on the seats which Hephaistos has wrought for them in the house of Zeus (17). The same word ἀγορή is used to express the divine and the human Assembly; the constitution of the two is exactly alike, unless any one should argue that the importance of Hêrê and Athênê in the inner Council, and the marked attendance of all the Nymphs in the general Assembly, show that political progress had made wider strides in Olympos than it had on earth (18). But the overwhelming power of the will of Zeus in the Assembly, where Poseidôn alone dares to question him (19), and where no one ventures a word in answer to him, brings me to one point in the character of the Homeric Assemblies which has given rise to a good deal of discussion, and about which I myself, among others, have had my own say elsewhere (20). This is the alleged extreme submission of the Assembly, and even of the chiefs, to the supreme King, Zeus on Olympos and Agamemnôn on earth. It is, I think, undoubtedly true that the primitive Greek Assembly, as set before us by Homer, does show far more of deference to the King than is to be found in the primitive Teutonic Assembly as set before us by Tacitus. We have seen that the whole conception and position of the Greek King was something higher than that of the Teutonic King. This is the kind of difference which we must always expect to meet with between one age and people and another. But we may remark that the Agamemnôn of the Iliad is something more than an ordinary King. The King of Mykênê who reigned over many islands and all Argos was, as it were, the *Bretwalda* of Hellas, *Basileus* in the later as well as in the earlier sense (21). And when we add that he is general of the confederate army on actual service, the fact that the Assembly should go on and retain any kind of independence, amid the discipline of actual warfare, is in itself no small matter. It surely proves more one way than is proved the other way by the fact that the King's power is more arbitrary in war-time than it was in time of peace. As for the polity of Olympos, the poet was clearly divided between two opposite ideas. Zeus the human God, who shared the feelings and passions of man, who hearkened to the prayer of Thetis and felt his heart moved with human sorrow for the fate of Sarpedôn (22), could be conceived only as a human King with all the surroundings of a human King. But Zeus in the elder conception, Zeus the God of the sky, the power spread over all and ruling over all, must speak with a voice of command which neither men nor Gods can gainsay. And, again to come down to earth, if the camp before Ilios might tend to give us an overweening idea of the authority of the Achaian King in the face of his Assembly, the Odyssey shows us, on the other hand, how low Achaian kingship could fall when the King himself was absent, and when his person had to be represented by the old age of his father and by the youth of his son. But it should be marked too that, in the anarchy of Ithakê, as long as the kingly power is in abeyance, the Assembly is in abeyance also (23). It might seem that King and Assembly were the two essential elements of lawful government, neither of which could stand without the other. But, after all, I think that the submission of the mass of the Achaian freemen to Agamemnôn and a few other great chiefs has been, if not exaggerated, at least misunderstood. It is not the submission of slaves, but the submission of children. It is not the submission of men who wish to oppose but who dare not; it is the submission of men who have not yet formed the wish to oppose. The speaking, to be sure, is mainly confined to a few great chiefs, and the opposition speaker Thersitês is roughly handled. But this is, I venture to think, not altogether peculiar to the military assembly of the Achaians. The real thing to be marked is that there should be any opposition speakers at all. There is no formal reckoning of votes; but I suspect that any formal reckoning of votes is a refinement belonging to a much later stage of political life. To shout or to clash the arms is the primitive way of declaring assent (24). Ages afterwards the will of the Spartan Assembly was declared, not by a formal vote, but by a shout (25); nay, down to our own day, in our Houses of Parliament, in the deliberative Assemblies of our Universities, the vote, the division, the scrutiny, is a mere secondary refinement; the Assembly first speaks its mind in Homeric fashion by a shout, and then it is open to any member to appeal—for an appeal it is in the strictest sense—from the primitive decision by the shout to the more certain test of actual voting. The Achaian King, to put the powers of the Assembly at their very lowest, cannot reign without gathering his people together, without setting his purposes before them, without at least learning whether his own will is the same as the will of his people. And herein is the essence of freedom. An Assembly of this kind will gather strength as it goes on; men whom their King has to persuade will some day refuse to be persuaded; men before whom Kings and chiefs speak and argue will some day speak and argue for themselves. The Assembly which, not in the feebleness of age but in the simplicity of childhood, still cries Aye to whatever is set before it will assuredly learn to cry No, whenever the time for crying No shall come.

We should better understand the nature of the Greek Assemblies in the Homeric times, if we had fuller accounts of the internal affairs of those kindred nations among whom the Homeric kingship went on after it had come to an end in Hellas itself. The Epeirot and Macedonian Assemblies, assemblies which, at different stages of their growth, were assemblies, first of tribes and then of nations, but never strictly assemblies of cities, must have had more in common with the early Teutonic Assemblies than anything to be found among the proper Hellênes. But we hardly know more of them than that they existed. Of the solemn pledge which bound together the Molossian king and people in the Assembly of Passarôn I have already spoken. The Macedonian Assemblies of which we read in history are either military assemblies which come together to hear charges brought before them by Alexander, or else they are assemblies held in the revolutionary times which followed Alexander's death to accept some successful candidate for the Crown, or to condemn some one whose career has been less lucky (26). All that we know is that there were such Assemblies, and that they did exercise a will of their own, since those whom Alexander himself accused were sometimes acquitted (27). But we must remember that of the internal state of Macedonia and Epeiros we know absolutely nothing. We hear of their foreign relations and of their dynastic revolutions, but of the ordinary working of government in those countries not a word is recorded. The precious notices that we have as to the political constitution of the Chaonians and Thesprotians come to us only from a short and incidental notice in Thucydides, which we should never have had, if he had not been called on to describe a military expedition in which those nations took a share. Our ignorance on these matters is specially to be lamented. It is plain that in these countries there was an opportunity for free government on a large scale, for the political life of a nation and not of a mere city, such as did not arise again for many ages. Of the local institutions of those lands and of their everyday working we have no account whatever. We know a great deal less of the Macedonian monarchy than we should know of the Frankish or the Old-English monarchy, if we had only their chroniclers, and not a single word of laws, charters, or letters. But without these last we should have a very vague notion indeed even of our own land. We should see that there were Kings and that there were Assemblies, but we should not see much more. Of the every-day working of local institutions we should know absolutely nothing. We are therefore quite unable to say what points of likeness or unlikeness the internal state of Macedonia or of Molossis may have shown to that of mediæval or of modern kingdoms. But the mere facts that there was a King, and that there was a national Assembly of some kind or other, are enough to show that the approach to the state of things in modern, or at least in mediæval, Europe must have been far nearer than anything else to be found in the early history of the Greek and Italian lands. It would seem as if the first steps had been taken towards a work which was only begun and not finished, and which had to be begun again ages afterwards. The conquests of Philip and Alexander, the close relations into which they brought their kingdom alike with the intellectual culture of Greece and with the political despotism of the East, doubtless did much to check the natural developement of national Macedonian life. The whole subject is a disappointing one; we see that something was begun and never finished, and we do not see in detail what was begun, or what hope there was of finishing it. But we do see that Macedonia stood alone among the chief nations of the ancient world, as the one which most nearly foreshadowed the political life of modern Europe, as the one great nation which had Kings and which is yet allowed to have been free (28).

The chance then of the developement of a constitutional government for a whole nation seems to have been lost in the one case in the ancient world where there was most hope for it. The political civilization of the two great peninsulas took the city as its ruling idea, and the political assemblies of Greece and Italy were assemblies of cities, or, at most, assemblies of confederations of cities. One of these, the most illustrious of all, the Assembly of the Democracy of Athens, still lives before us in its minutest details. We know the laws which regulated its constitution; we know the rules which were followed in its procedure. We have living pictures of the course of its debates; we can listen to the very words by which it was stirred as they fell from the lips of the greatest of orators and statesmen. In the Ekklêsia which listened to Periklês and Dêmosthenês we feel almost as much at home as in an institution of our own land and our own times. At least we ought to feel at home there; for we have the full materials for calling up the political life of Athens in all its fullness, and within our own times one of the greatest minds of our own or of any age has given its full strength to clear away the mists of error and calumny which so long shrouded the parent state of justice and freedom. Among the contemporaries and countrymen of Mr. Grote it is shame indeed if men fail to see in the great Democracy the first state which taught mankind that the voice of persuasion could be stronger than a despot's will, the first which taught that disputes could be settled by a free debate and a free vote which in other lands could have been decided only by the banishment or massacre of the weaker side. It was the Democracy of Athens which taught the world that there was, in the words of its own great historian, such a thing as constitutional morality. The man who, in any age or in any land, does aught for the cause of right or freedom, may cherish as his brightest thought that he is walking in the path in which Solôn, Kleisthenês, Aristeidês, and Periklês walked before him. They walked before us, but there were none who walked before them. The Assembly of Athens, called together and guided in its procedure by established and written laws, grew doubtless step by step out of the more irregular assemblies of the heroic times; but we now for the first time come across the personal agency of living men;

we now have no longer to talk vaguely about growth and tendencies and developements; we stand face to face with men who, each in his own day, wrought a great and noble work for his own age and for all ages. That the glory of such a work was too bright to last we have already seen. The life of a nation is less brilliant than the life of a city, but, for that very reason, the nation outlives the city. Our national life has been spread over fourteen hundred years, and we trust that it is still far from being run out. The real life of Athens lasted at the most for two hundred years (29); and yet there are moments in which all that we have won by the toils of so many generations seems as if it would be felt to be but a small thing beside a single hour of Periklês.

The Democracy of Athens was in truth the noblest fruit of that self-developing power of the Greek mind which worked every possession of the common heritage into some new and more brilliant shape, but which learned nothing, nothing of all that formed its real life and its real glory, from the Barbarians of the outer world. Men tell us that Greece learned this or that mechanical invention from Phœnicia or Egypt or Assyria. Be it so; but stand in the Pnyx; listen to the contending orators; listen to the ambassadors of distant cities; listen to each side as it is fairly hearkened to, and see the matter in hand decided by the peaceful vote of thousands—here at least of a truth is something which Athens did not learn from any Assyrian despot or from any Egyptian priest. And we, children of the common stock, sharers in the common heritage, as we see man, Aryan man, in the full growth of his noblest type, we may feel a thrill as we think that Kleisthenês and Periklês were, after all, men of our own blood—as we think that the institutions which grew up under their hands and the institutions under which we ourselves are living are alike branches sprung from one stock, portions of one inheritance in which Athens and England have an equal right. In the Athenian Democracy we see a popular constitution taking the form which was natural for such a constitution to take when it was able to run its natural course in a commonwealth which consisted only of a single city. Wherever the Assembly really remains, in truth as well as in name, an Assembly of the whole people in their own persons, it must in its own nature be sovereign. It must, in the nature of things, delegate more or less of power to magistrates and generals; but such power will be simply delegated. Their authority will be a mere trust from the sovereign body, and to that sovereign body they will be responsible for its exercise. That is to say, one of the original elements of the State, the King or chief, now represented by the elective magistracy, will lose its independent powers, and will sink into a body who have only to carry out the will of the sovereign Assembly. So with another of the original elements, the Council. This body too loses its independent being; it has no ruling or checking power; it becomes a mere Committee of the Assembly, chosen or appointed by lot to put measures into shape for more easy discussion in the sovereign body. As society becomes more advanced and complicated, the judicial power can no longer be exercised by the Assembly itself, while it would be against every democratic instinct to leave it in the arbitrary power of individual magistrates. Other Committees of the Assembly, Juries on a gigantic scale, with a presiding magistrate as chairman rather than as Judge, are therefore set apart to decide causes and to sit in judgement on offenders. Such is pure Democracy, the government of the whole people and not of a part of it only (30), as carried out in its full perfection in a single city. It is a form of government which works up the faculties of man to a higher pitch than any other; it is the form of government which gives the freest scope to the inborn genius of the whole community and of every member of it (31). Its weak point is that it works up the faculties of man to a pitch so high that it can hardly be lasting, that its ordinary life needs an enthusiasm, a devotion, too highly strung to be likely to live through many generations. Athens in the days of her glory, the Athens of Periklês, was truly "the roof and crown of things;" her democracy raised a greater number of human beings to a higher level than any government before or since; it gave freer play than any government before or since to the personal gifts of the foremost of mankind. But against the few years of Athenian glory we must set the long ages of Athenian decline. Against the city where Periklês was General we must set the city where Hadrian was Archon.

On the Assemblies of other Grecian cities it is hardly needful to dwell. Our knowledge of their practical working is slight. We have one picture of a debate in the popular Assembly of Sparta, an Assembly none the less popular in its internal constitution because it was the assembly of what, as regarded the excluded classes of the State, was a narrow oligarchy. We see that there, as might be looked for, the chiefs of the State, the Kings, and yet more the Ephors, spoke with a degree of official, as distinguished from personal, authority which fell to the lot of no man in the Assembly of Athens (32). Periklês reigned supreme, not because he was one of Ten Generals, but because he was Periklês. From another cause a greater weight of official authority was placed in the hands of the magistrates of the Federal Democracy of Achaia than was ever entrusted to the magistrates of the single city Democracy of Athens. The meetings of the Federal Assembly were far less frequent than those of the Assembly of Athens; it was therefore needful to clothe the Senate and the magistrates, above all the chief magistrate, the General, with far higher powers than were held at Athens by Senators, Archons, or even Generals (33). And there is another difference which brings the later, the Federal, form of Greek democracy into the closest relations with the political developements of modern times. The Federal democracy was as far from hitting on the subtle device of representation as the city democracy was. Every citizen had a right to appear in the general Assembly of the League as well as in the local Assembly of his own city. But it is plain that such a right as this, when applied to a League spread over all Peloponnêsos and some cities beyond Peloponnêsos, was a right which, by the mass of those who held it, could seldom or never be exercised. The Assembly seems, as a rule, to have been attended mainly by those who had wealth and leisure enough to take distant journeys, and by the inhabitants of the particular city in which the Assembly was held. Sometimes the Senate seems to have acted as the

Assembly; it might so happen that an Assembly was summoned, and that none but Senators came. Those who are familiar with the constitution of the University of Oxford know very well that it often happens that a Convocation—that is, an Assembly of all Doctors and Masters—is really attended by none but members of Congregation, the smaller resident and official body (34). In cases of this kind the larger body does not lose its right as long as its members take care to exercise it on occasion; but it may be easily lost, if the right is not at least occasionally exercised, and, even where it is not lost, its exercise is apt to be looked upon with a certain degree of jealousy on the part of the smaller body. Thus we find an unusually large meeting of the Achaian Assembly spokèn of with a kind of surprise, if not of dislike (35); and it is not uncommon to hear an outcry against the appearance of non-resident members in the academical Convocation. No pretensions of this kind on the part of a smaller body could possibly arise in the Assemblies of Athens or of Uri.

In fact the Federal period of Grecian history is one which is richer than almost any other in analogies bearing directly on the developement of our own constitution. It illustrates the law by which, unless the device of representation is brought in, an originally democratic constitution, if it is applied to a large territory, can never keep its true democratic character. Its citizens cannot come frequently and regularly together, so as to carry on an orderly government like that of Athens. Perhaps the Assembly becomes, as that of Rome did in the end, an ungovernable multitude, incapable of debate, whose meetings are always accompanied by acts of violence, and are at last put an end to in the interests of order, if not of freedom. Or perhaps the democracy shrinks up, I will not say into an oligarchy, but into an aristocracy, simply because it is impossible that the mass of the nominal members of the Assembly should ever really attend its meetings. The Achaian League, in its form as pure a democracy as Athens or Uri, became, in its practical working, the best model of a liberal aristocracy, ruling by sufferance. And a process exactly the same went on in the early Assemblies of England and other Teutonic countries. As marks grew into shires and shires into kingdoms, the general body of freemen who had been accustomed to attend in the Assemblies of the smaller body were not formally deprived of their right to attend in the Assemblies of the larger body. But as tribes grew into nations and Ealdormen into Kings, the Assemblies of their kingdoms grew into bodies which were yet more incapable of really coming together than the general body of the free citizens of the Peloponnesian cities. I can see nothing to show that the right of the common freeman to take his place in the general Assembly of the nation was ever formally taken away in our own country. But I can see that, in the nature of things, it gradually died out. I can see that, as in Achaia the Federal Assembly shrank up, as a rule, into an Assembly of the Senators and a few other leading men, so in England the national Assembly, the *Mickle Gemót* of the whole nation, shrank up into a gathering of few besides the King's Thegns (36). But I can see also, in both cases, that, on special occasions, the Assembly again swelled into something far greater. The citizens of London or Corinth, of Winchester or Aigion, asserted and exercised their old right when the Assembly was held within the walls of their cities. And, on a few great days, when the heart of the nation was stirred to its depths, we see armed multitudes which no building, no city, could contain, taking part, as of old, in the election of Kings, in the banishment of public enemies, in the declaration of war and peace (37). That in our own land the right was exercised only by fits and starts is simply what was to be looked for from the unfixed and informal nature of our early institutions in general. But the right went on; it cannot be said to have wholly vanished, as long as the people were called on to cry Yea, Yea, even though there was no thought of their crying Nay, Nay, at the election and consecration of Kings. It must not be forgotten that Henry the Eighth was chosen King by the shout of the assembled people as truly as Hengest or Cerdic could have been (38).

What took place in our own land took place also in the kindred lands beyond the sea. Among the Franks, as has been traced out by the great constitutional historians of Germany, the old Assemblies, national and local, went on after the Frankish conquerors had settled themselves on Gaulish soil. And we see, from the language constantly used under the Carolingian Emperors and Kings, that the right and duty of the common freeman to attend in the general Assembly was never formally taken away, that the great gathering of the *Märzfeld* or the *Maifeld* was still in theory the gathering of the whole Frankish people, deciding the affairs of the nation by the voice of the nation itself. But we can see too how the general Assembly of the whole Frankish realm lost step by step the real life, the practical power, the effective control over the royal will, which had belonged to the military Assemblies of the immediate followers of Chlodwig. The right of the Assembly to say Yea or Nay is not taken away by any formal act, but it sinks at the outside into giving a formal Yea to what the King and his inner Council have already decreed (39). In this, as in so many other things, there is a real cycle in human affairs. As there is an early time, an early stage, in which the Assembly has not yet formed the wish to oppose, so there is a later stage in which it has perhaps lost the wish and has certainly lost the spirit and the power. So in the lesser Assemblies of the *Gau* or the Hundred, the judicial functions which had once belonged to the whole Assembly came gradually to be vested in a select body which grew up through the sheer unwillingness of the general mass of the freemen to attend and exercise their rights in their own persons (40).

In short, experience shows that the purely democratic system, which does such great things for a wandering band, a single city, or a small district, becomes out of place when it is applied to all the inhabitants of a large country. Unless the happy device of representation is hit upon, the primitive democracy, directly by the working of its democratic character, shrinks up into despotism or oligarchy. The primary Assembly is the natural form of free government for the wandering band, for the group of households settled in their mark, for the tribe gathered within the walls of a city. It begins to break down when it is applied even to a *Gau* or Canton of a larger size; it utterly breaks down when it is applied to a nation. The representative Assembly is as much the natural form of free government for the greater society as the primary Assembly is for the smaller.

The analogies which have crowded on me in the course of the present lecture have hindered me from following so strict a chronological order as I have done at other times. I have been dealing with Greek and Teutonic matters at once. But it is my special business to point out the analogies between them. And in no case is the analogy more striking than in the point with which we are now dealing. All European political societies start from the one common possession, the Assembly of the tribe. This, among a people who take to the common life within a walled town, goes on as the Assembly of the city. The constitution which, under these circumstances, grows out of the primitive elements, may be aristocratic or democratic, as may happen, but kingship in a city-commonwealth cannot last long after the political instincts of the people are fully awakened and sharpened. If many cities join together in a League, the Federal Assembly of the League will most likely be formed after the type of the Assemblies of the particular cities, modified by all those consequences which flow from the greater distance at which the place of meeting will now be from the mass of the citizens. So, among a people who do not adopt the city-life, who at least do not make it the ruling principle of their political life, the old state of things goes on as long as the tribe, the mark, the hundred, the shire, still keep any distinct political being. As the tribes grow into a nation, the national Assembly, if by no other cause, yet through the mere working of the law of distance, shrinks up into a gathering of a few chief men, and the smaller Assemblies go on simply as subordinate local bodies, and perhaps themselves die out altogether in course of time. But in the system of city-commonwealths, there was one means of keeping up a greater vitality in the old institutions than could be kept up in the tribal or national system. In the general Assembly of the Achaian League, each city had a single and equal vote (41). In the later Lykian League, by a refinement which forestalls some very modern political controversies, the vote of each city, according to its size, counted as one, two, or three (42). But in either case the vote of the city had its fixed value, which was no way affected by the number of its citizens which might happen to appear in any particular Assembly. In the Assembly of the League Corinth had one vote, whether one Corinthian or a thousand were there to give it. This refinement seems never to have been adopted in the Teutonic Assemblies; it is in truth a refinement far too refined for the stage of things to which they belong. But it is plain that this method of voting made the Assembly come as near to the nature of a representative body as it could come without actually being one. When Corinth had a single vote, whether few or many Corinthians were there to give it, it might easily be arranged that those citizens of Corinth who actually appeared in the Assembly might practically be the representatives of the greater number of citizens who stayed at home. The lack of the real representative system would hardly be felt; the grievance, if any, would be one which experience shows that the representative system does not necessarily heal, but which the Lykian constitution did heal, the grievance that Corinth had no greater weight in the Assembly than the smallest town in the League (43). Thus, though the Assembly might shrink up into a gathering of a small body of chief men, those chief men might practically be the delegates of the local Assemblies of their several cities (44). But there is no sign that in the Teutonic Assemblies any such refinement was ever thought of as that which gave separate votes to the separate cities of the League. It is a refinement far more likely to arise in a system of cities, with the sharply-defined separate being of each, than under the larger system of tribes or districts. When therefore a Teutonic Assembly shrank up into an Assembly of the King's Thegns and other chief men, there could be no such softening of the oligarchic process as the Achaian system allowed. But, for that very reason, the true representative system was all the more needful, and, by the process inherent in all healthy and really living constitutions, it grew up as it was needed.

I have spoken of the allotment of separate votes to the separate cities of the Achaian and Lykian Leagues as one of the characteristics of the Federal period of Greece. It certainly distinguishes the Federal democracy of Achaia from the single city democracy of Athens. But it also appears in all its fulness in the Assemblies of the Roman Commonwealth. In the Comitia of the Centuries, the military Assembly, where the People came together in military array, where the value of each man's vote was decided by the nature of his military service, and the nature of his military service was decided by the amount of his property, the votes taken were not the votes of individuals, but the votes of the artificial units, the Centuries. So in the Comitia of the Tribes, where men were ranged, not according to their place in battle but according to the local divisions of the State, it was again the votes of the Tribes that were taken. So again, in that later form of the Comitia in which Tribes and Centuries were intermingled, the only point which concerns us is that here too the votes were the votes of Tribes and Centuries, not of single citizens (45). At Rome then, as in Achaia, it was perfectly possible that those citizens of a distant tribe who appeared in any particular Assembly may have practically been representatives of their neighbours who stayed away, commissioned to vote on their behalf. This is one of several points in which the Roman Commonwealth, with its city franchise extended over so large a territory, has more in common with the Federal than with the single commonwealths of Greece. Another point in which Rome bears more likeness to Achaia than to Athens is to be found in the independent powers which were kept to the last by the Senate and by the several magistrates. Nowhere indeed did the three elements—the kingly power, held in commission by the curule magistrates, the power of the Senate, and the power of the People—stand out more distinctly than they did at Rome down to the last days of the Commonwealth. The forms of Roman political partizanship are a witness to their vitality. At Rome we hear of a

Popular party and of a Senatorial party. At Athens such names would have been meaningless. There was doubtless at Athens an aristocratic, or more truly an oligarchic, party, which would have been well pleased to overthrow the popular government altogether. But such a party could in no wise profess itself the champion of the yearly Senate of Five Hundred, nor could it shelter itself under its authority (46). A truer analogy to the Roman Senate would be found in the Senate of Areiopagos, whose members sat for life, and which was formed, in a manner nearly the same as that in use at Rome, out of those citizens who had held the highest magistracies. But, for that very reason, the course of change at Athens gradually brought down this ancient Senate to be little more than a venerable shadow (47). Two facts distinctly show how strong the traditions both of the kingly and the senatorial power remained at Rome during the whole time of the commonwealth. A check was needed on the arbitrary powers of the Consuls. Rome found the remedy, not in lessening the powers of the Consuls, but in setting up an opposition magistracy as the embodiment of plebeian rights, the Tribune no less powerful to forbid than the Consul was powerful to command. Again, it is almost more striking that the Senate, made up as it was of men who had been in the first instance chosen to their offices by the voice of the People (48), could ever come to be looked on as a power antagonistic to the People. In the later days of the Commonwealth, if the Senate was an aristocratic body, it was purely by the sufferance of the People that it was so. Those who had the choice of Consuls, Prætors, Censors, and High Pontiffs had the remedy in their own hands. A jealousy of the Senate may indeed have lingered on as a mere survival from the far-gone days when the Senate was a purely patrician body. But I believe also that one most important cause of the difference in this respect between Rome and Athens was that, as I have before said, Rome was not in the same strict sense a city commonwealth, but that it had in it something of a Federal element. As long as the Roman Commonwealth lasted, the popular Assembly remained the supreme elective and legislative body, the highest and final authority of the Commonwealth. But it never, like the Assembly of Athens, drew to itself all the powers of the State; it never brought down the Senate to be a mere Committee of its own body, and Consuls and Censors to be mere instruments of its will. It was not in the nature of things that it should do so. Setting aside the effect of any difference between the Roman and the Athenian national character, the Roman Assembly could not become what the Athenian Assembly became. The free inhabitants of so large a district must have formed, even in early times, a body too large either to be gathered together so often as the Athenian Assembly was, or in the same way to discharge the duties of a deliberative Assembly when it did come together. It could not allow the same free power of debate and amendment. It could not do more than say Yea or Nay to the proposals of the magistrate by whom it was summoned. It could not possibly exercise the same constant care over all the departments of the state. It could not take points of detail into its consideration in the same way that the Athenian Assembly did. In a word the Athenian Assembly was the *Government*. Dêmos was sovereign; he was, as he rather liked to be called, King or Tyrant (49). The Archons had sunk to such mere routine functions as hardly to be political officers at all. The Generals were the ministers of the Sovereign Assembly; the Prytaneis were merely its chairmen; the Senate was merely its committee. The real ruling power was the Assembly itself. But at Rome, as in Achaia, the Assembly was simply the power which acted for legislative and elective purposes, when legislative and elective acts were needed. The Senate was the Government, the body which carried on the ordinary management of the State, with the Consuls and other great magistrates as its ministers. At Rome, as at Athens, the power of peace and war rested with the Assembly. But its power in this, as in other matters, did not go beyond the final power of saying Yea or Nay to a definite proposition laid before it. All the preliminary steps, the receiving and listening to foreign ambassadors, the listening to the arguments of private citizens on one side or the other, all which at Athens formed such an important part of the business of the Assembly, was at Rome part of the business of the Senate. Under the Roman system, the great speeches of Periklês and Dêmosthenês, like the great speeches of Cicero, might still have been addressed to the people. But the debate between Kleôn and Diodotos (50), between Nikias and Alkibiadês (51), between Euryptolemos and the accusers of the Generals (52), which at Athens were spoken to the people assembled under no roof but the sky, must at Rome, like the debate between Cato and Cæsar, have gone on only within the walls of the senate-house (53).

The Roman Assembly died of the disease of which every primary Assembly in a large country must die. It became too large for its functions; it became a mob incapable of debate, and in which its worst elements got the upper hand. But its death-blow came from those pretended popular chiefs who made use of the mutual jealousies of Senate and People to trample both Senate and People under foot. Yet it is to the honour alike of the Roman Senate and of the Roman Assembly that the Cæsars dreaded both of them. And it is to the special honour of the Roman Assembly that, while the Cæsars kept on the Senate, which they deemed that they could turn to their own ends, the Assembly they found it needful utterly to sweep away (54). Be it an aristocratic Senate or a democratic Assembly, there must be some good thing in any institution which a despot fears. The Teutonic Assemblies on the other hand simply died out; there were no Julii or Claudii to trample them out. In nearly every Western country the old primary Assemblies gave way to representative Assemblies founded on the principle of Estates. Those Estates were in most countries three—the Clergy, the Nobles, and the Commons, the Commons being for the most part only the citizens of the chartered towns. In some cases however, where there was a numerous and independent yeomanry, they also had a share in the representation. Thus in Sweden, the four Estates, the House of Peasants being one of them, lasted, whenever the genuine constitution of the country was in force, down to within a very few years past. As in all such cases, the constitution of the Estates differed in different countries; there were perhaps hardly any two countries where their constitution was exactly the same in every detail; but one general principle runs through all, the principle that the Assembly should consist of representatives of all the Estates or classes of men of which the body-politic is held to consist. In England, on the other hand, the course of things was somewhat different; the primitive Assembly never died out; it never was trampled out; it simply—through the natural working of causes of which I have already spoken—shrank up into a narrow body. Through that law of shrinking up, the old democratic Assembly lived on to become the aristocratic element in a new form of the constitution. That is to say, I believe that the primitive Assembly was, by lineal personal succession, continued in the Witenagemót, and that the Witenagemót is, by lineal personal succession, continued in the House of Lords. I will not here enlarge on this seeming paradox, on which I have spoken at some length elsewhere (55); but I think that, if we grasp this doctrine, we shall better understand some of the points in which English history differs from the history of most other European nations. The doctrine is that, while elsewhere the old Assemblies actually died out and the constitution of Estates arose in its stead as something new, in England the Assembly, in its contracted form, itself lived on to form one of the Estates.

That is to say, the Lords are simply those among the members of the old Assembly—that is, those among all free Englishmen—who never lost the right of personal attendance. These were the Bishops and parliamentary Abbots, the Earls, and such other persons as the King chose personally to summon. This free right of summons in the King has been hampered by the strange doctrine of lawyers that, if a man is summoned once, his descendants must needs be summoned for ever and ever. Alongside of the body so formed another body gradually arose, in which those who had failed to keep on the right of personal attendance made their appearance by representation (56). Hence we better see how it came about that in England there is no Nobility, no *Noblesse* or *Adel* in the foreign sense. Seats in the House of Lords have become either official or hereditary; but there is no noble class, such as there is or has been in other lands. Hence also we can better understand how it came to pass that the true system of three Estates never could be established in England. Besides other reasons which made it hard to establish a real parliamentary Estate of the Clergy, one clearly was that the highest members of that estate already had official seats in another branch of the Parliament. Through this accident, as I said in my first lecture, came the bicameral constitution of the English Parliament, the fact that it is a Parliament of two Houses, and not of one, three, or four. What arose in England by the circumstances of our history has been reproduced in other lands by direct imitation. The good or evil of such a system is a question which does not belong to Comparative Politics, but to the practical politics of our own day. But it is not out of place to say that we have a great advantage in the fact that our system has come down to us through the facts of our history and has not been the invention of any clever constitution-maker. No one perhaps, if he had to make a constitution afresh, would invent exactly such a body as our House of Lords. But the fact that our House of Lords exists gives it a great advantage over Upper Chambers whose constitution may be theoretically much better, but which have to be artificially called into being. And one thing I think is often forgotten when these matters are discussed, but which cannot be too constantly borne in mind. In an ordinary kingdom or commonwealth the question between one and two Chambers is simply a question in which way the Legislature is likely to do its duty best. In a Federal State the two Chambers are absolutely necessary. Where there is a twofold sovereignty, the sovereignty of the united nation and the sovereignty of the States or Cantons which make it up, each sovereignty must be represented in the Legislature. There must be the House of Representatives, the *Nationalrath*, representing the nation, and with its numbers apportioned to the numbers of the nation, and there must be the Senate or *Ständerath*, representing the States, and in which each State, great or small, must have an equal voice. To abolish or modify the English or the Prussian House of Lords might be a wise or a foolish step; but it would not be the utter overthrow of the existing political system. Notwithstanding such a change, the constitutional monarchy of England or of Prussia might go on untouched. But to abolish, or essentially to modify, the American Senate or the Swiss *Ständerath* would be the utter overthrow of the existing political system of the American or the Swiss Confederation. The House of Representatives or the *Nationalrath* standing by itself would represent the united nation only, without any representation of the independent States. The happy device of the two Federal Chambers gets rid of all the difficulties which beset all the ancient confederations and the Swiss and American Confederations themselves in their earlier forms. The Achaian system distinctly sacrificed the greater cities to the smaller. The Lykian system, wonderful step as it was, had a tendency to sacrifice the smaller cities to the greater. But with the two Federal Chambers, one representing the sovereignty of the nation, the other representing the sovereignty of the States, numbers cannot be sacrificed to cantonal rights, neither can cantonal rights be sacrificed to numbers. Each element in the Federal state is a check upon the other; each can throw out any measure which would hurt its own interests; neither can carry any measure which would hurt the interests of the other. The American Senate, with the special executive powers which it holds apart from the House of Representatives, has a further strength and dignity of its own, beyond that which belongs to it as one House in the Federal legislature representing one element in the Federal State. The Swiss *Ständerath* has no such special powers; it rests solely on its general position as one necessary element of the Federal system. As such, the loss of it would at once upset the balance between the two elements of the state. In a word the Federal system would be destroyed.

In most parts of the world the primary Assembly, democratic or aristocratic, is now a thing of the past. Since the kingdoms and commonwealths of Europe began to settle down into something like their present shape, the old primary Assemblies have gradually died out or have lingered on only in the form of survivals.

In this form we can still point to them in our own land. It may be held that the *Scirgemót* has come to an end by the bill which takes away the ancient election by the show of hands, from which the later refinement of taking the poll was a mere appeal. The ancient election of the King by the voice of the people at his crowning has, since the sixteenth century, sunk into the mere form of an acknowledgement. But, as long as the parish vestry ever comes together, the Assembly of the Mark has not utterly died away. Older than the Assembly of the Shire and of the Kingdom, it has, in its primitive form, outlived both of them. In other lands more important traces of the old state of things may be seen. But it should be noticed that, even in the free cities, though primary Assemblies were by no means unknown—the Parliament of Florence was one famous example among many—yet they never played the same important part which they played in the commonwealths of old Greece. No mediæval city that I know of was regularly ruled by a democratic Assembly in the way that Athens was. The form which the democratic principle took in most of the Italian cities was rather that of making all citizens eligible for office, perhaps of giving all citizens a share in the great offices in their turn, rather than the Athenian principle of giving the people as a body the general direction of the affairs of the Commonwealth. Provided magistracies were filled by men freely chosen or drawn, by men to whom the people thought that it could safely trust its affairs, it did not fear to clothe them with very large legal powers, and even to wink at vigorous and arbitrary action beyond the letter of the law. The people itself in its Parliament met only now and then, when it suited those who were in power to call it together. And, when it came together, its first and only act most commonly was to bestow a special commission with extraordinary powers on some corporate Pittakos or Sulla (57). Where the ancient state of things lingered on longest, where it lingers on still, was, not within the walls of cities, but in those homes of freedom at either end of the great Teutonic realm where men never fall away from the institutions of their earliest fathers. In the lowlands of Friesland and on the heaths of Ditmarsen, the old freedom and its embodiment, the old primitive Assemblies, lived on till the fifteenth and sixteenth centuries. In the mountain dales of Uri and on the hill-sides of Appenzell they live on still. Do not suspect me of any yearning for the exploded dreams which once saw in the primitive Switzerland a land peopled by a separate race, enjoying a separate freedom, altogether distinct from the rest of their brethren around them. Uri, Schwyz, and Unterwalden are but three small districts—they hardly amount to tribes — of the Alemanni in which, through a strange and happy combination of circumstances, the ancient freedom never wholly died out. The three lands were members of the Roman Empire, of the German Kingdom, of the Swabian Duchy Parts of them even were, at various times, in subjection to lesser lords. For ages their highest ambition was to win the *Reichsfreiheit*, to be released from all such intermediate lords, and to be able to boast that they had no King but Cæsar. But allegiance to inferior lords, much less allegiance to the Empire, in no way interfered with the popular constitutions of the three lands within their own bosoms. By a number of favouring circumstances, the mere local freedom of a mark or a hundred grew into the absolute freedom of a sovereign commonwealth. As such it still abides, modified only by the obligations of the Federal tie. Of those primitive Assemblies, which I hold it as one of the great privileges of my life to have looked on with my own eyes, I have often spoken elsewhere. I will now only say that it is a moment when all that one has read and thought comes before him as a living thing, when, beneath the canopy of heaven, he hears the mighty voice of an assembled people binding themselves in solemn form to obey the laws which they themselves have made (58).

The democratic Assembly therefore to this day still remains in its fulness. Of the aristocratic primary Assembly Europe now contains no example; but we must remember that, in the last century, it too existed in all its fulness. Poland and Venice, no less than Sparta and Corinth, still kept that form of Assembly in which, not every member of the nation, but every member of a privileged body within the nation, had a right to appear in his own person. The great meeting of the whole Polish nobility which came together to choose the Polish King, oligarchic as it was with regard to the excluded classes, came, after all, nearer to a primary Assembly of a whole nation than anything to be found elsewhere. It was the gathering of a body far greater than the whole body of citizens in the small commonwealths where alone the democratic primary Assembly still lingered on. Its military character, the fierceness and turbulence ascribed to it, its gathering in the open air, all form a marked contrast with the otherwise kindred institution which formed the supreme authority of the island commonwealth. The civic aristocracy, if it was narrow and unscrupulous, was at least calm, regular, and orderly. No contrast can more plainly point out the city life as the life of the higher civilization. But neither in Venice nor in Poland could the aristocratic primary Assembly boast of having its roots in any remote past. Both were comparatively modern; but both were natural political developements of the state of things which gradually grew up in the two commonwealths (59). Both are bodies which show that, as a democratic Assembly may be representative, so an aristocratic Assembly may be primary. In fact, as I have before said, the difference between aristocracy and democracy is a difference which simply concerns the excluded classes. The ruling order in either case, whether it consists of all the citizens or only of part of the citizens, may develope every variety of political institution within its own bosom.

The primary Assembly, of whatever kind, is in its own nature sovereign. It is the gathering together of the whole nation, or of the whole ruling part of the nation. The whole power of the nation is therefore vested in it. It is only gradually and by slow steps that there arises that distinction between legislative, executive, and judicial powers on which such stress is laid in the refined political theories of modern times. And in no country perhaps is the distinction fully carried out. It certainly is not so in our own. The primitive Assemblies described by

Tacitus were courts of justice as well as deliberative bodies. So were all Assemblies of the kind, great and small. In the Frankish Assemblies we have seen that it was only step by step, as the great mass of the freemen began to grow slack in their attendance and to deem their duties a burthen, that a separate class of judges arose in order to ensure that there should always be some one ready to do justice between man and man (60). That great offenders were called upon to answer for their crimes before the general Assembly of the whole realm, was a matter of course. So in our own land, our ancient Witenagemóts not only made laws, not only chose and deposed Kings, Ealdormen, and Bishops, but sat in judgement on state offenders and pronounced sentences of outlawry or confiscation. And that branch of our Legislature which is the personal descendant of the ancient Gemót still keeps its judicial authority in matters both criminal and civil (61). The newer, the more popular, branch shares the judicial authority only in an indirect way. It exercises it by its share in Acts which are judicial in substance though legislative in form, bills of attainder and of pains and penalties. It exercises it too by its share in that anomalous jurisdiction by which each House undertakes the defence of its own privileges. In the smaller local Assemblies, after they had ceased to be sovereign, the business must always have been mainly judicial. We must remember that, carefully as we now distinguish the functions of legislator, judge, juror and witness, it was only by slow degrees that they were distinguished. All grew out of the various attributes of an Assembly which, as being itself the people, exercised every branch of that power which the people has, at sundry times and in divers manners, entrusted to the various bodies which, directly or indirectly, draw their authority from that one sovereign source. In all times and in all places power can have no lawful origin but the grant of the people. The difference between a well and an ill-ordered commonwealth lies in this. Have the people wisdom and self-control enough to see that, in reverencing and obeying all the powers of the State in their lawful exercise, they are in truth doing homage to themselves and giving the fullest proof of their fitness to discharge the highest right of men and citizens?

## LECTURE VI.

## MISCELLANEOUS ANALOGIES.

I HAVE now gone through the main analogies which strike us in the chief political institutions of those three great branches of the Aryan family to which our inquiries have been mainly given. I have dealt with the general conception of the State, with the powers of the King or other chief, and with those of the Assembly of the People. On all these points I hope that I have made it, to say the least, probable that the institutions of the several branches of the family all contain traces of a common origin, relics of a common primæval stock, which have grown up into various forms under the influence of diversities of time, place, and circumstance. In this last lecture I purpose to seek for some other analogies in points which come under the general head of politics in the wide sense, but which do not exactly come under the head of political constitutions. I have now chiefly to deal with the various orders and classes of men, a subject which is closely connected with the varieties to be found in forms of government, but which still is in idea something separate from them. The idea of the smaller Council in primitive times, the idea of the second or Upper Chamber in the refined constitutions of later days, are both of them ideas which easily blend with the idea of hereditary distinctions of birth. But the two things are in their own nature separate. It is quite possible, both in the earlier and in the later state of things, that certain families may be acknowledged as noble and may be entitled to whatever honours and privileges the custom of the country may attach to nobility of birth, without those honours and privileges taking the form of any special share in the government. Men may be honoured on account of their birth; their birth may even give them legal privileges; while at the same time the Council or Upper Chamber may be formed of men picked out, not for their birth but for their age, their personal merit, or any other standard which may be chosen, not shutting out the blind working of the lot. But, though the two ideas are in this way perfectly distinct, they have a great tendency in practice to run into one another. Wherever a noble class, whatever may be its origin, is acknowledged at all, it always has a tendency to win for itself, if not a legal, at least a practical, preference for posts of authority. In fact, this voluntary preference for certain families in the disposal of elective offices is one of several ways in which nobility has grown up. It is the most usual way in which what we may call a secondary nobility grows up, after an earlier and immemorial nobility has lost its privileges. A nobility of birth, of whose origin no account can be given, but which must be accepted as one of the primary facts of political history, makes way for a nobility of office, which again in its turn grows into a nobility of birth. Of this process history supplies many cases, and the rule applies equally when the offices which are the source of nobility are bestowed by the gift of the King and when they are bestowed by the choice of the people. Of the latter process the most illustrious example is the way in which at Rome, after the legal privileges of the patricians had ceased, there arose a new nobility composed of patricians and plebeians alike. We see the same thing in our own land in the way in which the immemorial nobility of the *Eorls* gave way to the later official nobility of the *Thegns*, and that in which the nobility of the Thegns gave way to another form of official nobility in the modern peerage. Both these cases agree in being cases of a later nobility supplanting an earlier one. But exactly the same process may be gone through when a nobility is formed for the first time. And it was in this way that the constitutions of not a few city commonwealths, that of Venice itself at their head, changed step by step from democracies into oligarchies (1).

The different ways in which a noble class has arisen in various nations and cities within historical times may thus help us to make some probable guesses as to the origin of nobility in those cases where nobility is strictly immemorial. But we cannot get beyond probable guesses. In a great number of cases nobility is strictly immemorial. We see a distinction within the class of freemen, a distinction which marks out certain families as holding a higher rank than the rest of their fellows, in the very earliest glimpses which we get of the political constitution of the commonwealth. It is so in all the three great cases with which we are mainly concerned. We cannot tell what was the origin of the peculiar privileges which belonged to an Athenian Eupatrid, to a Roman Patrician, or to an English Eorl. We may conjecture, we may theorize, we may even infer with a high degree of probability, but we cannot dogmatically assert (2). All that we can say is that, in the first glimpses which we get of Grecian, Italian, and Teutonic history, we see the distinction between the noble and the common freeman at least as clearly marked as the distinction between the common freeman and the classes which were beneath him. I speak thus vaguely, because, for our present purpose, we may put together all who stand below the rank of the common freeman, from the mere personal slave upwards. I need hardly say that, in all discussions of this kind, slavery is to be taken for granted. Slavery has been the common law of all times and places till, within a few centuries past, it has, among most of the nations of the Western Aryan stock, either died out or been formally abolished (3). And we must further remember what the earliest form of slavery, before slavery has been aggravated by the slave trade, really is. The prisoner of war who, according to the military code of a rude age, might lawfully be put to death—the criminal who has forfeited his life to the laws of the state of which he is a member—is allowed, whether out of mercy or out of covetousness, to exchange death for life in bondage. Then the family feeling, so strong in setting up one stock, steps in no less strongly for the pulling down of another, and the man who has forfeited his own freedom is held to have forfeited the freedom of his children also. Thus arises the class of personal slaves, mere chattels either of the commonwealth or of an individual master.

And it is no less easy to understand how, under the different circumstances of different tribes and cities, other classes may arise whose condition is better than that of the mere slave, but still is not equal to that of the least distinguished among the class that is fully free. Of course I am here speaking of personal, not of political, freedom. In the sense in which I now use the words "fully free," a Venetian *cittadino*, a Lacedæmonian περίοικος, was as fully free as if he had a voice in the government of the commonwealth. He was subject to laws which he had no voice in making; he had to obey magistrates whom he had no voice in choosing; but he had no personal master either in the commonwealth or in any of its members. I am now speaking of the various degrees of personal dependence, freedmen, *liti*, villains, and so forth, who hold a place between that of the mere slave and that of the lowest full freeman (4). Such classes may be formed in various ways, by raising the slave, by pressing down the smaller freemen, by admitting strangers or conquered enemies to a state intermediate between mere bondage and full freedom. Such classes have been formed in these various ways within historical times, and we may reasonably conjecture that the same processes went on before written history began. But we cannot do more than conjecture. The threefold distinction between the noble, the common freeman, and the classes below the common freeman is one of the primary facts with which we start alike in Greece, in Italy, and among our own forefathers (5). The fact is a matter of history; its causes we can at the most explain only by reasoning from analogies and survivals.

A class of nobles is clearly implied in the description of the Teutonic nations given by Tacitus, even though we explain the word *principes* of elective chiefs (6), who however would pretty certainly be, as a rule, chosen from among the members of the noble order. And the threefold division of the noble, the common freeman, and the unfree, appears, sometimes drawn out in a formal manner, in many of the earliest records of our race. We find it in its most marked form in the Scandinavian legend which makes the mythical forefathers of the three classes, Jarl, Karl, and Thrall, the offspring of three distinct acts of creation on the part of the Gods (7). Among ourselves we find from the very beginning, *Eorl* and *Ceorl*, gentle and simple, as an exhaustive division of the free population. It is plain that the distinction was thoroughly well marked and was universally understood. And yet it is utterly impossible to say in what the privileges of the *Eorlas* consisted. There is nothing to make us think that they were oppressive; they may well have been purely honorary. But all analogy and probability would lead us to think that the *Eorlas* would have a practical preference, a preference which might even be practically exclusive, in the choice of leaders both in peace and war, just as the noblest among the noble, the kingly house, had an exclusive preference for the post of the highest leader of all. The same marked distinction of a noble class meets us equally in our pictures of the earliest Greek society, and we find the same distinction living on into the historic ages. In the Greek commonwealth of which we know most, that of Athens, our earliest historical picture sets before us the rule of the nobles, the Eupatrids, as an exclusive and oppressive oligarchy. The harshness of its rule was first modified by the reforms of Solôn, and all traces of ancient distinctions were swept away by the later reform of Aristeidês. We have no historical account of the origin of the distinction which parted off the Eupatrid *gentes* at Athens from the excluded plebeian mass. But the whole circumstances of the story may lead us to think that in this case the patriciate was a body of old citizens, as opposed to the new citizens who had gradually settled around them. In the history of a city, when either history or legend traces it up to its first beginnings, there is commonly a stage in which new comers are freely welcomed to all the rights of citizenship, which is followed by a stage in which those rights are found to be far too precious to be thus given away at random. The first stage is well set forth in the Roman story by the legend of the Asylum of Romulus. The second stage is most probably marked by the exclusive dominion of the Athenian Eupatrids and the Roman Patricians. The original citizens have kept all privileges to themselves, and have thus become an aristocratic order in the midst of the unprivileged body of plebeians which has gradually gathered round them. To break down, step by step, all traces of this original inequality was the work of the founders of the democracy. But here again we may mark the characteristic difference between Athens and Europe. At Athens all distinctions of the kind were utterly swept away; every trace of inequality was wiped out; every political office without exception was thrown open to every citizen. The Eupatrid *gentes* remained as religious and social unions, cherishing the sacred traditions which each traced up to its legendary patriarch. Some special priestly offices still remained hereditary in particular families. But every office which carried with it any shred of political power was open to every citizen without distinction of birth and fortune. Yet it is no less true that, long after the establishment of the pure and perfect democracy, the Assembly, which disposed of every office according to its sovereign will, did, as a rule, choose men of the ancient houses to direct the counsels and command the armies of the commonwealth. No more speaking proof can be found of that inherent influence of birth and wealth, which survives the wiping out of all legal distinctions, an influence which legislation cannot give and which legislation by itself cannot take away. The people, of its own will, placed at its head men of the same class as those who in the earlier state of things had ruled it against its will. Periklês, Nikias, Alkibiadês, were men widely differing in character, widely differing in their relations to the popular government. But all alike were men of ancient birth, who, as men of ancient birth, found their way, almost as a matter of course, to those high places of the State to which Kleôn found his way only by a strange freak of fortune.

At Rome we find quite another story. There, no less than at Athens, the moral influence of nobility survived its legal privileges; but, more than this, the legal privileges of the elder nobility were never wholly swept away, and the inherent feeling of respect for illustrious birth called into being a younger nobility by its side. At Athens one stage of reform placed a distinction of wealth instead of a distinction of birth: another stage swept away the distinction of wealth also. But the reform, at each of its stages, was general; it affected all offices alike, save those sacred offices which still remained the special heritage of certain sacred families. At Rome the change was done bit by bit. No one law threw open all offices to plebeians. One by one, this and that office was thrown open; but some offices were never made the subject of any such special enactment; those offices therefore seemed the exclusive possession of the patricians. Among the priestly offices, the Pontificate, an office held for life and which was indirectly of high political importance, was thrown open to plebeians, and was bestowed, like the yearly magistracies, by the election of the people. So the augurship, as all the world knows, was held by the plebeian Cicero. But the Flamens, officers whose religious sanctity was great but whose political importance was small, remained to the last exclusively patrician. And among temporal magistracies, Curule Ædiles, Prætors, Consuls, Censors, and Dictators, might all freely be plebeians; but that occasional office in which, at moments few and far between, the ancient kingship again rose visibly to light was never opened to the Commons. Not only was the Interrex to the last an exclusively patrician officer, but in his election none but the patrician Senators had a share. An

Interregnum was, in the fully developed commonwealth, so rare an event that it perhaps never suggested itself to the mind of any reformer to bring forward a special enactment decreeing that a plebeian might be Interrex (8). And, in default of such special enactment, the office would necessarily remain confined to patricians, just as much as the consulship had been before the Licinian Laws. This way of doing things bit by bit, and the occasional anomalies to which it gives birth, is eminently characteristic of the Roman constitution, just as it is of our own. But it stands in marked opposition to the symmetrical democracy of Athens.

At Rome again we may mark, what we have no sign of at Athens, but what has a perfect parallel among ourselves, the growth of a new nobility of office after the exclusive privileges of the old patriciate had come to an end. The Roman Plebs, so largely composed of the inhabitants of allied and conquered cities who had been admitted in a mass to the plebeian franchise, naturally contained many families which were, in wealth and in nobility of descent, the equals of the proudest patricians. Such a class as this could hardly have existed, at least not in anything like the same degree, in a Commons like that of Athens. After the union of the Attic towns, the civic territory of Athens never grew, and her Commons must have been mainly formed of settlers in the city itself. We therefore find nothing at Athens answering to the plebeian houses of Lutatius, Pompeius, and Octavius, of Porcius of Tusculum and Tullius of Arpinum. When the great magistracies were opened to the plebeians, it was mainly by plebeians of this class that they were filled, and out of them, combined with the old patricians, a new nobility arose. Every descendant of a curule magistrate, whether patrician or plebeian, was *nobilis*; he had the *jus imaginum*, the right of exhibiting the images of his forefathers who had held high office, the number of which formed the measure of his nobility. Thus grew up a new noble class, clothed with no legal privilege, but which gradually became as well marked in practice as ever the old patricians had been, and which looked on the great offices of the commonwealth as no less its own exclusive right. In the later days of the commonwealth the consulship of a *new man*, a man whose forefathers had never held curule rank, though forbidden by no law, and though the new man might be Caius Marius himself, seemed as strange as the consulship of a Lutatius or a Licinius had once been (9). The nobility of birth had given way to the nobility of office, and the nobility of office had grown into a new nobility of birth.

The parallel to this change in our own early history is to be found in the way in which the old immemorial nobility of the *Eorlas*, the origin and the nature of whose privileges are both shrouded in the mist of the earliest antiquity, gave way to the new nobility of office, the nobility of the *Thegnas*. The *Eorlas*, a nobility patrician in the strictest sense, gave way in England to a class who owed their rank to the favour of the King, just as at Rome the patricians gave way to a class who owed their rank to the favour of the people. But the origin of the Thegns itself supplies one of our best analogies, if not with Roman, at least with Achaian antiquity. This analogy is one of which I have so often spoken elsewhere that I may perhaps be forgiven if I now pass it over in a few words. The *Comitatus* stands out in Tacitus as one of the primitive institutions of our race, and the *Gesiðas*, in later phrase the *Thegnas*, of Teutonic antiquity, the personal following of the King, Ealdorman, or other chief, form the exact parallels of the ἑταῖροι and θεράποντες of the Homeric Achaians (10). The parallel here is as close as a parallel can be; only it does not seem that in early Greece the institution of the *Comitatus* ever rose to the same political importance which it reached in England. There is no sign that those companions of the chiefs who stand out with such prominence in Homer became the source of any of the later forms of nobility which we find in the Greek cities. There is nothing to make us think that the Eupatrid Houses of Athens traced their descent in any special way from the ἑταῖροι and θεράποντες of Thêseus or Menestheus. The *comitatus* is, in truth, an institution which is not well suited for the atmosphere of a city life. It takes personal chieftainship for granted; it needs the personal chief to gather around. But the spirit of a civic aristocracy tends to equality among its own members; it surrounds the whole ruling body with a dependent class, but it does not love to surround particular men with personal dependents. The same causes which made kingship come so soon to an end in the Greek commonwealths hindered the *comitatus*, the natural offshoot of kingship, from filling any great place in later Greek history. Among the Teutonic nations the case was widely different. As kingship grew and flourished, the *comitatus* grew and flourished with it, till in some lands the King was for a season overshadowed by his own following. The *comitatus*, in one shape or another, became the root of every form of nobility in Western Europe, remembering that, among the nobilities of Western Europe, one order as proud as any of them, the civic patriciate of the island Rome on the Venetian lagunes, is not to be reckoned. In our own land the King's Thegns became really the ruling order, till the older nobility of the *Eorlas* was forgotten, and their name became confined to the rank next to the King, to the great officers who in earlier days had borne the more ancient title of Ealdormen (11). It shows how completely the notion of personal service became the standard of the new nobility that the word *Thegn* itself, in its first meaning simply *servant*, came to have its later force of *noble* or *gentle* (12). What went on in our own land went on also among our kinsfolk beyond the sea. The companions, the *antrustions*, of the Frankish Kings, changed step by step into the later nobility of feudal vassals. Under the strong hand of the early Karlings, the royal power kept its own, but presently, as kingdoms split off from kingdoms, as offices changed into fiefs, as the commonwealth changed into a society of Lords and Vassals of various ranks, the sovereign became simply the highest lord among them; the new nobility not only supplanted the old, but it crushed alike the body of the commonwealth and its head; it trampled King and people alike under foot (13). And it is worth noticing that, just at the point of transition, when the old nobility was sinking and when the new nobility was as yet hardly rising, there was a time when birth seems to have been less thought of than it ever was before or after, and when men of lowly origin seem to have risen with unusual ease (14). But when the time came for the growth of the new nobility, it grew faster, and it more utterly ate out all earlier and healthier elements than it did in England. In England, under our native Kings, the tendency was to closer union, while in Gaul the tendency was to separation. And, if there had been any tendencies the other way, the strong hand of the Conqueror, even in the act of giving feudal ideas and feudal relations a wider scope, took care that they should never endanger either the power of the King or the security of the Kingdom.

If we turn to Rome, we shall find there but small traces of the *Comitatus* in its Achaian or its Teutonic shape. It may be that the devotion of the Romans to the commonwealth, and to the commonwealth only, hindered the growth of any institution founded on a tie purely personal, at all events between men of equal or nearly equal rank, like Achilleus and Patroklos, like Brihtnoth and the Thegns who fell around him at Maldon. Yet we may perhaps see something like it in the special bodyguard of noble youths which legend places around the early Kings and Dictators, around Romulus in the spot which was to be Rome's *comitia*, and around Aulus Postumius on the day of slaughter by Regillus (15). The client relation too springs from the same personal tie as the *comitatus*; only there is the wide difference that in this case the client stands at an unpassable distance of rank beneath his patron. In the Hellenic and the Teutonic system advance in age and exploits might raise the *man* to the level of his lord; but nothing could raise the client to the level of his patron. No patrician ever stooped to the client relation; we may doubt whether, in the early days of the commonwealth, any full citizen did. Yet the lowly clientage of the Roman patrician and the noble following of the Hellenic or Teutonic leader may really come from the same source, and may both alike be parts of the common primæval heritage. If this be so, it shows how easily institutions which are in their origin the same may, under different circumstances, develope in different directions. There is something romantic, chivalrous, sentimental—none of these are good words to express the idea, but I know of none better—in both the early Hellenic and the early Teutonic state of society. Of this there is no trace in the more purely political society of Rome. It is the same kind of difference as that which I have already noticed between the Roman King and his Hellenic or Teutonic brother. The difference is no doubt partly owing to the fact that our first glimpses both of Hellenic and of Teutonic life belong to an earlier stage than our first glimpses of Roman life. But this is not all. The institution took utterly different courses among the three nations, according to the several circumstances of each. In Teutonic Europe it grew and flourished; it became the groundwork of nobility; it became one main element in producing the whole fabric of what, for want of a better word, we may call feudal society. It grew and flourished, because the personal chieftainship which it implies grew and flourished. It reached its highest point of external splendour, though its real spirit had already passed away, at the coronation of a mediæval Emperor, when Kings and Electors did their personal service to the anointed Lord of the World. In Greece, on the other hand, it died out as kingship died out. Achilleus and Menelaos had their *Thegnas* and *Gesiðas;* none such surrounded Miltiadês or Epameinôndas; but we see them again in the Companions who fought around the Macedonian Alexander (16). Under the stern, practical, political, mind of Rome, the institution took another and a worse form. The general idea which forms the groundwork of the whole thing survived. There was still the relation of faithful service on one side, of faithful protection on the other; but they appear in a shape from which all that made the *Comitatus* the groundwork of modern society has wholly passed away. The client is a true Thegn; the patron is a true *Hlaford:* but his thegnship is of so literal and lowly a kind as to be fit only for the freedman, the stranger, or at most the citizen of the very lowest rank (17).

Out of this institution of the *Comitatus* grew the nobility of modern Europe, and specially that Old-English nobility of Thegns which supplanted the older nobility of the Eorls. In England, as at Rome, a nobility of office supplanted the nobility of birth: only in the commonwealth of Rome it was the nobility of office bestowed by the people, while in the English kingdom it was the nobility of office bestowed by the King. The King could not in strictness make an *Eorl*, because he could not change a man's forefathers, but he could make a Thegn, as he now can make a Duke. Now what was it that hindered the nobility thus formed from becoming a real nobility? What saved us from a *noblesse* or *Adel* in the foreign sense? For I repeat that in England we have, in strictness, no nobility; we have no class which keeps on from generation to generation in the possession of exclusive privileges, either political or social. Our peerage is not a nobility in the sense in which nobility is understood in foreign lands. It is not only a rank to which any man may rise, but it is a rank from which the descendants of the hereditary holders must as a matter of course come down. Political privilege belongs only to one member of a family at a time; honorary precedence does not go beyond one or two generations. This is not nobility in the sense which that word bears in those lands where all the descendants of a noble are noble for ever. Why then did not the Thegnhood of England grow into a nobility such as that which in other lands grew out of the same elements? One answer doubtless is that the Norman Conquest thrust down the native Thegnhood, the growing nobility of England, to a secondary place in the social and political scale. In so doing it wrought for us one of the greatest of blessings. It gave us a middle class spread over the whole country. While in most continental lands it was only in the chartered towns there was any class intermediate between the noble and the peasant, often none between the noble and the villain, in England the ancient lords of the soil, thus thrust down into the second rank, formed that great body of freeholders, the stout gentry and yeomanry of England, who were for so many ages the strength of the land. But why did not a nobility of the foreign type grow up among the Norman Conquerors themselves? That great law of William which made every man in the land the man of the King had much to do with it; but paradoxical as it may sound, I conceive that the very power and dignity of the peerage has had a good deal to do with it also. Elsewhere nobility was primarily a matter of rank and privilege, with which political power might or might not be connected.

But in an English peerage the primary idea is political power; rank and privilege are a mere adjunct. The peer does not hold a mere rank which he can share with his descendants; he holds an office, which passes to his next heir when he dies, but which he cannot share with any man while he lives. The peer then, not a mere noble, but a legislator, a counsellor, and a judge, holds a distinct place in the State which his children can no more share with him than any one else. Hence in England we have but two classes, Peers and Commoners, those who hold the office and authority of a peer and those who do not. The children of a peer come under this last head as much as other men; they are therefore Commoners. The very existence of the peerage of itself hinders the existence of a nobility in the true sense of the word.

If then the Norman Conquest had never happened, it is most likely that the native Thegnhood of England would have grown up into a nobility of the foreign type. If the wisdom of the Norman Conqueror had not preserved our ancient institutions, if it had not thus been possible that the House of Lords of our later constitution could grow out of the Witenagemót of our earlier constitution, it is most likely that a nobility of the foreign type would have grown up among the Norman conquerors themselves. As it is, we have had no nobility, but we have had a peerage; I might almost say that we have had an aristocracy. I say almost and not altogether, because England is a kingdom and not a republic. I once heard it said that in a republic there could be no aristocracy except "an aristocracy of wealth." I treasured up the saying as one of the shallowest that I ever heard. I put it alongside of another saying, the saying of one who argued that ancient Bern must have been a democracy because it was a republic. I should rather say that it is only in a republic that a real aristocracy can exist. Corinth and Rome, Venice and Genoa, Bern and Nürnberg, bear out what I am saying. The nobles who cringed at the court of the Great King at Paris, or at the lesser courts of his imitators in the petty despotisms of Germany and Italy, had no right to the name of an aristocracy. Aristocracy is the rule of the best; they were not the best, and they did not rule. But in aristocratic commonwealths, in the proud city which floats on the waves of the Hadriatic, in the hardly less proud city which looks forth from her peninsula on the snows of her once vassal mountains, in Byzantine Venice and Teutonic Bern, there was for ages something which it needed no great straining of language to call the rule of the best. Morally best indeed I do not say, but best so far as this, that, narrow as was the government of those commonwealths, fenced in as the power of the State was within a circle of exclusive houses, those houses at least knew how to rule, and how to hand on the craft of the ruler from generation to generation. Their rule was in itself unjust, because it was exclusive, narrow, and selfish. It was often oppressive; but it was never oppressive with the frantic and purposeless oppression of many a personal despot. It was in some respects more galling than the yoke of a despot, but it was so simply because the yoke of one master is in itself less galling than the yoke of many. But, as regarded the members of the ruling order, no other form of government supplied such a school of rulers. The patrician was born to rule; but he was born to rule, not according to his own caprice, but according to the laws of the ruling order of which he was only one member among many (18). Such a system tended to dwarf the powers of men of the very highest order; but it tended at once to raise and to regulate the powers of all but the very highest class. It checked the growth of heroes and of exceptionally great men, but it fostered the growth of a succession of men who were great enough for their own position, but not too great. In an aristocratic commonwealth there is no room for Periklês; there is no room for the people that hearkened to Periklês; but in men of the second order, skilful conservative administrators, men able to work the system which they find established, no form of government is so fertile. But such a commonwealth, where the power of strengthening the ruling order by new blood either does not exist or is but sparingly exercised, commonly degenerates in the end, though the causes of the degeneracy are not exactly the same as those which bring about the degeneracy of democratic commonwealths. The day of glory of the aristocratic commonwealth may be longer than the day of glory of a democracy, but its decay will be even more hopeless. As its ruling families die out, as those which survive lose their strength—two processes which must sooner or later affect every exclusive body—the dregs of an oligarchy become even baser than the dregs of a democracy. There was at least some difference in dignity and courage between the fall of Venice and the fall of Unterwalden.

I maintain then that aristocracy, in its true sense, is something essentially republican, something to which a monarchic state can present only a faint approach. So far as a monarchic state is aristocratic, as our own country has been at some times, it can only be in proportion to the degree that, through the lessening of the powers both of the Crown and of the people, it approaches to the nature of a commonwealth in the hands of certain ruling families. A government like the old French monarchy, where a noble class has hateful social and civil privileges, but where those privileges carry with them no political power, is not aristocratic in any political sense. Where an external power, that of the King, can ennoble, and where that external power is politically supreme, there is no aristocracy in the sense which the word bore in the mouth of a Greek thinker. Poland, and Sweden at some stages of its history, came nearer to aristocratic government than any other states which acknowledged a King. But a Chian or a Venetian aristocrat would hardly have owned their constitutions as kindred with his own. The true aristocracy, the aristocracy of a commonwealth, may, as we have seen, arise in several ways. A body of older citizens, like the original patriciate of Rome, may keep—for a time or for ever—all the powers of the commonwealth in their own hands to the exclusion of the Commons who grow up around them. In a city of late foundation, like Bern, where there is a noble element in the population from the beginning, a patriciate may grow up which may gradually draw all power into its own hands. Or, without any reference to earlier nobility, a patriciate may, as at Venice, arise among the citizens themselves, simply by the process of confining office, whether by law or only in practice, to the descendants of certain families which have gained exclusive possession of it. But, when a patriciate has arisen by any of these means, it seems essential to its being that no new members can be admitted to the body except by its own act. Few aristocracies have been so exclusive as never to admit any new houses or individuals to a share in their own privileges. The Claudian house at Rome, the house of Morlot at Bern, were strangers who were received not only to citizenship but to nobility. And at Venice and Nürnberg new families were, down to the last days of the commonwealth, received from time to time within the pale of the ruling order (19). But in all these cases the aristocracy enlarged itself by its own act and deed, by the exercise of its sovereign power. When the noble class can be enlarged by the external will of a personal sovereign, it shows that the noble class is not, exclusively and by itself, the ruling body in the state. In a state which has a King at its head, there may be a peerage; there may be a nobility; there cannot, if words are used in their true meanings, be an aristocracy.

This last lecture must be a desultory one. I have now only to point out some of the analogies which are to be found among the particular institutions of the nations with which we are concerned. Let us take for instance the institution of the *wergild*, the price of blood. This is one of those institutions which we have every reason to believe are common to the whole Aryan family, and which may indeed be traced back beyond the bounds of the Aryan family. That criminal jurisprudence which in highly civilized societies takes so elaborate a shape grows out of that desire of private vengeance which it is one of its main objects in its fully developed growth to check, and even to punish. A man is slain; the passion of vengeance is awakened; the right—the duty, as it seems in their eyes—of avenging the slain man naturally falls to those who have lost most by his death, to his immediate kinsfolk, the men of his own family or household. As the social and political circle widens, the right and the duty are handed over from the mere household to the *gens*, the tribe, and the nation. And at each stage, as the right and duty of vengeance is thus handed over to men who, at each stage, are less and less stirred by the mere passion, vengeance loses more and more of its character as vengeance, and puts on more and more of the character which punishment bears in fully civilized societies, a preventive and corrective interference of the public authority on behalf of the public good. So with other wrongs; in a state of nature each man who is wronged must right himself by the strong hand; each man has the right of war and peace in his own person. Again, as the social and political circle widens, the wrong of each man becomes something which does not concern himself only, but concerns also the *gens*, the tribe, and the nation. Thus, by slow degrees, the right of each man to defend himself against a wrong-doer grows into the right of the State to defend itself against the wrong doings of its own members by legal punishment and against the wrong doings of other states by regular war. But it is only in highly civilized communities that the right of private vengeance is wholly taken away, and that the right of defence—that is the right of private warfare—is kept within the narrowest bounds of undoubted necessity. Our law, the law of every country, allows that there are extreme cases in which private homicide in the form of self-defence is not a crime. That is to say, it is the duty of the citizen to give up to the Commonwealth the duty of his protection whenever the Commonwealth can protect him: but, in any case where the Commonwealth cannot protect him, the natural right revives, and it is allowed that he may protect himself. But it is only in the highest state of civilization that the natural rights of private vengeance and private war can be cut down within this very narrow limit. For a long time the Commonwealth steps in, not so much to forbid as to regulate and soften the natural right which it admits. The Mosaic Law fully admits the right of the avenger of blood: all that it does is to set apart certain cities of refuge whither the slayer may flee and be safe. If he is overtaken before he can reach the asylum, the law does nothing to stay the arm of the avenger (20). Our own early laws, the early laws of most nations, do not wholly forbid a man to help himself with the strong hand; they only limit the right to certain extreme cases, to certain specially inexpiable wrongs, to certain cases where legal means have been tried and have failed. By the law alike of Athens, of Rome, and of England, a man might without crime slay the defiler of the purity of his own household (21): by the law alike of Athens and of Rome every citizen might slay the Tyrant who had trampled the Commonwealth under foot and had made law powerless to defend or to avenge (22). In cases of wrongs between man and man the State steps in as an arbitrator before it steps in as a judge. It tries to persuade the injured man to abate somewhat of his wrath against the wrong-doer; it strives to make him accept something less than the full satisfaction of his vengeance; it gradually fixes the amount of compensation with which the injured man shall be satisfied. But it is only when civilization has reached a high pitch indeed that the vengeance of the injured man is made wholly to give way to the remedial interference of the State, that every crime is looked on as a crime against the Commonwealth, whose punishment is the business of the Commonwealth and of the Commonwealth alone.

The *appeal of murder* and of other crimes, with its accompaniment the *wager of battle*, was an instance of the regulated right of private war which, though it had long fallen into disuse, was actually removed from our Statute-Book only within the present century. Here the right of vengeance was recognized, though it was recognized in such a form as gave it somewhat of the nature of a legal trial. The appeal was brought by the injured person in his own name; he sought for redress for the private wrong, and, as the one who had suffered for the wrong, he had the right of pardoning the offender. And this mode of procedure went on alongside of that with which alone we are now familiar, that in which the crime is dealt with as a wrong done to the King as head of the Commonwealth, in which the prosecution is made in the name of the King, and in which the King alone has the right of pardon (23). Of that limiting of the right of private war which took the form of judicial combat, and which was afterwards corrupted back again into the baser form of the private duel, we find few or no traces in early Greek or Roman antiquity. This is probably another result of the quicker developement of things in the city commonwealths of Greece and Italy, as compared with the tribal system of our own forefathers. But the old Roman Law allowed the principle of *talio*, the Mosaic doctrine of an eye for an eye and a tooth for a tooth, and it recognized the right of the injured person either to exact the penalty or to admit of some form of compromise (24). This brings us at once to the doctrine of the *wergild*, a doctrine common to the Greece of Homer and to the Germany of Tacitus, and which, we cannot doubt, is a portion of the primitive Aryan inheritance. The *wergild* is an appeal from the passion of vengeance to a less fierce, if more sordid, passion, to the love of gain. The man who has forfeited his life to the vengeance of the injured kinsman may perhaps stay his vengeance by offering gifts in its stead; he may buy back his own life at a price. In the Homeric times, the man whose son or father had been slain might—perhaps was bound to—receive the gifts of atonement offered by the slayer, and the slayer, when he had paid those gifts, could dwell in peace among his people (25). It seems here to be implied that custom at least demanded that the proffered atonement should be accepted. This was an advance on the kindred war-law of the same age, according to which the conqueror might accept the bondage of the conquered instead of his blood, but might also slay him without reproach (26).

The next step plainly is for the Commonwealth to step in, for the law to enforce the duty of accepting the atonement, and perhaps, as another step, to regulate the amount of the atonement, instead of leaving the injured man to wring what he could out of the wrong-doer. In our earliest glimpse of Teutonic law we seem to see a further advance; the crime is recognized as a wrong done to the commonwealth as well as to the individual, and the King or other head of the State receives his share of the atonement as well as the kindred of the slain man (27). In our own ancient laws the subject is gone into with the utmost minuteness. The ancient *talio* has given way to an elaborate scale of prices, according to which every form of bodily injury, small or great, may be atoned for by the payment of the appointed sum in money (28). And the penalty to be paid by the man-slayer is regulated with a minute regard to the rank of the person slain and to his supposed consequent value. The life of every man, like the oath of every man, was of some value; but the life and the oath of the man of higher rank was of more value than the life and the oath of the man of lower rank (29). The price of one Thegn was equal to that of several churls, and so on in an ascending scale, till we reach the mighty penalty which alone could atone for the death of the King. Mark too that differences of race come in as well as differences of rank; in the lands where the Englishman and the Briton dwelled side by side, the blood of the Englishman was rated at a higher price than the blood of the Briton of his own rank (30). Mark too that care was taken that the penalty should be paid to those who, in the eye of the law, had undergone the wrong; the price of the slave was paid to his master; the price of the freeman was paid to his kinsfolk; but the price of kingly blood was not only heavier than the price of other men, but it had to be paid twice over, to the kinsfolk who had lost one of their house and to the commonwealth which had lost its leader. And in this last case the payment of the *wergild* might rise to the rank of an affair between commonwealth and commonwealth. War between sovereign states is simply the natural right of self-defence, which still goes on in a state of things where the contending parties have no common superior to decide with authority between them. But the vengeance of the Commonwealth, like the vengeance of the individual, may be bought off; and we have at least two cases in early English history, where an invader, seeking vengeance for the blood of a royal kinsman, stayed his hand on the payment of the appointed *wergild* which custom had fixed for the shedding of royal blood (31). No feature of our ancient jurisprudence plays a more important part than this in our earlier laws; none has so utterly vanished without leaving any trace of itself in modern legislation. As the Commonwealth, and the King as its head, have taken the place of the actual sufferer or his kinsman, as—in criminal as distinguished from civil jurisprudence—the idea of compensation has given way to the idea of punishment whether remedial or vindictive, the notion of vengeance to be bought off by a payment has utterly died away. Yet it may be well to remember that, as late as the fifteenth century, a private dispute between two English noblemen was decided by open warfare on a battle-field in Gloucestershire, and the wrong done to the wife of one of them by the slaughter of her husband was in the end made up by a payment which in earlier times would have passed for his *wergild* (32).

In this case we have, beyond doubt, an institution which is at once Hellenic and Teutonic, and which is at once Hellenic and Teutonic, not by borrowing or imitation, not by like causes producing like effects, but because Hellên and Teuton alike inherited it as part of a common stock, a stock, it would seem, not even peculiar to the Aryan family. We may end our survey by looking back to some points which have more connexion with the subject of the early part of this lecture. We may end with a glance at some of the striking analogies which are to be seen in the political relations of states in ages far distant from one another, and which, there can be no doubt, are to be explained, not by common inheritance from a common stock, but by the operation of like causes leading to like effects. We have seen that there is every reason to believe that the distinctions within the Commonwealth, the noble, the freeman, and the slave—perhaps also some of those intermediate stages which part off the mere slave from the common freeman—are really part of the common Aryan heritage. At least we cannot go back, by the help either of history or of legend, to any stage either of Greek, of Teutonic, or of Italian history in which those distinctions are not to be found. But the relations which rise up between the Commonwealth and those, whether individuals or commonwealths, which lie outside its pale, though they present a series of most striking and most instructive analogies, are necessarily the results of the circumstances under which each commonwealth finds itself, and can have no claim to be looked on as parts of the common heritage. We have already seen that, as cities began to arise in the Teutonic lands, and as, through the decline of the royal power, those cities began to approach to the character of independent commonwealths, many of the phænomena of the old city system of Greece were called again into being. Many of those analogies were to be seen in full force within the memory of men now living; some of them have lingered on to our own time. There is commonly a stage in the history of a city Commonwealth, that stage which in the Roman legend is represented by the Asylum of Romulus, in which the new-born city is liberal of its franchise to strangers who are ready to throw in their lot to the new community, and so to add to its strength. Then comes a stage in which citizenship begins to be too highly valued to be given to all who ask for it, when the original citizens shrink up into an oligarchic body, with a large mass around them, who share only an imperfect citizenship, or no citizenship at all. Gradually, as at Rome, or suddenly, as at Athens, the unenfranchised or half enfranchised classes win for themselves equality of rights with the old citizens, and the work of Kleisthenês or Licinius is done. Or perhaps no such revolution takes place; perhaps a change takes place the other way, and the mass of the citizens gradually lose the rights which they had once enjoyed. That is to say, the Commonwealth developes either in an oligarchic or in a democratic direction. But, in either case, a time comes when its developement seems to stop, when the idea of any general extension of citizenship is an idea which is no longer heard of, when the civic franchise, aristocratic or democratic, becomes an hereditary privilege which is at most doled out now and then as a special favour, the reward of special merit. Or perhaps, in a meaner state of things, it becomes a matter of purchase and sale, and thereby of profit to the privileged class. Thus there arises an excluded class, strangers in the place where perhaps they were born, where their forefathers may even have lived for several generations. Such a class we have seen in the μέτοικοι of the ancient Greek cities; they might be seen, perhaps they may still be seen by way of a feeble survival, in those whom many an English borough distinguished from the hereditary freemen by the name of *foreigners* (33). The two things are essentially the same, differing only in the value of the franchise from which the stranger is shut out. And that again depends on the difference between a community which forms a sovereign commonwealth and one which, whatever its internal constitution may be, is, as regards all national matters, merely part of a greater whole. The μέτοικος at Athens was shut out from the privileges of a sovereign commonwealth, while he had to bear burthens in which the hereditary burgher had no share. He had no voice, he had no means of obtaining a voice, in the affairs of the political society in which he lived. But the foreigner in an English borough, whether the local privileges from which he was shut out were precious or worthless, lay under a disqualification which was purely local. He lay under no disqualification as a member of the Commonwealth at large; if he had no share in the election of the representatives of his own town, he could at any moment, by buying a forty-shilling freehold, become an elector of any county in England which he chose. And, through later enactments, other franchises, the parliamentary franchise among them, franchises dependent on residence and careless about descent, have grown up by the side of the old franchise of the hereditary freemen. And these new franchises have become so much more valuable as to make the old burghership seem contemptible. The freemen of an English borough are in most places looked upon as an inferior class; yet it is they who answer to the Athenian Eupatrids and the Roman Patricians; the other inhabitants are but μέτοικοι or plebeians by their side. The principle is the same in both cases; mere residence gives no claim to admission to the civic community, whether that civic community be a sovereign commonwealth or the pettiest municipality. In both cases the franchise, whatever it may be worth and whatever it carries with it, can be had only by the appointed means, means easier doubtless in most of the English cases than they were in the analogous case in Greece. Still in neither case does the civic franchise belong to every man who chooses to go and dwell within the civic boundary. It may not always be purely a matter of birth; but it is always something which cannot be taken up at the mere will of the stranger. It always requires that particular qualification which is fixed by the custom of the civic community, be that qualification birth, marriage, servitude, special purchase, or special grant.

All distinctions of this kind have, through later English legislation, lost all practical importance, and they have become mere materials for enquiries such as that on which we are now engaged. But in another part of Europe, in the land which among all modern states preserves to us at once the most precious relics of the old Teutonic world and the most striking analogies with the old Hellenic and Italian world, a close parallel to this feature, as to so many other features of Greek political life, is still to be seen in its fulness. It is naturally among those cities and districts which have grown into the Confederation of Switzerland that we find the most instructive illustrations which modern political life can give us of the working of city—in many cases we should rather say of village—communities. The *Niedergelassenen* in Switzerland, those Swiss citizens who are settled in *Gemeinden* or *Communes*—parishes or *Markgenossenschaften*—of which they have not the hereditary burghership, answer exactly to the Greek μέτοικοι. And, in the late debates on the reform of the Federal Constitution, many proposals were brought forward to remedy a state of things by which a number not far short of half of the Swiss people are, in many important respects, strangers in the places where they themselves dwell, and where it may happen that their forefathers have dwelt for many generations (34). But this state of things is the exact parallel to those which we have just been speaking of in Greece and in England. It is of the essence of a *Gemeinde* or *commune*, of a borough or a village community, one perhaps owning a considerable estate in *folkland* or *ager publicus*, that the stranger should be admitted to membership of the community only on such terms as the community itself may think good. In a sovereign community the power thus to bind and loose can be relaxed only by its own will and pleasure; in a community which forms part of a greater sovereign whole, it may of course be modified or taken away by an act of the supreme Legislature. In the old days of the Swiss Confederation, the days of the *Staatenbund*, when there was no common Federal Legislature or Executive, when no part of the internal sovereignty of the Cantons had been given over to any central power, the citizen of one Canton who settled in another Canton must have been as strictly a μέτοικος as a Corinthian who settled at Athens. He had no voice either in the cantonal or the communal affairs of the place in which he lived, any more than if he had settled in a spot beyond the bounds of the Confederation. The existing Federal Constitution gives every Swiss citizen equal Federal and Cantonal rights, in whatever part of the Confederation he may settle. But communal matters are left to the legislation of the Canton or of the *commune* itself; all that the Federal Constitution provides is that the μέτοικος shall not be, as he was at Athens, subject to any special μετοίκιον, any special tax laid on the μέτοικος and in which the citizen bears no share. The laws of different Cantons, the customs of different *communes*, may of course differ on these points; some *communes* are more chary of granting or selling their franchise than others; but everywhere the *Niedergelassene* is still, in communal matters, a μέτοικος; the mere fact of residence and contribution to the local taxes no more gives him the full communal franchise than it makes him a freeman of an English borough. The two higher franchises, those of the Confederation and the Canton, he enjoys as fully as any native; to the lower franchise of the *commune* he can be admitted only by special grant or by the effect of some special enactment.

In the like sort, as long as the old Confederation lasted, some other features of old Greek and Italian political life were still to be seen in all their fulness. If there still are μέτοικοι in Switzerland, down to 1798 there were περίοικοι. Of course we may see a relation equivalent to the *perioikic* relation whenever any state, be it Venice or England, holds dependencies whose inhabitants have no voice in the general government, especially if they have no means of obtaining that voice, even by taking up their abode in the ruling country (35). But distance makes a great difference both in the appearance and in the reality of things. We may question the right by which Venice bore rule over Cyprus, or that by which England bears rule over India. But, granting that such rule exists, it is not to be expected that the inhabitants of Cyprus or of India should have a voice in the affairs of Venice or of England. The full nature of the *perioikic* relation does not come out except in a state of things where the name can be applied geographically as well as politically, in those cases where the subjects really dwell round about or near the home of their rulers. The dominions of Venice on the mainland of Italy present an approach to the old *perioikic* relation. Still the island city always remained isolated from the Continent; Venice never became part of continental Venetia in the same sense in which Florence was part of Tuscany or Bern part of the Lesser Burgundy. It is in mediæval Italy, in Switzerland down to 1798, and, to some extent also, among the free cities of Germany, that we see the *perioikic* relation, just as it stood between Sparta and the other Laconian towns. As Sparta ruled over Amyklai and Epidauros Limêra, so Florence ruled over Pisa and Bern ruled over Lausanne. Nay more, a very few years back, down to the last changes in Germany, the cities of Lübeck and Hamburg held the small district of Vierlande in *Condominium* (36). They held it in partnership as a joint possession, the government of which might be exercised conjointly or alternately as the ruling powers may think fit. In the like sort, in the old state of things in Switzerland, various districts were held, not only by this or that Canton singly, but by two or more Cantons, or by all the Cantons of the Confederation, in the same joint ownership. And mark again that, in all these cases, the internal constitution of the ruling State made no difference. As Athens had her subjects—though not strictly her περίοικοι—no less than Sparta, so democratic Uri had her own subjects, and her share in the common subjects of the Confederation, no less than aristocratic Bern. In all this we have a lively image of the state of things in old Greece, except that I do not remember that the *condominium*, the joint sovereignty or rather the joint ownership, has its parallel there. This fact is to be taken in connexion with a fact to which Mr. Grote has called attention, that the acquisition of dominion by purchase, so common in mediæval history, is rare in the history of Greece. (37) I conceive the cause of the difference to be that in old Greece and Italy the ideas of property and government had not got mixed together in the way in which they were mixed together in mediæval times. The Roman People might make itself the landowner of the soil of a conquered commonwealth; it might add the *folkland* of the conquered to its own *folkland*, or it might part it out as *bookland* among its own citizens; but the right of government remained a distinct thing from the right of property. It remained something which could not be, as in mediæval times, granted, sold, or enfeoffed, along with the land. But we have seen how in mediæval times, as the feudal idea took root and grew, the right of government came to be looked on as a property, while the possession of landed property came to be looked on as carrying with it a kind of right of government. When government was thus looked on as a possession, there seemed no reason why a rich commonwealth might not buy the sovereign rights and powers of a spendthrift prince, just as it might buy his landed estate or his manorial privileges. In this way, Bern and other cities largely bought out the neighbouring territorial nobility, besides often conquering them in warfare. The new corporate lord, the Commonwealth, stepped into the place of the old personal lord; it was clothed with all his authority, and it commonly contrived that the authority which thus passed to it should grow, rather than lessen, in its hands. So, when the same notion of property in sovereignty was fully established, there was no reason why two or more commonwealths might not hold the sovereignty of a town or district in partnership, just as two or more personal owners might hold a field or a house in partnership. In this way the purchase of territory, and with it of sovereignty, and the holding of sovereignty in partnership, if not absolutely unknown in the elder state of things, became at least far more familiar and important in the later. And, through the greater complication of mediæval jurisprudence—a complication which for the most part grew out of this same confusion of the ideas of property and sovereignty—there arose an endless variety of relations between princes, towns, independent and subject districts, to which there is no parallel in the simpler state of things in Greece and Italy (38). Still, as often as there arose a system of separate towns and districts, independent of, or but slightly controlled by, the central power of the Emperor, we find in mediæval Europe a lively image of the relations between a Greek or Italian city and its Greek or Italian subjects, an image of the relation of Sparta to her Laconian *περίοικοι* or of Rome to her Italian allies (39). And in Switzerland and the neighbouring lands this system went on in all its fullness till the French invasion came to sweep away the old state of things, to sweep away its worst evils for ever, its good points only for a moment. The League itself, its several Cantons, the allied cities and confederations, all had their subjects, their *Unterthanen*, in Greek phrase their *περίοικοι*. It was not only aristocratic Bern or Basel that thus ruled, sometimes over men of their own blood and language, in all cases over men who were not savages or heathens, but sharers in the common faith and civilization of Europe. If the Bear held a firm grasp on the lands from the Aargau to the Leman Lake, if for a moment he held—and Europe may now sigh that he did not keep—the shore which so proudly fronts Lausanne and Chillon (40), the bull of Uri had planted his foot no less firmly on the Levantine valley. So too the confederate village communities of the Upper Wallis lorded it over their Welsh neighbours lower down the river, and the Three Leagues of Rætia bore a rule perhaps sterner than all over the Italian valley to the south of them. The Valtelina alone has failed to rise from bondage to the highest freedom of all; yet incorporation with constitutional Italy, nay, even subjection to France and Austria, was a good exchange for the rule of its former masters. In all these lands, whether well or ill governed in detail, the principle of government was the same. The internal state of the subject district might range from something very like bondage to a large amount of local self-government; but all alike were περίοικοι, in so far as the sovereignty was neither vested in the community itself nor in a prince whom it could claim as its own. In all alike, the sovereign was a commonwealth beyond their borders, a corporate lord, who, whether he ruled well or ill, ruled in his own interest and not in the interest of his subjects. Such a rule is not necessarily oppressive, though there is every temptation to make it so. But it is in any case irksome and degrading; it is the story of Rome over again; the rule of a single despot, where there is at least the chance of the personal virtues of a well-disposed despot, is better than the systematically selfish rule of an alien commonwealth. The rule of a single man, of a man so exalted as to seem like a being of another order, is less irksome than the rule of a body of men who seem to be in no way privileged above their subjects. And in one respect the experience of earlier and later days has been reversed. Democratic Athens was at least a better ruler of dependencies than oligarchic Sparta (41). But the common bailiwicks of Switzerland were always better off when the bailiff, the *Vogt*, the *harmost*, who was sent to rule them came from aristocratic Bern or Zürich than when he came from democratic Uri or Unterwalden. A patrician of Bern was at least a man who knew men and things; he was one of a class who were taught the art of ruling from their birth. The peasant harmost from a democratic Canton had too often bought his office of his countrymen, and had to repay and enrich himself at the cost of his temporary subjects. In the Greek case we must remember that Athens wisely sent no harmosts at all to her dependent allies, and the little evidence that we have tends to show that the foreign administration of Sparta was harsher than that of other Dorian and aristocratic cities (42). But everywhere we learn the same lesson, the inconsistency of commonwealths which boast themselves of their own freedom and exalt themselves at the cost of the freedom of others.

I have thus gone through my subject as fully, I trust, as the nature and limits of the course prescribed to me would allow. But that is of course very imperfectly. In a course of lectures like this no subject can be dealt with exhaustively; no subject can be set forth in all its bearings; nothing can be traced in detail from its beginning to its end. The object of the lecturer is rather to awaken curiosity than to gratify it, rather to show what is to be learned than to attempt to teach it in all its fullness. All that he can hope to do is to choose a few of the many aspects of his subject, and to take care that his treatment of them, though necessarily imperfect, shall be accurate as far as it goes. Thus much I trust that I have done; to some I may have suggested a new line of thought; to others I may have suggested new illustrations of a line of thought on which they had already entered. It will be enough if I can, by this present line of argument, bring home to any mind the great truth which it has been the chief business of all that I say or write to set forth by various arguments, the truth that history is one, and that every part of it has a bearing on every other part. No one, I think, who has followed me will deem that the institutions of ancient Greece and Italy are at all lowered from their place of dignity, by being shewn to be the same in their origin, the same in many of their details, as the institutions of our own forefathers. We shall not think the less highly of the studies which form the groundwork of all our studies, if we give them their due place and no more, if we treat them as only branches of one great study, records of one great heritage in which England and Germany have their share alongside of Rome and Athens. I do not shut out the other branches of the common family, those who came before us, those whose destiny it may be to come after us, those whom, after so long a separation, we have again met in the far off Eastern world. I do not shut my eyes to the strong likelihood that much that is common to the various branches of the Aryan family comes from sources common to the Aryans along with other divisions of mankind. But I leave researches of this kind to inquirers of wider ken than my own. It is enough for me to keep myself on ground on which I can be sure of my footing, and to trace out, at least in the form of a rough, though I would hope a suggestive, sketch, the main points of political instruction to be gathered from the history of the three branches of the common stock which have, each in its turn, held the foremost place among civilized men. It is enough if I have led any to look on the earlier forms of the institutions of our own people, on the kindred forms of the common institutions of their kindred races, not as something which is utterly passed and gone, not as something which is cut off from us by an impassable barrier of time and place, but as something which is still living, something in which we ourselves share, something of which we still reap the fruit, as a heritage which has descended to us from unrecorded times, as the still abiding work of the fathers and elder brethren of our common blood.

# THE UNITY OF HISTORY.

The revival of learning in the fifteenth and sixteenth centuries marks, as is agreed on all hands, one of the great epochs in the history of the mind of man. It is easy to exaggerate the extent of the revival itself; it is easy to dwell too exclusively on the bright side of its results; but the undoubted fact still remains none the less. That age was an age when the spirit of man cast away trammels by which it had long been fettered; it was an age when men opened their eyes to light against which they had been closed for ages. A new world was opened; or, more truly, a world which men never had forgotten, but which had become to them a world of fable, was suddenly set before them in its true and living reality. The Virgil, the Aristotle, the Alexander, of legend gave way to the true Virgil, the true Aristotle, the true Alexander, called up again to life in their writings and in their deeds. We are indeed apt greatly to exaggerate the ignorance of earlier times, but in one point it is hardly possible to exaggerate the importance of the change. It must have been like the discovery of a new sense, like the discovery of a new world of being, when the treasures of genuine Greek literature were, for the first time, thrown open to the gaze of Western Christendom. The twelfth century had its classical revival as well as the fifteenth; but the classical revival of the twelfth century hardly ever went beyond a more accurate knowledge, a more happy imitation, of the elder specimens of that Latin tongue which was still the tongue of religion, government, and learning. To William of Malmesbury and John of Salisbury the voice of Homer was dumb, and the voice of Aristotle spoke only at third-hand with a Spanish Saracen to his dragoman. Such knowledge of Greek as fell to the lot of Robert Grosseteste and Roger Bacon was looked on as a prodigy; and, whatever was its amount, it certainly did not extend to any familiar knowledge of the masterpieces of Hellenic poetry, history, or oratory (1). That revival of learning which brought the men of our Northern world face to face with the camp before Ilios and with the Agorê of Athens was indeed a revolution which amounted to hardly less than a second birth of the human mind.

Yet the revival of learning, rich and manifold as have been its fruits, had its dark side. I speak not of its immediate results, political and ecclesiastical, in its native land of Italy. Better indeed by far was the honest barbarism of the darkest age than the guilty splendours of Lorenzo and of Leo, where all the blaze of art and poetry and learning strive in vain to gloss over the overthrow of freedom and the foul abuse of sacred things. I speak rather of the effects of the classical revival of those days directly on the pursuit of learning, on those studies of Greek and Roman literature and art which became the all in all of the intellect of the age. It at once opened and narrowed the field of human study. It led men to centre their whole powers on an exclusive attention to writings contained in two languages, and for the most part in certain arbitrarily chosen periods of those two languages. In its first stage it devoted itself too exclusively to the mere literature of those two languages, as opposed to the solid lessons of their political history. But, in all its forms and stages, it fostered the idea that the languages, the arts, the history, of Greece and Rome, at certain stages of their being, were the only forms of language, art, and history which deserved the study of cultivated men. It led to the belief, not perhaps fully put forth in words, but none the less practically acted on, that those two languages, and all that belonged to them, had some special privilege above all others—that the studies which were honoured by the ambiguous name of 'classical' were fenced off from all others by some mysterious barrier—that they formed a sacred precinct which the initiated alone might enter, and from which the profane were to be jealously shut out. Such a state of feeling, a feeling which has even now far from died out, could not fail to lead to mere contempt, and thereby to mere ignorance, of everything beyond the sacred pale. And, what is more, it hindered any knowledge of the true nature of those things which were allowed a place within the sacred pale. It led to a cutting off of so-called 'classical' studies from all ordinary human pursuits and human interests. And of this cutting off we still feel the evil effects. Men persuaded themselves, not only that 'classical' models in literature and art were amongst the noblest and most precious works of human genius, but that they were the only possible standards of excellence. Whatever did not conform to their pattern was worthless and barbarous; the exclusive votaries of classical art and literature deemed that they were branding it with the heaviest reproach when they called it Gothic. They thus cut themselves off from long and stirring volumes of the world's history; they cut themselves off from forms of art and language no less worthy of their homage than those which they deemed alone worthy to receive it. They learned to look with scorn on the works of men of their own land, their own blood, and their own faith. They stifled art and literature by arbitrary rules drawn from models, perfect indeed in their own time and place, but which were utterly inappropriate when creeds and tongues and feelings had altogether changed. Let any one who would thoroughly take in how low the taste of Englishmen had fallen under the dominion of the exclusive classical fashion turn to those passages in the Spectator where Addison chances to speak of the history, the manners, the art, the religious belief, of Englishmen in earlier days. Then let him turn, and see how even then nature asserted her rights against the deadening yoke of fashion, in those passages in which the same man called on his astonished age to acknowledge an outpouring of the true Homeric spirit in the English lay of Chevy Chace (2).

But, more than all this, the exclusive study of 'classical' models hindered men from gaining any living knowledge of the classical models themselves. It has been wittily said that they believed that all 'the ancients' lived at the same time. Certain it is that the habit of constantly classing together Greece and Rome—that is, Greece and Rome during a few arbitrarily chosen centuries of their history—in opposition to all other times and places led to an utter forgetfulness of the wide gap by which Greece and Rome were parted asunder. Men forgot the difference between the Ionian singer and the Augustan laureate; they held up Homer and Virgil as poets of the same class, whose merits and defects could be profitably compared together. They would have been amazed indeed to be told that the true parallel for the tale of the wrath of Achilleus was to be looked for in the Lay of the Nibelungs or in the stirring battle-songs of Saulcourt and Maldon. They would have deemed it a degradation to entertain the thought that the vulgar tongues of England and Germany were kindred tongues, of equal birth and claiming equal honour, with the sacred languages of Latium and Attica. They would have deemed it, not so much a degradation as an utterance of open madness, had they heard that those sacred languages were but dialects of one common mother-speech, that its elder offspring was to be looked for in the tongues of lands which the Macedonian conqueror had barely grazed, and, more wondrous still to tell, in the fast-vanishing speech of a few men of strange tongue by the Eastern shore of the Baltic Sea (3).

On us a new light has come. I do not for a moment hesitate to say that the discovery of the

Comparative method in philology, in mythology—let me add in politics and history and the whole range of human thought—marks a stage in the progress of the human mind at least as great and memorable as the revival of Greek and Latin learning. The great contribution of the nineteenth century to the advance of human knowledge may boldly take its stand alongside of the great contribution of the fifteenth. Like the revival of learning, it has opened to its votaries a new world, and that not an isolated world, a world shut up within itself, but a world in which times and tongues and nations which before seemed parted poles asunder, now find each one its own place, its own relation to every other, as members of one common primæval brotherhood. And not the least of its services is that it has put the languages and the history of the so-called 'classical' world into their true position in the general history of the world. By making them no longer the objects of an exclusive idolatry, it has made them the objects of a worthier, because a more reasonable, worship. It has broken down the middle wall of partition between kindred races and kindred studies; it has swept away barriers which fenced off certain times and languages as 'dead' and 'ancient;' it has taught us that there is no such thing as 'dead' and 'living' languages, as 'ancient' and 'modern' history; it has taught us that the study of language is one study, that the study of history is one study; it has taught us that no languages are more truly living than those which an arbitrary barrier fences off as dead; it has taught us that no parts of history are more truly modern—if by modern we mean full of living interest and teaching for our own times—than those which the delusive name of 'ancient' would seem to brand as something which has wholly passed away, something which, for any practical use in these later times, may safely be forgotten.

My position then is that, in all our studies of history and language—and the study of language, besides all that it is in other ways, is one most important branch of the study of history—we must cast away all distinctions of 'ancient' and 'modern,' of 'dead' and 'living,' and must boldly grapple with the great fact of the unity of history. As man is the same in all ages, the history of man is one in all ages. The scientific student of language, the student of primitive culture, will refuse any limits to their pursuits which cut them off from any portion of the earth's surface, from any moment of man's history since he first walked upon it. In their eyes the languages and the customs of Greece and Rome have no special privilege above the languages and the customs of other nations. They do but take their place among their fellows, as illustrations of the universal laws which bear rule over human nature and human speech. But let us come to history more strictly so called, to the history of man as a political being, to the history of our own quarter of the globe and our own family of nations. The history of the Aryan nations of Europe, their languages, their institutions, their dealings with one another, all form one long series of cause and effect, no part of which can be rightly understood if it be dealt with as something wholly cut off from, and alien to, any other part. There is really nothing in certain arbitrarily chosen centuries of the history of Greece and Italy which ought to cut them off, either for reverence or for contempt, from any other portion of the history of the kindred nations. There is nothing to make the so-called 'ancient' history a separate study from the history of so-called 'modern' times. 'Ancient' history calls for no special powers for its mastery; it calls for no special method for its study. The powers which are needed for the mastery of ancient history are the same as those that are needed for the mastery of modern history. The method, the line of thought, the habits of research and criticism, which are needed for the one are equally needed for the other. Knowledge is, in both cases, gained by the exercise of the same faculties, and by the use of the same process in their exercise. So too it is with language. There is not, as the world in general seems to think, anything special or mysterious about the Greek and Latin tongues, or about those particular stages of those tongues which are picked out to receive the name of classical. The accurate knowledge of one language can be gained only by the same means as the accurate knowledge of another. It does not need two sets of faculties, but one and the same set, to enable us to master the inflexions of the tongue of Homer and the kindred inflexions of the kindred tongue of Ulfilas.

No language, no period of history, can be understood in its fulness, none can be clothed with its highest interest and its highest profit, if it be looked at wholly in itself, without reference to its bearing on those other languages, those other periods of history, which join with it to make up the great whole of human, or at least of Aryan and European, being. The tie which binds together the Greek and the Latin languages is doubtless closer than that which binds either of them to any other member of the great family. But the tie is simply closer in degree; it is in no way different in kind. We are at last learning that our scientific knowledge of the speech of Greece is imperfect unless we add to it a scientific knowledge of the speech of England, and that our knowledge of the speech of England is imperfect unless we add to it a scientific knowledge of the speech of Greece. We are learning that Greek and Roman history do not stand alone, bound together by some special tie, but isolated from the rest of the history of the world, even from the history of the kindred nations. We are learning that European history, from its first glimmerings to our own day, is one unbroken drama, no part of which can be rightly understood without reference to the other parts which come before and after it. We are learning that of this great drama Rome is the centre, the point to which all roads lead, and from which all roads lead no less. It is the vast lake in which all the streams of earlier history lose themselves, and from which all the streams of later history flow forth again. The world of independent Greece stands on one side of it; the world of modern Europe stands on the other. But the history alike of the great centre and of its satellites on either side can never be fully grasped, except from a point of view wide enough to take in the whole group, and to mark the relations of each of its members to the centre and to one another. As it is with the language, so it is with the history. Our knowledge of the history of Greece is mperfect without a knowledge of the kindred history of England, and our knowledge of the history of England is imperfect without a knowledge of the kindred history of Greece. Rome is the centre; Rome is the common link which binds all together; and yet, while learning this, while learning more truly and fully the place and dignity of Rome, we are learning too to cast away the superstition which once looked on her language as the one guide and key to all other languages and to all human knowledge. We have learned that all members of the great family are alike kinsfolk, entitled to stand side by side on equal terms. We have learned that Angul and his brother Dan (4) may march boldly and claim of right to speak face to face with their cousin Hellên, and have no need to be smuggled in by some back-way through the favour of their other cousin Latinus.

I here stop to answer one possible objection. Is it, I may be asked, needful for the student of history or of language to be master of all history and of all language? Must he be equally familiar with the tongue, the literature, the political constitutions, the civil and military events, of all times and places? Such an amount of knowledge, it may well be argued, can never fall to the lot of man. And some may go on to infer that any doctrine which may even seem to lead to such a result must be in itself fruitless. Now to be equally familiar with all history and all language is of course utterly beyond human power. But it is none the less true that the student of history or of language—and he who is a student of either must be in no small degree a student of the other—must take in all history and all language within his range. The degrees of his knowledge of various languages, of various branches of history, will vary infinitely. Of some branches he must know everything, but of every branch he must know something. Each student will have his own special range, the times and places which he chooses for his special and minute study. Of these he will know everything; he will master every detail of their history in the minutest way from the original authorities. The choice of such ages and countries for special study will of course depend upon each man's taste and opportunities; one may choose an earlier, another a later time; one may choose the East, another the West; one may choose a heathen, another a Christian period; but all are fellow-workers, if only they all remember that, beyond the something of which they must needs know everything lies the everything of which they need only know something. No man can study the history of all ages and countries in original authorities. To the man who is most deeply versed in historic lore there must still be many periods of which his knowledge is vague, imperfect, and gained at second-hand. When a subject is so vast, it cannot be otherwise. Some branches must in every case be primary and some secondary; which are primary and which are secondary will of course differ in the case of each particular student. It is enough if each man, while thoroughly mastering the branches of his own choice, knows at least enough of the other branches to have a clear and abiding conception of their relation to his own special branches and to one another. And the thorough knowledge of one period, the habit of minute research and criticism among contemporary authorities, undoubtedly gives a man a power which leads him better to see his way through the periods which he has to take at second-hand, and to feel by a kind of instinct where second-hand writers may be freely followed and where they must be used with caution. A man who is thoroughly master of the periods which to him are primary will readily grasp the leading outlines and the true relations of the periods which to him are secondary. The one point is that of no period of history worthy of the name, of no part of the record of man's political being, can he afford to know nothing. I have said that a knowledge of the history of Greece is imperfect without a knowledge of the history of

England, and that a knowledge of the history of England is imperfect without a knowledge of the history of Greece. But I do not say that the knowledge need be in each case the same in amount, or even the same in kind. With many men one must be primary and the other secondary; one will be a study to be mastered in its minutest detail, while the other will be something of which it is enough to know the main outlines and to grasp the true relations of each period to the others. And as it is with history, so it is with language. The philologer will have certain languages of which he is thoroughly master, with whose literature he is familiar, and in which his tact can distinguish the nicest peculiarities of dialects and periods and particular writers. Of other tongues he will have no such minute knowledge; he may be unable to compose a sentence in them, perhaps even to construe a sentence in them; yet he may have a very real and practical knowledge of them for his own purpose. That purpose is gained if he thoroughly grasps their relations to other languages, the main peculiarities which distinguish them, and the position which they hold in the general history of human speech.

Looking then at the history of man, at all

events at the history of Aryan man in Europe, as one unbroken whole, no part of which can be safely looked at without reference to other parts, we shall soon see that those branches of history which are too often set aside as something distinct and isolated from all others do not lose but gain in dignity and importance, by being set free from the unnatural bondage, by being brought into their natural relation to other branches of the one great study of which they form a part. Let us look at the history of the Greek people and the Greek tongue. Some men speak as if that history came to an end on the field of Chairôneia, while others will graciously allow that the life of Greece lingered on to be burned up for ever among the flames of Corinth. Some speak as if the whole life of the Greek tongue was shut up within those few centuries which, by an arbitrary distinction, we choose to speak of as 'classical.' Some indeed draw the line very narrowly indeed. There was one Greek historian before whose eyes the history of the world was laid open as it never was to any other man before or after. There was one man who, in the compass of a single life, had been as it were a dweller in two worlds, in two wholly different stages of man's being. To the experience of Polybios the old life of independent Greece, the border warfare and the internal politics of her commonwealths, had been the familiar scenes of his earlier days. His childhood had been brought up among the traditions of the Achaian League, among men who were fellow-workers with Markos and Aratos. His birth would almost fall in days when Megalopolis stood, under the rule of Lydiadas, as an independent unit in the independent world of Hellas. The son of Lykortas, the pupil of Philopoimên, may have sat as a child on the knees of the deliverer of Sikyôn and Corinth. He could remember the times when the tale of the self-devotion of their illustrious tyrant must have still sounded like a trumpet in the ears of the men of the Great City (5). He had himself borne to the grave the urn of the last hero of his native land, cut off, as Anaxandros or Archidamos might have been, in border warfare with the rebels of Messênê (6). He could remember times when Macedonia, perhaps even when Carthage, was still an independent and mighty power, able to grapple on equal terms with the advancing, but as yet not overwhelming, power of Rome. He lived to see all swept away. He lived to see Africa, Macedonia, and Greece itself, either incorporated with the Roman dominion or mocked with a shadow of freedom which left them abject dependents on the will of the conquering people. He saw the dominion of the descendants of Seleukos, the truest heirs of Alexander's conquests, shrink up from the vast empire of Western Asia into the local sovereignty of a Syrian kingdom. He saw Pergamos rise to its momentary greatness and Egypt begin the first steps of its downward course. He saw the gem of Asiatic history, the wise Confederation of Lykia, rise into being after the model of the state in which his own youth had been spent. He lived to stand by the younger Scipio beside the flames of Carthage, and, if he saw not the ruin of Corinth with his own eyes, he lived to legislate for the helpless Roman dependency into which the free Hellenic League of his youth had changed (7). The man who saw all this saw changes greater than the men who lived in the days of Theodoric and Justinian, or the men who lived in the days of the elder Buonaparte. And yet there are scholars, men devoted to 'ancient' and 'classical' learning, who have been known to cast away from them the writings of the man who saw all this, because forsooth they were 'bad Greek,' because they did not conform in every jot and tittle to the standard of some arbitrarily chosen point in the history of a language which has lived a life of well nigh three thousand years. As if the form were more precious than the substance; as if the changes in a language were not the most instructive part of the history of that language; as if it were not as unreasonable to call the Greek of Polybios 'bad Greek' because it is not the Greek of Thucydides as it would be to call the Greek of Thucydides 'bad Greek' because it is not the Greek of Homer. But let us rise above trammels such as these; let us take a wider and a worthier view of the long history of the most illustrious form of human speech. Let us remember that the despised Greek of Polybios gives us an instance of a law which has gone on from his day to ours. Thucydides, Xenophôn, Dêmosthenês, wrote and harangued in the dialect which came most naturally to their lips, in the dialect of their daily life. The History of Polybios is as little written in the dialect which came most naturally to his lips as is the History of Trikoupês. The language of an Arkadian inscription is something wholly different from the language of the contemporary History (8). That is to say, the dialect of Athens had already made that complete conquest of Hellenic prose literature which it has kept ever since. The classical purist may smile when I apply the name of Attic to the long succession of writers of Macedonian, Roman, and Byzantine date. But so it is; the style and spirit may change; the vocabulary may be corrupted by strange and barbarous intruders; but the mere forms of words still remain Attic. The latest Byzantine writer really differs less from Xenophôn than Xenophôn differs from Herodotus. Even the language of a modern Greek newspaper, in its vain attempts to call back a form of speech which has passed away, is Attic to the best of its ability. Its aim is to reproduce the Greek of Plato and Xenophôn, not the Greek of Herodotus or of Pindar. What higher tribute can be paid to the great writers of the short sunshine of Athenian glory, than that the dialect of their one city should for two thousand years have thus set the standard of Greek prose writing, that it should thus keep up one ideal of Hellenic purity among the many and shifting forms of speech which were the native dialects of the men who used it? But the full extent, the full worth, of such a tribute can never be fully understood by those who cast away with contempt whatever does not fully come up to an ideal whose full perfection of course was unattainable except in its native time and place. The man who would fully take in the influence of the Greek tongue and the Greek mind on the history of the world must look far beyond the narrow range of time and place within which classical purism would confine him. Let him see how, in the earliest days of Greek colonization, the tongue and the arts of Greece found themselves a home on every coast from the isle of Cyprus to the peninsula of Spain. Let him look on the greater isle of Sicily, twice the battle-field between the East and the West, between Africa and Europe, between the Semitic and the Aryan man (9). Let him see the native tribes gradually absorbed by kindred conquerors and neighbours, till the distinction between Sikel and Sikeliot died away, till the whole island was gathered into the Hellenic fold, a land whose Hellenic life failed not under the rule of Carthaginian, Roman, Saracen, and Norman, and where the tongue in which the victories of Hierôn had been sung to the lyre of Pindar lived on to record the glories of the house of Hauteville on the walls of the Saracenic churches of Palermo (10). Look again at the Phokaian settlement in Gaul; see how, among a race far more alien than the kindred Sikel, the arts and letters of Greece held their place for ages, and how some glimmerings from the Massalian hearth may even have reached, not indeed to our own forefathers, but to our predecessors in our own island. See the long history of the Massalian commonwealth itself; how the spirit of the men who sailed away from the Persian yoke lived on in their kinsfolk who withstood the might of Cæsar, and sprang again to life in later times to withstand the sterner might of Charles of Anjou (11). From the western extremity of Greek colonization let us look to the eastern; let us turn our eyes from the northern shore of the

Mediterranean to the northern shore of the Inhospitable Sea. The Greek kingdom of Bosporos and the Greek commonwealth of Cherson have passed so utterly out of memory that we may doubt whether, when, eighteen years back, those lands were in every mouth, there was one among the warriors and tourists and writers of a day who knew that, in compassing the fortress of Sebastopol, he was treading on the ruins of the last of the Greek republics. Yet it is something to remember that, ages after Athens and Sparta and Thebes had been swallowed up in the dominion of Rome, ages after their citizens had exchanged the name of Hellênes for the name of Romans, the fire once lighted at the prytaneion of Megara still burned on, that one single commonwealth still lived, Greek in blood and speech and feeling, the ally but not the subject of the lords of the Old and the New Rome (12). Thus far we have seen the free Greek settle on distant shores, and carry with him the freedom of his own land. But we must look also to other times and lands, when the Greek tongue and Greek arts were scattered through the world, but without carrying Greek freedom with them. Yet it was something that, before Greece yielded to her Macedonian master, he had himself to become a Greek, to be adopted into the great religious brotherhood of Greece, and to be chosen, with at least the outward assent of her commonwealths, to be their common leader against the Barbarian (13). The arms which overthrew her old political freedom carried her tongue and her culture through the kingdoms of the East. The centres of Grecian intellectual life moved from the banks of the Ilissos and the Eurôtas to the banks of the Orontês and the Nile. Even the barbarous Gaul, the descendant of the invaders of her Delphic temple, was brought in his new home within her magic range, and his Asiatic land deserved to be spoken of as the Gaulish Greece (14). Thus that artificial Greek nation arose, sometimes Greek in birth, always Greek in speech and culture, which so long divided the dominion of the world, and which, after ages of bondage, has again sprung to life in our own day. It is something too to see how truly Greece led captive, not only her Macedonian but her Roman conqueror; to remember how the first Roman historians recorded Roman legends in the Greek tongue, and how well nigh every Roman poet went to Greece as the fount of his inspiration. But our view will not stop with the Augustan or with the Flavian age. If we would see how truly Greece conquered Rome, we must see the two Imperial saints of heathendom, Marcus in his camp by the Danube and Julian in his camp by the Rhine, choosing the tongue of Greece, and not of

Rome, to receive the witness of the time when the prayer of the wise man was answered, and when philosophers held the dominion of the world. But from them we must turn away to the records of the Faith which the one persecuted and the other cast aside. Those conquests which made the Greek tongue the literary tongue of civilized Asia caused that it should be in the Greek tongue that the oracles of Christianity should be given to the world, and that Greek should be the speech of the earliest and most eloquent preachers of the Faith. The traditions of Greece and Rome, the conquests of Macedonian warriors and of Christian Apostles, all came together when the throne and the name of Rome were transferred to a Greek-speaking city of the Eastern world, and when the once heathen colony of Megara was baptized into the Christian capital of Constantine. There went on that long dominion of the laws of Rome, but of the speech, the learning, and the arts of Greece, the dominion of the city which those who scorned and overthrew her political power none the less revered as their intellectual mistress. We have not gone through the history of Greece till we have read the legends carved in her tongue on the monumental stones of Ravenna, and blazing in all the glory of the apses of Venice and Torcello (15). We have not taken in how thoroughly

Greece leavened the world, till we read how the panegyrist of the Norman Conqueror tells us that the spoils of England were of such richness that they would not have disgraced the Imperial city, and that even Greek eyes might have looked on them with wonder (16). The Empire of Greece has passed away, but her changeless Church remains, the Church which still speaks the tongue of Paul and of Chrysostom, the Church which still sends up her prayers in the words of the liturgies of the earliest days, the Church which still keeps her Creed free from the interpolations of later times (17), and which, alone among Christian Churches, can give to her people the New Testament itself, and not man's interpretation of it. And now again the Hellên, disguised for ages under the Roman name, has once more stood forth as a nation, a nation artificial indeed as regards actual blood, but a nation well defined by its Greek speech and its Greek religion. And, if regenerate Hellas has in some points failed, what has been the cause of her failure? Mainly because regenerate Hellas has, in the zeal of her new birth, forgotten her long continuous being. It is, above all things, the dream of the irrecoverable past, the dream of the exclusively classic past, which has checked the progress of the ransomed nation. A Greece which could utterly forget Athens and Sparta, which could look on herself simply as one of the Christian races rescued, or to be rescued, from the bondage of the Infidel—a Greece which could look on herself, and which was allowed to look on herself, simply as the yoke-fellow of Servia and Bulgaria—would be far more likely to hold up her head among the nations of Europe than a Greece that still dreams of Thermopylai and Marathôn, hard as the lesson must be when her strife for freedom was one in which the very soil of Thermopylai and Marathôn was again dyed with the blood of vanquished barbarians.

Surely in such a view as this we learn how truly history is one; surely such a survey teaches us how the whole drama hangs together, how ill we can afford to look at any one of its scenes as a mere isolated fragment, without referring to the scenes before and after it. And surely too we pay the highest homage to 'ancient' days, to 'classic' days, to the nation which stood forth as the first teacher of the human mind and to the tongue which was the instrument of its teaching, not by shutting them up within the prison of a few centuries, but by tracing out their influence on the history of all time, by showing how close is the bearing of those 'ancient' times upon the modern world around us, and how the language which we falsely speak of as 'dead' has in truth never died, but still lives on, as it has ever lived through the revolutions of so many ages. But we shall feel the oneness of history even more, if we turn from Greece and her influence on mankind to the influence of the other 'ancient' and 'classical' people, to the long and abiding life of that other tongue which is even more strangely spoken of as 'dead.' Let us look at Rome, not the mere 'classic' Rome of a generation or two of imitative poets, but the true Eternal City, the Rome of universal history. And in this view, it is again no small witness to the true oneness of history that much that we have already looked at as Greek we must look at from another point as Roman. The influence of Greece on the later world, deep and lasting as it has been, has been largely an indirect influence, an influence of example and analogy. No modern nation is governed by the laws of Lykourgos or the laws of Solôn; no modern state can directly trace its political being either to Athenian democracy or to Macedonian kingship. But Rome still lives in the inmost life of every modern European state. Two abiding signs of her rule stand out on the very surface of the modern world, and need no thought, no searching into records, to bring them before the eyes of every man. Three of the foremost nations of Europe still speak the tongue of Rome, in forms indeed which have parted off into independent languages, but which are none the less living witnesses of her abiding rule, as not only the conqueror but the civilizer of the Western lands. And among all the nations which speak her tongue, among many too to whom her tongue is strange, the city of the Cæsars and the Pontiffs is still looked up to as their religious metropolis, though no longer as their temporal capital. Let us look at the history of Rome and of her language. We may say of Rome, in a truer sense even than of Greece, that her sound has gone out into all lands, and her words unto the ends of the world. In the view of universal history, the century or two of its 'classic' purity seem but as a moment in the long annals of the Imperial tongue. We might indeed be tempted to wipe out altogether the days of her 'classical'—that is, her imitative—literature, as a mere episode in the history of the undying speech of Rome. We might be tempted to say that the genuine literature of Italy went into a *katabothra* when the Camenæ wept over the tomb of Nævius, and that it came out again when the dominion of the stranger Muses had passed away, and when the inspiration of Prudentius and Ambrose was drawn from sources at least not more foreign than the well of Helikôn (18). The old Saturnian echoes which sang how it was the evil fate of Rome which gave her the Metelli as her Consuls, ring out again in those new Saturnian rimes which sing the praises of Imperial Frederick and set forth the reforming policy of Earl Simon (19). The truly distinctive character of the Latin tongue was not stamped on it by its poets, not even by its historians and orators. The special calling of Rome, as one of those poets told her, was to rule the nations; not merely to conquer by her arms, but to govern by her abiding laws. Her truest and longest life is to be looked for, not in the triumphs of her Dictators, but in the edicts of her Prætors. The most truly original branch of Latin literature is to be found in what some might perhaps deny to be part of literature at all, in the immediate records of her rule, in the text-books of her great lawyers, in the Itineraries of her provinces, in the Notitia of her governments and offices. The true glory of the Latin tongue is to have become the eternal speech of law and dominion. It is the tongue of Rome's twofold sovereignty and of her twofold legislation, the tongue of the Church and the Empire, the tongue of the successors of Augustus and of the successors of Saint Peter. It has been, wherever King or Priest could wrap himself in any shred of her Imperial or her Pontifical mantle, the chosen speech alike of temporal and of religious rule. In the hymn of the Fratres Arvales, in the 'lex horrendi carminis' of the earliest recorded Roman formula (20), we get the beginnings of that long series of witnesses of her twofold rule, as alike the temporal and the spiritual mistress of the Western world. In the eyes of universal history the truest triumphs of the Latin tongue are to be found in lands far away from the seven hills, far away even from the shores of the Italian peninsula. The tongue of Rome, the tongue of Gaius and Ulpian rather than the tongue of Virgil and Horace, has become the tongue of the Code and the Capitularies, the tongue of the false Decretals and of the true Acts of Councils, the tongue of Domesday and the Great Charter, the tongue of the Missal and the Breviary, the tongue which was for ages in Western eyes the very tongue of Scripture itself, the tongue in which all Western nations were content to record their laws and annals, the tongue for which all those nations which came within her immediate dominion were content to cast away their native speech. It is this abiding and Imperial character of the speech of Rome, far more than even the greatest works of one or two short periods in its long life, which gives it a position in the history of the world which no other European tongue can share with it. But this its position in the history of the world can never be grasped except by those who look on the history of the world as one continuous whole. It is unintelligible to those who break up the unity of history by artificial barriers of 'ancient' and 'modern.' Much that in a shallow view of things passes for mere imitation, for mere artificial revival, was in truth abiding and unbroken tradition. Of all the languages of the earth, Latin is the last to be spoken of as dead. It was but yesterday the universal speech of science and learning; it is still the religious speech of half Western Europe; it is still the key to European history and law; and, if it is nowhere spoken in its ancient form, it still lives in the new forms into which it grew in the provinces which Rome civilized as well as conquered. It was a wise saying that the true scholar should know, not only whence words come, but whither they go (21). The history of the Latin language is imperfect if it does not take in the history of the changes by which it grew into the tongue of Dante and Villani, into the tongues of the Provençal Troubadour and the Castilian Campeador, and into that later but once vigorous speech which gave us the rimes of Wace and the prose of Joinville, and which still lives in so many of the statutes and records and legal formulæ of our own land.

In truth, as the full meaning and greatness of the Roman history cannot be grasped without a full understanding of history as a whole, so the history of Rome is in itself the great example of the oneness of all history. The history of Rome is the history of the European world. It is in Rome that all the states of the earlier European world lose themselves; it is out of Rome that all the states of the later European world take their being. The true meaning of Roman history as a branch of universal history, or rather the absolute identity of Roman history with universal history, can only be fully understood by giving special attention to those ages of the history of Europe which are commonly most neglected. Men study what they call Greek and Roman history; they study again the history of the modern kingdoms of England and France. But they end their Roman studies at the latest with the deposition of Augustulus; sometimes they do not carry them beyond Pharsalia and Philippi. Their study of English history they begin at the point when England for a moment ceased to be England; their French studies they begin at some point which teaches them that the greatest of Germans was a Frenchman. In every case, they begin both at some point which leaves an utter gap between their 'ancient' or 'classical' and their 'modern' studies. To understand history as a whole, to understand how truly all European history is Roman history, we must see things, not only as they seem when they are looked at from Rome and Athens, from Paris and London, but as they seem when they are looked at from Constantinople, from Aachen, and from Ravenna. In that last-named wondrous city we stand as it were on the isthmus which joins two worlds, and there, amid Roman, Gothic, and Byzantine monuments, we feel, more than on any other spot of the earth's surface, what the history of the Roman Empire really was. It is in the days of the decline of the Roman power—those days which were in truth the days of its greatest conquests—that we see how truly great, how truly abiding, was the power of Rome. When we see how thoroughly the conquered Roman led captive his Teutonic conqueror, we see how firm was the work of Sulla and of Augustus, of Diocletian and of Constantine. We see it alike when Odoacer and Theodoric shrink from assuming the titles and ensigns of Imperial power, and when the Imperial crown of Rome is placed upon the head of the Frankish Charles. We see it in our own day as long as the *cognomen* of a Roman family, strangely changed into the official designation of Roman sovereignty, still remains the highest and most coveted of earthly titles. To know what Rome was, to feel how she looked in the eyes of other nations, it is not enough to read the hireling strains in which Horace sends the living Consul and Tribune to drink nectar among the Gods, or those in which Virgil and Lucan bid him take care on what quarter of the universe he seats himself (22). Let us rather see how Rome, in the days of her supposed decay, looked in the eyes of the men who overthrew her. Let us listen to the Goth Athanaric, when, overwhelmed by the splendours of the New Rome, he bears witness that the Emperor is a God upon earth, and that he who dares to withstand him shall have his blood on his own head (23). Let us listen to Ataulf in the moment of his triumph, when he tells how he had once dreamed of sweeping away the Roman name, of putting the Goth in the place of the Roman, and Ataulf in the place of Augustus, but how he learned in later days that the world could not be governed save by the laws of Rome, and how the highest glory to which he now looked was to use the power of the Goth in the defence of the Roman Commonwealth (24). And so her name and power lives on, witnessed in the Imperial style of every prince, from Winchester to Trebizond, who deemed it his highest glory to deck himself in some shreds of her purple; witnessed too, when her name passes on not only to her subjects, allies, and disciples, but to the destroyers of her power and faith; when Timour, coming forth from his unknown Mongolian land, sends his defiance to the Ottoman Bajazet and addresses him by the title of the Cæsar of Rome (25). But it is not in mere names and titles that her dominion still lives. As long as the law of well nigh every European nation but ourselves rests as its groundwork on the legislation of Servius and Justinian—as long as the successor of the Leos and the Innocents, shorn of all earthly power, is still looked to by millions as holding their seat by a more than earthly right—so long can no man say that the power of Rome is a thing of days which are gone by, or that the history of her twofold rule is the history of a dominion which has wholly passed away.

In tracing out the long history of the true middle ages, the ages when Roman and Teutonic elements stood as yet side by side, not yet mingled together into the whole which was to spring out of their union—in treading the spots which have witnessed the deeds of Roman Cæsars and Teutonic Kings—many are the scenes which we light upon which make us feel more strongly how truly all European history is one unbroken tale. There are moments when contending elements are brought together in a wondrous sort, when strangely mingled tongues and races and states of feeling meet as it were from distant lands and ages. I will choose but one such scene out of many. Let us stand on the Akropolis of Athens on a day in the early part of the eleventh century of our æra. A change has come since the days of

Periklês and even since the days of Alaric. The voice of the orator is silent in the Pnyx; the voice of the philosopher is silent in the Academy. Athênê Promachos no longer guards her city with her uplifted spear, nor do men deem that, if the Goth should again draw nigh, her living form would again scare him from her walls (26). But her temple is still there, as yet untouched by the cannon of Turk and Venetian, as yet unspoiled by the hand of the Scottish plunderer. It stands as holy as ever in the minds of men; it is hallowed to a worship of which Iktinos and Kallikratês never heard; yet in some sort it keeps its ancient name and use: the House of the Virgin is the House of the Virgin still. The old altars, the old images, are swept away; but altars unstained by blood have risen in their stead, and the walls of the cella blaze, like Saint Sophia and Saint Vital, with the painted forms of Hebrew patriarchs, Christian martyrs, and Roman Cæsars. It is a day of triumph, not as when the walls were broken down to welcome a returning Olympic conqueror; not as when ransomed thousands pressed forth to hail the victors of Marathôn, or when their servile offspring crowded to pay their impious homage to the descending godship of Dêmêtrios (27). A conqueror comes to pay his worship within those ancient walls; an Emperor of the Romans comes to give thanks for the deliverance of his Empire in the Church of Saint Mary of Athens. Roman in title, Greek in speech — boasting of his descent from the Macedonian Alexander and from the Parthian Arsakês, but sprung in truth, so men whispered, from the same Slavonic stock which had given the Empire Justinian and Belisarius—fresh from his victories over a people Turanian in blood, Slavonic in speech, and delighting to deck their Kings with the names of Hebrew prophets (28)—Basil the Second, the Slayer of the Bulgarians, the restorer of the Byzantine power, paying his thank-offerings to God and the Panagia in the old heathen temple of democratic Athens, seems as if he had gathered all the ages and nations of the world around him, to teach by the most pointed of contrasts that the history of no age or nation can be safely fenced off from the history of its fellows (29). Other scenes of the same class might easily be brought together, but this one, perhaps the most striking of all, is enough. I know of no nobler subject for a picture or a poem.

We might carry out the same doctrine of the unity of history into many and various applications. I have as yet been speaking of branches of the study where its oneness takes the form of direct connexion, of long chains of events bound together in the direct relation of cause and effect. There are other branches of history which proclaim the unity of the study in a hardly less striking way, in the form of mere analogy. Man is in truth ever the same; even when the direct succession of cause and effect does not come in, we see that in times and places most remote from one another like events follow upon like causes. European history forms one whole in the strictest sense, but between European and Asiatic history the connexion is only occasional and incidental. The fortunes of the Roman Empire had no effect on the internal revolutions of the Saracenic Caliphate, still less effect had they on the momentary dominion of the house of Jenghiz or on the Mogul Empire in India. Yet the way in which the European Empire and its several kingdoms broke in pieces has its exact parallel in those distant Eastern monarchies. After all real dominion in the West had passed away from the New Rome, Gothic and Frankish Kings bore themselves as lieutenants of the absent Emperor. It was by Imperial commission that Ataulf conquered Spain and that Theodoric conquered Italy, and Odoacer, Chlodwig, and Theodoric himself, bore the titles of Consul and Patrician, no less than Boetius and Belisarius. So in later times we see the Duke of the French at

Paris owning a nominal homage to the King of the Franks at Laon, and at the same time attacking, despoiling, leading about as a prisoner, the King whom he did not dare deprive of his royal title (30). We see Princes of Aquitaine and Toulouse so far vassals of the King of Laon as to date their charters by the years of his reign, but not caring to speak a word for or against their master in his struggle with their rebellious fellow-vassal. We see in times far nearer to our own a Roman Emperor and King of Germany addressed in terms of the lowliest homage, and served, as by his menial servants, by princes some of them mightier than himself, princes who never scrupled to draw the sword against a Lord of the World who, as such, held not a foot of the earth's surface. We see the parallels to this when the dominion of Jenghiz is split up into endless fragments which still remember the name of their lawful sovereign. It is brought in all its fulness before our eyes when the Emir Timour, scrupulously forbearing to take on him any higher title, thus far respects the hereditary right of the Grand Khan who follows him as a single soldier in his army (31). We see it when every Moslem prince who has grasped any fragment of the old Saracenic Empire dutifully seeks investiture from the Caliph of his own sect—when Bajazet the Thunderbolt stoops to receive his patent as Sultan from the trembling slave of the Egyptian Mamelukes, and when Selim the Inflexible obtains from the last Abbasside a formal cession of the rank and style of Commander of the Faithful (32). We see it in events which have more nearly touched ourselves. We see it in the history of our own dealings with the land where we won province after province from princes who owned a formal allegiance to the heir of Timour. We see it in the way in which we ourselves have dealt with the heir of Timour himself, first as a pampered pensioner, lord only within the walls of his own palace, and at last as a criminal and a prisoner, sent to a harder exile than that of Glycerius in his bishoprick or of the last Merwing in his cloister.

One word more. The fashion of the day, by a not unnatural reaction, seems to be turning against 'ancient' and 'classical' learning altogether. We are asked, What is the use of learning languages which are 'dead'? What is the use of studying the records of times which have for ever passed away? Men who call themselves statesmen and historians are not ashamed to run up and down the land, spreading abroad, wherever such assertions will win them a cheer, the daring falsehood that such studies, and no others, form the sole business of our ancient

Universities. They ask, in their pitiful shallowness, What is the use of poring over the history of 'petty states'? What is the use of studying battles in which so few men were killed as on the field of Marathôn (33)? In this place I need not stop for a moment to answer such transparent fallacies. Still even such falsehoods and fallacies as these are signs of the times which we cannot afford to neglect. The answer is in our own hands. As long as we treat the language and the history of Greece and Rome as if they were something special and mysterious, something to be set apart from all other studies, something to be approached and handled in some peculiar method of their own, we are playing into the hands of the enemy. As long as we have 'classical' schools instead of general schools of language, as long as we have schools of 'modern' history instead of general schools of history (34), as long as we in any way recognize the distinctions implied in the words 'classical' and 'ancient,' we are pleading guilty to the charge which is brought against us. We are acknowledging that, not indeed our whole attention, but a chief share of it, is given to subjects which do stand apart from ourselves, cut off from all bearing on the intellect and life of modern days. The answer to such charges is to break down the barrier, to forget, if we can, the whole line of thought implied in the distinctions of 'ancient,' 'classical,' and 'modern,' to proclaim boldly that no languages are more truly living than those which are falsely called dead, that no portions of history are more truly 'modern'—that is, more full of practical lessons for our own political and social state—than the history of the times which in mere physical distance we look upon as 'ancient.' If men ask whether French and German are not more useful languages than Latin and Greek, let us answer that, as a direct matter of parentage and birth, it is an imperfect knowledge of French which takes no heed to the steps by which French grew out of Latin, and that it is an imperfect knowledge of Latin which takes no heed to the steps by which Latin grew into French. Let us answer again, not as a matter of parentage and birth, but as a matter of analogy and kindred, that it is an imperfect knowledge of German which takes no heed to the kindred phænomena of Greek, and that it is an imperfect knowledge of Greek which takes no heed to the kindred phænomena of German. If they ask what is the use of studying the histories of petty states, let us answer that moral and intellectual greatness is not always measured by physical bigness, that the smallness of a state of itself heightens and quickens the power of its citizens, and makes the history of a small commonwealth a more instructive lesson in politics than the history of a huge empire. If we are asked what is the use of studying the events and institutions of times so far removed from our own, let us answer that distance is not to be measured simply by lapse of time, and that those ages which gave birth to literature, and art, and political freedom are, sometimes only by analogy and indirect influence, sometimes by actual cause and effect, not distant, but very near to us indeed. Let us give to the history and literature of Greece and Rome in their chosen periods their due place in the history of mankind, but not more than their due place. Let us look on the 'ancients,' the men of Plutarch, the men of Homer, not as beings of another race, but as men of like passions with ourselves, as elder brethren of our common Aryan household. In this way we can make answer to gainsayers; in this way we can convince the unlearned and unbelieving that our studies are not vain gropings into what is dead and gone. Let us carry about with us the thought that the tongue which we still speak is in truth one with the tongue of Homer; that the Ekklêsia of Athens, the Comitia of Rome, and the Parliament of England, are all offshoots from one common stock; that Kleisthenês, Licinius, and Simon of Montfort were fellow-workers in one common cause—let all this be to us a living thought, as we read the records either of the earlier or of the later time—and we shall find that the studies of our youthful days will still keep an honoured place among the studies of later life, that the heroes of ancient legend, the worthies of ancient history, lose not, but rather gain, in true dignity by being made the objects of a reasonable homage instead of an exclusive superstition.

# NOTES.

## LECTURE I.

(1) Page 6.—Max Müller, Oxford Essays, 1856, p. 27. "The English name for 'mill' is likewise of considerable antiquity, for it exists not only in the O. H. G. *muli*, but in the Lithuanian *malunas*, the Bohemian *mlyn*, the Welsh *melin*, the Latin *mola*, and the Greek μύλη." Supposing the word not to be found beyond the Western branch of the Aryan family, it still seems quite impossible that the word could have got into these various languages by any means but that of original kindred. Examples of wider range might have been found; but this has the example of being so perfectly clear, and of needing no philological practice to see the likeness between the different cognate words.

(2) Page 9.—The connexion between the Greek *Charis* and *Charites* and the Sanscrit *Harits* is discussed by Müller, Science of Language, ii. 369–376, 381–383; Cox, Aryan Mythology, i. 48, 210; ii. 2. Mr. Cox, as usual, goes somewhat further than Professor Müller. I can see no difficulty in looking on the Greek word χάρις and its Greek cognates as sprung from the same original root *ghar* as the Sanscrit *Harits* and their Sanscrit cognates, and at the same time

believing that the mythological *Charis* and *Charites* arose after the appellative χάρις had received its particular Greek meaning. *Charis* and the *Charites* would thus be strictly personifications, like the other personifications compared with them in the text. The *Harits* and the *Charites* have thus a connexion, the general connexion which exists between any two words sprung from the same root. I cannot see with Mr. Cox (i. 210) that we are bound to see the same kind of connexion between them which there is between *Dyaus* and *Zeus*.

(3) Page 10.—The solar theory has undoubtedly been pressed too far; on the other hand, it has been made the subject of a good deal of jesting which is much more foolish than any possible vagaries of the theory itself. The true rule seems to be this; it is not safe to set down as a solar myth every story which, by some ingenious process, *may* be made to fit in with the requirements of a solar story. I believe that this might be done with a little trouble with almost every tale in history or fiction. I have myself tried (see Fortnightly Review, November, 1870) to do as much with the story both of Harold Hardrada and of Harold the son of Godwine. One might argue that Augustus the Strong was a solar hero, on the strength of the 360 children whom he is said to have left behind him. These might fairly pass for the days of the year, all the more so as the most famous of them was undoubtedly the son of *Êôs* or the Morning, in the person of Aurora von Königsmarck. Many of the solar explanations which have been put forth seriously seem to me to be of exactly the same kind as these sportive ones. The case is changed when philology comes to the help of mythology, and when the names and epithets of the hero and his attendants show beyond doubt that the story is solar.

This is the distinction which is more than once drawn by Professor Müller. Thus the solar character of Phoibos-Apollôn runs through every detail. But I cannot see the same evidence for the solar character of Achilleus and Odysseus.

(4) Page 14.— For the happy name "survivals" we have to thank Mr. Tylor. No line of argument can well be more convincing, and it will be seen that in other lectures I have made a large use of it for my own purposes.

(5) Page 15.—Müller, Science of Language, i. 223–226.

(6) Page 16.—Let the science rather go nameless than bear the burthen of such a name as, for instance, *Sociology.*

(7) Page 22.—See Growth of the English Constitution, 92, ed. ii. It can hardly be needful to expose for the thousandth time either the notion that the Three Estates are King, Lords, and Commons, or the silly joke of calling the newspapers the Fourth Estate.

(8) Page 22.—See Growth of the English Constitution, 96, 98.

(9) Page 25.—I must confess that I say this at second hand, as I have not studied the Crusading Jurisprudence for myself. But it is plain that in no other time or place was there the same opportunity for bringing in a system of Feudal Law—if any one likes the phrase, of introducing the Feudal System—which was supplied by the Frank Conquest of Palestine. Elsewhere feudal notions gradually grew up, and they gradually spread from one country to another. Thus

in England the feudal ideas, which were already growing up before the Norman Conquest, were greatly strengthened and put into shape through the Norman Conquest. But there was nothing like the bringing in of a wholly new jurisprudence at a single blow. In Palestine, on the other hand, where of course Mahometan law and custom went for nothing, the Crusaders had the opportunity of legislating afresh from the beginning, and the most perfect of feudal codes was the natural result. The lands conquered from the Eastern Empire by the Crusaders and other Western adventurers, from Apulia to Cyprus, offered a field for feudal legislation only one degree less open than the lands conquered from the Mahometans. The Assizes of Jerusalem themselves became the law of the Kingdom of Cyprus, whose Kings of the House of Lusignan continued the nominal succession of the Kings of Jerusalem. See Gibbon, c. lviii. vol. xi. p. 91, ed. Milman.

(10) Page 27.—The magistrates were called in Romance *Capitouls.* The name *Capitolium* is graven in large letters on the front of the building itself, a building of no great age. I have not specially studied the local history of Toulouse, but I can hardly think that the *Capitouls,* whatever we make of the *Capitolium* itself, can be a direct inheritance from Roman times. Indeed, according to Thierry (Tiers État, ii. 1, Eng. Trans.), the *Consuls* of Toulouse were only established in 1188. There was also a Capitol at Köln, the name of which survives in the church of Saint Mary Capitoline.

(11) Page 28.—I learned this from an inscription in the church of Saint Salvi at Alby. The style is "major et consules." On the consular governments in the cities of Southern Gaul see the chapter of Thierry just quoted. He

speaks of the Mayor as an addition to the original consular government which came in first in the Aquitanian cities under Norman or English rule.

(12) Page 29.—On the modern corruption of the German language I have said something in my second series of Historical Essays, p. 269.

(13) Page 31.—See Forsyth, History of Ancient Manuscripts, p. 25.

(14) Page 32.—I said something on this matter many years ago in the two first chapters of the First Book of my History of Architecture; but I should not now talk about "Pelasgian."

## LECTURE II.

(1) Page 39.—See the remarks of Grote, ii. 289–302, on the effects of the geographical character of Greece on its history. See also the first chapter of Curtius, especially the remarkable passage at page 13:

"Euphrat und Nil bieten Jahr um Jahr ihren Anwohnern dieselben Vortheile und regeln ihre Beschäftigungen, deren stetiges Einerlei es möglich macht, dass Jahrhunderte über das Land hingehen, ohne dass sich in den hergebrachten Lebensverhältnissen etwas Wesentliches ändert. Es erfolgen Umwälzungen, aber keine Entwickelungen, und mumienartig eingesargt stockt im Thale des Nils die Cultur der Aegypter; sie zählen die einförmigen Pendelschläge der Zeit, aber die Zeit hat keinen Inhalt; sie haben Chronologie, aber keine Geschichte im vollen Sinne des Worts. Solche Zustände der Erstarrung duldet der Wellenschlag des ägäischen Meeres nicht, der, wenn einmal Verkehr und geistiges Leben erwacht ist, dasselbe ohne Stillstand immer weiter führt und entwickelt."

(2) Page 40.—The second chapter of Curtius and the appendix to the first volume should be read. But I see no reason to doubt the received version, which makes European Hellas the mother-land of the Asiatic Hellênes.

(3) Page 40.—Of the Phœnician occupation of the Ægæan

islands there seems no doubt. See Thucydides, i. 8; Herodotus, iv. 147. Thasos, with its gold mines, is a well-known case; the authorities are collected in the article on Thasos in the Dictionary of Geography. I venture to think that the Homeric Catalogue might enable us to draw a map of the islands as far as they had been already wrested from Phœnician and other præ-Hellenic occupants. It appears from vv. 645–680 that Crete, Rhodes, Kôs, and several other of the southern islands, were already Hellenic, though the language used of Rhodes would seem to imply that the Hellenic settlement had been made not very long before. Chios and Samos were clearly not yet Hellenic, and Lesbos is a conquest of Achilleus himself. (Iliad, ix. 271.)

The Hellênes were doing in these islands in præ-historic times what they afterwards did in Sicily and Cyprus. They were fighting the battle of the Aryan against the Semitic man; and all the more so because the Phœnicians had doubtless established themselves in all these islands, except perhaps Cyprus, at the cost of Sikels, Karians, and other nations more or less akin to the Greek.

(4) Page 40.—See Historical Essays, Second Series, p. 90.

(5) Page 41.—The exact limits of Greek colonization should be noted. It spread gradually over the whole coast of the Mediterranean Sea and its great gulfs, except when there was some manifest hindrance. Thus, on the eastern and southern coasts of the Mediterranean the Greeks were cut off from colonization by the presence of Phœnicians and Egyptians, except in the lands between Egypt and the Carthaginian dominions, which did receive Greek colonies in the form of the Kyrênaic Pentapolis. It will be at once

seen that, while no part of the Mediterranean coast was more thickly set with Greek colonies than Southern Italy, Northern Italy contained few or none. The Greek origin of Pisæ on the one coast and of Spina on the other is at best doubtful, and in no case did they play any part as Greek cities worthy to be compared with the famous cities which won the name of Magna Græcia. This plainly shows that, in the days of Greek colonization, the occupants of Northern Italy—Etruscan, Gaulish, Umbrian, or Latin—were much stronger than those whom the Greek colonists found in the South. Another point to notice is that Greek colonization succeeded best in those lands where the former inhabitants were more or less closely akin to the Greeks. Thus Sicily and the Ægæan coast became really Greek countries, while in Libya and on the Euxine the Greek colonies always remained mere scattered settlements in a barbarian land.

(6) Page 41.—Notwithstanding all that has been said about Egypt and the East, I see no more reason than I did five-and-twenty years ago to derive the origin of Greek architecture from any barbarian source. The Ionic capital indeed may perhaps come from the East. But if so, the Greeks made it thoroughly their own, and they were the first to give it any form which, in the words of the text, really deserved the name of art.

(7) Page 41.—That is of course the *κτῆμα ἐς ἀεὶ* of Thucydides himself (i. 22). The fact that such a history as that of Thucydides could be written at such an early stage of prose literature is in itself one of the greatest facts in Greek or in human history. The man himself was of course above his contemporaries; but in no other contemporary society could room have been found for such a man. I may

refer to the third Essay in my second series of Historical Essays.

(8) Page 41.—I have said something on this head in the fifth and sixth essays of the same series. But the real witness to the lasting results of Alexander's career is to be found in the Histories of Mr. Finlay. An inhabitant of modern Athens seeks to trace out the causes of the state of things which he sees around him and of the events in which he had himself played a part, and he has to go back to the conquests of Alexander as his beginning.

(9) Page 42.—It must always be remembered that, till the modern Hellenic revival, the name of Ἕλλην was altogether unknown as the name of the Greek nation. All through Byzantine, Frank, and Ottoman times, their one name was Ῥωμαῖοι—Romans by virtue of the unrepealed law of Antoninus Caracalla.

(10) Page 42.—I accept the legend so far as this, that it expresses, in a legendary form, a policy by which Rome grew from the beginning—the policy of incorporation.

(11) Page 43.—"The reign of Cæsar and of Christ was restored," says Gibbon (c. lii., vol. x., 86, Milman), in recording the recovery of Antioch by Nikêphoros Phôkas. This exactly expresses the state of the case.

(12) Page 44.—The phrase of "Urbs æterna" is common in Ammianus. See xiv. 6, and a note of Lindenbrog for other instances.

(13) Page 44.—I believe that there are still people—perhaps those who talk about "Goths, Huns and Vandals" as if they were all the same—who fancy that the Goths were destroyers. Let them study the famous passage of Cassiodorus (vii. 15); only let them not fancy that the description there given has anything to do with Gothic architecture in the technical sense.

(14) Page 45.—See Growth of the English Constitution, p. 9, ed. 2.

(15) Page 46.—It should always be remembered that the three Scandinavian kingdoms, like the two Nether-Dutch kingdoms of Belgium and the Netherlands, were among the few European states which passed undisturbed through the storms of 1848. From 1660 to 1848 Denmark was the one country where despotism was really lawful; and in 1848 Frederick the Seventh had, as his first act, given his people a constitution of his own free will, before revolutions had began elsewhere. The wars and negotiations which have gone on since 1848 have had nothing to do with the state of Denmark itself, but wholly with its relations to the two border Duchies. And it should be further remarked that the discontent in those Duchies came to a head at the very moment of the proclamation of free institutions in Denmark. The cause is obvious. Under the despotism Kingdom and Duchies fared alike, and there were even times when the German element seemed to be preferred to the Danish. In a Parliament representing both the Kingdom and the Duchies the German element would always have been out-voted. The like would be the case with the Romance Cantons of Switzerland, if their equality as sovereign States did not protect them. Hence the strong

opposition of those Cantons to the proposed changes in the Federal Constitution.

(16) Page 47.—I assume this here; I have gone more fully into the matter in my Growth of the English Constitution, of which this position is the main argument.

(17) Page 47.—For Ælfred's description of the modest way in which he laid his laws before his Witan, see Norman Conquest, i. 51.

(18) Page 47.—See Growth of the English Constitution, 34.

(19) Page 47.—I have elsewhere collected some instances of the notion of Britain as another world (Norman Conquest, i. 556). It may be well to give some more instances from earlier writers. The form of speech begins with Virgil's "Penitus toto divisos orbe Britannos." (Ecl. i. 67.) So Velleius (ii. 46) speaks of Cæsar as going into Britain, "alterum pene imperio nostro ac suo quærens orbem." Lucan probably means the same thing less directly, when he speaks (ii. 294) of "diductique fretis alio sub sidere reges." So Florus (iii. 10): "Quasi hic Romanus orbis non sufficeret, alterum cogitavit." (We hear again of "Romanus orbis" and even of "Imperator Romani orbis," in Vopiscus, Aurelian, 26, 28.) So Jornandes (11) also speaks of Cæsar: "Pene omnem mundum suæ ditionis subegit, omniaque regna perdomuit, adeo ut extra nostrum orbem in Oceani sinu repositas insulas occuparet." So elsewhere (5) he opposes "Britannia" to "noster orbis." We find the same way of speaking in Greek authors also. Josephus (Bell. Jud. ii. 16, 4) makes Agrippa, when enlarging on

the Roman power, say, *σκέψασθε δὲ καὶ τὸ Βρεττανῶν τεῖχος, οἱ τοῖς Ἱεροσολύμων τείχεσι πεποιθότες· καὶ γὰρ ἐκείνους περιβεβλημένους ὠκεανὸν καὶ τῆς καθ' ἡμᾶς οἰκουμένης οὐκ ἐλάσσονα νῆσον οἰκοῦντας, πλεύσαντες ἐδουλώσαντο Ῥωμαῖοι.* So Plutarch, Cæsar, 23, *προήγαγεν ἔξω τῆς οἰκουμένης τὴν Ῥωμαίων ἡγεμονίαν.* Diôn, on the other hand (lxii. 4), puts language of the same kind into the mouth of Boadicea: *τοιγαροῦν νῆσον τηλικαύτην, μᾶλλον δ' ἤπειρον τρόπον τινὰ περίῤῥυτον, νεμόμενοι, καὶ ἰδίαν οἰκουμένην ἔχοντες, καὶ τοσοῦτον ὑπὸ τοῦ ὠκεανοῦ ἀφ' ἁπάντων τῶν ἄλλων ἀνθρώπων ἀφωρισμένοι, ὥστε καὶ γῆν ἄλλην καὶ οὐρανὸν ἄλλον οἰκεῖν πεπιστεῦσθαι.* So, at a later time, we find Orderic (723 c.) saying that the preaching of the Crusade "Angliam quoque, aliasque maritimas insulas nequivit latere, licet undisoni maris abyssus illas removeat ab orbe." (The monk of St. Evroul, born in Shropshire, and who afterwards visited Crowland, is perhaps describing his own feelings in his several voyages over the abyss.) And, as the Archbishop of Canterbury is several times called "alterius orbis papa" or "apostolicus," so, in a passage of Eadmer (Hist. Nov. l. ii. p. 422, Migne) the conviction of William Rufus that the Bishop of Rome had no jurisdiction in his realm of England takes this form, "Nec enim putabat *apostolicum* orbis posse in regno suo esse cujuslibet juris, nisi permissus a se." Britain was out of the world, and the "Pope of the world" had therefore nothing to say to it.

All this is much more than rhetoric; it is more even than national or territorial feeling. Our insular position has been one of the greatest facts of our history; it has caused a distinction between us islanders and our neighbours on the Continent which is independent of all distinctions of race, language, or religion, and which is often found at cross purposes with all of them. We feel at once that there are some points, great and small, in which we stand by ourselves in opposition to continentals, simply as continentals. This is a fact which should carefully be borne in mind, because some points of difference between ourselves and our kinsfolk on the mainland, which are really owing simply to our geographical isolation, have been set down as proofs of imaginary Roman or British influences in England.

(20) Page 48.—See Norman Conquest, i. 279.

(21) Page 48.—On this head see note B in the Appendix to the first volume of the Norman Conquest. The particular titles which the English Kings took, in order to set forth their independence of the continental Empire, were doubtless borrowed from that Empire. But the general conception of Britain as a separate Empire was the natural result of its geographical position.

(22) Page 49.—It will be remembered that the great moment of triumph in the life of Charles the Great was when the Ambassadors of the Eastern Emperor Michael addressed him according to the full Imperial style (Eginhard, Annals, 812): "Aquisgrani, ubi ad Imperatorem venerunt . . . . . . more suo, id est Græca lingua, laudes ei dixerunt, *Imperatorem* eum et *Basileum* appellantes." Charles was strong and Michael was weak. Three generations later, when the tables were rather turned between Basil the Macedonian and Lewis the Second who reigned in Italy only, the Imperial titles became the subject of a long dispute. The controversy is given at length in the Chronicle of Salerno (Pertz, iii. 521). Basil is offended because Lewis

had called himself "Imperator Augustus" in a letter. The Carolingian Emperor, in his answer, goes to the root of the matter. His salutation runs: "Lodoguicus, divina ordinante providentia, Imperator Augustus Romanorum, dilectissimo spiritualique patri nostro Basilio, gloriosissimo et piissimo æque Imperatori Novæ Romæ." He says that it does not matter what either of them is called, but rather what either of them is. Still, as his brother Basil has raised the question about the title of Emperor ("quia de imperatorio nomine multa nobis scripsisti"), he argues the point at length. The Byzantine position is "neminem appellandum *Basilea* nisi eum quem in urbe Constantinopoli Imperii tenere gubernacula contigisset." The Western Emperor answers that a study of Greek books will show him that all manner of Kings, good and bad, from Melchizedek to the Kings of the Goths and Vandals, all bore the title of *Basileus.* He objects to be called merely *Rix*—a form which throws some light on the difference of sound which must already have arisen between the Latin *Rex* and the Greek ῥήξ—and then argues the point minutely:

"Postremo scito, quia qui *Riga* quemquam appellat, quid dicat nec ipse novit. Siquidem etiam si linguis omnibus more apostolorum, immo angelorum, loquaris, cujus linguæ sit *Rix*, vel cui dignitati sonus ille barbarus congruit quod *Rix* dicitur, interpretari non poteris, nihil enim est hoc, nisi forte ad idioma propriæ linguæ tractum, *Riga* regem significare monstraveris. Quod si ita est, quia non jam barbarum sed Latinum est, oportet ut, quum ad manus vestras pervenerit, in linguam vestram fideli translatione vertatur. Quod si factum fuerit, quid aliud nisi hoc nomine βασυλευς interpretabitur? Quod non solum Veteris sed et Novi Testamenti omnes interpretes attestantur. Unde si in alienis personis hoc detestaris vocabulum, stude et omnibus tam Latinis libris quam Græcis sive *Rigis* sive βασυλευς nomen eradere, nam nihil *Rex* in lingua Latina resonat, quam quod Græca dicitur βασυλευς." [The spelling of βασυλευς with an υ is another illustration of Greek pronunciation. In modern Greek the two sounds are the same.]

I need hardly say that the same controversy went on in one form or another for several ages. Thus John Kinnamos (lib. iv. pp. 247, 248, A.D. 1652) calls Frederick Barbarossa only ῥήξ 'Αλαμανῶν, but speaks of him as wishing to be thought Emperor (τοῦ 'Ρωμαίων αὐτοκράτορος προσαρμόσειν αὐτῷ τὸ ἀξίωμα οἰηθεὶς . . . . τῇ αὐτοκράτορος πάλαι ἐποφθαλμίζων ἀρχῇ). He goes on to tell us that none but the Emperor had any right to appoint the Pope (οὐδενὶ γὰρ ἄλλῳ, ὅτι μὴ βασιλεῖ 'Ρωμαίων, ἀρχιέρεα περιβεβλῆσθαι τῇ 'Ρώμῃ ἐφεῖται); but that, through the contempt into which the Empire had fallen (ἐξ ὅτου ὀλιγωρία τῶν ἐν Βυζαντίῳ βασιλέων τὸ τοιοῦτον ἀπεσβήκε ἔθος), this was now the case no longer. One of the oddest forms of the dispute is when the Council of Basel in 1437 addresses the Emperor John Palaiologos as "Imperator Romæorum" (Letters of Thomas Beckington, ii. 19, et al.). I conceive that this use of the Greek form was to avoid calling him "Imperator Rom*an*orum;" somewhat in the same way as I have known strict Anglican theologians who would not have called the ecclesiastical Establishment of Scotland a *Church*, according to the Saxon pronunciation, but who had no scruple against calling it by the Anglian or Danish form *Kirk*. In an earlier letter in the same series (i. 285) Richard the Second addresses Manuel Palaiologos as "Imperator Constantinopolitanus."

(23) Page 49.—Besides the important part which the Servians and Bulgarians—for the Bulgarians may be practically

reckoned as a Slavonic people—played in the affairs of the Eastern Empire, the modern history of Russia is very like its history in the ninth and tenth centuries acted over again. Then, as in later times, Russian fleets covered the Euxine and threatened Constantinople. A variety of causes, crowned by the Mogul invasion in the thirteenth century, broke up the Russian power and directed its chief energies elsewhere. The wars of the Russians with their Tartar enemies, and their final recovery of the Euxine coast, form the exact parallel to the advance of the Christians in Spain and the recovery of Granada. And besides Russia, we must remember the great European position held by Poland under the House of Jagellon in the fifteenth and sixteenth centuries.

(24) Page 51.—All these stories are familiar from the legendary history of Rome in the first book of Livy and elsewhere. It is hard to say how far they are strictly native Italian legends, how far they were devised after the Romans had become familiar with Greek literature. The story which makes Numa a pupil of Pythagoras is of course only an unlucky guess, the chronological absurdity of which is exposed by Livy himself.

(25) Page 51.—Tacitus, Germania, 3: "Fuisse apud eos et Herculem memorant, primumque omnium virorum fortium ituri in prœlia canunt . . . . Ceterum Ulyssem quidam opinantur, longo illo et fabuloso errore in hunc Oceanum delatum, adisse Germaniæ terras, Asciburgiumque, quod in ripa Rheni situm hodieque incolitur, ab illo constitutum nominatumque. Aram quinetiam Ulyssi consecratam, adjecto Laertæ patris nomine, eodem loco olim repertam, monumentaque et tumulos quosdam, Græcis litteris inscriptos, in confinio Germaniæ Rhætiæque adhuc exstare;

quæ neque confirmare argumentis, neque refellere in animo est: ex ingenio suo quisque demat, vel addat fidem."

(26) Page 53.—I have here tried to bring together a few of the most obvious words which all, or many, of the Aryan languages have in common. On *timber* and *ear* see Müller, Oxford Essays, 1856, 25–27. The former word, in the form *timbrian*, is the word commonly used in Old-English for building, whatever be the material used. So Cnut "ferde to Assandune and let *timbrian* ðar an mynster of stane and lime;" and so Eadward "getimbrode" the West Minster itself. (From the etymological connexion of this word with *timber* some people have oddly argued that all buildings built in England up to sunset on St. Calixtus' Day, 1066, must have been made of wood.) *Tame, hound, deer*, the two latter of which are words which have come down from a wider to a more special meaning, are good examples of common Aryan words. The *bull*—I was thinking of him in his noblest office, as furnishing the standard and the war-horn of Uri —does not appear by that name in Greek or Latin, but I believe that he is to be found in the primitive speech of Lithuania. One may doubt too whether the name of the *lion* is to be looked on as wholly borrowed from the South; the beast himself is certainly a genuine European animal, whose "retreat" has been traced out by a happy union of historical and physical evidence in the hands of Mr. Dawkins.

(27) Page 53.—With the words of Herodotus (ix. 62) before us—λήματι μέν νυν καὶ ῥώμῃ οὐκ ἕσσονες ἦσαν οἱ Πέρσαι—followed up by the marked way in which he presently speaks of the native Persians as the only trustworthy part of the barbarian host, we may be tempted

to infer that, as between Aryan and Aryan, the struggle between Greek and Persian was not so unequal, and that the armies of the Great King were rather weakened than strengthened by the mixed multitude which cumbered the action of the real men of Iran. By the time of Alexander, as Mr. Grote truly says, the Persian infantry seem to have lost their old personal prowess, but the cavalry still meet the mounted Companions of Alexander on equal terms. The regenerate Persians of the Sassanid period—all the stronger because their dominion was so much smaller, and therefore more strictly national, than that of the Achaimenids—were, as I need not stop to show, the one foe that met Rome on really equal terms.

(28) Page 53.—The death of the sun is an obvious form of the "daily tragedy" of his course. The home of the sun in the West comes out in the well-known verses of Stesichoros (see Mure, iii. 251);

> 'Αέλιος δ' 'Υπεριονίδας δέπας ἐςκατέβαινε
> χρύσεον, ὄφρα δ' ὠκεανοῖο περάσας,
> ἀφίκοιθ' ἱερᾶς ποτὶ βένθεα νυκτὸς ἐρεμνᾶς·
> ποτὶ ματέρα κουῤιδίαν τ' ἄλοχον
> παῖδάς τε φίλους.

(29) Page 54.—Setting aside the relations of language, and looking only to the political and geographical state of Europe, the position of the Aryan Celts and that of the non-Aryan Iberians is almost exactly the same. Each forms the main element in one of the great nations of Europe; France is essentially Celtic; Spain is essentially Iberian. But the Celtic and Iberian essence is in both cases covered over by a varnish which is mainly Roman but partly Teutonic. The true Celt, unmixed and unaltered, keeping his own language and

his unbroken national being, is to be found only in certain corners of Gaul and Britain, just as the Iberian, unromanized and unteutonized, is found only in certain corners of Gaul and Spain. The case of the Fins is somewhat different. One independent European nation, that of the Hungarians, is of Finnish descent, while the other Fins linger only in corners, like the unmixed Celts and Iberians. But the Hungarians are not, like the Romanized Celts and Iberians of France and Spain, a nation which came into Europe in the course of præ-historic migrations, and which has exchanged its language for that of conquerors of historic times. They are a race of non-Aryan conquerors, who have made their way into Europe at a comparatively late time, and who still keep their non-Aryan language.

(30) Page 54.—On the upper course of the Rhine we find the Swiss Cantons and their allies, and specially the Rætian Confederacy of the Three Leagues, now forming part of the greater confederation as the Canton of Graubünden. At the other end of the stream we find the Confederation of the Seven United Provinces, now turned into the Kingdom of the Netherlands. Each confederation alike was a mere offshoot from the Empire and the Kingdom of Germany, which circumstances enabled to win and keep a fuller degree of independence than the other members of the Empire. The two were formally recognized as independent of the Empire at the same time, namely by the Peace of Westphalia. And, placed thus at the two ends of the Empire, the two confederations represent severally the two great branches of the Teutonic race, High and Low. The point to be remembered is that neither Switzerland nor Holland was a separate state from the beginning. But there is this difference between them: the United Provinces became inde-

pendent of the Empire by virtue of the great and independent position which had been won by their sovereigns the Dukes of Burgundy; it is therefore less unnatural that their republican constitution has changed back again into a monarchy. But the independence of the Old League of High Germany arose through the casting off of all immediate princely rule, and the owning of no King but Cæsar till the time came when Cæsar himself could be cast off also. Thus the republican freedom of the cities and lands (*Städte und Länder*) on the borders of Germany, Italy, and Burgundy has lived on, under various forms, to our own day.

(31) Page 56.—I have quoted the passage from Prokopios which records this early English—most likely Kentish—embassy to Constantinople at vol. i. p. 30 of the Norman Conquest.

(32) Page 56.—The position and extent of the Empire under Justinian and his immediate successors is one of those points which cannot be too often insisted on. People have their heads so full of the vulgar confused notions about "Greeks of the Lower Empire" that they find it hard to understand the fact that in the sixth century the Roman Emperor—Imperator Cæsar Flavius Justinianus Augustus—though he held his court in the New Rome and not in the Old, ruled in fact as well as in name over the whole Mediterranean coast of Europe, Asia, and Africa, saving some parts of Gaul and Spain. Gades, Carthage, and Antioch again obeyed a single master. It was a great lack in the old edition of Spruner's *Hand-Atlas* that there was no general map of the Empire at this time. This defect is fully made up in the new edition which is now publishing.

(33) Page 57.—Of Aëtius, him to whom the groans of the Britons were sent, Jornandes (34) gives this account:—"Aetius ergo patricius tunc præerat militibus, fortissimorum Mœsiorum stirpe progenitus, in Dorostina civitate, a patre Gaudentio, labores bellicos tolerans, Reipublicæ Romanæ singulariter natus, qui superbiam Suevorum Francorumque barbariem immensis cædibus servire Romano Imperio coegisset." Prokopios himself also (Bell. Vand. i. 3) gives us his panegyric, along with the contemporary Bonifacius:

*Στρατηγὼ δύο Ῥωμαῖοι ἤστην, Ἀέτιός τε καὶ Βονιφάτιος, καρτερώ τε ἐς τὰ μάλιστα καὶ πολλῶν πολέμων ἐμπείρω τῶν γε κατ' ἐκεῖνον τὸν χρόνον οὐδενὸς ἧσσον. τούτω τὼ ἄνδρε διαφόρω μὲν τὰ πολιτικὰ ἐγενέσθην, ἐς τοσοῦτον δὲ μεγαλοψυχίας τε καὶ τῆς ἄλλης ἀρετῆς ἡκέτην ὥστε, εἴ τις αὐτοῖν ἑκάτερον ἄνδρα Ῥωμαίων ὕστατον εἴποι, οὐκ ἂν ἁμάρτοι· οὕτω τὴν Ῥωμαίων ἀρετὴν ξύμπασαν ἐς τούτω τὼ ἄνδρε ἀποκεκρίσθαι τετύχηκε.*

We are apt to look upon the West-Gothic kingdom as something specially Spanish. But, till the conquest of Aquitaine by Chlodwig, it was at least as much Gaulish as Spanish. The Gothic capital was the Gaulish Tolosa; and there were more truly "no Pyrenees" then than at any time before or since.

(34) Page 57.—Jornandes, 36. "A parte vero Romanorum tanta patricii Aetii providentia fuit, cui tunc innitebatur respublica Hesperiæ plagæ, ut undique bellatoribus congregatis adversus ferocem et infinitam multitudinem non impar occurreret. His enim adfuere auxiliares Franci, Sarmatæ, Armoritiani, Litiani, Burgundiones, Saxones, Riparioli, Ibriones, quondam milites Romani, tunc vero jam in numero auxiliariorum exquisiti, aliæque nonnullæ Celticæ vel Germanicæ nationes."

There is something very strange in the appearance of the Sarmatians; but it is not for me to dispute the assertion of the historian that they were there, especially as it is convenient for my argument that they should have been there.

The grievous thing is that in this great struggle between Aryan and Turanian men, there were Aryans, Teutons, Goths, on the Turanian side.

(35) Page 57.—On Alaric's march to Athens, see Zôsimos, v. 6.

(36) Page 59.—On the influence of Massalia on the neighbouring Gauls, see Strabo, iv. 1. His words are very strong:—*ὥςθ' ἡ πόλις μικρῷ μὲν πρότερον τοῖς βαρβάροις ἀνεῖτο παιδευτήριον, καὶ φιλέλληνας κατεσκεύασε τοὺς Γαλάτας, ὥςτε καὶ τὰ συμβόλαια Ἑλληνιστὶ γράφειν· εὖ δὲ τῷ παρόντι καὶ τοὺς γνωριμωτάτους Ῥωμαίων πέπεικεν, ἀντὶ τῆς εἰς Ἀθήνας ἀποδημίας ἐκεῖσε φοιτᾶν φιλομαθεῖς ὄντας.* He speaks no less strongly of the Roman influence on the Gaulish tribes in that neighbourhood:—*Ἐπικρατεῖ δὲ τὸ τῶν Καουάρων ὄνομα, καὶ πάντας οὕτως ἤδη προςαγορεύουσι τοὺς ταύτῃ βαρβάρους, οὐδὲ βαρβάρους ἔτι ὄντας, ἀλλὰ μετακειμένους τὸ πλέον εἰς τὸν τῶν Ῥωμαίων τύπον, καὶ τῇ γλώττῃ καὶ τοῖς βίοις, τινὰς δὲ καὶ τῇ πολιτείᾳ.*

Elsewhere (iii. 2), he sets forth the progress of Roman influences among the tribes of southern Spain:—*οἱ μέν τοι Τουρδιτανοὶ, καὶ μάλιστα οἱ περὶ τὸν Βαῖτιν, τελέως εἰς τὸν Ῥωμαίων μεταβέβληνται τρόπον, οὐδὲ τῆς διαλέκτου τῆς σφετέρας ἔτι μεμνημένοι. Λατῖνοί τε οἱ πλεῖστοι γεγόνασι, καὶ ἐποίκους εἰλήφασι Ῥωμαίους· ὥςτε μικρὸν ἀπέχουσι τοῦ πάντες εἶναι Ῥωμαῖοι.*

(37) Page 60.—Any questions of this kind I should wish

to leave open till philologers have determined the exact degree of affinity, if there be any, between the two great groups of inflexional languages, the Aryan and Semitic. Till then we shall do wisely to collect and classify facts, but to abstain from theories, and, above all things, we must take care not to be led away by particular likenesses here and there, which may turn out to be accidental. The only scientific process is to find out what is the common possession of the Aryan nations, what is the common possession of the Semitic nations. When we have done this, we shall be able to see what the two great families have in common, but not before.

(38) Page 65.—Annals, iv. 33. "Nam cunctas nationes et urbes populus, aut primores, aut singuli regunt: delecta ex his et consociata Reipublicæ forma laudari facilius quam evenire, vel, si evenit, haud diuturna esse potest." Yet a large part of the argument of Aristotle, in the fourth book of the Politics, goes on the assumption that the best form of government will be something of a mixed kind. The ideal *πολιτεία* described in his ninth chapter is a mixture of aristocracy and democracy, and he lays down (iv. 12. 6) the exactly opposite doctrine to that of Tacitus,—*ὅσῳ ἂν ἄμεινον ἡ πολιτεία μιχθῇ τοσούτῳ μονιμωτέρα.* So, at an earlier stage of his argument (ii. 6), he says, *ἔνιοι μὲν οὖν λέγουσιν ὡς δεῖ τὴν ἀρίστην πολιτείαν ἐξ ἁπασῶν εἶναι τῶν πολιτειῶν μεμιγμένην, διὸ καὶ τὴν τῶν Λακεδαιμονίων ἐπαινοῦσιν·* and he goes on to describe the way in which the three forms of government were held to be united in the constitution of Sparta. Isokratês too, throughout the Areiopagitic and Panathenaic discourses, where the object is to contrast what he looks on as the corrupt democracy of his own time with the truer democracy of a past time

(*ἐκείνην τὴν δημοκρατίαν, ἣν Σόλων μὲν ὁ δημοτικώτατος γενόμενος ἐνομοθέτησεν*, A. 17; *ἡ βεβαιωτέρα καὶ δικαιοτέρα δημοκρατία*, A. 30, &c. &c.), which he conceives (Π. 159) to have lasted for a thousand years, once or twice uses the same kind of formula more than once. Thus in Π. 139, *κατεστήσαντο γὰρ δημοκρατίαν οὐ τὴν εἰκῇ πολιτευομένην . . . . ἀλλὰ τὴν τοιούτοις μὲν ἐπιτιμῶσαν, ἀριστοκρατίᾳ δὲ χρωμένην*, and again Π. 165, he speaks of Lykourgos, &c., *τήν τε δημοκρατίαν καταστήσαντος παρ' αὐτοῖς τὴν ἀριστοκρατίᾳ μεμιγμένην, ἥπερ ἦν παρ' ἡμῖν, καὶ τὰς ἀρχας οὐ κληρωτὰς ἀλλ' αἱρετὰς ποιήσαντα.* This last seems to be Isokratês' great distinction between a good democracy and a bad one. Yet at Athens all the really important offices were filled by election.

On the other hand it is possible, as in the old Polish constitution, to make a mixed government which shall combine the bad points, without the good, of all the three forms by themselves—a King without real power, but with large means of irregular influence; a people brought down to serfdom; a nobility forming a narrow oligarchy as regards the rest of the nation and a frantic mob among themselves.

(36) Page 66.—It is now hardly needful to prove that the *Germania* of Tacitus, though it doubtless contains sarcastic touches here and there, is no mere dream of a Roman dissatisfied with the state of things at Rome, but an essentially faithful description of the Teutonic race when it first made its appearance in history. The deeper we search into Teutonic antiquities, whether on our own island or on the mainland, the more fully do we find the statements of the Roman historian borne out. The best commentary on the *Germania* is the first volume of Waitz's *Deutsche Verfassungsgeschichte.*

(40) Page 68.—I do not remember finding the word *ἄναξ* anywhere in Greek prose, except in the Evagoras of Isokratês, 88, where he uses *ἄναξ* and *ἄνασσα* almost like the vulgar use of the words prince and princess. *τῶν ἐξ αὐτοῦ γεγονότων οὐδένα μετέλιπεν ἰδιωτικοῖς ὀνόμασι προςαγορευόμενον, ἀλλὰ τὸν μὲν βασιλέα καλούμενον, τοὺς δὲ ἄνακτας, τὰς δὲ ἀνάσσας.*

(41) Page 69.—See Growth of the English Constitution, 32, 171, and below.

(42) Page 69.—The Old-English *rice*, the same as the High-Dutch *reich*, seems now to survive only in the ending of the word *bishopric;* but in Northern English *cynerice*, in various spellings, went on till a very late time. *Ricsian*, *rixian*, is the Old-English verb = *regere*.

(43) Page 70.—See Max Müller, Oxford Essays, p. 24, and see below, note 64 on Lecture IV.

(44) Page 70.—Massmann (Ulfilas, 728) explains the Gothic *reiks* by "ein Mächtiger, Oberster, Herrscher; vornehm, angesehen, mächtig."

(45) Page 71.—The Athenian *ἡλιαία*, which Greek etymologists (see Suidas in *ἡλιαστής*) were tempted to connect with *ἥλιος*, is of course the same word as *ἁλία*, connected with *ἁλής* and other kindred words.

(46) Page 72.—On the various names, *ἀγορά* for one of them, by which the Achaian Federal Assembly is called by Polybios, see History of Federal Government, i. 263.

(47) Page 72.—The Latin *frater* and English *brother*

seem at first sight to have no Greek cognate, as its place in the literal sense has been usurped by ἀδελφός. But the word appears, in the form of *φράτηρ* or *φράτωρ*, to express a member of one of the union of *gentes* known as *φράτραι* or *φρατρίαι*, of which I have said more at p. 103. It might almost be in either sense that Nestôr (Iliad, ix. 63) uses the negative word;

> *ἀφρήτωρ, ἀθέμιστος, ἀνέστιός ἐστιν ἐκεῖνος,*
> *ὃς πολέμου ἔραται ἐπιδημίου ὀκρυόεντος.*

But when in ii. 362 he bids Agamemnôn—

> *κρῖν' ἄνδρας κατὰ φῦλα, κατὰ φρήτρας, Ἀγάμεμνον,*
> *ὡς φρήτρη φρήτρηφιν ἀρήγῃ, φῦλα δὲ φύλοις·*

we could not better express *κατὰ φῦλα, κατὰ φρήτρας*, than by saying "according to shires and hundreds."

(48) Page 72.—Besides ἵππος and *equus*, there once was a Teutonic cognate in the Old-English *eoh*, Old-High-Dutch *ehu*, of which the former form is found in the song of Maldon; but I am not aware that any words answering to *eques* or *chevalier* were formed from it.

(49) Page 73.—On this class of words see Norman Conquest, vol. i. pp. 74, 172, 582. To those there collected I may add the feminine "seniorissa" from a document quoted by Waitz, *Deutsche Verfassungsgeschichte*, iv. 207. See also Thirlwall, History of Greece, i. 134. A most curious case of the way in which words of this sort have become mere survivals is shown in the poem in the English Chronicles which I have quoted at i. 625 of the History of the Norman Conquest. There Eadward the Martyr is spoken of in the same breath as "cild únweaxan," and as "eorla ealdor."

(50) Page 73.—The chief of the Assassins, "rex Accinorum, id est de Assasis" (Roger of Howden, iii. 181; "Assisini Saraceni," Roger of Wendover, iii. 46), appears in Brompton (1268), as "Senex de monte, non pro ætate sic dictus sed pro sapientia et gravitate, Princeps gentis orientalis quam *Hassisinos* vocant;" and he is made (see also Rymer, i. 62) to write a letter beginning "Vetus de monte Principibus Europæ et omni populo Christiano salutem."

(51) Page 73.—Of these two forms the earlier expresses the sentiment, the later the mere fact. We might compare the difference between *chieftain* and *captain.*

(52) Page 74.—See Norman Conquest, iv. 694.

(53) Page 74.—See Norman Conquest, i. 269, ii. 388, iii. 472.

# LECTURE III.

(1) Page 77.—The definition of aristocracy given by Aristotle (Pol. iv. 7. 2–5)—*τὴν γὰρ ἐκ τῶν ἀρίστων ἁπλῶς κατ' ἀρετὴν πολιτείαν, καὶ μὴ πρὸς ὑπόθεσίν τινα ἀγαθῶν ἀνδρῶν, μόνην δίκαιον προσαγορεύειν ἀριστοκρατίαν,*—distinctly shuts out any such *ὑποθέσεις ἀγαθῶν ἀνδρῶν* as age, wealth, or birth. But he clearly feels that such a government of the actually best is something merely ideal; and he seems to hold the best form of government to be that form of *πολιτεία*—his *πολιτεία* being the same as the *δημοκρατία* of Polybios and others (see Growth of the English Constitution, p. 166)—which leans towards aristocracy. In this offices are filled by election and not by lot, and they are filled with regard not to riches only but to merit: *ὅπου γε μὴ μόνον πλουτίνδην ἀλλὰ καὶ ἀριστίνδην αἱροῦνται τὰς ἀρχάς.* Aristocracy, in Aristotle's idea, was something wholly distinct from oligarchy, the government of the few, the government of mere wealth or birth, without regard to merit. Still the tendency of even the ideal aristocracy would unavoidably be to give predominance to birth and wealth; for, without ruling whether there is or is not such a thing as strictly hereditary capacity, it is certain that some kinds of capacity, especially political capacity, are not only likely to be more easily recognized, but are likely really to be thicker on the ground

where birth and wealth afford special opportunities for their culture. Aristotle's definition of εὐγένεια is ἀρχαῖος πλοῦτος καὶ ἀρετή (iv. 8, 9), and again (iii. 13, 3), εὐγένειά ἐστιν ἀρετὴ γένους: oligarchy, the corruption of aristocracy, looks only to birth or wealth without regard to merit. So, to turn to a writer of a time when all questions about aristocracy and democracy had become mere speculative talk, Diôn Chrysostom, in his discourses addressed to Trajan, has his definition of aristocracy and of oligarchy. He follows Aristotle in the doctrine of the three forms of government, each of which has its corruption, and he thus defines aristocracy (i. 47): δευτέρα δε ἀριστοκρατία καλουμένη οὔτε ἑνὸς οὔτε πολλῶν τινων, ἀλλὰ ὀλίγων τῶν ἀρίστων ἡγουμένων, πλεῖον ἀπέχουσα ἤδη τοῦ δυνατοῦ καὶ τοῦ συμφέροντος. He then defines oligarchy as ὀλιγαρχία, σκληρὰ καὶ ἄδικος πλεονεξία, πλουσίων τινῶν καὶ πονηρῶν ὀλίγων ἐπὶ τοὺς πολλοὺς καὶ ἀπόρους σύστασις. Plutarch (περὶ Μον. κ.τ.λ. 3) makes the threefold division μοναρχία, ὀλιγαρχία, δημοκρατία, of which the corruptions are τυραννὶς, δυναστεία, ὀχλοκρατία.

I need hardly say that the vulgar use of the word "aristocracy," to mean, not a form of government but a class of society, has no countenance from Aristotle or from any other writer who attends to the meaning of the words which he uses. A kindred vulgarism has lately crept in, with still less excuse, by which the word "democracy" also is used to express, not a form of government but a class of society.

(2) Page 77.—Livy, ii. 1. "Libertatis originem inde magis, quia annuum imperium consulare factum est, quam quod deminutum quidquam sit ex regia potestate, numeres. Omnia jura, omnia insignia, primi consules tenuere; id modo cautum est ne, si ambo fasces haberent, duplicatus terror videretur." Dionysios (iv. 73) very clearly brings out

the nature of the consulship as a continuation of kingship. He makes Brutus counsel the Romans *μεταθέσθαι τοὔνομα τῆς πολιτείας . . . . καὶ τοὺς μέλλοντας ἕξειν τὴν ἁπάντων ἐξουσίαν, μήτε βασιλεῖς ἔτι μήτε μονάρχους καλεῖν, ἀλλὰ μετριωτέραν τινὰ καὶ φιλανθρωποτέραν αὐτοῖς θέσθαι προσηγορίαν· ἔπειτα μὴ ποιεῖν γνώμην μίαν ἁπάντων κυρίαν, ἀλλὰ δυσὶν ἐπιτρέπειν ἀνδράσι τὴν βασιλικὴν ἀρχήν.* In c. 75 (cf. below, note 30 on Lecture IV.) he distinctly calls the consular power *βασιλεία.* I see that the phrase of putting the kingly power in commission has occurred also to Sir Henry Maine.

(3) Page 78.—Something of this divided kingship belonged to all the curule magistrates, all of whom shared in some degree in the outward insignia of the kingly office. These are discussed at length by Dionysios, iv. 74. The doctrine of the *Imperium* and the *Lex regia*, handed on from the days of the Kings through the whole time of the Commonwealth, undoubtedly made the transition to the Empire more easy.

(4) Page 78.—Tacitus, Annals, i. 2. "Posito Triumviri nomine, consulem se ferens, et ad tuendam plebem tribunicio jure contentum; ubi militem donis, populum annona, cunctos dulcedine otii pellexit, insurgere paullatim, munia Senatûs, magistratuum, legum, in se trahere, nullo adversante."

(5) Page 78.—No doubt there were cases in which the powers of the Senate were purposely lessened in particular points; as, for instance, by the *Lex Hortensia* of B.C. 268 ("Lex Hortensia lata est, qua cautum est, ut plebiscita universum populum tenerent, itaque eo modo legibus exæquata sunt," Gaius, i. 2). But there was no tendency at

Rome seriously to interfere with the position of the Senate as the *government* of the Commonwealth, as distinguished from its legislature. This is a marked point of difference between Rome and Athens, and one of which I have said something in a later lecture. See p. 228.

(6) Page 79.—Arnold's Rome, ii. 388. "And thus the event seems to have given the highest sanction to the wisdom of the Hortensian laws: nor can we regard them as mischievous or revolutionary, when we find that from the time of their enactment the internal dissensions of the Romans were at an end for a hundred and fifty years, and that during this period the several parts of the constitution were all active; it was a calm not produced by the extinction of either of the contending forces, but by their perfect union."

(7) Page 79.—Arnold's Rome, iii. 63. "Twice in history has there been witnessed the struggle of the highest individual genius against the resources and institutions of a great nation, and in both cases the nation has been victorious. For seventeen years Hannibal strove against Rome; for sixteen years Napoleon Buonaparte strove against England. The efforts of the first ended in Zama, those of the second in Waterloo."

This is the opening of the noblest historical narrative in our language, Arnold's narrative of the Hannibalian War. I may perhaps be doing a good service by reminding the present generation that such a narrative exists. Of course the comparison between Hannibal and Buonaparte applies solely to the genius of the two men, not at all to their objects: Hannibal fought for Carthage, Buonaparte fought for himself.

(8) Page 80.—No Roman, no Latin—that is, no full citizen and no one who had a reasonable hope of citizenship—turned against Rome, though more than once both Romans and Latins, individual citizens and individual colonies, seemed inclined to shrink from the struggle. This is a marked contrast to the state of things in the Greek cities, where a party is so constantly found in league with the enemy. It is of course not fair to compare the warfare between one Greek city and another with the struggle of Rome against the wholly alien power of Carthage. But even in the Persian war there was in most Greek cities either a medizing party or, at all events, a Hippias or a Dêmaratos ready to seek his own restoration by the help of the Barbarian. The weakness of Rome lay in that she was, in the words of Tiberius in Tacitus (Annals, iii. 6), an "imperator populus." The subject states of Italy, to say nothing of the Gauls, were naturally ready to join Hannibal.

(9) Page 82.—See Norman Conquest, i. 128.

(10) Page 83.—To seek for barbarian aid against fellow Greeks was a thing which was often done, but it was a thing which might always be turned to the discredit of those who did it. It was like Francis the First and Lewis the Fourteenth joining with the Turks against the Empire. And the real feeling of common Greek brotherhood which underlay all occasional dealings of this kind comes out very strongly on occasion. We see it through the whole history of the Retreat of the Ten Thousand, both in the tie which kept the army together and in the fellow-feeling shown between them and the various Greek cities to which they come on their march. We see it again in the Athenian decree against Arthmios of Zêleia; while it is the pervading spirit

of all the discourses of Isokratês. Take, for instance, his oration, or rather letter, to Philip, the whole tone of which assumes the Greeks as forming one whole, and the Barbarians as another, while the Macedonians, under their Greek King, are rightly enough looked on as something between the two. One passage (150) is very strong. Philip is called on to look on all Greece as his country, and to risk everything on its behalf—*ἅπασαν τὴν Ἑλλάδα πατρίδα νομίζειν, ὥσπερ ὁ γεννήσας* [Hêraklês] *ὑμᾶς, καὶ κινδυνεύειν ὑπὲρ αὐτῆς ὁμοίως ὥς περ ὑπὲρ ὧν μάλιστα σπουδάζεις.* Isokratês indeed was little more than a dreamer; still he is a good witness when it is a sentiment of which we are speaking. But the sentiment comes out in a much more practical shape in the two noble declarations of Kallikratidas, that no Greek should be enslaved by his means, and that he would do his best to reconcile the contending Greek powers, that they might no longer cringe to the barbarian. Xen. Hell. i. 6, 7. *Καλλικρατίδας ἀχθεσθεὶς τῇ ἀναβολῇ καὶ ταῖς ἐπὶ τὰς θύρας φοιτήσεσιν, ὀργισθεὶς καὶ εἰπὼν ἀθλιωτάτους εἶναι τοὺς Ἕλληνας, ὅτι βαρβάρους κολακεύουσιν ἕνεκα ἀργυρίου, φάσκων τε, ἢν σωθῇ οἴκαδε, κατά γε τὸ αὐτῷ δυνατὸν διαλλάξειν Ἀθηναίους καὶ Λακεδαιμονίους, ἀπέπλευσεν ἐς Μίλητον.* i. 6. 14.—*Καλλικρατίδας οὐκ ἔφη, ἑαυτοῦ γε ἄρχοντος, οὐδένα Ἑλλήνων ἐς τοὐκείνου δυνατὸν ἀνδραποδισθῆναι.*

(11) Page 84.—The whole argument of Aristotle assumes that the commonwealth will be a city, and neither more nor less—neither a mere village nor yet a nation. The three are contrasted together in several places. Thus we read in the Politics (ii. 2, 3) — *διοίσει δὲ τῷ τοιούτῳ καὶ πόλις ἔθνους, ὅταν μὴ κατὰ κώμας ὦσι κεχωρισμένοι τὸ πλῆθος, ἀλλ' οἷον Ἀρκάδες.* So, again (iii. 3, 5), when he is dis-

cussing the definition of *πόλις*, he says *οὐ γὰρ δὴ τοῖς τείχεσιν· εἴη γὰρ ἂν Πελοποννήσῳ περιβαλεῖν ἓν τεῖχος. τοιαύτη δ' ἴσως ἐστὶ καὶ Βαβυλὼν καὶ πᾶσα ἥτις ἔχει περιγραφὴν μᾶλλον ἔθνους ἢ πόλεως.* And again, when he is discussing the possible size of a commonwealth (vii. 4, 11) *ὁμοίως καὶ πόλις ἡ μὲν ἐξ ὀλίγων λίαν οὐκ αὐτάρκης (ἡ δὲ πόλις αὔταρκες), ἡ δὲ ἐκ πολλῶν ἄγαν ἐν τοῖς μὲν ἀναγκαίοις αὐτάρκης, ὥσπερ ἔθνος, ἀλλ' οὐ πόλις· πολιτείαν γὰρ οὐ ῥᾴδιον ὑπάρχειν· τίς γὰρ στρατηγὸς ἔσται τοῦ λίαν ὑπερβάλλοντος πλήθους, ἢ τίς κῆρυξ μὴ Στεντόρειος;*

The opposite idea to that of Aristotle is found in a glossary of the tenth century in Eckhart (Res Franciæ Orient. ii. 999), where "pagus" is defined to be "provincia absque muro."

(12) Page 84. — There is a certain shade of difference between "oppressed nationalities" and "oppressed nations." A people suffering under an oppressive government of their own race and speech would no doubt be an "oppressed nation," but they would not be what is called an "oppressed nationality." By an "oppressed nationality" I conceive is meant a people who are under a government which not only is oppressive but is oppressive in a particular way. The "oppressed nationality" deems itself wronged, because the government under which it finds itself refuses its claim to count as a nation. In this sense Poland is, and Hungary once was, an "oppressed nationality." But though the home government of Russia or of Austria might be never so bad, no one would speak of Russia or of Austria as an "oppressed nationality." An "oppressed nationality" then is a nation whose oppression takes the particular form of not dealing with it as a nation. The distinction is a real one; but the use of the abstract word "nationality,"

which has quite another meaning, is a very awkward way of expressing what is meant.

(13) Page 85.—This is one of the points in ancient politics which, with our ideas, we find it hardest to understand. In modern times conquest, or submission of any kind, almost always involves more or less of incorporation with the conquering state. The country which is conquered or otherwise annexed may be allowed to retain its laws; in the case of actual conquest it may retain them as a matter of sufferance; in the case of voluntary union, like that of England and Scotland, it may retain them as a matter of treaty; but in either case the difference of law is a mere local difference between two parts of the same state. In modern politics there is hardly such a thing as a state which retains its separate government untouched in all its branches, which is capable of legislating for itself, perhaps even of changing its form of government at pleasure, but which has no will of its own in international concerns, which is bound at the very least to follow the lead of another state in matters of peace and war, perhaps is even bound to contribute men or money at the bidding of the ruling state. But this was the case between Athens and her allies in the fourth century B.C.; it was the relation between Rome and her Italian allies down to the Social War; and the relation between Sparta and her Peloponnesian allies did not widely differ from it, though their position was certainly more favourable. The state still remains a state; it is absolutely untouched in all that forms a separate state; only it is hindered from exercising the ordinary powers of a state in relation to other states. Such a relation need not involve any practical oppression towards any member of the inferior state, though it gives occasional opportunities for

such oppression on the part of officers of the ruling state. A city in this case could of course at any moment act for itself, and refuse to obey the commands of the ruling city, at the risk of being conquered afresh and being brought down to a worse bondage. We better understand the case of more complete subjection, where the subject state is ruled by a harmost, proconsul, satrap, bailiff, or other officer of the ruling state. But, even in this case, the whole machinery of the subject state often went on as something more than a mere municipality; it was still a city which was subject to the ruling city. In modern ideas, the inhabitants of the conquered or annexed country become subjects of the government of the ruling state, fellow-subjects of its older members.

(14) Page 85.—The incidental expressions of Isokratês bring this out strongly. The Greeks of some unknown, and most likely mythical, time were (Paneg. 90) *ἴδια μὲν ἄστη τὰς αὐτῶν πόλεις ἡγούμενοι, κοινὴν δὲ πατρίδα τὴν Ἑλλάδα νομίζοντες εἶναι.* So, in the discourse addressed to Philip (150; see above, note 10), he tells him, *προσήκει τοῖς μὲν ἄλλοις τοῖς ἀφ' Ἡρακλέους πεφυκόσι καὶ τοῖς ἐν πολιτείᾳ καὶ νόμοις ἐνδεδεμένοις ἐκείνην τὴν πόλιν στέργειν ἐν ᾗ τυγχάνουσι κατοικοῦντες, σὲ δ', ὥσπερ ἄφετον γεγενημένον, ἅπασαν τὴν Ἑλλάδα πατρίδα νομίζειν.* *Πατρίς*, in Isokratês' own day, was not the word which was commonly applied to all Hellas, but only to each man's own city. He uses it in that sense in several places in this same discourse (111, 121, and elsewhere); and still more strikingly when, in his discourse to Philip (72), he says that Konôn *τὰ τείχη τὰ τῆς πατρίδος ἀνώρθωσεν.* But there had been, or ought to have been, a time when all Hellas had been the *πατρίς* of every Greek.

(15) Page 85.—Livy (xxxviii. 53), in recording the departure of Scipio to Liternum, only speaks of the "necessitas aut subeundi judicii aut simul cum patria deserendi." But Seneca (Epist. xiii. 1) distinctly uses the word *exile.* "Quidni ego admirer hanc magnitudinem animi, qua in exsilium voluntarium secessit et civitatem exoneravit? Eo perducta res erat, ut aut libertas Scipioni aut Scipio libertati faceret injuriam. Neutrum fas erat: itaque locum dedit legibus, et se Liternum recepit, tam suum exsilium reipublicæ imputaturus quam Hannibalis." So of Tiberius, Tacitus (Ann. iv. 58) says, "neque enim tam incredibilem casum providebant, ut undecim per annos libens patria careret." See Merivale, v. 251.

(16) Page 86.—This is one of the most striking points of difference between France and England, and one of the best signs of the difference between the Frankish conquest of Gaul and the English conquest of Britain. As a rule, the chief towns of France have continued their uninterrupted existence and importance from Roman and Gaulish times. They have not always kept their relative position to one another; still Paris, Lyons, Marseilles, Bourdeaux, Rouen, and a crowd of others, have always kept up their importance as the capitals at least of their surrounding districts. The older city has very seldom been outstripped by a younger rival, in the way in which the local capitals of Yorkshire, Lancashire, Warwickshire, and Staffordshire, have been outstripped among ourselves. The old Celtic post became the Roman city, and the Roman city has lived on uninterruptedly to our own time as the chief place in its own district. And of these cities a large proportion—most of those which do not, like Paris or Châlons, lie in or beside a

river—occupy the high sites where the Gaulish hill-fort was first placed. Such are Bourges, Chartres, above all, Laon. We may say the same of Gaulish cities beyond the limits of the French kingdom, as Geneva, Lausanne, and Sitten. In England the phænomena are quite different. The Roman towns in Britain do not seem to have so universally occupied Celtic sites as they did in Gaul; and it would also seem that the Celt of Britain did not feel that special attachment to high places which was felt by the Celt of Gaul. We have a few cities, like Lincoln and Exeter, in which a lofty site has been successively occupied by Briton, Roman, and Englishman; and among these we may reckon London, where the original city, with the cathedral crowning the hill, is really a nearer approach, though a very feeble one, to Bourges or Chartres, than is at all common in England. And there are many hill sites which the Briton occupied, but which did not grow into Roman cities. In Gaul the great camp of Uleybury might have grown into a city like Laon, and Dorchester might have been built on the top of Sinodun instead of at its foot. But that the tendency to occupy lower sites is not only Roman, but also British, is shown by the sites of at least two of the episcopal churches of Wales. No greater contrast can be thought of to Bourges and Chartres than the sites of Llandaff and Saint David's. Then too, owing to the destroying nature of the English Conquest, the occupation of the English towns has scarcely ever been continuous. Some of the Roman towns, like Wroxeter and Silchester, were destroyed, and their sites were never again occupied. Others, like Bath and Chester, were occupied afresh, after having lain waste for several centuries. In everything the contrast between English and French towns is one of the most striking witnesses to that utter gap between one state of things and another, which was caused in Britain by the character of the English conquest, but which has nothing answering to it in the history of Gaul.

(17) Page 86.—Thucydides, ii. 15, τὸ δὲ πρὸ τούτου ἡ ἀκρόπολις ἡ νῦν οὖσα πόλις ἦν. On the whole subject of the change from the hill-sides to lower positions, see Grote, ii. 144-148. In western Europe there cannot be a better study of the general change than is to be found at Le Mans, where the Gaulish fort, the Roman, and the mediæval city, may all be traced, each being an enlargement of its predecessor, and each coming lower down from the top of the hill.

(18) Page 87.—I have ventured to quote the well-known Homeric contrast between Dardaniê and Ilios, as illustrating the change from Old to New Salisbury. Norman Conquest, i. 318.

(19) Page 87.—Sophoklês, Œd. Col. 694. ἐν τᾷ μεγάλᾳ Δωρίδι νά-Σῳ Πέλοπος.

(20) Page 87.—See Grote, ii. 147. So Maine, Ancient Law, 125. "It may not perhaps be an altogether fanciful idea when I suggest that the Cyclops is Homer's type of an alien and less advanced civilization; for the almost physical loathing which a primitive community feels for men of widely different manners from its own usually expresses itself by describing them as monsters, such as giants, or even (which is almost always the case in Oriental mythology) as demons." Cf. Arist. Pol. i. 2-6. The Kyklôpes of course are an extreme case; and the traditions about them, as about other beings of the same kind, most likely refer, like the

stories of the Trolls of the North, to some memory of the earlier non-Aryan races whom the Hellênes most likely found in the land. But the references in the Homeric poems to the nations on the west coast of Asia, kindred as they undoubtedly were, are all tinged by a certain feeling of superiority, though how slight that feeling is cannot be fully understood, except by comparing Homer's way of speaking with that of the tragedians. We get notices also (see Odyssey, xiv. 315; xv. 426-452) of European neighbours, the friendly Thesprotians and the hostile Taphians, conceived in the same spirit. So the preface of Thucydides throughout conceives the earlier state of Hellas as being something lower than that described in the Homeric poems (see Grote, ii. 47), but as something of which traces still remained in his own time among the ruder members of the Greek nation.

(21) Page 87.—Δῆμος in Homer constantly means the land, *πίων δῆμος* and the like, and it is not uncommonly distinguished from *πόλις*, or perhaps used as including *πόλις* —*πολῆΐ τε πάντι τε δήμῳ*.

(22) Page 87.—On the Attic Dêmoi, see below, p. 403.

(23) Page 88.—See History of Federal Government, i. 133.

(24) Page 89.—See the well-known notice of the Lokrians, Ætolians, and Akarnanians in Thucydides, i. 5, and cf. iii. 94.

(25) Page 89.—The foundation of Megalopolis (see History of Federal Government, i. 200) is a matter of history, and the names of the towns which contributed

inhabitants to it are given at length by Pausanias, viii. 27. Xenophôn (Hell. iii. 2, 27) mentions that Elis in his time was still unwalled, and Diodôros (xi. 54) gives the date of its foundation in the archonship of Praxiergos, B.C. 471. His words are Ἠλεῖοι πλείους καὶ μικρὰς πόλεις οἰκοῦντες εἰς μίαν συνῳκίσθησαν τὴν ὀνομαζομένην Ἦλιν. Strabo (viii. 3) is more precise, and he extends the remark to many others among the Peloponnesian cities. Ἦλις δὲ ἡ νῦν πόλις οὔπω ἔκτιστο καθ' Ὅμηρον, ἀλλ' ἡ χώρα κωμηδὸν ᾠκεῖτο . . . . . ὀψὲ δέ ποτε συνῆλθον εἰς τὴν νῦν πόλιν τὴν Ἦλιν, μετὰ τὰ Περσικὰ, ἐκ πολλῶν δήμων. σχεδὸν δὲ καὶ τοὺς ἄλλους τόπους τοὺς κατὰ Πελοπόννησον πλὴν ὀλίγων, οὓς κατέλεξεν ὁ ποιητὴς οὐ πόλεις, ἀλλὰ χώρας ὀνομάζει, συστήματα δήμων ἔχουσαν ἑκάστην πλείω, ἐξ ὧν ὕστερον αἱ γνωριζόμεναι πόλεις συνῳκίσθησαν οἷον τῆς Ἀρκαδίας Μαντίνεια μὲν ἐκ πέντε δήμων ὑπ' Ἀργείων συνῳκίσθη· Τεγέα δ' ἐξ ἐννέα· ἐκ τοσούτων δὲ καὶ Ἡραία ὑπὸ Κλεομβρότου, ἢ ὑπὸ Κλεωνύμου· ὡς δ' αὔτως Αἴγιον ἐξ ἑπτὰ ἢ ὀκτὼ δήμων συνεπολίσθη· Πάτραι δὲ ἐξ ἑπτὰ, Δύμη δὲ ἐξ ὀκτώ· οὕτω δὲ καὶ ἡ Ἦλις ἐκ τῶν περιοικίδων συνεπολίσθη μία τούτων. The different words used by Strabo to express the earlier state of things, δῆμοι, κωμηδὸν, περιοικίδες, are worth noticing. The last at least could hardly be applicable. Elis, in the Homeric Catalogue, is the name, not of the city, but of the district; nor is the word πόλις applied to the Arcadian communities, but neither is χώρα.

Kemble (Saxons in England, i. 49) remarks that "generally speaking in Greece the origin of the πόλις lies in what may be called the compression of the κῶμαι. The ἀγορά is on the space of neutral ground where all may meet on equal terms." He makes the remark to illustrate the growth of the Teutonic *Gau* (see below, note 72 on Lect. III.) out of component *marks*. He also refers to the formation of Rome out of the three local tribes.

(26) Page 89.—The four or five earlier communities by the union of which the city of Mantineia was said to have been founded were heard of again when it suited the policy of Sparta to break up a powerful neighbour. Xenophôn tells the story, Hell. v. 2, 7. *ἐκ δὲ τούτου καθηρέθη μὲν τὸ τεῖχος, διῳκίσθη δ' ἡ Μαντίνεια τετραχῇ, καθάπερ τὸ ἀρχαῖον ᾤκουν.* He goes on to say how each village (*κώμη*) sent its separate contingent to the Lacedæmonian army, and how well the Mantineian oligarchs liked the change, as delivering them from democracy and demagogues. But in the Homeric Catalogue (ii. 607) both Tegea and Mantineia appear as integral wholes.

*καὶ Τεγέην εἶχον, καὶ Μαντινέην ἐρατεινήν.*

That the same was the case with Sparta is well known from the words of Thucydides, i. 10, when he speaks of Sparta as *κατὰ κώμας τῷ παλαιῷ τῆς Ἑλλάδος τρόπῳ οἰκισθεῖσα* even in his own day. The names of the original five villages seem to be given by Pausanias, iii. 16, 9, but the words of the Catalogue (581) seem rather to point to Lakedaimôn and Spartê as having once been separate communities.

*οἳ δ' εἶχον κοίλην Λακεδαίμονα κητώεσσαν,*
*Φάρην τε, Σπάρτην τε, πολυτρήρωνα τε Μέσσην.*

All these cases, in which a city was formed by the union of several villages, must be carefully distinguished from the union of the Attic towns. Elis, Mantineia, and the rest were formed either by actually joining together neighbouring villages, or by causing the inhabitants of more distant places to remove their dwellings to the new city. In Attica nothing of the kind happened. The towns went on as they did before, only they ceased to exist as political communities, and all their citizens received the franchise of Athens.

(27) Page 89.—That there were Macedonian cities which had made progress enough in city life to be enrolled as members, though perhaps in some degree as dependent members (see History of Federal Government, i. 193), of a Greek confederation is plain from the description which Xenophôn (v. 2, 12) gives of the steps taken by Olynthos in the formation of the league which the Spartans put down. *ἐκ τούτου ἐπεχείρησαν καὶ τὰς τῆς Μακεδονίας πόλεις ἐλευθεροῦν ἀπὸ Ἀμύντου τοῦ Μακεδόνων βασιλέως.* But the local divisions of Macedonia and Epeiros are all tribe divisions (see Thuc. ii. 99), and the village life which went on even among the purely Greek neighbours of the Epeirots was clearly the ruling life in both countries.

(28) Page 90.—Of the analogy between the Greek *μέτοικοι*, the *Niedergelassenen* in Switzerland, and the "foreigners," as they were often called, in many English boroughs, I have spoken more at large in another Lecture (see p. 284). The main point is that mere residence in all cases goes for nothing. How little it counted for in the ideas of Greek political thinkers is shown by the incidental words of Aristotle (Pol. iii. 1, 3), *ὁ δὲ πολίτης οὐ τῷ οἰκεῖν που πολίτης ἐστίν· καὶ γὰρ μέτοικοι καὶ δοῦλοι κοινωνοῦσι τῆς οἰκήσεως.* He goes on to speak of those *μέτοικοι* who, by the terms of special treaties, enjoyed special rights, the *connubium* and *commercium* or any others. *οὐδ' οἱ τῶν δικαίων μετέχοντες οὕτως ὥστε καὶ δίκην ὑπέχειν καὶ δικάζεσθαι· τοῦτο γὰρ ὑπάρχει καὶ τοῖς ἀπὸ συμβόλων κοινωνοῦσι· καὶ γὰρ ταῦτα τούτοις ὑπάρχει. πολλαχοῦ μὲν οὖν οὐδὲ τούτων τελέως οἱ μέτοικοι μετέχουσιν, ἀλλὰ νέμειν ἀνάγκη προστάτην.* This last is the well-known disqualification of the *μέτοικοι* at Athens, which forbade them from suing in any court in their own names, and required them to appear through a citizen patron.

(29) Page 90.—Something of this kind happened at some stage or other of the history of most Grecian cities. I quote the most illustrious case of all (Arist. Pol. iii. 2, 3): *ὅσοι μετέσχον μεταβολῆς γενομένης πολιτείας, οἷον Ἀθήνησιν ἐποίησε Κλεισθένης μετὰ τὴν τῶν τυράννων ἐκβολήν· πολλοὺς γὰρ ἐφυλέτευσε ξένους καὶ δούλους μετοίκους. τὸ δ' ἀμφισβήτημα πρὸς τούτους ἐστὶν οὐ τίς πολίτης, ἀλλὰ πότερον ἀδίκως ἢ δικαίως.*

(30) Page 90.—Take the case of the orator Lysias at Athens, a *μέτοικος* who had shown himself as good an Athenian patriot as if he had come in a straight line from Erechtheus, who first had full citizenship voted to him, and then lost it on the ground of an informality in the vote. Phôtios 262 (p. 490, Bekker); *γράφει μὲν μετὰ τὴν κάθοδον Θρασύβουλος πολιτείαν αὐτῷ, ὁ δὲ δῆμος ἐκύρωσε τὴν δωρεάν. Ἀρχῖνος δὲ, διὰ τὸ ἀπροβούλευτον εἰσαχθῆναι τὸ ψήφισμα, γράφεται παρανόμων τὴν δωρεάν· καὶ ἐπεὶ κατεγνώσθη τὸ ψήφισμα, τῆς μὲν πολιτείας ὁ Λυσίας ἀπελαύνεται, τὸν λοιπὸν δὲ χρόνον κατεβίω ἰσοτελὴς ὤν.* That is to say, he remained a *μέτοικος*, shut out from the political franchise, but exempted from the special burthens laid upon his class, and paying only the same tax as the citizens. That there could be any doubt or question about granting full citizenship to such a man shows how high a privilege the grant was held to be. On the other hand there is an early case of the way in which grants of citizenship, which must have been practically honorary, were made to foreign princes in the enfranchisement of the Thracian Sadokos, son of Sitalkês, which is recorded by Thucydides, ii. 29. *ὁ Νυμφόδωρος τήν τε τοῦ Σιτάλκου ξυμμαχίαν ἐποίησε καὶ Σάδοκον τὸν υἱὸν αὐτοῦ Ἀθηναῖον.* So ii. 67, *τὸν Σάδοκον τὸν γεγενημένον Ἀθηναῖον.* All this is made sport of by Aristophanês, Acharn. 145:

> ὁ δ' υἱὸς, ὃν Ἀθηναῖον ἐπεποιήμεθα,
> ἤρα φαγεῖν ἀλλᾶντος ἐξ Ἀπατουρίων,
> καὶ τὸν πατέρ' ἠντιβόλει βοηθεῖν τῇ πάτρᾳ.

We hear much more of this in later times.

In oligarchic Sparta the grant of citizenship was of course far more rare and precious than in democratic Athens. Yet we find an instance in Herodotus (ix. 33) where the full Spartan citizenship is granted to the Eleian prophet Tisamenos and his brother Hêgias. But the story shows how rare such a favour was, and with what difficulty the Spartans brought themselves to grant it: *Σπαρτιῆται δὲ πρῶτα μὲν ἀκούσαντες δεινὰ ἐποιεῦντο.* There is a later instance in the case of Diôn of Syracuse (Plutarch, Diôn, 49) which shows how completely such artificial citizenship, when once granted, was looked on as the same thing as citizenship by birth. Hêrakleitos sets up Gaisylos as fitter to command the Syracusan forces than Diôn, on the ground of his being a Spartan. Diôn, who had, like Tisamenos, been admitted to Spartan citizenship, answers *ὡς εἰσὶν ἄρχοντες ἱκανοὶ τοῖς Συρακουσίοις, εἰ δὲ πάντως δέοι καὶ Σπαρτιάτου τοῖς πράγμασιν, αὐτὸς οὗτος εἶναι κατὰ ποίησιν γεγονὼς Σπαρτιάτης.* Compare also the jest of Gorgias of Leontinoi (Arist. Pol. iii. 2, 2) on the ease with which citizens were made at Larissa; *ἔφη, καθάπερ ὅλμους εἶναι τοὺς ὑπὸ τῶν ὁλμοποιῶν πεποιημένους, οὕτω καὶ Λαρισσαίους τοὺς ὑπὸ τῶν δημιουργῶν πεποιημένους· εἶναι γάρ τινας λαρισσοποιούς.* We cannot help contrasting all this with the ease with which strangers are naturalized both in European kingdoms and American commonwealths. But this is part of the difference between a city and a nation. The true parallel to the citizenship of Athens or Sparta is not naturalization as a British subject, but admission to the local freedom of a borough.

(31) Page 91.—On this *ξυνοίκισις* of Attica, one of the great events in the history of Greece and of the world, see Historical Essays, Second Series, p. 119.

(32) Page 91.—On the momentary union of Argos and Corinth in B.C. 393, see Xenophôn, Hell. iv. 4, 6, and the remarks of Grote, ix. 462. The expressions of Xenophôn are remarkable, even though they may express only the feelings of an oligarchic party, as they show the natural repugnance of the Greek mind to any such union of separate cities. *αἰσθανόμενοι ἀφανιζομένην τὴν πόλιν, διὰ τὸ καὶ τοὺς ὅρους ἀνασπᾶσθαι καὶ Ἄργος ἀντὶ Κορίνθου τὴν πατρίδα αὐτῶν ὀνομάζεσθαι, καὶ πολιτείας μὲν ἀναγκαζόμενοι τῆς ἐν Ἄργει μετέχειν, ἧς οὐδὲν ἐδέοντο, ἐν δὲ τῇ πόλει μετοίκων ἔλαττον δυνάμενοι, ἐγένοντό τινες αὐτῶν, οἵ ἐνόμισαν οὕτω μὲν οὐκ ἀξιοβίωτον εἶναι.* Certainly there is no other case in Grecian history where two commonwealths were fused together in this way; and we should be glad to have some details of the process, momentary as the union proved. One can hardly understand an actual union of two cities so far apart from each other, and there cannot well be such a thing as a confederation of two. Mark again the complaint of the discontented Corinthians that they were no better than *μέτοικοι* in their own city.

(33) Page 92.—I have traced out the early history of these two Leagues in my History of Federal Government. Among the Ætolians we have seen that Greek city life was hardly at all developed. The Achaian League, on the other hand, was from the beginning a League of cities in the strictest sense; but then they were cities so small that they had no chance of maintaining their independence as perfectly independent commonwealths.

(34) Page 92.—See History of Federal Government,

i. 630. The annexation of Sparta, which made the League take in the whole of Peloponnêsos, must have held out temptations too strong for human nature to withstand. But from that time the history of the League is largely made up of secessions, and movements in the direction of secessions, on the part of Sparta, and of complaints against the Federal power brought by Sparta before the Roman protector.

(35) Page 93.—The distinction in German political language between *Staatenbund* and *Bundesstaat* is one which Greek itself might envy. In the *Staatenbund,* such as the American Union was up to 1789 and the Swiss Confederation up to 1848, the members of the League are joined together on such terms and for such purposes as may be agreed on, and their common affairs are administered by a Federal Diet or Congress. Still each State remains perfectly independent in all its internal concerns, and each may even keep the right of separate dealing with foreign Governments. There is nothing which can be strictly called a Federal *Government.* In the *Bundesstaat,* on the other hand, though each State remains sovereign and independent within the range of such powers as it does not hand over to the Federal authority, yet, within the range of those powers which are handed over to the Federal authority, the whole body forms a single commonwealth under a Government, with its executive, legislative, and judicial branches, acting as a sovereign and independent power within its own range. Most of the Greek confederations in the later days of Greece seem to have been fairly entitled to the name of *Bundesstaat.*

(36) Page 94.—See Historical Essays, Second Series, p. 146.

(37) Page 96.—Veii seems to have been as large as Rome, but then Veii was the great march city of Etruria, just as Rome was the great march city of Latium. So Megalopolis was founded on the Spartan march of Arcadia. But certainly, setting Etruria aside, Capua is the only Italian city at all on a level with Rome, till we get down to the great Greek cities of the South. The nearness of the great Greek cities to one another is brought forcibly home to us by the story of Philolaos and Dioklês, told by Aristotle (Politics, ii. 12. 8, 9). Philolaos was buried at Thebes, on a spot from which the Corinthian territory could be seen. Aigina, as all the world knows, was the eyesore of Peiraieus. But perhaps the clearest picture of the physical smallness—that is, in truth, the moral greatness—of the Greek commonwealths is that drawn by Servius Sulpicius in his letter to Cicero (Ep. ad Div. iv. 5)—"Ex Asiâ rediens quum ab Ægina Megaram versus navigarem, cœpi regiones circumcirca prospicere. Post me erat Ægina, ante Megara, dextra Piræeus, sinistra Corinthus." His comment is "quæ oppida quodam tempore florentissima fuerunt, nunc prostrata et diruta ante oculos jacent." We might have looked for the reflexion that all had once been independent commonwealths, but that they now all formed parts of the Roman dominion. The truth is that they did not all as yet form part of the Roman dominion. See Note 40.

(38) Page 96.—This is clearly set forth in the third chapter of Mommsen's History of Rome. He gives a vivid picture of the origin of the old Italian towns. The story is essentially the same in Italy, Greece, and Gaul; only Italy lagged behind Greece, while Gaul, till the Roman civilization was brought in from without, lagged behind Italy. The Latins began with a *Markgenossenschaft,* and

the town, like the British *oppidum*, was at first a mere place of defence in case of the attacks of enemies. "Diese Plätze, die natürlich auch zugleich die heiligen Stätten der Markgenossen einschlossen und die wir uns übrigens als regelmässig unbewohnt oder schwach bewohnt zu denken haben, begegnen uns unter den Namen der 'Berge' (*montes*) und 'Bauten' (*pagi*, von *pangere*), der 'Burgen' (*arces*, von *arcere*) und 'Ringe' (*urbes*, von *urvus*, *curvus*, *orbis*), und sie sind die Grundlage der vorstädtischen Gauverfassung in Italien geworden, welche in denjenigen Italischen Landschaften, die zum städtischen Zusammensiedeln erst spät und zum Theil noch bis auf den heutigen Tag nicht vollständig gelangt sind, wie im Marserland und in den kleinen Gauen der Abruzzen, noch einigermassen deutlich sich erkennen lässt."

Even Rome itself was, from the beginning, a place of meeting rather than a place of dwelling to the greater part of its citizens. So far Rome and Athens are alike; but the Athenian franchise could not, from a whole crowd of causes, be extended beyond the original towns of Attica, while circumstances allowed the Roman franchise to be, in the end, extended as far as the Roman dominion was. Long before Rome had become the head even of Italy, districts had been admitted to citizenship which were further from Rome than any part of Attica was from Athens.

(39) Page 96.—I here accept Mommsen's view as to the origin of Rome. On the tendency of these border districts and states to become ruling states over their neighbours and kindred, see Historical Essays, First Series, p. 220.

(40) Page 97.—The great legal division is into *cives* and *peregrini*. The *peregrini*, up to the Social War, included, first, the *Latins*—no longer, of course, the old confederacy of that name, but the communities which enjoyed the *Jus Latii* in any part of the Roman dominion; these were half citizens who had a right, under certain circumstances, to claim citizenship; secondly, the *Socii*, the allied states of Italy, of which we have already spoken, and which received citizenship after the Social War; thirdly, the *Provincials*, the subjects of Rome out of Italy, who were placed under the rule of Roman Proconsuls or other governors, and whose earlier institutions, though seldom wholly swept away, remained as the institutions of mere municipalities and no longer of distinct commonwealths. It must always be remembered that both the full citizenship of Rome and the inferior Latin and Italian franchises could be conferred either on individuals or communities in any part of the Roman dominions. And we should also remember how many principalities and commonwealths, though surrounded by Roman territory and practically dependent on Rome, retained their formal independence till very late times. Thus the Lykian League lived on till the reign of Claudius, and the commonwealths of Rhodes and Byzantion till the reign of Vespasian.

Gaius i. 28, remarks that "Latini multis modis ad civitatem Romanam perveniunt." The peculiarity of the Latin condition is, that the Latins, though not citizens, could, if the necessary conditions were fulfilled, claim citizenship of right, while Italians and Provincials, like the Greek μέτοικοι, could receive it only of special favour.

(41) Page 98.—We have the speech of Claudius in favour of a larger extension of citizenship among the Gauls, as it is reported by Tacitus (Ann. xi., 25), and we have the fragments

of the actual speech, found on a brass tablet at Lyons, and printed at the end of the eleventh book in Orelli's edition. The difference between the two versions is instructive, as it helps to show how far the speeches in the classical writers are to be taken as real reports of what was actually said. The general drift of the argument is the same; but the language is altogether different, and even the particular examples chosen are different. As the genuine speech is imperfect, it may, in its complete state, have contained more than it now does of the matter which is found in Tacitus; but it is singular that Tacitus should have left out the very curious story which makes Servius Tullius the same person as the Etruscan Mastarna, which is found in the original speech. Both however alike set forth the policy of Rome in gradually extending her citizenship to her allies and subjects. The passage which I had specially in my eye may come from Claudius; it certainly comes from Tacitus. "Quid aliud exitio Lacedæmoniis et Atheniensibus fuit, quamquam armis pollerent, nisi, quod victos pro alienigenis arcebant? At conditor noster Romulus tantum sapientia valuit, ut plerosque populos eodem die hostes, dein cives habuerit." The last sentences in Tacitus, which are also much to our purpose, are undoubtedly Claudian in substance, though Tacitus has put them into much better language. "Omnia, Patres Conscripti, quæ nunc vetustissima creduntur, nova fuere; plebei magistratus post patricios; Latini post plebeios; ceterarum Italiæ gentium post Latinos. Inveterascet hoc quoque: et quod hodie exemplis tuemur, inter exempla erit."

As for the edict of Antoninus Caracalla, by which all the free inhabitants of the empire became Roman citizens, I am glad to find Sir Henry Maine (Ancient Law, 144) protesting against the common tendency to underrate its effects. "I may be permitted to remark that there is little foundation for the opinion which represents the constitution of Antoninus Caracalla conferring Roman citizenship on the whole of his subjects as a measure of small importance." To Sir Henry Maine the edict is of importance chiefly as having "enormously enlarged the sphere of the Patria Potestas." To me it comes more home as having extended the Roman name to all the inhabitants of the Empire. The name *Romanus,* as opposed to *Barbarus,* in the Teutonic codes, and the name of Ῥωμαῖος, still the true name of the people who have only latterly revived the name of Ἕλληνες, are the direct results of the edict. And, but for that edict, Roderic the West-Goth would not have appeared in Saracenic eyes as the King of the Romans; the Seljuk Sultans of Ikonion would not have called themselves Sultans of *Roum*; nor would the Roman name have still remained the received name of the Ottomans and their empire in the further East. That edict created a territorial *Romania,* instead of a mere local *Roma.* The edict, in short, is a great landmark in the history of the world; still, as far as any political privilege went, the franchise bestowed by it was altogether worthless.

(42) Page 98.—I need not show that, as long as the commonwealth lasted, the vote of the Roman citizen, in whatever *comitia* it was to be given, could be given nowhere but in the proper place, in or close to Rome. It has been perhaps less commonly remarked that, when the vote had become of very little worth, Augustus devised a means by which citizens at a distance might give their votes at home, and have them sent them to Rome by something, I suppose, like sealed voting-papers. So Suetonius tells us (Aug. 46) "Italiam . . . . jure ac dignatione urbi quodam modo pro parte aliqua adæquavit: excogitato genere suffragiorum,

quæ de magistratibus urbicis decuriones colonici, in sua quisque colonia ferrent, et sub diem comitiorum obsignata Romam mitterent."

Of this way of voting one would gladly have some further details. One would like to know what the mechanical process was, and whether any means were taken to hinder any tampering with the votes on the part of the decurions. The device may be looked on as a sign of the decay of public spirit; for it is no bad test of the worth of a man's vote whether he will take a little trouble to give it. Still the possibility of voting about laws and magistrates elsewhere than at Rome, like the discovery which was made somewhat later, that it was possible to choose an Emperor elsewhere than at Rome, is one of the signs of the gradual pulling down of the supremacy of the local city.

(43) Page 99.—See Historical Essays, Second Series, pp. 264, 321.

The verses of Mæcenas are preserved by Seneca, Epistles, xvii. 1.

"Debilem factito manu,
Debilem pede, coxa,
Tuber adstrue, gibberum,
Lubricos quate dente:
Vita dum superest, bene est,
Hanc mihi, vel acuta
Si sedeam cruce, sustine."

The philosopher calls this "turpissimum votum," "miserrimum," "contemptissimum." The last lines, as well as the commentary of Seneca which follows, should be noticed as throwing light both on the familiarity and the nature of crucifixion.

(44) Page 101.—Aristotle however (Pol. i. 25) fully recognizes the village—that is, as we shall presently see, the

γένος—as a natural stage intermediate between the family and the city. Ἡ μὲν οὖν εἰς πᾶσαν ἡμέραν συνεστηκυῖα κοινωνία κατὰ φύσιν οἶκός ἐστιν . . . . ἡ δ' ἐκ πλειόνων οἰκιῶν κοινωνία πρώτη χρήσεως ἕνεκεν μὴ ἐφημέρου κώμη· μάλιστα δὲ κατὰ φύσιν ἔοικεν ἡ κώμη ἀποικία οἰκίας εἶναι. . . . . . ἡ δ' ἐκ πλειόνων κωμῶν κοινωνία τέλειος πόλις. But throughout his treatise in general we hardly hear so much as we might have expected about the γένος as a distinct element in the commonwealth.

(45) Page 102.—The Celtic clans seem to be distinguished from the other forms of the common institution by the strength and permanence of the family and hereditary feeling. Among the Teutonic nations the notion of kindred seems to have died out very early, as it no doubt died out early in fact, among the *marks* or *gemeinden;* and at Rome, though the *gens* always remained a *gens,* the feeling of kindred was much slighter than in the Celtic clan. Above all, there was nothing at Rome which in any way answered to the chief of the clan.

(46) Page 102.—For village communities in the East I must refer to the second and fourth lectures in Sir Henry Maine's book. Of the Western form of the institution we shall find more to say as we go on.

(47) Page 103.—I know of no name for the village community, either in English or in German, which at all translates the Greek and Latin names. The *Geschlechter* of the German towns of course answer admirably, in the history of those towns, to the Greek γένη and Latin *gentes,* but then they belong wholly to that after-growth of Teutonic municipality of which I shall have to speak towards the end of this lecture; they have nothing to do with the early state of political developement of which we are now speaking.

(48) Page 103.—On the patronymic names of *marks* in England see Kemble, Saxons in England, 159, and Appendix A. at the end of the volume. The principle of formation is this: the eponymous hero, say Dodda, gives his name to the *gens*, the Doddingas, exactly as Alkmaiôn does to the Alkmaiônidai; the Teutonic patronymic *ing* answers exactly to the Greek ιδης. Then a settlement of the Doddingas most commonly forms its name by adding one of the common-place endings, as *ham* or *tun*, Doddingaham, Doddingatún, which last is actually found in the various places named Doddington. Sometimes, however, as Tooting, Woking (Totingas, Wocingas), &c., the name of the *gens* is found without any ending, just like the Greek Βραγχίδαι. The names which come directly from the name of an ἐπώνυμος, as *Finsbury* (Finnesburh), are rarer. These last must of course not be confounded with places which are named after mere mortal owners. These are common enough, but they are not so common among the original Saxon and Anglian settlements as they are among the Danes of Lincolnshire and the Flemings of Pembrokeshire. And, as Kemble points out, the *ing* form, being so common, has sometimes thrust itself in where it has no right; as Ab*ing*don and Hunt*ing*don for Abb*an*dun and Hunt*an*dun.

The same patronymic *ing*, in various shapes, is also found in many Continental names. One most interesting class is that which has been worked out by Bluntschli (*Staats- und Rechtsgeschichte der Stadt und Landschaft Zürich*, i. 25, referred to by Mr. Grote, iii. 16), who shows, by tracing the names through various forms, that the ending *ikon*, or *iken*, common in the old Zürichgau, is a corruption of *inghoven;* as Dellikon, for Tellinghoven, exactly answering to our Gillingham and Doddington. Another set will be found in Dithmarschen among the *gentes* or *Geschlechter* by whom the land was settled. See the Chronicle of Johann Adolfi, surnamed Neocorus (edited by Dahlmann, Kiel, 1827), i. 224 Some of the names have the *ing* form, as *Dickbolingmanschlecht*, *Wittingmanschlacht*, &c.

See also Norman Conquest, i. 562, f.

(49) Page 104.—On this matter should be read the essay of Mommsen, *Die Römischen Eigennamen*, in his *Römische Forschungen*. But I cannot follow him when he makes the addition of the name of the *dêmos* at Athens (Δημοσθένης Δημοσθένους Παιανιεύς, for example) equivalent to the *nomen* or gentile name at Rome. Παιανιεύς is not a gentile name as such. It may happen to be so, inasmuch as many of the *dêmoi* answered to *gentes;* but in itself it is not gentile but local. Παιανιεύς in truth is not a *name* at all; it is merely a description, while the gentile name Claudius or Julius is strictly the *nomen* of its bearer. Except that the membership of the *dêmos* was strictly hereditary, Δημοσθένης Δημοσθένους Παιανιεύς would exactly answer to Morgan ap Morgan of Llanfihangel or to John Johnson of Beckington, at that stage of nomenclature when only the son of a John could be called Johnson, and when the son of Robin Johnson would be called Richard Robinson. A Roman was never described by his local tribe or other local description, unless through the chance of a local description becoming a *cognomen*, such as Maluginensis and such like. The Athenian again was never spoken of as Παιανιεύς, except as a mere description by which he was introduced. No one would go on saying that Δημοσθένης Παιανιεύς, still less that Παιανιεύς, did so and so; while we do say in Latin that "Caius Julius," and even that "Julius," did so and so. The arrangement again of the names at Athens and at Rome shows the difference. At Athens a man is Δημοσθένης Δημοσθένους Παιανιεύς. At Rome he is not "Caius Lucii filius Julius," but "Caius Julius Lucii filius."

Then the *cognomen*, if he have one, is added: "Caius Julius Lucii filius Cæsar." It is the *Cæsar*, in short, not the *Julius*, which answers to the Παιανιεύς. The only difference is that at Athens every man had a demotic name, and the demotic name was necessarily local, while at Rome a man had not neccessarily a *cognomen*, and the *cognomen* was not necessarily local. The difference is really implied in Mommsen's own remark (p. 7):

"Bei den Griechen schwankt noch das gentilische Ethnikon: es findet sich -εύς, -ίδης, -ιος neben einander; die Italiker, vor allem mit der ihnen eigenen Strenge die Römer haben das Suffix -*ius* im gentilischen Ethnikon ausschliesslich durchgeführt."

That is to say, the demotic description, not being a *nomen* or gentile name, but a legalized local *cognomen*, takes various endings according to the name of the *dêmos* from which it is formed; the *nomen* or gentile name, being strictly gentile, takes always the one ending in *ius*, answering to the Greek ίδης and to the Teutonic *ing*.

Mommsen makes a remark just before (pp. 5, 6) which is striking, and, to say the least, worth looking into. This is that, in such phrases as "Marcus Marci," Δημοσθένης Δημοσθένους, there was at first no ellipsis of *filius* or υἱός. The name in the genitive case is simply the genitive expressing property; it is, as he calls it, a *Herrenname*, pointing out under whose *potestas* or *mund* the person spoken of was. That which is under the *potestas* may be wife, son, slave, ox, or field, and the formula is the same for all. *Cæcilia Marci, Marcus Marci*, are the same form ("sprachlich und rechtlich gleichartig") as *ager Marci*, or, I suppose, as *Marci por*. If it be so, it would be worth finding out whether the formula which names the grandfather as well as the father, "Caius Julius Lucii filius Sexti nepos," came in through those cases where the father was himself still in the *potestas* of the grandfather.

(50) Page 104.—See the passages collected by Niebuhr (i. 327, i. 606 of the English translation), passages which undoubtedly prove that there was not necessarily any real kindred among all the members of a *gens*. So too there is force when he says that, if Cicero had believed all the members of a *gens* to have a common origin, he would hardly have thought it enough to say, as he does in the Topica, 6, "Gentiles sunt qui inter se eodem nomine sunt." Adoptions and enfranchisements, even if the *gens* was never enlarged in any way but these two, would be enough to hinder there being any real connexion by blood among all the members of the *gens*. But Niebuhr is clearly wrong in inferring from this that the *gentes* were purely artificial divisions. Mr. Grote puts the case far better when he says (iii. 74):—"The basis of the whole was the house, hearth, or family—a number of which, greater or less, composed the gens or genos. This gens was therefore a clan, sept, or enlarged, and partly factitious brotherhood." The description given by Curtius, *Griechische Geschichte*, i. 250, would very well describe the nature of a *gens*, if he had not made the *Stammvater* and the *Sippschaft* alternative. He begins by saying, "Jedes Geschlecht umfasste eine Gruppe von Familien, welche entweder wirklich von einem Stammvater herrührten oder sich in alter Zeit zu einer Sippschaft vereinigt hatten." He then mentions the chief ties, religious and civil, and adds, "Es war ein grosses Haus, eine enggeschlossene heilige Lebensgemeinschaft." The well known passage of Varro, "ab Æmilio homine orti Æmilii ac gentiles," expresses the idea of the whole thing, and it matters not whether the supposed Æmilius, or rather Æmilus, was a real man or not. A *gens* may even have invented a forefather for itself, as pedigree-makers do now; but if so, they did it simply in imitation of *gentes* which had real known forefathers. Every Julius was not necessarily

descended from either a real or a mythical Julus, but the *gens Julia* had none the less for its kernel a body of real kinsmen who either were, or pretended to be, descended from a Julus, but who admitted, by adoption or naturalization, some members who neither were nor pretended to be his descendants.

In the passage referred to in the Topica Cicero adds to his definition of *gentiles*, "Qui ab ingenuis oriundi sunt" and "Quorum majorum nemo servitutem servivit." But this definition is given simply as the definition of the gentile right to inheritance. In a wider sense, the freedman who bore the name of the *gens* was surely a member of it. Compare the dispute between the patrician and plebeian Claudii in Cicero de Oratore, i. 39, and the remarks of Mr. Long in the Dictionary of Antiquities, 568. In other parts of the article he follows the notion of Niebuhr.

(51) Page 104.—On the importance of legal fictions, especially in an early state of society, see the second chapter of Sir Henry Maine's Ancient Law.

(52) Page 104.—In the cases of adoption we commonly find that the adopted son was already a kinsman of his artificial father, a sister's son or the like. But, on the one hand, there was no need that there should be any such connexion; and, if there was, the nephew or other kinsman was as much a stranger to the *gens*, his admission to its legal and religious rites was as purely artificial, as when the adopting parent chose some one who had nothing to do with himself. But in either case the adopted son became, as far as a fiction of law could make him, the real son of his new parent. He became such for every purpose legal, social, and religious. That is to say, the *gens* was an institution originally founded

on community of blood, but in certain cases an artificial kindred was allowed to take the place of a natural one.

The orations of Isaios, the second and third, for instance, throw great light on the process of adoption at Athens. In the second, Περὶ τοῦ Μενεκλέους κλήρου, the adopted son describes the process (18); *ποιησάμενος εἰσάγει με εἰς τοὺς φράτορας παρόντων τούτων, καὶ εἰς τοὺς δημότας με ἐγγράφει, καὶ εἰς τοὺς ὀργεῶνας.* So in vii. 17, 20, another claimant describes his adoption; *ὡς ἐμὲ ἐποιήσατο υἱὸν ζῶν αὐτὸς καὶ κύριον τῶν αὐτοῦ κατέστησε καὶ εἰς τοὺς γεννήτας καὶ εἰς τοὺς φράτορας ἐνέγραψε. . . . . καὶ ἐπειδὴ θαργήλια ἦν, ἤγαγέ με ἐπὶ τοὺς βωμοὺς εἰς τους γεννήτας τε καὶ φράτορας.* The *ὀργεῶνες* mentioned in one of the above extracts, were the religious officers of the *φρατρίαι*. See Suidas *in voce*, who says, *περὶ τῶν ὀργεώνων γέγραφε καὶ Φιλόχορος· τοὺς δὲ φράτορας ἐπάναγκες δέχεσθαι καὶ τοὺς ὀργεῶνας καὶ τοὺς ὁμογάλακτας οὓς γεννήτας καλοῦμεν.* It does not seem clear whether the bodies among whom the adopted son was to be admitted to membership had the power of rejecting him. Probably they would have it at first, but it would sink into a mere form. This, as is well known, actually happened at Rome, where the adoption needed the formality of a *lex curiata*.

(53) Page 104.—See note 47 on Lecture II.

(54) Page 106.—There can be no doubt that the political effects of the Roman practice of using the gentile name as the real *nomen* were most important. The *nomen* stamped a man as belonging to a certain gens. He could not be spoken of without himself and others being reminded of the gens to which he belonged. At Athens an Alkmaionid himself knew, and everybody else knew, that he was an Alkmaionid,

but they were not in the same way reminded of it every time he was spoken of. There can be no doubt that this had a great effect on the hereditary character which we see so strongly marked on the great Roman families. We know beforehand the policy which a Fabius, a Valerius, or a Claudius must follow. The same thing revives in the Middle Ages, when surnames revive. The truth is that there is nothing so really aristocratic as a surname. And this bears on a remark which I have made in the last Lecture, that a real aristocracy can exist only in a republic. When the title of a peer is changed in each generation (sometimes, as in the case of the first Duke of Leeds, several times in the same life-time), the *gentile* sentiment may possibly live on within the family itself, but it is quite lost among the outer world, who have to ask at each stage who he is. No doubts of the kind can arise when a man, instead of a mere title, inherits the name of Fabius, Erlach, or Reding.

(55) Page 106.—See above, note 26.

(56) Page 107.—On the Doric tribes see Grote ii. 479, O. Müller, Dorians ii. 76 (Eng. Gr.) The point is that, as the three tribes, Hylleis, Pamphyloi, and Dymanes, seem to have been found in all Dorian settlements everywhere—a point which seems to be fully proved by Herod. v. 68—it would follow that these tribes are older than the migrations which took the Dorians into Peloponnêsos and Crete. In this last we must remember that the threefold division was recognized in the time of Homer, witness the Δωριέες τε τριχάϊκες of the Odyssey (xix. 174). That is to say, these tribes must be as old or older, than the occupation of the primitive northern Dôris and we may be inclined to suspect that they were older, because their names bear no relation to the names of the

four old Dorian towns. We are thus led to look upon these tribes as the oldest known elements of the Dorian people, and it would seem that in every Dorian settlement members of each of these tribes took a share. And the name of the Pamphyloi would seem to show that that tribe at least was an aggregate made up of smaller tribes. These tribes, or at least the ὠβαί of which they were formed, went on to the very latest times. The local divisions, handed on from the præ-Dorian time, went on alongside of them, like the Attic δῆμοι, or like the local tribes of Rome alongside of the *gentes*. The difference, of course, was that in this case the divisions of the conquerors and of those of the conquered went on together, while at Athens we have no sign of conquest. The ὠβαί answered to φρατρίαι and *curiæ*. O. Müller refers to Athênaios iv. 19, for the use of the word φρατρία to express a Spartan ὠβά. Dêmêtrios of Skêpsis there speaks of σκιάδες at the Karneian festival, each of which contained three ὠβαί. I do not know that this proves much. But I must go with O. Müller against Mr. Grote in holding that the famous ῥήτρα in Plutarch, Lyk. 6, proves that the ὠβαί were thirty. I can get no other meaning out of it. The whole passage is remarkable, as giving the technical Spartan names for the different parts of the Spartan State; φυλὰς φυλάξαντα καὶ ὠβὰς ὠβάξαντα τριάκοντα, γερουσίαν σὺν ἀρχαγέταις καταστήσαντα, ὥρας ἐξ ὥρας ἀπελλάζειν . . . . δάμῳ δ' ἀγορὰν εἶμεν καὶ κράτος. Plutarch goes on to explain that ἀρχαγέται means the Kings, and that ἀπελλάζειν means ἐκκλησιάζειν; but he cannot avoid the belief that Lykourgos divided the Spartan people into tribes and ὠβαί, just as it is a common English belief that Ælfred divided England into shires and hundreds.

(57) Page 107.—I think I can see something of the kind in

the story of the Pelasgian inhabitants of Attica in Herod. vi. 137, Thucydides ii. 17 (where see Arnold's note), Pausanias i. 28, 3, Strabo ix. 1 (ii. 241). εἴρηται δ' ὅτι κἀνταῦθα φαίνεται τὸ τῶν Πελασγῶν ἔθνος ἐπιδημῆσαν· καὶ ὅτι ὑπὸ τῶν 'Αττικῶν Πελαργοὶ προσηγορεύθησαν διὰ τὴν πλάνην. The use of the rare word 'Αττικοί reminds one of the remarkable distinction drawn by Dikaiarchos or Athênaios (Geographi Græci Minores, i. 99) between 'Αττικοί and 'Αθηναῖοι; but that would not seem necessarily to point to any difference in race.

(58) Page 107.—On the Ionic tribes, and the question of their being castes, compare Thirlwall ii. 6, Grote iii. 69. But there seems nothing to connect these tribes with the local political parties of which we hear in the time of Solôn and Peisistratos.

(59) Page 108.—See Grote iv. 177, Curtius i. 311, who appropriately calls them *Ortsgemeinden*. He contends for, or rather takes for granted, the strict decimal system which has been inferred from the well-known passage in Herodotus v. 69, δέκα δὲ τοὺς δήμους κατένεμε ἐς τὰς φυλάς. To me it seems that Herodotus meant to assert a decimal system, but that he was mistaken in his fact. It is a kind of fact about which it is very easy to go wrong, as in the memorable case when a Parliament of Edward the Third fancied that there were fifty thousand parishes in England. The point is that, though the new Ten Tribes were artificial, made by Kleisthenes for the occasion, yet they were made up of Dêmoi which were not artificial, but which existed already. It was the evils which had arisen a little time before from prevalence of local party-divisions in Attica which made Kleisthenês determine that the Tribes which were now to form the component

elements of the commonwealth should be made up of districts which did not lie close to one another. The tribes are therefore not examples of local contiguity (though the Dêmoi of which they are formed are; see above, note 22), but as examples of the opposite principle, they assume its existence.

(60) Page 108.—Curtius, *Griechische Geschichte*, i. 311. "Sie [the new tribes] hatten mit Abstammung und Herkunft nichts zu thun. Sie waren nichts als die Einheiten, welchen gewisse Gruppen ländlicher Bezirke (Demen) untergeordnet wurden. Diese Bezirke oder Ortsgemeinden hatten längst bestanden: es waren zum Theil alte Zwolfstädte Atticas, wie Eleusis, Kephisia, Thorikos, oder sie trugen ihre Namen von den Geschlechtern, welche vorzugsweise in denselben begütert waren, wie Butadai, Aithalidai, Paionidai."

(61) Page 108.—That is to say, in all political arrangements the Tribe formed an unit, without any reference to the Dêmoi contained in it. The analogy of Rome would lead us to think that this had not been the case with the old Tribes; for at Rome the Curia remained a political unit, with its distinct vote in the Comitia of the Curiæ. For military purposes too the Tribe formed an unit, though the men from each Dêmos may likely enough have been ranged together.

(62) Page 109.—See Mommsen's treatment (*Römische Geschichte*, i. 33) of the traditions about the three original Roman tribes, Ramnes, Titienses, and—if they be original—Luceres. The original legend, the topography of which at least there seems no reason to doubt, comes out in Dionysios ii. 50. οἱ δὲ περὶ τὸν Ῥωμύλον καὶ Τάτιον τήν τε πόλιν εὐθὺς ἐποίουν μείζονα, προσθέντας ἑτέρους αὐτῇ δύο λόφους, τόν τε Κυρίνιον κληθέντα καὶ τὸν Καιλίον· καὶ διελόμενοι τὰς οἰκήσεις χωρὶς

*ἀλλήλων, δίαιταν ἐν τοῖς ἰδίοις ἑκάτεροι χωρίοις ἐποιοῦντο. Ῥωμύλος μὲν τὸ Παλάτιον κατέχων, καὶ τὸ Καίλιον ὄρος· ἔστι δὲ τῷ Παλατίῳ προσεχές. Τάτιος δὲ τὸ Καπιτώλιον, ὅπερ ἐξ ἀρχῆς κατέσχε, καὶ τὸν Κυρίνιον ὄχθον.* It will be remembered that the space between the two was the Comitia, and that the gate of Janus was opened in time of war to allow the allied communities to give help to one another.

(63) Page 109.—The difference between genealogical and local tribes is well brought out by Dionysios, iv. 14, when he is describing the changes made by Servius:—Ὁ δὲ Τύλλιος . . . . *εἰς τέσσαρα μέρη διελὼν τὴν πόλιν . . . . τετράφυλον ἐποίησε τὴν πόλιν εἶναι, τρίφυλον οὖσαν τέως, καὶ τοὺς ἀνθρώπους ἔταξε τοὺς ἐν ἑκάστῃ μοίρᾳ τῶν τεττάρων οἰκοῦντας, ὥσπερ κωμήτας, . . . . καὶ οὐκ ἔτι κατὰ τὰς τρεῖς φυλὰς τὰς γενικὰς στρατιωτικά, ὡς πρότερον, ἀλλὰ κατὰ τὰς τέσσαρας τὰς τοπικάς, καὶ τὰς ὑφ' ἑαυτοῦ διαταχθείσας ἐποιεῖτο, ἡγεμόνας ἐφ' ἑκάστης ἀποδείξας συμμορίας, ὥσπερ φυλάρχους ἢ κωμάρχας.*

(64) Page 109.—The usual version of the coming of the Claudian tribe places it a few years after the driving out of the Kings. Mommsen, however (*Römische Forschungen,* 72), refers it to a much earlier time, following the tradition preserved by Suetonius, Tib. 1. "Inde [Regillis] Romam recens conditam cum magna clientum manu commigravit, auctore Tito Tatio consorte Romuli." Mommsen's words are:—

"Das Factum selbst scheint glaubwürdiger als die meisten übrigen Angaben in diesem älteren Theil der Annalen, aber natürlich war dasselbe ursprünglich zeitlos überliefert und ist nur von dem spätern falschen Pragmatismus mit dem Sabinerkrieg des Poplicola verknüpft worden—die Einwanderung des claudischen Stammes muss viel früher fallen, dass eine der Landtribus ältester Einrichtung nach ihn benannt ist und das Geschlecht, obwohl es in den älteren Fasten keine hervorragende Rolle spielt, doch bereits im J. 259 in der Consulartafel erscheint."

It might be said in answer to this that family vanity would be likely to thrust back the incorporation of the Claudii with the Roman State to an earlier time, while, if the Claudii had been Sabines simply in the sense of being Titienses—the statement in Suetonius, as it stands, is clearly a mixture of two stories—it is not easy to see how the tale of their later origin could arise. Anyhow the accounts given by Livy and Dionysios set clearly before us the kind of process which would happen in such a case—the addition at once of a Patrician gens and of a local tribe. Livy (ii. 16) thus tells the story; "Attus Clausus, cui postea Ap. Claudio fuit Romæ nomen . . . . ab Regillo, magna clientium comitatus manu, Romam transfugit. His civitas data agerque trans Anienem; vetus Claudia tribus, additis postea novis tribulibus, qui ex eo venirent agro, appellata." The migration is again referred to in speeches in iv. 3, x. 8. So Dionysios, v. 40, *ἀνήρ τις ἐκ τοῦ Σαβίνων ἔθνους πόλιν οἰκῶν Ῥήγιλλον, εὐγενὴς καὶ χρήμασι δυνατὸς, Τίτος Κλαύδιος, αὐτομολεῖ πρὸς αὐτοὺς, συγγένειάν τε μεγάλην ἐπαγόμενος, καὶ φίλους καὶ πελάτας συχνοὺς αὐτοῖς μεταναστάντας ἐφεστίοις, οὐκ ἐλάττους πεντακισχιλίων τοὺς ὅπλα φέρειν δυναμένους . . . . ἀνθ' ὧν ἡ βουλὴ καὶ ὁ δῆμος εἴς τε τοὺς πατρικίους αὐτὸν ἐνέγραψε, καὶ τῆς πόλεως μοῖραν εἴασεν ὅσην ἐβούλετο εἰς κατασκευὴν οἰκιῶν· χώραν τ' αὐτῷ προσέθηκεν ἐκ τῆς δημοσίας τὴν μεταξὺ Φιδήνης καὶ Πικεντίας, ὡς ἔχοι διανεῖμαι κλήρους ἅπασι τοῖς περὶ αὐτὸν, ἀφ' ὧν καὶ φυλή τις ἐγένετο σὺν χρόνῳ, Κλαυδία καλουμένη.*

The other new local tribes, formed out of allies or subjects admitted to citizenship, were added pretty constantly down to B.C. 299, when the Tribes Aniensis and Terentina were added (Livy, x. 9). There is then a gap till B.C. 241, when the last two Tribes, Velina and Quirina, were added (Livy, Epit. 19). This marks a stage in the history of commonwealths in general, the stage when they feel that they have no further need of fresh citizens, and when the selfish and exclusive feeling begins to prevail (see pp. 251, 252). But in this case it should be remembered that these successive additions had made the *ager Romanus* reach, and indeed outstrip, the fullest extent of territory which could be occupied by a single city-community.

(65) Page 113.—See Norman Conquest, iv. 415. The whole history of the word is drawn out by Gibbon, chap. 21 (vol. iii. p. 402, Milman).

(66) Page 113.—It is a certain trial of faith to believe that the word "heathen" has nothing to do with the Greek ἐθνικός:—but it is, in its different forms, good English, good High-German, and good Gothic; *háiþno* from *háiþi*.

(67) Page 115.—I have discussed this elsewhere at some length.—Norman Conquest, ii. 587.

(68) Page 115.—Even Anselm is "Anglorum Archiepiscopus," at least in the mouths of Irishmen and of the Pope. See Eadmer, Hist. Nov. Lib. ii. pp. 393–414, Migne. On the specially territorial style of the Bishops of the South-Saxons see Norman Conquest, ii. 592.

The territorial styles of many American and colonial Bishops are therefore, from an English or British point of view, more primitive than those which are taken from cities.

(69) Page 116.—I have touched somewhat slightly on the

nature of the Mark in the History of the Norman Conquest, i. 83, and still more slightly in the Growth of the English Constitution, p. 10. The great English authority on the subject is, of course, Mr. Kemble's chapter on the Mark, in the first volume of his Saxons in England. Before that, the nature of the early Teutonic settlements had been worked out by various German writers, from Jacob Grimm (*Deutsche Rechtsalterthümer*, 495 et seqq.) onwards, especially in the chapter of Waitz in the first volume of his *Deutsche Verfassungsgeschichte, Das Dorf, die Gemeinde, der Gau*. Since Mr. Kemble wrote, the subject has been dealt with more at large, though, on the whole, from a somewhat different point of view, in the great works of Maurer, *Einleitung zur Geschichte der Mark-, Hof- und Stadtverfassung* (München, 1854), *Geschichte der Markenverfassung in Deutschland* (Erlangen, 1856), *Geschichte der Dorfverfassung in Deutschland* (Erlangen, 1866), for which works Sir Henry Maine, in his Village Communities, has become a sort of sponsor to English readers. The *Mark*, in its strictness, is of course the boundary, the strip of uncultivated land left between the land occupied by one settlement and the land occupied by its neighbour, The *Markgenossenschaft* is the body of settlers, that is, in my view, the *gens* or clan, by whom the land was first occupied. Here we have the lowest territorial and political unit, to be found alike in India, Greece, Italy, Germany, and England, and out of the union of which with other *marks*, cities, tribes, and nations gradually grew.

(70) Page 117.—The common occupation of land by the members of the *Markgenossenschaft* has been the point which, since the researches of Maurer (see *Einleitung*, 40), and more lately of Nasse and Sir Henry Maine, has drawn to itself most attention. This concerns me only as being the earliest form

of *folkland*—a name which should never be uttered without a feeling of thankfulness to the memory of John Allen—of which I have said a word or two in the History of the Norman Conquest, i. pp. 83, 94, 589, and on the political aspect of which I have found something to say at p. 139 of the Growth of the English Constitution.

(71) Page 117.—The original kindred between the members of the *Markgenossenschaft*, allowing of course, for adoptions and admissions (on which see Maurer, *Dorfverfassung*, i. 175, cf. *Einleitung*, 13), is strongly set forth by Mr. Kemble, i. 56. "I represent them to myself as great family unions, comprising households of various degrees of wealth, rank, and authority: some, in direct descent from the common ancestors, or from the hero of the particular tribe; others, more distantly connected, through the natural result of increasing population, which multiplies indeed the members of the family, but removes them at every step further from the original stock; some, admitted into communion by marriage, others by adoption; others even by emancipation; but all recognizing a brotherhood, a kinsmanship or *sibsceaft;* all standing together as one unit in respect of other, similar communities; all governed by the same judges and led by the same captains; all sharing in the same religious rites, and all known to themselves and to their neighbours by one general name."

Mr. Kemble refers to the passage of Cæsar, vi. 22, "Neque quisquam agri modum certum, aut fines habet proprios; sed magistratus ac principes in annos singulos *gentibus cognationibusque hominum* qui una coierint quantum et quo loco visum est agri attribuunt, atque anno post alio transire cogunt." This passage is, of course, of importance as bearing on the history of the occupation of land. I am concerned with it as distinctly pointing to the *Markgenossenschaft* as an association founded on kindred, and as actually using the word *gens* in what can be meant only for its technical Roman sense. There is also the passage of Tacitus (Germania, 7), "Non casus, nec fortuita conglobatio turmam aut cuneum facit, sed familiæ et propinquitates," which is referred to by Waitz (*Deutsche Verfassungsgeschichte*, i. 44), whose own words are:—

"Doch auch innerhalb der Gemeinde konnte die Familie ihre Bedeutung haben; Nachwirkungen des ältern Zustandes finden wir auch noch in späterer Zeit. Tacitus sagt, dass im Heer der Deutschen die einzelnen Haufen sich nach Familien und Verwandtschaften bildeten; während schon die Eintheilung nach Hundertschaften bestand, die vorherrschende war, hatte doch auch diese älteste natürlichste Verbindung ihre Geltung, und das war möglich, da die Familienglieder leicht zur gemeinschaftlichen Ansiedelung sich verbanden, Kinder und Vettern zusammenblieben, wenn sie nicht zur Auswanderung oder zum Ausbauen genöthigt wurden. Weiter aber werden wir auch nicht gelangen; wir werden unten sehen, dass die Familie in den Verhältnissen des Rechts noch von grosser durchgreifender Wichtigkeit war; aber alles nur innerhalb der Gemeinde." Waitz quotes a passage from the Lex Alamannorum (tit. 84, col. 232, Georgisch), "Si qua contentio orta fuerit inter duas genealogias de termino terræ eorum," where the two "genealogiæ" are to come before the "comes de plebe ista" (the Gaugraf?) and settle the matter by single combat. In England we have the *mægð* in its narrower sense, on which Lappenberg (to whom Waitz also refers) has a remarkable passage (p. 583), which I must quote in full in the original, because it is so strangely cut short in Mr. Thorpe's Translation, ii. 328.

"Zu den ältesten Districtsbenennungen, welche der Shire vorangingen, gehörte noch die 'Maegthe,' ein Land, welches die Genossen eines Geschlechtes oder Stammes, eine Magenschaft, wie sie im Kriege zusammen gefochten und erobert hatten, so im Frieden zusammen erhielten." [He here refers to the passages from Cæsar and Tacitus quoted above.] "Wir finden diese Bezeichnung gewöhnlich schon auf die grössern sächsischen, nicht aber auf die von den Angeln besetzten Provinzen angewandt, doch zuweilen noch im ältern Sinne, wie bei der Maegthe der Meanwaren. Dass sich eine wirkliche, bei den Angelsachsen jedoch nur in seltenen Spuren noch nachzuweisende Verwandtschaft unter diesen neben einander siedelnden Geschlechtern durch Erbrecht, Wergeld, politische Bürgschaften, Näherrechte und andere mit jenen verknüpfte Einrichtungen lange erhalten konnten, zeigen uns viele Beispiele, selbst noch des spätern Mittelalters, in den Kluften, Vetterschaften und ähnlichen Familienverbindungen germanischer Stämme, um nicht auf entfernteres hinzuweisen; woraus wir gleichfalls wahrnehmen, wie zuletzt, bei grösserer Beweglichkeit der Habe und selbst des Landeigenthumes, die Verwandtschaft nur als Bezeichnung einer politischen Verbindung übrigblieb."

See also the articles *Mearc*, *Mægð*, and *Magenschaft*, in Schmid (*Gesetze der Angelsachsen*), who however seems wholly to cast aside Kemble's notions about the mark. But it would, I think, be hard to get over Kemble's fact (i. 55, 56) that there was a *Mearcmót* and a *Mearcbeorgh*, the hill where the *gemót* of the mark was held. So Sir Henry Maine (Village Communities, 175) says of the *marks* in the East: "At the outset they seem to be associations of kinsmen, united by the assumption (doubtless very vaguely conceived) of a common lineage. Sometimes the community is unconnected with any exterior body, save by the shadowy bond of caste. Sometimes it acknowledges itself to belong to a larger group or class. But in all cases the community is so organized as to be complete in itself."

I need hardly enlarge on the *mund* of our forefathers, and its analogy with the Roman *potestas.* But the Teutonic *filius familias* did not, like the Roman, remain for ever under the *mund* of his father. When he himself became a member of the State, a citizen and a soldier, emancipation took place of itself. See Waitz, i. 39.

(72) Page 118.—The Tithing and the Hundred are parts of the ancient constitution which are much more perplexing than the *mark* and the *gau.* I will only refer to Zöpfl, *Geschichte der Deutschen Rechts-Institute,* 97, 112, 121; Waitz, i. 37; Lappenberg, i. 585 of the original, ii. 329 of the English translation; Kemble's chapter on the Tithing and Hundred; Bluntschli, *Staats- und Rechtsgeschichte der Stadt und Landschaft Zürich,* i. 24; Maurer, *Einleitung,* 59, and the article Hundred, in Schmid, where it is strange to see him quoting the false Ingulf. Waitz suggests that the passages in Cæsar and Tacitus which speak of *centum pagi* have arisen out of some misconception, and I cannot help fancying that where Tacitus (Germania, 12) speaks of the "centeni singuli ex plebe comites" who were attached to the princes for judicial purposes, there is also some confusion, and that Tacitus misunderstood a statement that there were some men present from each hundred.

(73) Page 118.—The *gau* is treated of by all our authors; Grimm, *Deutsche Rechtsalterthümer,* 496; Eichhorn, *Deutsche Staats- und Rechtsgeschichte,* 49; Zöpfl, *Geschichte der Deutschen Rechts-Institute,* 95, 108, 121, 148; Maurer, *Einleitung,* 54 (Comparative Philology will hardly allow us to believe that

*gau* is the same as the Greek γέα or γῆ)—and for the history of a particular *gau*, and its breaking up into several smaller *gauen*, see Bluntschli, i. 20. Waitz (i. 49) gives the definition of a *gau*—"Nicht von dem Boden, der Vertheilung des Territoriums ist dies ausgegangen, sondern so weit die Völkerschaft wohnte, reichte ihr Gau. So nothwendig wie mit dem deutschen Volk ein deutsches Land, Deutschland, gegeben ist, so nothwendig entstehen mit der Zertheilung des Volks nach Stämmen und der Stämme in Völkerschaften auch jene territorialen Abtheilungen, die wir Gaue nennen."

(74) Page 119.—I suppose that no one will dispute this as to the formation of the *gau* out of *marks* and the kingdom out of *gauen*. Those are the two essential elements; about the hundred the case may be less clear, and Waitz (i. 48) seems to look on it as a division of the *gau*. Yet, as we seem everywhere to find something between the *gau* and the tribe, it seems not unlikely that the intermediate association, φρατρία, *curia*, or hundred, may also have been strictly an association, and not a division. But I do not care to insist upon this point, as long as it is understood that in the other cases the greater unit is made up by the union of the smaller units, and that the smaller units are not formed by the division of the greater. Kemble has a vigorous passage on the way in which the smaller groups grew into the larger, "a process repeated and continued until the family becomes a tribe and the tribe a kingdom."

(75) Page 120.—On *Ealdormen* and *Heretogan*, see Norman Conquest, i. 579. Cf. the note on Æthelred of Mercia, i. 563. *Ealdorman* is the word used by Ælfred to express the *Satrapæ* of Bæda, v. 10. There can, I think, be no doubt that *Heretoga*, the High-Dutch *Herzog*, is the word which Tacitus meant to express by *Dux*.

(76) Page 121.—The well-known passage of Bæda, describing the Old-Saxons, which I have quoted elsewhere (see Norman Conquest, i. 579), gives a vivid picture of a people who choose a single chief in war-time only. The Satraps or Ealdormen put one of their own body at their head in war-time—"peracto autem bello, rursum æqualis potentiæ omnes fiunt." I shall have to speak of this state of things again in my next Lecture (see p. 164), but I will meanwhile give a description of the Old-Saxon constitution from the Life of Saint Lebuin (Pertz, ii. 361), by an author of the tenth century, which, if it can be trusted, gives a distinct picture of a true Federal government. But the strange thing about it is that, not only the nobles and the common freemen are, as we should have expected, represented in the Federal Assembly, but also the class below the common freemen, a class of whom I shall have to speak in a later Lecture (see pp. 249, 458). But, even if the writer should be mistaken on this point, the whole picture can hardly be imaginary. It will be at once noticed that we have here, what is not to be found in any other contemporary assembly, a case of real representation; but this is only what we might have expected in a constitution so strictly federal. The whole passage stands thus:—

"Erat gens ipsa, sicuti nunc usque consistit, ordine tripartito divisa. Sunt denique ibi, qui illorum lingua edlingi, sunt qui frilingi, sunt qui lassi dicuntur, quod in Latina sonat lingua, nobiles, ingenuiles, atque serviles. Pro suo vero libitu, consilio quoque, ut sibi videbatur, prudenti singulis pagis principes præerant singuli. Statuto quoque tempore anni semel ex singulis pagis, atque ex iisdem ordinibus tripartitis, singillatim viri duodecim electi, et in unum collecti, in media Saxonia secus flumen Wiseram, et locum

Marklo nuncupatum, exercebant generale concilium, tractantes, sancientes, et propalantes communis commoda utilitatis, juxta placitum a se statutæ legis. Sed etsi forte belli terreret exitium, si pacis arrideret gaudium, consulebant ad hæc quid sibi foret agendum."

(77) Page 121.—On the kindred Frisian *Seelands* and their liberties, see the account in Eichhorn, § 285*b* (vol. iii. pp. 265–271), and on Dithmarschen itself (Maurer, *Einleitung*, p. 289). It was said of its people, in good Nether-Dutch, which ought not to need a translation for any Englishman, "De Didtmarschen leven sunder Heren and Hovedt, unde dohn wadt se willen." Dithmarschen was conquered by Frederick the Second of Denmark and his uncle Duke Adolf of Holstein, in 1559. In 1499 the free people of that land had utterly driven back the invasion of King John and Duke Frederick. The history of both these events may be read in the native tongue of the district in the Chronicle of Johann Adolfi. Adolfi lived in the latter half of the sixteenth century, so that he was contemporary or nearly so with the latter of the two events with which we are concerned. The heading of the book which records the victory (i. 447) runs thus: "Datt Veerde Boock Dithmerscher Historischer Geschichte, belangende eigentlicken uund wahrhafften Bericht der herlichen unde wunderlichen Victorien der Dithmerschen, unde der erbermlichen unde schrecklichen Nedderlage Koning Johans uth Denemarken unde seines H. Broders Frederichen, Hertogen tho Holstein." The sadder narrative of 1559 (ii. 151) is ushered in thus, "Dat Soste Bock geloff- unde denkwerdiger Geschichte, so sich im Ditmerschen begeven unde thogedragen, alleine de lateste Beide unde Eroveringe des Landes belangende." He adds the motto from Sallust, "Potior visa est periculosa libertas

quieto servitio," and ends with the chronogram "DIthMarsIae LIbertas rUIt."

(78) Page 121.—When I come to go on with my History of Federal Government, I trust to deal—far better than I could have dealt ten years back—with the traces of the old Teutonic constitution as it was, partly preserved, partly won back, both in the original Three Lands, and among the confederate *Gemeinden* in Graubünden and Wallis. These two countries, as not being surrounded with such a blaze of mythical glory as the Three Lands, have drawn to themselves far less attention, but their political history is perhaps even more instructive.

(79) Page 122.—This change makes the difference between the subject of the first book of Zeuss (*Die Deutschen und die Nachbarstämme*), headed *Das Alterthum*, and the second headed *Die neuen Umgestaltungen*. The novelty is the gathering together of the various scattered branches of the German nation of which we read in Cæsar and Tacitus, into those greater wholes—whether we call them nations or confederations—Franks, Allemans, Saxons, &c., which play the chief part in the history of the third century B.C. Zeuss's words (303) are:—

"Im westlichen Germanien weichen seit dem Anfang des dritten Jahrhunderts nach und nach die alten Namen der Völker anderen wenigen, aber ausgebreiteten. Die einzelnen Theile des vielgegliederten Stammes haben sich hier in grössere Körper vereinigt, deren Unterschied für die folgende Zeit bleibend wird. Zu dieser Umgestaltung im Innern kommt ein Fortdrängen gegen die äusseren Umgebungen; die neuen Völker haben auch ihre früheren Sitze geändert und in erweiterndem Streben nach Aussen sich in neue Stellungen fortbewegt."

(80.) Page 122.—Besides our own island, this description would apply to the lands between the Alps and the Danube, and to all the Teutonic lands on the left bank of the Rhine. The Roman cities lived on, and the neighbourhood of the Romance-speaking lands must have had some influence; otherwise the phænomena of these lands must have been nearly the same as those of Britain.

(81) Page 123.—Something has been done on this head by Sir Henry Maine, in the lecture on the Process of Feudalization, the fifth in the Village Communities. But the growth, both of the manor and of the ecclesiastical parish, needs thoroughly working out. Both of course are innovations; but lawyers deal with the *mark* just as they deal with the kingdom, and assume the lord, as they assume the King, to be the root and source of everything, instead of being a comparatively late intruder, who has crept in unawares. But the process by which the parish priest came to be the president of the *Mearcgemót*—for such, one cannot doubt, the parish vestry really is—must be stranger still.

(82) Page 125.—We have the fact that the word *Gau* is not found in English of any date. And we have the facts that the word *shire*, which answers to it, does not mean an association, but a division (from *sciran, shear*), that it is applied to other and smaller divisions besides *gauen* or counties, and that in the sense of *gau*, it is found as early as the Laws of Ine, 36–39. On the other hand, the *shire* is called in Latin *pagus*, the same word which expresses the Continental *gau;* and it forms, like the *gau*, the division out of the union of which the kingdom is made up. If I rightly understand Mr. Kemble's chapter on the "Gá or Scir," the *gau* and the *shire* are the same division looked at from two different points of view

2 E

The *gau* becomes a shire when it becomes part of a larger whole; or again when, as happened to many of the Continental *gauen*, a *gau* is cut up into several smaller *gauen*, or has its boundaries otherwise altered. Thus, when the great *Thurgau* was divided, the *Zürichgau*, and the other smaller *gauen* which were made out of it, would be literally *shires*—parts *shorn* off from a greater whole. It is certain too that, though we find the word *scír* as early as the time of Ine, it is only from about the tenth century that we find it actually added to the names of districts. It is certain also that there are many English counties to which the name *shire* has never been applied down to our own times. It is further certain, as Mr. Kemble has shown, that we have traces of earlier divisions —divisions earlier than the tenth century—which sometimes agree with, and sometimes differ from, our present divisions. (See Kemble, i. 78–84.) The inference I make from all this is the same which I made in Appendix E to the first volume of the Norman Conquest, namely that those shires which are not called after a town, but which have a territorial name of their own, are strictly *gauen*, or, when they are mediatized kingdoms, groups of *gauen*. Thus, in Kent and Sussex, the *lathe* and the *rape*, divisions between the hundred and the county, would answer to the *gau*. Elsewhere, where the county is called after a town, it is strictly a *shire*, something shorn off or otherwise divided afresh. Thus, as I have tried to show in the Appendix already referred to, the Mercian counties are strictly *shires*, divisions mapped out afresh by Eadward the Elder, after the recovery of the country from the Danes. Thus again, we do not hear of Yorkshire by that name till the second half of the eleventh century. It was a *shire*, shorn off from the original Northumberland, part of which still kept the elder name. And it is a shire which was further shorn into smaller shires, one of which, Richmondshire, could not have borne that name till the foundation of Richmond Castle after the Norman Conquest. But, on the other hand, looking on Yorkshire in its older estate as the kingdom of Deira, we may look on it as made up of earlier *gauen*, Elmet, Craven, Cleveland, and so forth. The *gau*, in short, is a natural association; the shire is an artificial division. The two may or may not coincide. But they very often do, and, in any case, the shire is the division which answers to and represents the *gau*, even when it represents it only by way of supplanting it.

In the Appendix of which I have already spoken I have said something about the names of particular counties. I have not mentioned there, though I think I have mentioned it elsewhere, that in the Chronicles and in the Exchequer Domesday, Devonshire is always spoken of as a shire (*Defenascír*), while Somerset and Dorset keep the tribal names (*on Sumorsætan, on Dorsætan*). And this is the more remarkable, because in the Exeter Domesday we do sometimes find such a name as "Summersetæ syra," so that the use of the tribal form in the Exchequer Domesday has the force of a correction.

Wherever, as I think really is the case in one or two instances, a modern French Department exactly answers to an ancient duchy or county, the distinction between the two would be exactly the same as that between the *gau* and the shire, and in the other case, when an ancient province was shorn into several departments, we see the creation of shires in the literal sense.

(83) Page 126.—See above, note 79.

(84) Page 126.—See Norman Conquest, i. 25-27. I have there quoted the description given by Henry of Huntingdon of the growth of East Anglia and Mercia; but the passage of

William of Malmesbury (i. 44) there referred to is worth giving at length :—" Annis enim uno minus centum, Northanhimbri duces communi habitu contenti, sub imperio Cantuaritarum privatos agebant; sed non postea stetit hæc ambitionis continentia, seu quia semper in deteriora declivus est humanus animus, seu quia gens illa naturaliter inflatiores anhelat spiritus. Anno itaque Dominicæ incarnationis quingentesimo quadragesimo septimo, post mortem Hengesti sexagesimo, ducatus in regnum mutatus, regnavitque ibi primus Ida, haud dubie nobilissimus, ætate et viribus integer; verum utrum ipse per se principatum invaserit, an aliorum consensu delatum susceperit, parum definio, quia est in abdito veritas: cæterum satis constat magna et vetere prosapia oriundum, puris et defæcatis moribus multum splendoris generosis contulisse natalibus."

(85) Page 128.—The truth that the Teutonic element in French exactly answers to the Romance element in English is somewhat disguised by the fact that, for some centuries past, it has been the fashion for English to borrow a crowd of French or Latin words, while the number of German, English, or other Teutonic words which have found their way into French during the same period is comparatively small. But, if we look to those words which make up the real substance of the two languages, we shall see that the analogy is a perfectly true one. There is however this difference. In English we have two, perhaps three, classes of Romance words which have become thoroughly naturalized—μέτοικοι admitted to the full franchise—while in French there is only one such class of Teutonic words. The number of Teutonic words which made their way into the Latin of Gaul during the time of the Gothic, Burgundian, and Frankish conquests, and which survive in the modern Provençal and French tongues,

is really very large, far larger than any one would think at first sight, far larger than the number of Celtic words which have crept in on the other side from the native languages of the country. Still, large as the infusion is, it is merely an infusion, and it in no way affects the essentially Latin character of the two modern languages of Gaul. But this Teutonic infusion into the Romance of Gaul answers to a threefold Romance infusion into the Teutonic of Britain. There is, first of all, the half-dozen words which the Romans left behind them, and which the English took up, just as we now take up native names for native things in India and elsewhere. Secondly, there is the larger group of Latin words, either ecclesiastical or expressing some foreign idea, which came in between the coming of Augustine and the coming of William. These two together would be outnumbered over and over again by the Teutonic—that is the Frankish—infusion in French. This is the natural result of the difference between a destroying conquest, like that of the English in Britain, and a colonizing conquest, like that of the Franks in Gaul. But the tables are turned the other way by the third, the Norman, infusion, under which I reckon those Romance words which it needs historical or philological knowledge to recognize for Romance words, as distinguished from those which, by their endings or otherwise, betray their foreign origin at first sight. All these three classes must be looked on as thoroughly naturalized in English, just as the Frankish words are naturalized in French. But one of the gradual results of the Norman Conquest and of the establishment of French for a while as the polite speech in England—events to which there is no parallel in France after it became France—has been to set a fashion of bringing in Romance words, and even Romance endings, into English, while nothing has ever set the fashion of bringing a German or English—as distinguished from an Old-Teutonic—infusion into French. For instance, we do not scruple to add a Romance ending to a Teutonic root, and thus to make such a mongrel word as *starvation*, while French adopts such a word as *meeting*, but it does not add on the ending *ing* to roots of its own. Still, the greater Romance infusion in English, and the lesser Teutonic infusion in French, both remain infusions, and do not affect the substance of either language. With a little care, Teutonic words may be avoided in French, and with somewhat more care, Romance words may be avoided in English. The opposite process in either language is impossible.

(86) Page 128.—The transitional days of European history, the days of the Wandering of the Nations and of the Frankish dominion, will not be fully understood as regards Italy, unless we bear in mind that Venice belongs, in all but geographical position, to the eastern side of the Hadriatic, and not to the western. The Venetian islands are the one piece of the earlier Western Empire which escaped Teutonic conquest. They remained part of the Eastern Empire—*ἡμεῖς δοῦλοι θέλομεν εἶναι τοῦ Ῥωμαίων βασιλέως*—till they were strong enough to build up a dominion of their own at the expense of both Empires.

(87) Page 129.—See the Essay on Ancient Greece and Mediæval Italy, in Historical Essays, Second Series.

(88) Page 130.—Nomenclature alone, without any help from recorded history, is commonly enough to tell us which of our towns are of purely English origin. A Roman site most commonly makes itself known, if not by some corruption of its earlier name, at any rate by the word *Ceaster* in its

various shapes. Of most of our purely English towns, like Bristol or Oxford, all we can say is, that we first hear of them at a given time, without having any record of their foundation. Of others, like Taunton in the eighth century, like the long string of places fortified by Eadward and Æthelflæd in the tenth century, we know when they became fortresses, but it does not follow that that was the time when they first became dwellings of men. Another class of towns grew up round some great monastery or, more rarely, as at Wells and Waltham, round a secular church. In the cases of Durham in the tenth century and New Salisbury in the thirteenth, church and city were founded together. But we have few towns in England of which we can safely say that they were called into being, like the cities founded by the Successors of Alexander, at the personal bidding of a King. Such however is Kingston-on-Hull, the work of the great Edward, and such also are several of the Welsh towns. In Bluntschli, *Staats- und Rechtsgeschichte der Stadt und Landschaft Zürich*, we can trace out the steps by which a city arose out of a royal house, a monastery, a church of secular canons, and a primitive *Markgenossenschaft*, all standing side by side.

(89) Page 130.—On the Five Boroughs, see Norman Conquest, i. 61; and on Lincoln, the greatest of them, iv. 208: on Exeter, and the chance which it had in 1068 of becoming the head of a confederation of boroughs, see iv. 138.

(90) Page 131.—The whole history of Bern, the greatest example in modern times of an inland city ruling over a great collection of subject towns and districts, is throughout eminently Roman. Lübeck, on the other hand, the head of the great commercial confederacy, as naturally suggests Carthage.

(91) Page 131.—On this phrase, the proper title of the old Swiss Confederation, see Historical Essays, First Series, 352. The name "Swiss" and "Switzerland," though they had long been in familiar use, did not form part of the formal style of the Confederation till 1803.

(92) Page 131.—Verona, I need hardly say, is *Dietrichs-bern;* and I have seen the Burgundian Bern called "Verona in montibus." The two names must surely have the same origin. The identification can hardly be so purely artificial as that which has turned Bormio into *Worms*. But what is the real origin? One thing alone is certain, that Bern has etymologically nothing to do with bears.

(93) Page 133.—This is a subject which I must some day find an opportunity of discussing at length. I trust that I have shown, in a paper in Macmillan's Magazine (July 1870), that the handing of Roman institutions to our own forefathers is simply impossible; but I find that, since then, the writer against whom I then argued, Mr. H. C. Coote, has again revived the notion, and supported it with the same curious plausibility against Dr. Brentano, in a paper on the Ordinances of some Secular Guilds of London, reprinted from the Transactions of the London and Middlesex Archæological Society.

(94) Page 135.—See Historical Essays, First Series, pp. 153, 154.

## LECTURE IV.

(1) Page 138.—See above, note 22 on Lecture II., and Bryce, Holy Roman Empire, 192.

(2) Page 139.—Bryce, Holy Roman Empire, 233.

(3) Page 140.—This is the way in which the comparative and superlative *βασιλεύτερος* and *βασιλεύτατος* are used in the Iliad. Thus, ix. 69:—

> Ἀτρείδη, σὺ μὲν ἄρχε, σὺ γὰρ βασιλεύτατός ἐσσι.
> καὶ μοὶ ὑποστήτω, ὅσσον βασιλεύτερός εἰμι. (ix. 160.)
> ἐς γενεὴν ὁρόων, μηδ' εἰ βασιλεύτερός ἐστιν. (x. 240.)

I do not profess to say off-hand that these forms are not to be found elsewhere in Homer; but it is certainly worth noticing that these three passages all come from the undoubtedly suspicious tenth book, and from the ninth, which Mr. Grote suspects, though I hold that Mr. Gladstone has made a good defence for it. The Homeric phrase is copied by Tyrtaios, Fragment iii. 7, *οὐδ' εἰ Ταντaλίδεω Πέλοπος βασιλεύτερος εἴη.*

(4) Page 140.—Württemberg, as not being the name of any nation or tribe, or territorial division, nor even, like Hannover and Naples, of a city, is surely the strangest royal title that ever was heard of. As for the true Saxony and Bavaria, one

might be inclined to call them, not so much divisions of the German nation, as nations whose union went towards forming the German nation. But it should always be remembered that even modern Bavaria in no way answers to ancient Bavaria, while the modern kingdom of Saxony has not a rood of ground in common with the Saxony which was subdued by Charles the Great.

(5) Page 140.—It must be remembered that the origin of the German and of the Italian kingdoms was quite different. The four strictly German kingdoms, Hannover, Saxony, Bavaria, and Württemberg, arose within living memory by the breaking up of the ancient Kingdom of Germany. But the kingdoms of Sardinia and the Two Sicilies, though part of what had come popularly and practically to be looked on as Italy, and though the continental Sicily actually contained the oldest Italy, were not formed by any dismemberment of the Italian kingdom. They arose in lands beyond its borders. The crowns of Sicily and Sardinia, as distinct kingdoms, helped, along with those of Rome, Germany, Italy, Burgundy, and Jerusalem, to make up the sevenfold diadem of Frederick the Second. Sardinia and Sicily answer rather to Bohemia and Prussia, kingdoms formed beyond the bounds of the proper German kingdom; and the application of the Sardinian name to the continental possessions of the Sardinian King, which was not uncommon before Piedmont grew into Italy, answers very closely to the process which has carried the Prussian name to the shores of the Elbe and the Rhine. In both cases the King's title was taken from a small and outlying part of his dominions.

(6) Page 141.—A King for a term seems unheard of,

except in the case of those mere survivals of kingship of which I have spoken further on. The reason no doubt is that it is felt that kingship, from the reason mentioned just below, conveys a sort of *character indelibilis.* The King might be deposed, but his deposition, though legal, was an extreme and unusual measure which was not contemplated on his admission to his office. He holds his office for life, subject to the unlikely chance of this extreme power being exercised. Such a tenure of this is something different in kind from a tenure for a term, or during pleasure, or even "quamdiu bene se gesserit."

(7) Page 141.—On Cæsar's desire to be a King, see Merivale, ii. 465. The dictatorships of Sulla and Cæsar would answer to what Aristotle calls (Pol. iii. 14,) *αἰσυμνητεία,* and defines as *αἱρετὴ τυραννίς,* and which forms one of the various kinds of kingship which he reckons up: but the *αἰσυμνητεία* was not necessarily held for life; *ἦρχον δ' οἱ μὲν διὰ βίου τὴν ἀρχὴν ταύτην, οἱ δὲ μέχρι τινῶν ὡρισμένων χρόνων ἢ πράξεων.* So Dionysios (v. 73), when he is trying to compare the Roman dictatorship to the Greek *αἰσυμνητεία, οἱ γὰρ αἰσυμνῆται καλούμενοι παρ' Ἕλλησι τὸ ἀρχαῖον, ὡς ἐν τοῖς περὶ βασιλείας ἱστορεῖ Θεόφραστος, αἱρετοί τινες ἦσαν τύραννοι· ᾑροῦντο δ' αὐτοὺς αἱ πόλεις, οὔτ' εἰς ἀόριστον χρόνον, οὔτε συνεχῶς, ἀλλὰ πρὸς τοὺς καιρούς, ὁπότε δόξειε συμφέρειν, καὶ εἰς πόσον χρόνον.* In his next chapter he goes on to discuss other cases of a temporary revival of kingly power under other names; *ἠναγκάζοντο παράγειν πάλιν τὰς βασιλικὰς καὶ τυραννικὰς ἐξουσίας εἰς μέσον, ὀνόμασι περικαλύπτοντες αὐτὰς εὐπρεπεστέροις. Θετταλοὶ μὲν γὰρ ἄρχους,* why not *ταγούς ;*] *Λακεδαιμόνιοι δὲ ἁρμοστὰς καλοῦντες, φοβούμενοι τυράννους ἢ βασιλεῖς αὐτοὺς καλεῖν· ὡς οὐδ' ὅσιον σφίσιν ὑπάρχον, ἃς κατέλυσαν ἐξουσίας ὅρκοις*

*καὶ ἀραῖς ἐπιθεσπισάντων θεῶν ταύτας πάλιν ἐμπεδοῦν.* In either case, whether the office was held for a time or for life, the holder of it was not necessarily succeeded by another *αἰσυμνήτης*. In truth the Roman Empire, down at least to Diocletian, was in form, as being in each case the subject of a special grant, a government of the same kind. A regular magistracy for life, such as that of the perpetual Gonfaloniere in the reformed Florentine Constitution of 1502, is by no means usual. The Spartan Kings and the Venetian Doge are not exceptions. The King and the Doge were not mere magistrates, but princes, though cut down to the lowest amount of power. Priesthoods, both at Rome and elsewhere, were commonly held for life; but that was because they were not magistracies.

(8) Page 141.—See Allen on the Royal Prerogative, 93-98.

(9) Page 142.—Waitz, *Deutsche Verfassungsgeschichte*, iii. 61. "Bei den germanischen Völkern, könnte man sagen, erlangte sie für den christlichen König eine ähnliche Bedeutung, wie in heidnischen Zeit die Zurückführung des königlichen Geschlechts auf die Götter gehabt hatte."

(10) Page 143.—Inquiry into the Rise and Growth of the Royal Prerogative in England. By John Allen. New edition, London, 1849.

(11) Page 143.—See Allen, pp. 14, 172.

(12) Page 145.—See the well-known verses in the Iliad (ii. 102) about the descent of the sceptre, which, if they do nothing else, show distinctly to my mind that the story of the Lydian origin of Pelops is no real primitive legend. Cf. i. 277:—

> μήτε σὺ, Πηλείδη, θέλ' ἐριζέμεναι βασιλῆϊ
> ἀντιβίην, ἐπεὶ οὔποθ' ὁμοίης ἔμμορε τιμῆς
> σκηπτοῦχος βασιλεὺς, ᾧτε Ζεὺς κῦδος ἔδωκεν.

ii. 205:

> εἷς βασιλεὺς, ᾧ ἔδωκε Κρόνου παῖς ἀγκυλομήτεω
> σκῆπτρόν τ' ἠδὲ θέμιστας, ἵνα σφίσιν ἐμβασιλεύῃ.

But the whole Iliad is full of such passages.

It is curious to read the comments of Diôn Chrysostom on the Homeric words. They are thoroughly characteristic of an age when Homer and everything else had become a subject of mere rhetorical display. His words (i. 3) are: *πάνυ γὰρ οὖν καλῶς σὺν ἄλλοις πλείοσιν Ὅμηρος, ἐμοὶ δοκεῖν, καὶ τοῦτο ἔφη, ὡς οὐχ ἅπαντας παρὰ τοῦ Διὸς ἔχοντας τὸ σκῆπτρον οὐδὲ τὴν ἀρχὴν ταύτην, ἀλλὰ μόνους τοὺς ἀγαθούς.* He goes on with a description of what a King ought to be. When one finds the Homeric doctrine of the transmission of the royal authority from Zeus confined to good Kings only, one is tempted to wonder at finding the Wickliffite tenet of dominion being founded on grace already set forth in a discourse addressed to Trajan.

I need hardly add that the succession of Jewish Kings from father to son, from David to the sons of Josiah, and of French Kings from Hugh Capet to Lewis the Tenth, are the most striking examples in history of direct succession in any royal house.

(13) Page 145.—It is worth while to read the account which Plutarch (Thêseus, 32) gives of the accession of Menestheus at Athens, and how he stirred the people up during the absence of Thêseus. He was himself sprung from the stock of Erechtheus; but he was, according to Plutarch's story, the earliest demagogue; *πρῶτος, ὥς φασιν, ἀνθρώπων*

*ἐπιθέμενος τῷ δημαγωγεῖν καὶ πρὸς χάριν ὄχλῳ διαλέγεσθαι.* Cf. Pausanias, i. 16, 5, 6. But in the Homeric Catalogue (ii. 552, and in iv. 328) he appears as a *διοτρεφὴς βασιλεύς* no less than anybody else. Presently we find another break in the hereditary succession of the Attic Kings through the accession of Melanthos; but here too the reigning King Thymoitês is described as being deposed or driven out (Paus. ii. 18, 9: Μέλανθος *τὴν βασιλείαν ἔσχεν, ἀφελόμενος* Θυμοίτην *τὸν* Ὀξύντου). In both cases the break in the succession seems to be irregular or revolutionary. I know of no case of orderly election of a Greek King in the Roman fashion.

(14) Page 145.—Aristotle (Pol. iii. 13) describes the heroic monarchies as *ἑκούσιαί τε καὶ πάτριαι γιγνόμεναι κατὰ νόμον*, and directly after (14), *αὕτη δ' ἦν ἑκόντων μὲν, ἐπί τισι δ' ὡρισμένοις, στρατηγὸς γὰρ ἦν καὶ δικαστὴς ὁ βασιλεὺς, καὶ τῶν πρὸς τοὺς θεοὺς κύριος.*

(15) Page 146.—Odyssey, i. 394.

> *ἀλλ' ἤτοι βασιλῆες* Ἀ*χαιῶν εἰσὶ καὶ ἄλλοι*
> *πολλοὶ ἐν ἀμφιάλῳ* Ἰ*θάκῃ, νέοι ἠδὲ παλαιοί.*

So amongst the Phaiakians (Odyssey, viii. 390):—

> *δώδεκα γὰρ κατὰ δῆμον ἀριπρεπέες βασιλῆες*
> *ἀρχοὶ κραίνουσι, τρισκαιδέκατος δ' ἐγὼ αὐτός.*

And they had already been spoken of as *σκηπτοῦχοι βασιλῆες*, viii. 40. Hesiod too (Works and Days, 200, 246, 259, 261), speaks of *βασιλῆες* rather as a class of whom there would be several in one state, than as holding a monarchy in the strict sense.

(16) Page 147.—We get the account of the *Interrex*, and

of his special mode of election by the patrician Senators, in Livy, iv. 43. He does not use the name in describing the first election of Consuls, but Dionysios (iv. 75, 76) gives the title to Spurius Lucretius, who, according to the story, presided at the Comitia. The words which he puts into the mouth of Brutus are remarkable: *μεσοβασιλέα ἑλοῦμαι τὸν ἀποδείξοντα τοὺς παραληψομένους τὰ κοινὰ, καὶ αὐτὸς ἀποθήσομαι τὴν τῶν Κελερίων ἀρχήν, ὁ δὲ κατασταθεὶς ὑπ' ἐμοῦ μεσοβασιλεὺς, συναγαγὼν τὴν λοχῖτιν ἐκκλησίαν, ὀνομασάτω τε τοὺς μέλλοντας ἕξειν τὴν μέλλουσαν βασιλείαν.* On this last word see above, p. 370.

(17) Page 148.—Livy, ii. 2. "Rerum deinde divinarum habita cura; et quia quædam publica sacra per ipsos reges factitata erant, ne ubiubi regum desiderium esset, regem sacrificulum creant. Id sacerdotium pontifici subjecere, ne additus nomini honos aliquid libertati, cujus tunc prima erat cura, officeret." He appears also as "rex sacrificulus" in Livy vi. 41, and as "rex sacrificus" in xl. 42; but that his real title was "rex sacrorum," appears from Livy himself (xxvii. 6), from Gellius (xv. 27), and Cicero (Pro Domo Sua, 14), who shows also that the "rex sacrorum," like the Interrex, always remained a patrician. That is to say, as the magistracies were thrown open to the plebeians one by one (see above, p. 254), it did not occur to any particular reformer to propose a law to throw open the office of "rex sacrorum," which was of no political importance. Dionysios (iv. 74) is emphatic on this last head. *ἵνα δὲ καὶ τοὔνομα τῆς βασιλικῆς ἐξουσίας πάτριον ὑπάρχον ἡμῖν, καὶ σὺν οἰωνοῖς αἰσίοις θεῶν ἐπικυρωσάντων παρεληλυθὸς εἰς τὴν πόλιν, αὐτῆς ἕνεκα τῆς ὁσίας φυλάττηται, ἱερῶν ἀποδεικνύσθω τις ἀεὶ βασιλεὺς, ὁ τὴν τιμὴν ταύτην ἕξων διὰ βίου, πάσης ἀπολελυμένος πολεμικῆς ἀσχολίας, ἓν τοῦτο μόνον ἔχων ἔργον, ὥσπερ ὁ βασιλεὺς,*

*τὴν ἡγεμονίαν τῶν θυηπολιῶν, ἄλλο δ' οὐδέν.* So Plutarch, Quæst. Rom. 63: *διὰ τί τῷ καλουμένῳ ῥῆγι σακρώρουμ (οὗτος δέ ἐστι βασιλεὺς ἱερῶν) ἀπείρηται καὶ ἄρχειν καὶ δημογορεῖν; ἢ τοπαλαιὸν οἱ βασιλεῖς τὰ πλεῖστα καὶ μέγιστα τῶν ἱερῶν ἔδρων, καὶ τὰς θυσίας ἔθυον αὐτοὶ μετὰ τῶν ἱερέων; ἐπεὶ δ' οὐκ ἐμετρίαζον, ἀλλ' ἦσαν ὑπερήφανοι καὶ βαρεῖς, τῶν μὲν Ἑλλήνων οἱ πλεῖστοι τὴν ἐξουσίαν αὐτῶν περιελόμενοι, μόνον τὸ θύειν τοῖς θεοῖς ἀπέλιπον. Ῥωμαῖοι δὲ παντάπασι τοὺς βασιλεῖς ἐκβαλόντες, ἄλλον ἐπὶ τὰς θυσίας ἔταξαν, οὔτ' ἄρχειν ἐάσαντες, οὔτε δημαγωγεῖν, ὅπως μόνον ἐν τοῖς ἱεροῖς βασιλεύεσθαι δοκῶσι, καὶ βασιλείαν διὰ τοὺς θεοὺς ὑπομένειν. ἔστι γοῦν τις ἐν ἀγορᾷ θυσία πρὸς τῷ λεγομένῳ Κομητίῳ πάτριος, ἣν θύσας ὁ βασιλεὺς, κατὰ τάχος ἄπεισι φεύγων ἐξ ἀγορᾶς.*

A more instructive case of political survival can hardly be conceived. A King is so needful for the religious part of his office, while a King clothed with any shred of political power is so hateful, that a King is made whose kingship seems to shut him out from the common rights and duties of citizens. (Cf. Livy, xli. 42.) A more speaking symbol of his exclusion could hardly have been devised than his offering his sacrifice, and then running from the Forum as from a place with which he had no further concern. We have a parallel to such a King in the Bishops who were kept at Iona and other Scottish monasteries, for the sole purpose of ordination, Bishops without any shadow of authority, and who were under the command of their ecclesiastical superior the Abbot.

Aristotle (Pol. iii. 14) speaks of this practice of cutting down the King to purely priestly functions as something usual in the Greek commonwealths:—*ὕστερον δὲ τὰ μὲν αὐτῶν παριέντων τῶν βασιλέων, τὰ δὲ τῶν ὄχλων παραιρουμένων, ἐν μὲν ταῖς ἄλλαις πόλεσι θυσίαι κατελείφθησαν τοῖς βασιλεῦσι μόνον, ὅπου δ' ἄξιον εἰπεῖν εἶναι βασιλείαν, ἐν τοῖς ὑπὲρ ὁρίοις* τῶν πολεμικῶν τὴν ἡγεμονίαν μόνον εἶχον. On this last clause see below, note 20.

(18) Page 149.—A still stronger proof would be that the Emperors themselves so constantly held the actual consulship, always once at least in each reign, and often much oftener; that, when they were not Consuls, they were invested with consular power; and that—though they could not be actual Tribunes because of the adoption of the plebeian Octavius into the patrician *gens Julia*—they not only held the tribunician power, but they looked on it as the main source of their authority. See below, note 42.

(19) Page 149.—The Spartan kingship was, in the ideas of Aristotle (Pol. iii. 14), a real kingship, not a mere survival, like the priestly kingships already mentioned. It is rather, in his eyes, the best example of a lawful kingship: ἡ γὰρ ἐν τῇ Λακωνικῇ πολιτείᾳ δοκεῖ μὲν εἶναι βασιλεία μάλιστα τῶν κατὰ νόμον, οὐκ ἔστι δὲ κυρία πάντων, ἀλλ' ὅταν ἐξέλθῃ τὴν χώραν, ἡγεμών ἐστι τῶν πρὸς τὸν πόλεμον, ἔτι δὲ τὰ πρὸς τοὺς θεοὺς ἀποδέδοται τοῖς βασιλεῦσιν. αὕτη μὲν οὖν ἡ βασιλεία οἷον στρατηγία τις αὐτοκρατόρων καὶ ἀΐδιός ἐστιν. Afterwards he calls it στρατηγία διὰ βίου, and ὡς εἰπεῖν ἁπλῶς στρατηγία κατὰ γένος ἀΐδιος. But, on the other hand, there is something remarkable in the way in which Herodotus (vi. 56–58) sums up the privileges of the Spartan Kings, without noticing that they do not take in anything which comes under the ordinary idea of government. Thucydides, on the other hand (i. 131), notices it as something strange that the Ephors had the power of arresting the King (ἐς μὲν τὴν είρκτὴν ἐσπίπτει τὸ πρῶτον ὑπὸ τῶν ἐφόρων· ἔξεστι δὲ τοῖς ἐφόροις τὸν βασιλέα δρᾶσαι τοῦτο), a comment which is the more remarkable as Pausanias was not King, but Regent. Xenophôn too looks on the

Spartan kingship as a real, though limited, kingship. Thus, at the beginning of the Agêsilaos (i. 1), he speaks of it as the only government which had really lasted, and that (see Growth of the English Constitution, p. 228) because the Kings did not seek for more power than the law gave them: *ἡ γὰρ πόλις οὐδεπώποτε φθονήσασα τοῦ προτετιμῆσθαι αὐτοὺς, ἐπεχείρησε καταλῦσαι τὴν ἀρχὴν αὐτῶν, οἵ τε βασιλεῖς οὐδεπώποτε μειζόνων ὠρέχθησαν ἢ ἐφ' οἷσπερ ἐξ ἀρχῆς τὴν βασιλείαν παρέλαβον. τοιγαροῦν ἄλλη μὲν οὐδεμία ἀρχὴ φανερά ἐστι διαγεγενημένη ἀδιάσπαστος οὔτε δημοκρατία οὔτε ὀλιγαρχία οὔτε τύραννις οὔτε βασιλεία· αὕτη δὲ μόνη διαμένει συνεχὴς βασιλεία.* The same fact is also insisted on in the treatise on the Lacedæmonian Commonwealth (15) which goes by his name, and he adds the custom of the monthly oath—like that of the Molossians—exchanged between the Kings and the Ephors on behalf of the city; *ὁ δὲ ὅρκος ἐστὶ, τῷ μὲν βασιλεῖ κατὰ τοὺς τῆς πόλεως κειμένους νόμους βασιλεύειν, τῇ δὲ πόλει ἐμπεδορκοῦντος ἐκείνου ἀστυφέλικτον τὴν βασιλείαν παρέξειν.* He adds—*αὗται μὲν οὖν αἱ τιμαὶ οἴκοι* [as opposed to his military command] *ζῶντι* [as opposed to the extravagant honours which he received after death.] *βασιλεῖ δέδονται, οὐδέν τι πολὺ ὑπερφέρουσαι τῶν ἰδιωτικῶν· οὐ γὰρ ἐβουλήθη οὔτε τοῖς βασιλεῦσι τυραννικὸν φρόνημα παραστῆσαι οὔτε τοῖς πολίταις φθόνον ἐμποιῆσαι τῆς δυνάμεως.* Dionysios, in the speech assigned to Brutus, which I have quoted several times, makes the deliverer speak of the consulship as following the model of the Spartan kingship. The power of the Roman Consul was certainly greater than that of the Spartan Kings. But an hereditary office is essentially different from one held by yearly election. The Spartan kingship was real kingship with its powers cut very short: the consulship was the kingly power put into perpetual commission.

(20) Page 149.—We have several notices of the Argeian Kings. Pausanias (ii. 19, 1) mentions that, from the reign of a certain King Mêdôn, the royal power became merely nominal, and that after Meltas, who is placed (Clinton. Fast. Hell. i. 249) in the days of Kleisthenês of Sikyôn, kingship was abolished altogether; *Ἀργεῖοι δὲ, ἅτε ἰσηγορίαν καὶ τὸ αὐτόνομον ἀγαπῶντες ἐκ παλαιοτάτου, τὰ τῆς ἐξουσίας τῶν βασιλέων ἐς ἐλάχιστον προήγαγον, ὡς Μήδωνι τῷ Κείσου καὶ τοῖς ἀπογόνοις τὸ ὄνομα λειφθῆναι τῆς βασιλείας μόνον. Μέλταν δὲ τὸν Λακίδου τὸν ἀπόγονον Μήδωνος τὸ παράπαν ἔπαυσεν ἀρχῆς καταγνοὺς ὁ δῆμος.* It is plain however that kingship went on much longer. There is a story told by Plutarch in his treatise *περὶ τῆς Ἀλεξάνδρου τύχης ἢ ἀρετῆς* (ii. 8), according to which kingship had such a hold at Argos that, when the old Hêrakleid line died out, another King was chosen, in obedience of course to divine signs; *ἐξέλιπεν Ἀργείοις ποτὲ τὸ Ἡρακλειδῶν γένος, ἐξ οὗ βασιλεύεσθαι πάτριον ἦν αὐτοῖς. ζητοῦσι δὲ καὶ διαπυνθανομένοις ὁ θεὸς ἔχρησεν ἀετὸν δείξειν· καὶ μεθ' ἡμέρας ὀλίγας ἀετὸς ὑπερφανεὶς καὶ καταρὰς ἐπὶ τὴν Αἴγωνος οἰκίαν ἐκάθισε, καὶ βασιλεὺς ᾑρέθη Αἴγων.* He has another reference to this election of Aigôn in his treatise on the Pythian oracles (5), where he speaks casually of *χρησμοῦ τινος ἐμμέτρου λεχθέντος, οἶμαι, περὶ τῆς Αἴγωνος τοῦ Ἀργείου βασιλείας.* But the most important notice is that in the well-known passage of Herodotus (vii. 148, 149), where he tells us how, on the coming of Xerxes, the Argeians claimed, if they joined in the defence of Greece, to have an equal share in the command with the Lacedæmonians. The Lacedæmonians answered that, as they had two Kings, while the Argeians had only one, the command could not be equally divided. Neither of the Spartan Kings could be deprived of his vote, but they were ready to allow the Argeian King a third vote along with their own two (*λέγειν*

σφὶ μὲν εἶναι δύο βασιλῆας, Ἀργείοισι δὲ ἕνα· οὔκων δυνατὸν εἶναι τῶν ἐκ Σπάρτης οὐδέτερον παῦσαι τῆς ἡγεμονίης· μετὰ δὲ δύο τῶν σφετέρων ὁμόψηφον τὸν Ἀργεῖον εἶναι κωλύειν οὐδέν). It would seem from this passage that the Argeian King, whatever his position may have been in other ways, at least retained the military command. The Spartans would never have proposed to give an equal vote with their own Kings to a magistrate whose functions were merely civil or priestly. The Argeian King would thus be one of the class spoken of by Aristotle in the extract in Note 17.

(21) Page 149.—We get a vivid mention of the King-archon at Athens and his functions in the opening of the oration of Lysias against Andokidês. He puts the possible case of so impious a person as Andokidês drawing the successful lot for this archonship: ἂν νυνὶ Ἀνδοκίδης ἀθῶος ἀπαλλαγῇ ἡμῶν ἐκ τοῦδε τοῦ ἀγῶνος καὶ ἔλθῃ κληρωσόμενος τῶν ἐννέα ἀρχόντων καὶ λάχῃ βασιλεύς. He goes on to speak of a great number of religious duties which the King had to discharge. But presently he has to bring in the word in its more usual sense; for he goes on to say that Andokidês, in the course of his travels, had been a flatterer of many Kings, among which class Dionysios of Syracuse is reckoned by implication (βασιλέας πολλοὺς κεκολάκευκεν, ᾧ ἂν ξυγγένηται, πλὴν τοῦ Συρακουσίου Διονυσίου). Dionysios, according to the orator, was a match for Andokidês, and would not be taken in by him.

The wife of the King-archon was *βασίλισσα*, as the wife of the Roman "rex sacrorum" was called "regina." (Cf. Pseudo-Dem. c. Neær. 98.)

Besides the King-archon, there was another survival of kingship at Athens in the form of the *Phylobasileis*, who seem to be the same as the βασιλεῖς spoken of in the law of Solôn quoted by Plutarch (Solôn, 19). Plutarch seems directly afterwards to speak of them as πρυτάνεις. Very little seems to be known about the nature of their duties, but it is with their kingly title alone that we are now concerned. They must, one would think, have been the Kings of the four Ionic tribes before they were thoroughly fused into one commonwealth, something like the local Under-kings of the West-Saxons. In any case, they are another instance of the kingly title continuing to be held after all kingly power had passed away, and that by magistrates who held no very important place in the commonwealth.

(22) Page 150.—Mommsen, probably with truth, looks on the whole legend of Romulus as comparatively late. The real ancient name of the city lurks in that of the *Ramnes*, and the ἐπώνυμος betrays his late origin by having his name formed from the later name of the city. However this may be, the legend which makes Romulus the son of Mars clearly shows an intermixture of Greek ideas. In the genuine Italian religion, not only is no man the son of a God, but there does not seem to be anything like generation or birth among the Gods themselves. The deities appear in pairs, male and female, and that is all; they are called "Patres" and "Matres" directly in their divine character. See Preller, *Römische Mythologie*, 50. The story of Numa and Egeria probably comes from the same hellenizing mint as the story of his having been a pupil of Pythagoras.

(23) Page 151.—I mean that there is nothing strictly mythical about these stories; the institutions of Ancus and Servius are real; their authors, and the dates assigned to them, may be fabulous, but there is nothing of divine or heroic legend about the story. We know, from the example

of undoubtedly real lawgivers like Solôn and Ælfred, that such lawgivers constantly draw, as it were, to themselves all manner of institutions, both earlier and later than their own times. On this ground we distrust the accounts of the legislations of Ancus and Servius; but, though they may not be historical, they are at least *quasi-historical.* See Historical Essays, First Series, p. 4.

(24) Page 151.—Whatever we make of the historical value of the stories of the Tarquinii and Servius, to say nothing of Numa, it is plain that they could have arisen only among a people who paid no regard whatever to birth in the appointment of their Kings, and among whom the choice of a stranger, or even of a slave, was at least theoretically not impossible. It will of course be remembered that Claudius got hold of an altogether different account of the origin of Servius; still, though he is not described as a slave, he is described as a stranger.

(25) Page 152.—There was a *gens Romilia* at Rome, but it was of little eminence and never produced a curule magistrate. I do not know that there is any evidence that its members claimed descent from the founders of the city.

(26) Page 153.—See the account in Herodotus (vi. 67) of the bitterness of the taunt addressed by Leotychidês to Dêmaratos, when he asks him *ὁκοῖόν τι εἴη τὸ ἄρχειν μετὰ τὸ βασιλεύειν.*

(27) Page 153.—See Fed. Gov. i. 433.

(28) Page 154.—I am not able to lay my hand on any better authority than that of Justin (ii. 7): "Post Codrum

nemo Athenis regnavit, quod memoriæ nominis ejus tributum est." If any such motive was avowed, it must have been a mere pretext, as the abolition of kingship was a step which was unavoidable sooner or later. Still we have the fact that the Roman story represents the last King as a hateful tyrant who was driven out for his crimes, while the Athenian story represents the last King as one who devoted his life for the safety of his country, and whose memory was ever after cherished with the deepest reverence. In short, the civic kingship was so impossible to last that neither a good nor a bad King could save it, and either the crimes or the virtues of a King might be assigned as a reason for getting rid of it.

(29) Page 154.—I see no reason to doubt the common story as to the gradual fall of the archonship at Athens from the old hereditary kingship to a magistracy needing so little either of personal qualification or of the charm of illustrious ancestry that any citizen of decent character was held to be fit to hold it. First we have the single Archon for life out of the old royal family; then the single Archon for ten years, still out of the old royal family; then the board of nine yearly Archons, aristocratic or democratic, chosen or taken by lot, according to the gradual stages in the developement of the commonwealth. The interposition of a *δυναστεία*, a single family from which magistrates were chosen, seems to have been a common stage between kingship and the fully developed commonwealth, first aristocratic, then democratic. The Corinthian Bacchiads are a well-known instance; but perhaps the most interesting example is that of the Chaonians in Epeiros (see below, note 36). We might also compare the tendency, even where there are no legal distinctions, to keep the great magistracies

in certain distinguished families, as was formerly the case with the Swiss democracies (see Growth of the English Constitution, p. 27). The difference, of course, is that in this last case the *δυναστεία* had no acknowledged existence. Tschudi or Attinghausen might practically be an *ἀρχικὸν γένος*; but this was simply because the electors habitually chose from among them: they had no privilege by law.

(30) Page 154.—In the Parian Chronicle (Boeckh, ii. 301) the Archons for life appear as Kings. It is only when the archonship becomes annual that the style is changed. The 48th entry stands thus: *βασιλεύοντος Ἀθηνῶν Αἰσχύλου ἔτους εἰκοστοῦ καὶ ἑνὸς, ἀφ᾽ οὗ κατ᾽ ἐνιαυτὸν ἦρχεν ὁ ἄρχων·* while in the 49th we have the usual form, *ἄρχοντος Ἀθήνησι Τλησία.* So Pausanias (vii. 2, 1) describes the sons of Kodros as disputing about the succession after his death, and uses the word *βασιλεύειν—οὐκ ἔφασκεν ὁ Νειλεὺς ἀνέξεσθαι βασιλευόμενος ὑπὸ τοῦ Μέδοντος.* What then was the difference between the Archon who was still called a King and the undoubted Kings who had gone before him? I conceive it to be that the King or Archon now became strictly responsible, as we have seen (see note 19) that the Spartan Kings were. In Greek ideas, the lack of responsibility seems to have been the essence of true kingship. Thus in the Persians of Æschylus (213), Atossa speaks of her son Xerxes as *οὐχ ὑπεύθυνος πόλει*, and we find this responsibility given as the actual definition of kingship by two later writers. Suidas, for instance, under the word *βασιλεία*, thus defines it—*βασιλεία ἐστὶν ἀνυπεύθυνος ἀρχή· οὐ μόνον δὲ ἐλευθέρους εἶναι τοὺς σπουδαίους ἀλλὰ καὶ βασιλέας. ἡ γὰρ βασιλεία ἀρχὴ ἀνυπεύθυνος, ἥτις περὶ μόνους ἂν τοὺς σόφους συσταίη.* So Diôn Chrysostom (i. 46): *βασιλεία δὲ ἀνυπεύθυνος ἀρχὴ, ὁ δὲ νόμος*

*βασιλέως δόγμα.* In this last we have a forestalling of the great doctrine of the Civil Law, though the Greek rhetorician does not stop to trouble himself with any theories about the "lex regia." I conceive that, though the King or Archon was still appointed for life, yet he became subject, like the magistrates who came after him, to the obligations of the formal *δοκιμασία* and *εὐθύνη*. This is quite another thing from a possible power of deposition, which, even if legally recognized, must always be something extraordinary and unusual. Some confusion between this state of things and the King-archon of the confirmed democracy may be traced in the words of the Pseudo-Demosthenês against Neaira (98): *ἐπειδὴ δὲ Θησεὺς συνῴκισεν αὐτοὺς καὶ δημοκρατίαν ἐποίησε καὶ ἡ πόλις πολυάνθρωπος ἐγένετο, τὸν μὲν βασιλέα οὐδὲν ἧττον ὁ δῆμος ᾑρεῖτο ἐκ προκρίτων κατ' ἀνδραγαθίαν χειροτονῶν.* This last statement leaves out of sight the fact that the kingship or archonship was confined to the single house of Kodros. In fact, at this stage of the Athenian constitution, the King or Archon, hereditary or at most chosen out of a single family, holding his office for life, but responsible for its administration, must have been exactly like the Spartan King, except that he had no colleague.

(31) Page 155.—See Historical Essays, Second Series, p. 126.

(32) Page 155.—Diôn Cassius (lxix. 16). Ἁδριανὸς . . . . *τὰ Διονύσια, τὴν μεγίστην παρ' αὐτοῖς ἀρχὴν ἄρξας, ἐν τῇ ἐσθῆτι τῇ ἐπιχωρίῳ λαμπρῶς ἐπετέλεσε.* That is to say, he was the *ἄρχων ἐπώνυμος* of the year.

(33) Page 155.—See Niebuhr, *Römische Geschichte*, i. 544, i. 509 of the English translation.

(34) Page 156.—See Historical Essays, Second Series, p. 127.

(35) Page 157.—The Presidency of the Senate and of the Assembly, the right of putting the question and deciding points of order, forms of itself an important distinction between the Roman Consuls and the Athenian Archons. The Archons, at all events after the establishment of the fullgrown democracy, never presided in the Assembly. That function belonged to the Prytaneis of the tribes in turn, as comes out strongly in the famous case of the presidency of Sôkratês in the debates after Arginousai. At Sparta, on the other hand, the debate recorded by Thucydides (i. 87) shows that this power was vested in the Ephors. It is plain that, if the powers of the Prytaneis and of the Archons had been in the same hands, the position of the magistrates who held those conjoint powers would have been far higher than that of either Prytaneis or Archons separately. It would have been inconvenient to place it in the hands of the Generals, the really highest executive magistrates of the Commonwealth, because it was perhaps already beginning to be felt that the position of Speaker and that of Leader of the House ought to be distinct. This came out still more strongly in the Achaian Assembly, where the Dêmiourgoi acted as Speakers, while the General acted as Leader of the House. See History of Federal Government, i. 296. I may perhaps be allowed to add that some remarks on this matter will be found in a letter from Sir George Lewis, the last which I had from him, which appears at p. 427 of his published Letters. My answer to that letter led to some changes in Sir George Lewis' views, which were embodied in the last thing which he wrote, the article on the Presidency of Deliberative Assemblies, which is referred to at p. 430 of

the Letters. I could have wished that all three, his letter and mine and that article, had appeared together.

The Roman magistrate also, the Consul in his Assembly and the Tribune in his, had a right of yet further importance, namely that he alone could make proposals to the Assembly. This, perhaps more than anything else, marks the far greater power of the Roman magistrates as compared with those of Athens.

(36) Page 159. Thuc. ii. 8. *Χάονες ἀβασίλευτοι, ὧν ἡγοῦντο ἐπ' ἐτησίῳ προστασίᾳ ἐκ τοῦ ἀρχικοῦ γένους Φώτυος καὶ Νικάνωρ.* See above, note 29.

(37) Page 159.—On the Epeirot League, see Hist. Fed. Gov. i. 150. I have there spoken of the oath of the Molossian Kings, as also in the Growth of the English Constitution, p. 229.

(38) Page 159.—Of the Macedonian Assemblies I shall have more to say in the next lecture.

(39) Page 159.—On the four Macedonian Commonwealths, see Hist. Fed. Gov. 661.

(40) Page 160.—Seleukeia, as the chief Eastern outpost of Western civilization, remained a free city with a republican constitution till a very late time. The decline and fall of the Seleukid monarchy no doubt did much to strengthen its independence. In the time of Tiberius, Tacitus (Annals, vi. 42) speaks of Seleukeia as a free commonwealth, with a Senate of three hundred and a popular Assembly. But, usually the two orders did not agree, and the Parthian Kings

sometimes stepped in to support the oligarchic interest. "Seleucenses, civitas potens, septa muris, neque in barbarum corrupta, sed conditoris Seleuci retinens. Trecenti, opibus aut sapientia delecti, ut Senatus; sua populo vis: et, quoties concordes agunt, spernitur Parthus; ubi dissensere, dum sibi quisque contra æmulos subsidium vocant, accitus in partem, adversum omnes valescit. Id nuper acciderat, Artabano regnante, qui plebem primoribus tradidit ex suo usu: nam populi imperium juxta libertatem; paucorum dominatio regiæ libidini propior est." Pliny too (Hist. Nat. vi. 30) speaks of it as "libera hodie ac sui juris Macedonumque moris."

(41) Page 160.—See Historical Essays, Second Series, pp. 180, 184.

(42) Page 161.—On the importance of the "potestas tribunitia" Tacitus speaks strongly, when he says (Annals, iii. 56): "Id summi fastigii vocabulum Augustus repperit, ne Regis aut Dictatoris nomen adsumeret, ac tamen adpellatione aliqua cetera imperia præmineret." He goes on to explain that the grant of the *tribunitia potestas* to Drusus was the same thing as naming him successor to the Empire. On the way in which the union of all powers grew into a power greater than any of them, compare the words put into the mouth of Tiberius himself a little before (iii. 53), "quia non Ædilis, aut Prætoris, aut Consulis partes sustineo: majus aliquid et excelsius a Principe postulatur."

There is a most curious discussion in John Lydus (De Magistratibus, i. 3) of the distinction between *τύραννος*, *βασιλεύς*, and *αὐτοκράτωρ*, and (in ii. 1–3) there is also a description of the powers granted to both the elder and the younger Cæsar. The passages are much too long to quote in full; but it should be noted that this writer, writing in Greek in the sixth century but in a thoroughly Roman character, distinctly denies the power of the Emperors to be either *βασιλεία* or *τυραννίς*. *ἔστι γὰρ βασιλέως μὲν τρόπος ὁ νόμος, τυράννου δὲ νόμος ὁ τρόπος. τὸ γὰρ τῶν Καισάρων ἤγουν αὐτοκρατόρων ἐπώνυμον οὐδὲ βασιλείας, ἀλλ' οὐδὲ τυραννίδος ἐστὶ σημαντικόν, αὐταρχίας δὲ μᾶλλον καὶ αὐθεντίας τοῦ διοικεῖν τοὺς ἐξανισταμένους κατὰ τῶν κοινῶν θορύβους ἐπὶ τὸ κάλλιον. ἐπιτάττειν τε τῷ στρατεύματι πῶς ἂν δέοι μάχεσθαι τοῖς ἐναντίοις·* imperare *γὰρ τὸ ἐπιτάττειν παρ' Ἰταλοῖς λέγεται, ἔνθεν ἰμπεράτωρ.* All this has the force of a protest, when we remember how familiarly the name of *βασιλεύς* had for ages been applied to the Emperors. Lydus very naturally sets down Marius and Sulla as Tyrants: but, what we should hardly have looked for, he sets down Romulus as a Tyrant also, and argues at some length that the Latin *Rex* answers to the Greek *τύραννος*. There is not a glimmering to be seen of the great dispute about *ῥήξ* and *βασιλεύς* three hundred years later.

(43) Page 161.—See above, note 18.

(44) Page 161.—Theodoric was undoubtedly Consul, though his patriciate stands out more conspicuously in history. Both he and Odoacer were Patricians by Imperial commission. For the patriciate of Odoacer see the fragment of Malchos in the Bonn edition, p. 235. The Senate asks Zênôn to bestow that rank on Odoacer; *πατρικίου τε αὐτῷ ἀποστεῖλαι ἀξίαν, καὶ τὴν τῶν Ἰταλῶν τούτῳ ἀφεῖναι διοίκησιν*, and the Emperor does so accordingly, *βασίλειον γράμμα περὶ ὧν ἠβούλετο πέμπων τῷ Ὀδοάχῳ, πατρίκιον ἐν τούτῳ τῷ γράμματι ἐπωνόμασε.* Of Theodoric the anonymous writer printed at the end of Ammianus (717) says; "Zeno recompensans Theodoricum, quem fecit patricium et consulem, donans

ei multum et mittens eum ad Italiam." He goes on calling him "Patricius" in a marked way. But Jornandes (57) emphatically brings out the consulship of Theodoric; "factus est consul ordinarius, quod summum bonum primumque in mundo decus edicitur."

(45) Page 161.—It was held to be the peculiar good luck of Boetius that he was not only Consul himself but saw his sons Consuls. See the Consolatio, ii. 3, 4.

(46) Page 161.—Jornandes (60) tells us pointedly how "Justinianus Imperator per fidelissimum Consulem vicit Belisarium, et perductum Witigim Constantinopolim Patricii honore donavit." So Prokopios (Bell. Goth. i. 5) pointedly marks that he was still Consul at the time of his conquest of Sicily, and that his year of office came to an end on the very day on which he entered Syracuse. *τῷ δὲ Βελισαρίῳ τότε κρεῖσσον λόγου εὐτύχημα ξυνηνέχθη γενέσθαι. τῆς γὰρ ὑπατείας λαβὼν τὸ ἀξίωμα ἐπὶ τῷ Βανδίλους νενικηκέναι, ταύτης ἔτι ἐχόμενος, ἐπειδὴ παρεστήσατο Σικελίαν ὅλην, τῇ τῆς ὑπατείας ἐσχάτῃ ἡμέρᾳ ἐς τὰς Συρακούσας ἐσήλασε.* He goes on to say, *οὐκ ἐξεπίτηδες μέντοι αὐτῷ πεποίητο τοῦτο, ἀλλά τις τῷ ἀνθρώπῳ ξυνέβη τύχη πᾶσαν ἀνασωσαμένῳ τὴν νῆσον Ῥωμαίοις ἐκείνῃ τῇ ἡμέρᾳ ἐς τὰς Συρακούσας ἐσεληλακέναι, τήν τε τῶν ὑπάτων ἀρχὴν, οὐκ ᾗπερ εἰώθει ἐν τῷ Βυζαντίου βουλευτηρίῳ, ἀλλ' ἐνταῦθα καταθεμένῳ ἐξ ὑπάτων γενέσθαι.*

(47) Page 161.—That Constantine held the office of General at Athens is recorded by his nephew Julian in his first oration, addressed to Constantius (8): *βασιλεὺς γὰρ ὢν, καὶ κύριος πάντων, στρατηγὸς ἐκείνων ἠξίου καλεῖσθαι, καὶ τοιαύτης εἰκόνος τυγχάνων μετ' ἐπιγράμματος, ἐγάννυτο πλέον ἢ τῶν μεγίστων τιμῶν ἀξιωθείς.* He goes on to speak of the

gifts of corn which Constantine made to the Athenians, *ἀμειβόμενος ἐπ' αὐτῷ τὴν πόλιν.* See Finlay, Greece under the Romans, 340.

(48) Page 161.—Plutarch, Cæsar, 60. *ἐκεῖνος οὐκ ἔφη βασιλεὺς ἀλλὰ Καῖσαρ καλεῖσθαι.*

(49) Page 161.—It is hardly needful to collect examples of this usage from the New Testament onwards, and indeed one or two have come incidentally in the extracts which I have already given. But it is worth noticing how completely the orations of Diôn Chrysostom addressed to Trajan assume the dominion of the Emperors to be a *βασιλεία*, though *βασιλεία* is throughout pointedly opposed to *τυραννίς*. In one place in the third oration (i. 46), after describing the oppressive ruler, Diôn says, *οὐκ ἄν ποτε εἴποιμι τὸν τοιοῦτον ἄρχοντα ἢ αὐτοκράτορα ἢ βασιλέα, πολὺ δὲ μᾶλλον τύραννον καὶ λευστῆρα, ὥς ποτε προςεῖπεν ὁ Ἀπόλλων τὸν Σικυώνιον τύραννον.* In another place in the second oration (i. 37), he incidentally brings out that solitary position of the Roman ruler which was so strikingly enforced by Mr. Goldwin Smith at the end of his famous review of Mr. Congreve. The good King is to do this and that for the public good, *πρὸς δὲ τοὺς ἄλλους βασιλέας, εἴ τινες ἄρα εἶεν, ἁμιλλᾶσθαι περὶ τῆς ἀρετῆς.* The difference between this writer and one so much later as John Lydus is the difference between a Greek rhetorician speaking in a loose way of things as he practically found them, and a Roman lawyer, who happened to write in Greek, but who still dealt with the legal and historical side of things from a purely Roman point of view.

(50) Page 161.—John Lydus (i. 4) points out the wearing of the diadem and the royal robes as an innovation of Dio-

cletian, adding that he thereby ἐπὶ τὸ βασιλικὸν ἢ τἀληθὲς εἰπεῖν ἐπὶ τὸ τυραννικὸν ἔτρεψεν. Compare Aurelius Victor, Cæsares, 39.

(51) Page 161.—The word *regnum* is applied to the imperial rule, even by Tacitus, though it would seem always with somewhat of sarcasm. Thus in the Annals (xii. 66) Locusta is said to have been "diu inter instrumenta regni habita" and again (xiii. 14) it is said of Pallas that "velut arbitrum regni agebat." But much earlier (Annals, i. 4) Tacitus speaks of the house of Augustus as "domus regnatrix" seemingly without any sarcastic meaning.

(52) Page 161.—The name *regia* is more than once applied by Tacitus to the Imperial dwelling. Thus in the Annals (xi. 29) Callistus, the former favourite of Caius, is described under Claudius as "prioris quoque regiæ peritus" and in xiv. 13 it is said of the palace of Nero "deterrimus quisque, quorum non alia regia fecundior exstitit." Here again there probably is sarcasm, but we must remember that the house of the Emperor was formally *regia* in his character of High Pontiff. If we leap from Tacitus to the next Latin writer who deserves the name of historian, we find, in the very first chapter of Ammianus which is preserved to us, the word *regia*, and pretty well every other derivative of *rex*, used as a matter of course, but *rex* itself never.

(53) Page 161.—In the opening chapter of Ammianus (xiv. 1) the name *regina* is twice applied to the Empress Eusebia. So again xvi. 10. So in xiv. 1, we read of "regia stirps" and in xix. 11 of "sella regalis."

(54) Page 161.—It is quite certain that no Emperor is

ever called *rex* by any Latin writer. That the title was given to Hannibalianus the nephew of Constantine is also quite certain (see the opening chapter of Ammianus and the Article in the Dictionary of Biography). At any time before the decree of Antoninus Caracalla, one would have said that he was meant to be King, not over Rome or Romans, but, like the sons of the Triumvir Antonius, over some of the provinces of the Roman Empire. But this seems hardly to apply, now that all the subjects of the Empire were alike Romans. Still this title stands quite by itself, and it is most striking to find the word *rex* never applied to the Emperor, though all its derivatives are so freely applied to his belongings.

(55) Page 162.—For the Roman appointments of Alaric see Zôsimos, v. 5, 31, vi. 7.

(56) Page 162.—The consulship of Chlodwig comes from Gregory of Tours, ii. 38. "Igitur Chlodovechus ab Anastasio imperatore codicillos de consulatu accepit, et in basilica beati Martini tunica blatea indutus est et chlamyde, imponens vertici diadema." He was saluted by the people "tanquam consul aut Augustus." The confusion between Consul and Augustus, in the mind either of Chlodwig or of Gregory, may remind one of the like confusion in the mind of Rienzi, when he called himself "candidatus Spiritûs Sancti miles, Nicolaus severus et clemens, Liberator Urbis, Zelator Italiæ, amator Orbis, et Tribunus Augustus." Cronica Sanese, 1347. Muratori, xv. 118. Chronicon Estense, ib. 441.

(57) Page 162.—See Bryce, Holy Roman Empire, 404. Joseph the Second was the last who bore this title, having

been elected in 1764, during the lifetime of his father, and becoming Emperor-elect on his death the next year.

(58) Page 163.—See Growth of the English Constitution, 17, 169.

(59) Page 163.—So the Peterborough Chronicle, 449. "Fram þan Wodne awoc eall ure cynecynn, and Suðanhymbra eac." The contrary process seems to be set forth by King Ælfred when he tells the story of Odysseus and Kirkê; "þa wæs þær Apollines dohtor, Iobes suna, se Iob wæs hiora cyning, and licette þæt he sceolde bion se hehsta god, and þæt dysige folc him gelyfde, forþam ðe he wæs cyne-cynnes, and hi nyston nænne oþerne god on þæne timan, buton hiora cyningas hi weorþodon for godas. Ða sceolde þæs Iobes fæder bion eac god, þæs nama wæs Saturnus, and his swa ilce æl cine hi hæfdon for god."

(60) Page 164.—See Norman Conquest, i. 593.

(61) Page 164.—See Waitz, *Deutsche Verfassungsgeschichte*, i. 68, 166.

(62) Page 165.—See above, note 76 on Lecture III.

(63) Page 165.—See Growth of the English Constitution, 34, 171.

(64) Page 166.—All people, save those who fancy that the name *King* has something to do with a Tartar *Khan* or with a "canning" or "cunning" man, are agreed that the English *Cyning* and the Sanscrit *Ganaka* both come from the same root, from that widely spread root whence comes

our own *cyn* or *kin* and the Greek *γένος*. The only question is whether there is any connexion between *cyning* and *ganaka* closer than that which is implied in their both coming from the same original root. That is to say, are we to suppose that *cyning* and *ganaka* are strictly the same word, common to Sanscrit and Teutonic, or is it enough to think that *cyning* is an independent formation, made after the Teutons had separated themselves from the common stock? The former view is maintained by Professor Max Müller, in the later editions of the Science of Language (ii. 285), with an array of German scholarship which it is hard to resist. On the other hand it is equally hard for an Englishman, looking to his own language only, to resist the obvious derivation of *cyning* as the direct offspring of *cyn*. See Norman Conquest, i. 583, Growth of the English Constitution, 171. The difference between the two derivations is not very remote, as the *cyn* is the ruling idea in either case; but if we make the word immediately cognate with *ganaka*, we bring in a notion about "the father of his people," which has no place, if we simply derive *cyning* from *cyn*.

(65) Page 167.—See the pedigrees of Æthelwulf in the Chronicles under the year 855. They go straight up to Woden, and thence to Noah and Adam; but Woden is not made to spring from Shem, Ham, or Japheth, but from Sceaf the son of Noah, who was born in the ark.

(66) Page 170.—Joshua ix. 2.

(67) Page 170.—Genesis xxxvi. 14. The Hebrew אַלּוּף from אֶלֶף *gens*, answers however better to *cyning* than to *heretoga*.

(68) Page 171.—See the instances which I have collected

in Note K in the Appendix to the first Volume of the Norman Conquest, and at page 172 of the Growth of the English Constitution. Another passage about the Goths will be found in Zôsimos, iv. 34. Frithigern is *ἡγεμών*, while he speaks of *'Αθάναριχόν τε πάντος τοῦ βασιλείου τῶν Σκύθων ἄρχοντα γένους*.

(69) Page 171.—This is the argument assumed throughout Dante's great treatise *De Monarchia.* See Historical Essays, First Series.

(70) Page 172.—See Norman Conquest, i. 26. Compare for Mercia also the account of the battle of Winfield, where Penda fell "and xxx cynebearna mid him, and þa wæron sume ciningas." This last notice comes from the Peterborough Chronicler only. We may again compare the description given by Ammianus (xvi. 12) of the Alemanni at the battle of Strassburg. Chnodomarius, the Bretwalda, so to speak, comes first; then some other chiefs by name; "Hos sequebantur potestate proximi Reges numero quinque, *Regalesque* [probably Æthelings] decem." The Batavians also in the same account have several Kings.

(71) Page 173.—See Growth of the English Constitution, 172.

(72) Page 173.—See the famous passage in the Iliad, ii. 188.

(73) Page 174.—I shall have to speak more fully of this in my last lecture.

(74) Page 175.—According to the famous doctrine of the Civil Law (Inst. i. 2. 6.) "quod principi placuit, legis habet vigorem; quum lege regia, quæ de ejus imperio lata est,

populus ei in eum omne imperium suum et potestatem concedat." With this lawyers' theory of the origin of the Empire one may well compare the pithy account given by Tacitus (Ann. i. 2) of its real origin: "Cæsar dux reliquus, posito Triumviri nomine, Consulem se ferens et ad tuendam plebem tribunicio jure contentum; ubi militem donis, populum annona, cunctos dulcedine otii pellexit, insurgere paullatim, munia Senatûs, magistratuum, legum, in se trahere, nullo adversante."

(75) Page 175.—See Norman Conquest, i. 584. It is worth while to compare the definition given by Suidas under the word *βασιλεύς*. *Βασιλεὺς μέγας, ὁ τῶν Περσῶν. τοὺς δὲ ἄλλους προσετίθεσαν καὶ τῶν ἀρχομένων τὰ ὀνόματα, οἷον Λακεδαιμόνιοι, Μακεδόνες.* He then goes on to distinguish *βασιλεύς* and *τύραννος*, and to point out how Pindar and others had applied the name *βασιλεύς* to tyrants.

(76) Page 176.—I suppose that Russia is now the only European state to which this description would apply, the only one where the sovereign can legislate by himself, without even the form of consulting a national assembly of any kind.

(77) Page 177.—See Norman Conquest, i. 23, 78, Growth of the English Constitution, 37.

(78) Page 177.—See Growth of the English Constitution, 153.

(79) Page 178.—See Norman Conquest, iv. 430.

(80) Page 179.—See Norman Conquest, i. 24.

(81) Page 179.—The recovery of southern Spain to the

Empire in the wars of Belisarius must always be borne in mind, if we wish to have an accurate notion either of the map of Europe or of the position of the Empire in the sixth and seventh centuries. See above, note 32 on Lecture II.

(82) Page 180.—See Norman Conquest, i. 78.

(83) Page 181.—"Mundi Dominus" was always the title of the mediæval Emperors. Take for instance the poem on Frederick Barbarossa published by Grimm (9), which begins "Salve, mundi domine; Cæsar noster, ave."

(84) Page 181.—The *kingdom* of Henry of Saxony and Rudolf of Habsburg, the greatest among the German Kings who never received the Imperial crown; not, in any strictness, the *Empire* of Charles and Otto. Yet the use of the title of Emperor by the head of a confederation of princes can hardly be wondered at.

(85) Page 182.—On the various names of the kingdoms which sprang up out of the divisions of the Frankish Empire, see Appendix T in the first volume of the History of the Norman Conquest, "Names of Kingdoms and Nations."

(86) Page 182.—I mean that, up to the extinction of the Hohenstaufen, the Empire followed that mixture of election and hereditary descent which was the law of all the Teutonic kingdoms. Then came a time during which birth was hardly regarded at all, though there was some faint approach to a dynasty in the Lüzelburg Kings of Bohemia. Then came the long period which begins in the middle of the fifteenth century, during which, though other candidates were often talked of, yet the Electors always chose an Austrian prince, com-

monly the heir of the Austrian Duchy, or, as in the case of Charles the Seventh, an unsuccessful claimant of that Duchy, or, as in the case of Francis the First, the husband of its Archduchess.

(87) Page 183.—See Norman Conquest, iv. 1695.

(88) Page 184.—I cannot be said to be speaking too strongly on this point, when it is remembered that, in a book on Italy by Lord Chief Justice Whiteside, Switzerland was spoken of as "a Confederation of small Kingdoms." It matters very little whether the writer really believed that there were twenty-two or twenty-five Kings in Switzerland, or whether he merely thought that the difference between kingdoms and commonwealths was of so little consequence that either word might be used indiscriminately for the other. In either case it is an extreme illustration of the common ignorance and carelessness about such matters. In the common notices of Swiss matters in the newspapers, the cantonal Government of Geneva—because it is from Geneva that the telegrams come—seems always to be confounded with the Federal Government. Would the same writers mistake the Governor of the State of New York for the President of the United States?

Besides the Commonwealths of Switzerland, we must not forget the Commonwealth of Andorra, now looking calmly, as a steady elder sister, on the commotions of the younger and less successful commonwealths on either side of her.

(89) Page 186.—On all these matters I would refer to the Essay on Presidential Government which stands last in my first Series of Historical Essays.

(90) Page 187.—The legitimate descent of Queen Eliza-

beth from Edward the Third through the house of York takes in nine generations of ancestors, two only of whom, her father and his grandfather Edward the Fourth, were Kings. And of them, only Henry himself came in by quiet succession. Her descent by the other line, that of Henry the Seventh, through the legitimated children of John of Gaunt, is still less kingly.

## LECTURE V.

(1) Page 191.—On the relations of the Achaian cities to the League, see History of Federal Government, i. 256.

(2) Page 192.—On the constitution of the Achaian Federal Assembly, see History of Federal Government. i. 263.

(3) Page 193.—We may see this process in England, as the small independent Kings and Ealdormen in Mercia sink into Ealdormen named by the central King of the Mercians, and again as the West-Saxon Under-kings of the royal house are also supplanted by Ealdormen. And the same process goes on as the several kingdoms are merged in one kingdom. The stages of this process are well marked in the cases of Mercia. From independent and conquering Kings like Penda and Offa, we come, in the days of Ælfred, to a King like Burhred, who is the man of the King of the West-Saxons; and then, between this sort of kingship and absolute incorporation, comes the stage represented by Æthelred and Æthelflæd. See Appendix F in the first volume of the Norman Conquest.

(4) Page 193.—The first Sunday in May is always the day of meeting for the *Landesgemeinde* of Uri, and the regular days of meeting for all the other *Landesgemeinden* come at the same time of the year. The distinctive peculiarities of

all the *Landesgemeinden* of which I have seen those only of Uri and Appenzell-Ausserrhoden are described at length by M. Rambert in an article in the *Bibliothéque Universelle* in the course of 1872.

(5) Page 195.—The mere slave, the *servus*, δοῦλος, or *þeow*, has, by the nature of the case, no political rights, because he has not even the common rights of humanity. But, besides the actual slave and the free μέτοικος who is a citizen of some other commonwealth, there is the large class of the *unfree*, filling up in various degrees the space between the mere slave and the full citizen. At Sparta we might reckon the περίοικοι, burghers of a subject township, and the Helots, slaves of the commonwealth but not slaves of individual masters, as representing severally a high and a low stage of this intermediate position. The Thessalian πενέσται, perhaps the Roman *clients*, would be other examples. So in the Teutonic system we find the *liberti* of Tacitus (Germ. 25), that is the *Lætas*, *Liten* or *Lazzen* (see page 249), on whom see Waitz (i. 179) and the chapter in Kemble on the Unfree. The class revives again at a later time in England in the form of the *villeins regardant* of our lawyers, a class formed on the one hand by raising the mere slave, the *þeow*, the *servus* of Domesday, and on the other hand by lowering the free *ceorl*, the *villanus* of Domesday.

One would have thought that it was inherent in this class to be without political rights, yet we have the strange statement about the Federal Diet of the Old-Saxons which I have quoted above.

Kemble (i. 185) defines slavery as " dependence, the being in the mund of another, and represented by him in the folcmót." This of course would take in classes much better off than the mere *þeow*.

(6) Page 196.—That is to say, the aristocratic commonwealth was democratic at its first starting. The Roman patricians, the *populus* or old citizens, of course began as a democracy among themselves, and their democratic character would not be affected by the presence of any class of the unfree, whether clients or mere slaves. They became an aristocracy, as there grew round them, in the form of the *plebs*, a body of men personally as free as themselves, but possessing only a lower political franchise.

(7) Page 197.—Waitz i. 36. "Wie das Heer nur das im Kriege befindliche Volk darstellt, so sind auch alle militärischen Verhältnisse nirgends von den übrigen Zuständen des Lebens zu trennen; immer befinden sich kriegerische und richterliche Gewalt in Einer Hand; wie das Volk Heer ist, die Versammlung des Volks Gericht, so ist der Richter auch Heerführer. Eine Eintheilung des Heers setzt daher stets eine gleiche des Volks voraus, die des Volks muss mit der des Landes identisch sein."

(8) Page 198.—It is hardly needful to point out that the famous Assembly of the Achaians in the second book of the Iliad is, in the nature of the case, a military assembly. But it is worth marking that it is *ἀγορή* in verse 51, 93, 96, *λαός* in 97–100, *στρατός* and *ἀγορή* both, in 207, and *πληθύς* in 278.

(9) Page 198.—The Macedonian military assembly is spoken of by Arrian, iii. 27, 2, 27, 3, as *πλῆθος* and *Μακεδόνες*, in 27, 4, it is *ἐκκλησία*.

(10) Page 198.—See Norman Conquest, ii. 103.

(11) Page 198.—I mean the Athenian process by which

the Generals chose ἐκ καταλόγου, from the list of citizens of the military age, such as they thought good to call upon for the particular expedition.

(12) Page 198.—This comes out very strongly in the history of the Athenian siege of Syracuse. The army in Sicily, though forming so large a part of the Athenian people, waits for and obeys the orders of the citizens who remained at home as submissively as the subjects of a despot could do.

(13) Page 199.—See the action of the Athenian Senate and People at Salamis in Herodotus, ix. 4 et seq. It is worth noting that the violence done to the Senator Lykidas, who proposed submission to the Persians, and still more the violence done by the Athenian women to his wife and children, are things altogether without parallel within the city itself.

(14) Page 199.—Thucydides, viii. 76, where the army at Samos acts for itself, and maintains the democracy after the oligarchic revolution in the city. Thrasyboulos and Thrasylos are made to say ὡς οὐ δεῖ ἀθυμεῖν ὅτι ἡ πόλις αὐτῶν ἀφέστηκε. They had just been elected Generals by the army, much as Camillus (Livy v. 46) is elected Dictator by the Roman Assembly at Veii, though the circumstances of the Roman migration to Veii are more like those of the Athenian migration to Salamis.

(15) Page 199.—For the Ætolian Federal Assembly held under the walls of the besieged city of Medeôn in B.C. 231, see History of Federal Government, i. 413.

(16) Page 202.—In the Teutonic mythology a God might

die, as appears from the famous case of Balder. In the Greek mythology there is no case of the death of a God, though the possibility of such a thing seems implied in one passage of the Iliad (v. 388), where Arês is spoken of as running a chance of being killed by the sons of Alôeus.

> *καί νύ κεν ἔνθ' ἀπόλοιτο Ἄρης, ἆτος πολέμοιο,*
> *εἰ μὴ μητρυιή, περικαλλὴς Ἠερίβοια,*
> *Ἑρμέᾳ ἐξήγγειλεν, ὁ δ' ἐξέκλεψεν Ἄρηα*
> *ἤδη τειρόμενον· χαλεπὸς δέ ἑ δεσμὸς ἐδάμνα.*

In the same speech both Hêrê and Aïdês are spoken of as being wounded by Hêraklês, and in the same book both Aphroditê and Arês are wounded by Diomêdês (336, 855).

(17) Page 203.—Iliad, xx. 10.

> *ἐλθόντες δ' ἐς δῶμα Διὸς νεφεληγερέταο,*
> *ξέστῃς αἰθούσῃσιν ἐφίζανον, ἃς Διὶ πατρὶ*
> *Ἥφαιστος ποίησεν ἰδυίῃσι πραπίδεσσιν.*

It was as needful in the divine as in the human Assembly that its members should be seated; when men began to stand up, there was then, as now, an end to all order. Iliad, xviii. 246.

> *ὀρθῶν δ' ἑσταότων ἀγορὴ γένετ', οὐδέ τις ἔτλη*
> *ἕζεσθαι, πάντας γὰρ ἔχε τρόμος.* Cf. ii. 96–100.

(18) Page 203.—See Growth of the English Constitution, 168.

(19) Page 203.—Iliad, xx. 13.

(20) Page 203.—See Historical Essays, Second Series, 83.

(21) Page 204.—For this comparison I might quote no

less an authority than King Ælfred, who looked on Odysseus as a King under the Emperor Agamemnôn. "Hit gebyrede gio on Troiana gewinne þæt þær wæs an cyning þæs nama Aulixes, se hæfde twa þioda under þam kasere. Þa ðioda wæron hatena Iðacige and Retie, and þæs kaseres nama wæs Agamemnon."

(22) Page 204.—Iliad, xvi. 434.

(23) Page 205.—Odyssey, ii. 26.

οὐδέ ποθ' ἡμετέρη ἀγορὴ γένετ' οὐδὲ θόωκος,
ἐξ οὗ 'Οδυσσεὺς δῖος ἔβη κοίλης ἐνὶ νηυσί.

(24) Page 206.—Tacitus, Germania, 11. "Si displicuit sententia, fremitu adspernantur; sin placuit, frameas concutiunt. Honoratissimum adsensus genus est, armis laudare."

(25) Page 206.—Thucydides, i. 87. κρίνουσι γὰρ βοῇ καὶ οὐ ψήφῳ.

(26) Page 208.—I will refer only to two examples, one of an Assembly which was held, and another of one which was not held, but which proves almost more than any of those which were held. Kassandros, having Olympias in his power, but having promised to spare her life, first holds an Assembly in which she is condemned to death in her absence; then, when she still demands a public trial, he shrinks from the effect which he knew that her presence would have upon the Assembly, and causes her to be put to death privately. Diod. xix. 51. ὁ δὲ Κάσσανδρος . . . . προετρέψατο τοὺς οἰκείους τῶν ἀνῃρημένων ὑπ' 'Ολυμπιάδος ἐν κοινῇ τῶν Μακεδόνων ἐκκλησίᾳ κατηγορεῖν τῆς προειρημένης γυναικός. ὧν

*ποιησάντων τὸ προσταχθὲν, καὶ τῆς Ὀλυμπιάδος οὔτε παρούσης οὔτε ἐχούσης τοὺς ἀπολογησομένους, οἱ μὲν Μακεδόνες κατεγίνωσκον αὐτῆς θάνατον . . . . εὐλαβεῖτο γὰρ ἅμα καὶ τὸ περὶ αὐτὴν ἀξίωμα καὶ τὸ τῶν Μακεδόνων εὐμετάβολον. τῆς δ' Ὀλυμπιάδος οὐ φαμένης φεύξεσθαι, τοὐναντίον δ' ἑτοίμης οὔσης ἐν πᾶσι Μακεδόσι κριθῆναι, ὁ Κάσσανδρος φοβηθεὶς μήποτε τὸ πλῆθος ἀκοῦον τῆς βασιλίσσης ἀπολογουμένης καὶ τῶν Ἀλεξάνδρου καὶ Φιλίππου πρὸς ἅπαν τὸ ἔθνος εὐεργεσιῶν ἀναμιμνησκόμενον μετανοήσῃ, κ.τ.λ.*

(27) Page 208.—Thus in Arrian, iii. 26, Philôtas is accused by Alexander before the Macedonian Assembly and is condemned, while in the next chapter Amyntas and several others are accused and acquitted.

(28) Page 210.—See Historical Essays, Second Series, 189.

(29) Page 212.—If we reckon from the legislation of Kleisthenês in B.C. 508 to the narrowing of the franchise by Antipatros in B.C. 322, the time is less than two hundred years; if we go back as far as Solôn in 594, we are still a good way under three hundred.

(30) Page 214.—See the definition of democracy given by Athênagoras in Thucydides, Growth of the English Constitution, 165. Most of the characteristics of democracy of which I have spoken in the text I have worked out more fully in the Essay on the Athenian Democracy in my Second Series of Historical Essays.

(31) Page 214.—One of the merits of democracy, according to Periklês in the Funeral Oration (Thuc. ii. 37), was

the room which it gave to the developement of individual character and ability, as opposed to the unvarying routine to which every man had to submit at Sparta. *ὄνομα μὲν διὰ τὸ μὴ ἐς ὀλίγους ἀλλ' ἐς πλείονας οἰκεῖν δημοκρατία κέκληται, μέτεστι δὲ κατὰ μὲν τοὺς νόμους πρὸς τὰ ἴδια διάφορα πᾶσι τὸ ἴσον, κατὰ δὲ τὴν ἀξίωσιν, ὡς ἕκαστος ἔν τῳ εὐδοκιμεῖ . . . ἐλευθέρως δὲ τά τε πρὸς τὸ κοινὸν πολιτεύομεν καὶ ἐς τὴν πρὸς ἀλλήλους τῶν καθ' ἡμέραν ἐπιτηδευμάτων ὑποψίαν, οὐ δι' ὀργῆς τὸν πέλας, εἰ καθ' ἡδονήν τι δρᾷ, ἔχοντες, οὐδὲ ἀζημίους μὲν λυπηρὰς δὲ τῇ ὄψει ἀχθηδόνας προστιθέμενοι.* He then goes on to speak of obedience to the laws and magistrates as one of the consequences of popular government. Modern writers very often charge democracy with doing the exact opposite to all these things, and especially with moulding all men according to one pattern. But it is commonly very hard to make out what modern writers mean by democracy, and it seems likely, on the whole, that Periklês knew best.

(32) Page 215.—I have referred to the debate in the Spartan Assembly recorded by Thucydides, i. 67–88. The body debating is the general Assembly of the Spartan citizens (*ξύλλογος σφῶν αὐτῶν ὁ εἰωθώς*), as distinguished both from the smaller bodies in the Spartan Commonwealth and from the general Assembly of the Lacedæmonian allies which appears in c. 119. The Corinthians and others are heard, and the Athenian Ambassadors are heard in answer. Then the Spartans debate among themselves; but the narrative seems to imply that no one spoke except the two great official persons, the King Archidamos and the Ephor Sthenelaïdas, and the latter seems to wind up the debate somewhat suddenly by his official authority. It should be noticed that, after the cry of Aye and Nay (see above, note 25) the Ephor professed—the historian hints that he merely professed

(*βουλόμενος αὐτοὺς φανερῶς ἀποδεικνυμένους τὴν γνώμην ἐς τὸ πολεμεῖν μᾶλλον ὁρμῆσαι*)—to be unable to distinguish which side "had it" and therefore he made the House divide. The words which I have quoted in the original should be noticed. Before the Ballot became law, one used sometimes to hear shallow people ask why, if electors were to vote by ballot, members of Parliament should not vote by ballot also. They forgot that it does not concern either of two electors to know how the other votes, while it does concern both of them to know how their representative votes. But in a primary Assembly there can be no objection to secret voting, if it be thought good on other grounds. And the story sounds as if Sthenelaïdas had somewhat unfairly made men vote openly, in order to carry his own purpose. It should be remembered that secret voting is the theory of the Oxford Convocation, that again being a primary Assembly.

In all our accounts of Athenian Assemblies we hear of many more speakers than in this at Sparta, and we never hear of any magistrates stepping in in the authoritative way as Sthenelaïdas did.

(33) Page 216.—On the powers of the Achaian General see History of Federal Government, i. 287.

(34) Page 217.—I have quoted this analogy and one or two others at p. 308 of the same work. In one of the cases there referred to, that of the non-residentiary members of the Cathedral Chapters, there is a clear tendency at work to bring about a better state of things.

(35) Page 217.—See History of Federal Government, i. 263.

(36) Page 219.—See Norman Conquest, i. 100–102.

(37) Page 219.—See History of Federal Government, i. 698. Norman Conquest, i. 592, ii. 330.

(38) Page 220.—See Norman Conquest, iii. 623.

(39) Page 221.—The changes in the Frankish Assemblies under the Merwings and Karlings are set forth in two chapters of Waitz, one in the second volume, headed *Die Gerichts-, Heer- und Reichs-Versammlungen*, the other in the third volume, headed *Der Hof und die Reichs-Versammlung*. The general result seems to be that the Assemblies greatly decayed under the Merwings, but that a new life was put into them by the Teutonic revival under the Austrasian Mayors and Kings. But, even under the Merwings, the old local assemblies seem to have gone on in their full vigour among the dependent nations (ii. 419; 439; 444; 455). That under the Karlings the Assembly retained, in theory at least, its old popular character is plain from a crowd of passages collected by Waitz, iii. 468 et seq.; and his general conclusion (iii. 486) is: "Man kann nicht zweifeln, dass es ein allgemeines Recht der Freien blieb, sich auf der grossen Jahresversammlung einzufinden: eben darum heisst sie die allgemeine, und von der Gesammtheit oder Menge des Volks ist öfter die Rede."

(40) Page 221.—Among the Bavarians and Allemans we find provisions enforcing attendance at the Assemblies. But these were not unknown even at Athens, as we see from the graphic description of Aristophanes in the opening scene of the Acharnians—

ὡς νῦν, ὁπότ' οὔσης κυρίας ἐκκλησίας
ἑωθινῆς ἔρημος ἡ Πνὺξ αὑτηΐ,
οἱ δ' ἐν ἀγορᾷ λαλοῦσι, κἄνω καὶ κάτω
τὸ σχοινίον φεύγουσι τὸ μεμιλτωμένον.

The appointment of special *Schöffen, Scabini, Échevins*, seems to have arisen from the necessity of insuring that some one should be ready to discharge the duties of the Assembly. See Waitz, iii. 487, iv. 325, and especially the chapter headed *Die Schöffen* in Savigny's *Geschichte des Römischen Rechts*. Savigny's distinct conclusion (i. 197) is that "der Unterschied lag nur darin, dass die Scabinen, als öffentliche Personen, die Verpflichtung hatten, als Schöffen den Gerichten beyzuwohnen, während es in der Willkühr der übrigen Freyen stand, zu erscheinen wenn sie wollten, nur mit Ausnahme der drey grossen Versammlungstage im Jahr, an welchen alle erscheinen mussten."

In the first page of Domesday, we find that in Kent those who were summoned to the *Scirgemót* and failed to appear were liable to forfeiture, provided the Assembly was held in the ancient place on Pennenden Heath. They were not bound to go further. "Si fuerint præmoniti ut conveniant ad sciram, ibunt usque ad Pinnedennam, non longius. Et si non venerint, de hac forisfactura et de aliis omnibus rex c. solidos habebit."

(41) Page 223.—See History of Federal Government, i. 211, 271. So Thucydides (i. 125) remarks that in the Assembly of the Lacedemonian Confederacy—which, though not a true confederation, made some approach to it as being an Assembly of independent states—each city great and small had an equal vote. ψῆφον ἐπήγαγον τοῖς ξυμμάχοις ἅπασιν ὅσοι παρῆσαν ἑξῆς, καὶ μείζονι καὶ ἐλάσσονι πόλει, καὶ τὸ πλῆθος ἐψηφίσαντο πολεμεῖν.

(42) Page 223.—This fact is preserved to us by Strabo and quoted in History of Federal Government, i. 209.

(43) Page 224.—See Hist. Fed. Gov. i. 272 and compare

the enfranchisement of the smaller Arcadian towns by Philopoimên, i. 626.

(44) Page 224.—Compare Hist. Fed. Gov. i. 270.

(45) Page 226.—So Livy (i. 43) remarks of the Comitia Centuriata of Servius: "non, ut ab Romulo traditum cæteri servaverant reges, viritim suffragium eadem vi eodemque jure promiscue omnibus datum est; sed gradus facti, ut neque exclusus quisquam suffragio videretur, et vis omnes penes primores civitatis esset." This passage takes for granted that the votes given in the Assembly will not be the votes of individuals but those of tribes or centuries, otherwise the word *viritim* might be misunderstood. In the Comitia of the local Tribes one man's vote was as good as another's within the tribe. So in the Comitia of the Centuries one man's vote was as good as another's within the century. But in the local tribes there was no distinction of birth or rank; while in the Comitia of Centuries care was taken that the vote of the few rich men who formed one century should be equal to the vote of the many poor men who formed another century. In this way it might be said that in the Assembly of the Tribes—and in that of the *Curiæ* also—votes were taken *viritim;* one man's vote was as good as another in a sense in which it was not so in the Assembly of the Centuries. One man's vote really did count for as much as another's, except so far as one tribe or *curia* might contain more citizens than another, a distinction which had nothing to do with birth or wealth.

(46) Page 227.—On the other hand, the yearly Senate is always spoken of as one of the specially democratic institutions of Athens, and, when the Four Hundred take possession

of the government, one of their first acts is to turn out the Senate by force. See Thucydides, viii. 69.

(47) Page 227.—On the lessening of the powers of the Areiopagos see Grote, v. 480 et seqq. The truth is that, in a body elected for life, a feeling which may be called aristocratic, though not necessarily oligarchic, can hardly fail to grow up. Each member, as he enters it, is gradually brought within the influence of the general sentiment.

(48) Page 228.—The Censors named the Senators, but it was usual for them at each census to place on the roll of Senators those whom the people had chosen to magistracies since the last census. The people thus indirectly chose the Senate.

(49) Page 229.—See the passages collected in a note at i. 264 of the History of Federal Government.

(50) Page 230.—Thuc. iii. 36–49.

(51) Page 230.—Thuc. vi. 8–28.

(52) Page 230.—Xen. Hell. i. 7.

(53) Page 230.—Sallust, Bell. Cat. 50–53.

(54) Page 231.—Under Augustus and Tiberius the comitia gradually became a mere name. Caius professed to restore the Assembly to its old powers, but after a while he took away his own gift. The words in which Diôn Cassius (lix. 20) describes this change are worth quoting; *ἀπέδωκε μὲν γὰρ τὰς ἀρχαιρεσίας αὐτοῖς· ἅτε δὲ ἐκείνων τε ἀργοτέρων ὑπὸ τοῦ*

*πολλῷ χρόνῳ μηδὲν ἐλευθέρως κεχρηματικέναι ἐς τὸ δρᾶν τι τῶν προσηκόντων σφίσιν ὄντων, καὶ τῶν σπουδαρχιώντων μάλιστα μὲν μὴ πλείονων ἢ ὅσους αἱρεῖσθαι ἔδει ἐπαγγελλόντων, εἰ δέ ποτε καὶ ὑπὲρ τὸν ἀριθμὸν γένοιντο, διομολογουμένων πρὸς ἀλλήλους, τὸ μὲν σχῆμα τῆς δημοκρατίας ἐσώζετο, ἔργον δ' οὐδὲν αὐτῆς ἐγίγνετο, καὶ διὰ τοῦτο ὑπ' αὐτοῦ αὖθις τοῦ Γαΐου κατελύθησαν· κἀκ τούτου τὰ μὲν ἄλλα καθάπερ καὶ ἐπὶ τοῦ Τιβερίου καθίστατο.*

(55) Page 232.—See Growth of the English Constitution, 162.

(56) Page 233.—Ib. 82. Norman Conquest, i. 102.

(57) Page 238.—Such for instance as the Parliaments which appointed the *Balie* which banished and restored Cosmo de' Medici. Sismondi, ix. 39, 44.

(58) Page 240.—See Norman Conquest, ii. 339. Growth of the English Constitution, 7.

(59) Page 241.—On the steps by which the Great Council of Venice, from its foundation in 1172, finally became, between 1286 and 1319, the primary Assembly of an aristocratic body, see Sismondi, iii. 289; Daru, Histoire de Venise, vi. 11–14. After this process, called *serrar del consiglio,* the Council consisted of all who were then members and their descendants. By this means several ancient families were shut out. As this oligarchic body grew, the older democratic Assembly, without being formally abolished, gradually went out of use.

I do not know enough of the history of Poland to be able to trace out in detail the steps by which the election of the King became vested in the general *Comitia* of the nobles, to the exclusion both of the Diet and of the rest of the nation. But it certainly was so from the extinction of the House of Jagellon.

(60) Page 242.—See above, note 40.

(61) Page 242.—The most important branches of the judicial power of the House of Lords seem likely to come to an end. That is to say, the separation between the legislative and the judicial branches of the Government will at last be fully carried out.

## LECTURE VI.

(1) Page 247.—See note 59 on Lecture V.

(2) Page 247.—I do not mean that I have any doubt that both the Eupatrids at Athens and the Patricians at Rome really had their origin in a body of old citizens, because there is quite proof enough in the way of inference and analogy to make it plain that such was the case. I mean that it is only from inference and analogy that we can say anything about the matter, that we have no records, such as we have of later times, nor even the witness of an intelligent observer from outside, such as we have in the case of the early days of our own forefathers.

(3) Page 248.—It should not be forgotten that both actual slavery, the state of the *þeow*, and the milder state of the villain died out in England, and was never formally abolished. Everybody knows this in the case of villainage, but I suspect that many people do not fully understand that actual slavery ever existed in England. When the Judges in the last century declared that there could not be a slave on English ground, they made an excellent piece of legislation, but it was essentially a piece of legislation, and its authors would perhaps have been amazed to hear of the Bristol slave-trade in the eleventh century and of Saint Wulfstan's labours to put it down.

(4) Page 249.—On the *liti* or *lazzi* see note 5 on Lecture V.

(5) Page 250.—See the description of the Old-Saxons quoted in note 76 on Lecture III. and compare the earlier description of the same people in Nithard, iv. 2: "Quæ gens omnis in tribus ordinibus divisa consistit; sunt enim inter illos qui edhilingi, sunt qui frilingi, sunt qui lazzi illorum lingua dicuntur; latina vero lingua hoc sunt: nobiles, ingenuiles, atque serviles." He goes on to speak of "frilingi lazzique, quorum infinita multitudo est."

(6) Page 250.—This is the view of Waitz, i. 86: "Die Fürsten sind von dem Adel durchaus verschieden. Ich setze das deutsche Wort, wo Tacitus 'principes' nennt. 'Nobiles' habe ich Adlige, 'nobilitas' Adel übersetzt. . . . . . . Die Fürsten (principes) werden in den Volksversammlungen gewählt."

(7) Page 250.—See Norman Conquest, i. 81.

(8) Page 255.—On the Interrex, see above, p. 147.

(9) Page 256.—I have referred to this story in Historical Essays, Second Series, ii. 92. The whole description in Sallust (Bell. Jug. 63, 64) is most remarkable. Fully to take it in, three things must be borne in mind. First, that the Consulship was in the free gift of the people themselves. Secondly, that Metellus was a plebeian. Thirdly, that Marius had risen from one post to another till he had reached the Prætorship, the office next in rank to the Consulship itself. Also it should be noticed that Sallust uses the word *Plebes*, no longer in opposition to *Patricii*, but in opposition to *Nobilitas*. Sallust tells us how Marius was elected to the post of military tribune and then goes on: "Deinde ab eo magistratu, alium post alium sibi

peperit: semperque in potestatibus eo modo agitabat ut ampliore quam gerebat dignus haberetur; tamen is ad id locorum talis vir (nam postea ambitione præceps datus est) consulatum appetere non audebat. Etiam tum alios magistratus plebes, consulatum nobilitas, inter se per manus tradebat. Novus nemo tam clarus neque tam egregiis factis erat, quin is indignus illo honore et quasi pollutus haberetur." He then goes on to tell how Metellus tried by friendly remonstrances to persuade Marius not to stand for the Consulship: "ne tam prava inciperet, neu super fortunam animum gereret, non omnia omnibus cupienda esse, debere illi res suas satis placere: postremo caveret id petere a populo Romano quod illi jure negaretur." At last he is betrayed into an insult: it would be time enough for Marius to stand for the Consulship when his own son the young Metellus could be his colleague; "Sæpius eadem postulanti fertur dixisse, ne festinaret abire; satis mature illum cum filio suo consulatum petiturum. Is eo tempore in contubernio patris ibidem militabat, annos natu circiter xx."

This language, in the mouth of one who was himself a plebeian, shows how thoroughly the new notion of nobility had supplanted the old. Metellus speaks to Marius as Appius Claudius might have spoken to a forefather of Metellus. It shows also how completely a mere customary prescription often seems to some minds to have more than the force of law, to be almost part of the order of nature.

(10) Page 257.—See Norman Conquest, i. 85 et seqq. Growth of the English Constitution, 42 et seqq.

(11) Page 259.—*Eorl* or *Jarl* is now held to be a contraction of *Ealdor* (see Max Müller, Science of Language, ii. 280, 7th ed.). It is quite in agreement with this that the shorter

form should prevail among the Danes, among whom names commonly appear in a shorter form than they do in English. And it would seem to follow from this derivation that the familiar jingle between *Eorl* and *Ceorl* is simply a jingle. But this is one of those facts which are simply philological. Historically, *Eorl*—that is, as the name of a particular office, as distinguished from the general sense of *noble*—is a distinct title from *Ealdorman*, the place of which it took. We first hear of *Eorlas* in the Danish hosts against which Ælfred fought. Then the title was borne, as might be expected, by the Danish chiefs who settled in Northumberland; lastly, under Cnut, it was extended to all England and supplanted *Ealdorman*. See Norman Conquest, i. 76, 277, 405, 646.

The word *Thegn*, as far as we are concerned, starts from the meaning of *servant*, and thence rises to its higher political and social meaning. But it would seem that the primary meaning of all was rather *man*, and thence *servant*, much like the word *man* itself in its relation to *lord*. Other cases are our *knave*, *Knabe*, and the Greek παῖς; or again *cniht*, *kneht*, which, starting from the notion of youth, has passed through that of service into the opposite meanings of the modern German *Knecht* and the English *knight*. Though *Thegn* seems never on the continent to have received the same fixed meaning as it did in England, yet the word in various forms is familiar enough, as we see from the *Degene* in the second stanza of the *Nibelungen-Lied*. A number of forms and uses of the word are collected in the old Thesaurus of Schilter (1738) under the word *Diu*.

(12) Page 259.—This meaning perhaps comes out most strongly in the use of the adjective *þegenlic*. Thus in the Song of Maldon (see Growth of English Constitution, p. 46) Offa is said to lie *thane-like* by his lord Brihtnoth;

He læg ðegenlice
ðeodne gehende.

And in a very remarkable document in Kemble's Codex Diplomaticus (iv. 54), describing the doings in a Scirgemót in Herefordshire, a woman named Eánwéne, whose son Eadwine was trying to dispossess her of some lands, says to three Thegns who are sent to her, "Doð þegenlíce and wel." That is, in modern language, "Act like gentlemen."

(13) Page 259.—The word *vassal* is, according to Waitz (iv. 205), of Celtic origin, and it seems to have started from the same point, and to have risen in much the same way, as our word *thegn*. In some cases (Waitz, iv. 229) "serviens," "servitium," and other cognate words are used as equivalents to it. But I must venture wholly to dissent from this great scholar when he says (210) that the vassalage of the Carolingian age had nothing whatever to do with the old *comitatus*.

"Mit der alten Gefolgschaft hat die Vassallität nichts zu thun; ohne Grund hat man in älterer und neuerer Zeit beide zusammengeworfen oder doch an einander geknüpft. Die Vassallität wird anders begründet, hat andere Folgen, hat zugleich eine viel weitere Ausdehnung als jene."

To me it seems that the difference between the two things is exactly the same as the difference between the Frankish kingship, while the Franks were still a wandering people, and the Frankish kingship, when its Kings held a territorial dominion over a large part of Europe and had begun to deck themselves with the Imperial titles of Rome. The character of the institution has in each case greatly changed, but it is still the same institution modified by change of circumstances. Indeed Waitz himself says pretty much what I mean when he says (198): "Darüber kann nach allem was vorliegt kein Zweifel sein, dass der Empfang von Beneficium an sich ein

Verhältniss naher persönlicher Verbindung, von Verpflichtung und Ergebenheit begründete, dem König gegenüber den allgemeinen Pflichten der Staatsangehörigen ein engeres persönliches Band hinzufügte. Dies aber erhielt in dieser Zeit seinen bestimmten Ausdruck, seine feste Form durch die Commendation oder den Eintritt in die Vassallität, die, ursprünglich auf andern Grundlagen erwachsen, jetzt in die engste Verbindung mit den Beneficien getreten, ja zu dem eigentlich charakteristischem Merkmal für diese geworden ist." I had not read this later part of Waitz's work when I wrote the second chapter of the History of the Norman Conquest, and, though it supplies a vast mass of illustration in detail, I see no reason to give up the view which I have there set forth after Palgrave and Kemble.

Waitz remarks (iv. 242) that the system of vassalage grew much faster in the Romance than in the purely Teutonic lands. This would naturally follow if, as I hold, the fully developed feudal relation arose by the union of a Roman and a Teutonic relation in the same person.

The way in which the feudal idea, the personal relation of *lord* and *vassal,* supplanted the strictly political notion of duty to the Commonwealth and to the King as its head is well put forth by Waitz, iv. 241. He quotes a variety of phrases showing how the King gradually came to be looked on chiefly in his character of lord. He might have added our old phrase of *Cynehlaford* and our modern phrase of "our Lord the King."

(14) Page 259.—I have said something on this head in the second volume of the Norman Conquest, p. 270. Compare also the remarks of Palgrave, Normandy, ii. 11.

(15) Page 260.—We seem to see a trace of the *comitatus*

in the "globus ferocissimorum juvenum" who surround Romulus in Livy, i. 12, and in the "delecta manus præsidii causa" who surround the Dictator Aulus Postumius in ii. 20.

(16) Page 262.—We seem to be at Ilios or at Maldon, when we read how, in the fight by the Granikos, the companion Dêmaratos (Arrian, i. 15, 9) gives his spear to Alexander when his own is broken: Δημάρατος δὲ, ἀνὴρ Κορίνθιος τῶν ἀμφ' αὐτὸν ἑταίρων, δίδωσιν αὐτῷ τὸ αὑτοῦ δόρυ.

(17) Page 262.—The Roman clients would be in old English phrase not so much *thegns* as *loaf-eaters.* The relation of the *loaf-eater* was surely a variety, though a very low variety, of the *comitatus;* and even a churl might have his *loaf-eaters*, as appears from the 25th law of Æthelberht: "Gif man ceorlæs hlaf-ætan ofslæhð, vi scillingum gebéte."

(18) Page 267.—At Bern the young patrician was literally apprenticed to political life by the singular institution of the *Ausserstand*, a copy of the real commonwealth with councils and magistrates of its own. The *Schultheiss* or chief magistrate of the mimic republic was commonly elected a member of the Great Council of the real one. See the account in Coxe's Travels in Switzerland, ii. 231. In his day, as in the earlier days of Bishop Burnet, travellers did not disdain to study the institutions of the country.

(19) Page 270.—I have before me, in a *Geographisches statistisch-topographisches Lexicon von Franken* (Ulm, 1801), iv. 46, a list of the twenty-three patrician families of Nürnberg, three of them had been admitted as lately as 1788, but none of these "novi homines" seem to have actually held seats in the Senate.

(20) Page 273.—Numbers xxxv. 9; Deuteronomy iv. 41; xix. 2; Joshua xx. 2. The right is however by the Hebrew law strictly confined to the slayer who hated not in times past the man whom he slew. It would therefore not cover the case of the old Teutonic *Fæhde.*

(21) Page 273.—The laws of Ælfred (42) set forth the general principle that no man is to appeal to force till he has tried legal means; "Eàc we beòdað, se mon se þe his gefàn hàm-sittendne wite, þæt he ne feohte ær þàm þe him ryhtes bidde." Then follow a number of rules regulating the cases in which private war is allowed, the last of which is, if he finds a man with his wife, daughter, sister, or mother; "And mon mòt feohtan orwìge, gif he gemèteð òðerne æt his æ̀wum wife betỳnedum durum oððe under ànre reòn, oððe æt his dèhter æ̀wumborenre, oððe æt his swister [æwum]-borenre, oððe æt his mèdder, þe wære tò æ̀wum wife forgifen his fæder." The Athenian law on this subject comes out in the First Oration of Lysias, where the slayer of Eratosthenês defends himself on the ground of the adultery of the slain man with his wife. The case is more remarkable because Eratosthenês offered money, which the husband refused, determining, as he said, to carry out the law; *οὐκ ἠμφισβήτει, ὦ ἄνδρες, ἀλλ' ὡμολόγει ἀδικεῖν, καὶ ὅπως μὲν μὴ ἀποθάνῃ ἠντιβόλει καὶ ἱκέτευεν, ἀποτίνειν δ' ἕτοιμος ἦν χρήματα. ἐγὼ δὲ τῷ μὲν ἐκείνου τιμήματι οὐ συνεχώρουν, τὸν δὲ τῆς πόλεως νόμον ἠξίουν εἶναι κυριώτερον, καὶ ταύτην ἔλαβον τὴν δίκην, ἣν ὑμεῖς δικαιοτάτην εἶναι ἡγησάμενοι τοῖς τὰ τοιαῦτα ἐπιτηδεύουσιν ἐτάξατε.*

The Roman law on this head comes out in the Lex Julia, which gives the power of slaying the adulterer to either the husband or the father. See Huschke, Jurisprudentiæ Antejustiniana, 560 et seqq. There in the "Mosaicarum et

Romanarum Legum Collatio" the rights of the father and the husband are carefully distinguished according to the rescripts of the Emperors and the opinions of the great lawyers.

(22) Page 273.—See History of Federal Government, i. 381.

(23) Page 274.—On all this see Allen's note on the Judicial Power, Royal Prerogative, 88.

(24) Page 275.—Leviticus xxiv. 19. See the article *Talio* in the Dictionary of Greek and Roman Antiquities.

(25) Page 275.—See the well-known passage, Iliad ix. 628.

> νηλής· καὶ μέν τίς τε κασιγνήτοιο φόνοιο
> ποινὴν, ἢ οὗ παιδὸς ἐδέξατο τεθνειῶτος·
> καί ῥ' ὁ μὲν ἐν δήμῳ μένει αὐτοῦ, πόλλ' ἀποτίσας,
> τοῦ δέ τ' ἐρητύεται κραδίη καὶ θυμὸς ἀγήνωρ,
> ποινὴν δεξαμένου·

(26) Page 276.—In Iliad, vi. 45, Adrêstos craves his life of Menelaos and offers a ransom—σὺ δ' ἄξια δέξαι ἄποινα—Menelaos is inclined to spare him but Agamemnon steps in and slays Adrêstos himself, and the poet approves the act.

> ὣς εἰπὼν ἔτρεψεν ἀδελφειοῦ φρένας ἥρως,
> αἴσιμα παρειπών·

Compare the slaughter of Lykaôn by Achilleus, Iliad xxi. 341–34. Achilleus, in the same spirit, refuses the ransom.

(27) Page 276.—Tacitus (Germania, 12), after mentioning the severer punishments awarded to traitors and

imitators of southern vices, adds: "Sed et levioribus delictis" [Mr. Kemble, i. 271, remarks that among these lesser crimes homicide must be reckoned], "pro modo, pœna; equorum pecorumque numero convicti multantur, pars multæ Regi, vel civitati pars ipsi, qui vindicatur, vel propinquis ejus exsolvitur." So 21: "Suscipere tam inimicitias, seu patris, seu propinqui, quam amicitias, necesse est: nec implacabiles durant. Luitur enim etiam homicidium certo armentorum ac pecorum numero, recipitque satisfactionem universa domus; utiliter in publicum; quia periculosiores sunt inimicitiæ juxta libertatem." On the growth of legislation on these matters, see Mr. Tylor on "Primitive Society" in the Contemporary Review, May, 1873.

(28) Page 276.—There is an elaborate scale of this kind in the earliest monument of English jurisprudence, the Laws of Æthelberht; but we find the degrees of bodily injury drawn out with no less care in the Laws of Ælfred three hundred years later. The series begins at No. 45 and goes on to the end of the collection of Laws. Schmid, 98.

(29) Page 276.—See the scale of Wergilds in the Laws of Ælfred, 27 et seqq. (Schmid, 86) and on the whole subject see Kemble's chapter on "Fæhde and Wergyld."

(30) Page 277.—See the Laws of Ine, 23, 24; 32, 33 (Schmid, 30, 34). We do not find this distinction in the Laws of Æthelberht, from whose realm the Britons had been swept away, nor in the Laws of Ælfred, by whose time the Britons under West-Saxon rule had become English, but we do find it in the Laws of Ine, in whose time all Somerset from the Axe south-westward was a recent conquest within which Englishman and Briton were still distinguished.

(31) Page 278.—On the royal *wergild,* and the payment made by the Kentishmen for the blood of Mul and by the Mercians for the blood of Ælfwine of Northumberland, see Kemble, i. 279–287.

(32) Page 278.—In the time of Edward the Fourth, the then Lord Berkeley with his followers met his neighbour and kinsman Lord Lisle with his followers at Nibley Green. A battle followed, in which Lord Lisle was defeated and slain. Lord Berkeley had in the end to compromise the matter by a money payment to the widow of the slain man. This is, as far as I know, the last example in England either of private war or of the payment of the *wergild.*

(33) Page 281.—In the choir of Brecon Priory church is the monument of a local worthy, one of whose merits is said to have been that he was a "zealous defender of the rights of the inhabiting burgesses against foreigners."

(34) Page 284.—See the article on Swiss Federal Reform in the British Quarterly Review, April, 1873.

(35) Page 286.—The relation of a British dependency to Great Britain is, even in the case of a colony enjoying the largest measure of self-government, *perioikic* in two points. The colony may be involved in a war in which it has no concern, and to which its consent is not asked, even in that indirect way in which the consent of the mother-country may be said to be asked to a war. It also receives a Governor—whatever may be the real amount of his powers—whom it does not choose and whom it cannot dismiss, while it has not, as Parliament and the constituencies have at home, any means of controlling those who appoint him. The Isle of Man and

the Channel Islands, dependencies which possess full internal self-government, but which still are liable to be legislated for by a Parliament in which they are not represented, are, by their geographical nearness to us, brought much more within the strict notion of *περίοικοι*. But such a dominion as India stands of course in a relation which is rather provincial than perioikic. Still there is a wide difference between the inhabitants of British dependencies of any kind and the subjects of Venice, Rome, or any other ruling city. The subjects of Rome or Venice, and in exactly the same way the subjects of Bern or Uri, were strictly subjects (*Unterthanen*); they not only had no voice in the affairs of the ruling state, but they had no means of obtaining any. But, in the case of British dependencies, the inhabitants are British subjects (*Cives*); their country may be said to be in a perioikic or provincial relation, but they themselves are not personally provincials or *περίοικοι*, because they are British subjects, and, if they take up their abode in the United Kingdom, they can at once exercise all the rights of British subjects.

(36) Page 287.—I have before me a pamphlet called *Verfassungs-Skizzen der freien und Hansestädte Lübeck, Bremen und Hamburg*, by Professor C. J. Wurm (Hamburg, 1841), where (p. 115) I find this comment: "Das beiderstädtische (Lübeck und Hamburg gemeinsam angehörende) Gebiet ist eine Anomalie, aber eben keine grössere als das Verhältniss der Herrschaft Kniphausen im deutschen Bunde." In the Low-Dutch of the Hanse Towns the subjects were called *Undersaten*.

(37) Page 288.—See History of Federal Government, i. 582–638.

(38) Page 290.—I forbear from enlarging minutely upon mediæval Swiss history, because I trust to have opportunities

of doing so more thoroughly, both in a longer and a shorter form. There is hardly any other part of the world which supplies such a varied form of political knowledge.

(39) Page 290.—It would call for more minute knowledge than we have to say what were the exact points of likeness and unlikeness between the Lacedæmonian *περίοικοι* and the Italian allies of Rome. The Italian allies no doubt retained full local self-government, subject only to any occasional interferences which the policy of Rome might deem called for. On the whole, their position might seem much better than that of the Laconian *περίοικοι*. At the same time we must remember that the *περίοικοι* had towns of their own, and there is one most remarkable passage in Herodotus, where they seem to be put much more nearly on a level with Sparta than any one would have expected. I mean where Dêmaratos (vii. 234) tells Xerxes that there are many cities of the Lacedæmonians, of which Sparta is the chief, and her men the bravest. Mr. Grote also remarks that we have no right to assume that the condition of all the perioikic towns was exactly the same. Some, like Amyklai, seem to have been favoured above others.

(40) Page 291.—It should not be forgotten that, during several years of the sixteenth century, Bern held the southern side of the Lake as well as the northern. These districts of Northern Savoy probably did not lose much at the time—unless we are to bring in theological controversies—by being given back from the rule of the Bernese aristocracy to that of their own Duke, but, had they then shared the fate of their brethren on the northern shore, they would probably share it still.

(41) Page 292.—See Historical Essays, 2nd Series, p. 143.

(42) Page 293.—Corinth at least could boast (Thucydides, i. 38) of the good terms on which she stood with all her colonies except Korkyra; *ἡμεῖς δὲ οὐδ' αὐτοί φαμεν ἐπὶ τῷ ὑπὸ τούτων ὑβρίζεσθαι κατοικίσαι, ἀλλ' ἐπὶ τῷ ἡγεμόνες τε εἶναι καὶ τὰ εἰκότα θαυμάζεσθαι. αἱ γοῦν ἄλλαι ἀποικίαι τιμῶσιν ἡμᾶς, καὶ μάλιστα ὑπὸ ἀποίκων στεργόμεθα.* And it is to be noticed that this language seems to imply a certain political authority on the part of Corinth over her colonies, which comes out more clearly when we find that the Corinthian colony of Potidaia received certain yearly magistrates from the mother-city (Thuc. i. 56: *τοὺς ἐπιδημιουργοὺς . . . οὓς κατὰ ἔτος ἕκαστον Κορίνθιοι ἔπεμπον*), and that even while Potidaia was a dependent ally of Athens. So little did Athens meddle with the internal constitutions of her dependencies.

## REDE LECTURE.

(1) Page 297.—It is plain, however, that something like Comparative Philology began with Roger Bacon, and even before him, with Giraldus Cambrensis. One could hardly ask for a better setting forth of the relation in which the Romance languages stand to the Latin than is given by the great friar in his Opus Tertium, c. 25 (p. 90, Brewer). "Et hoc videmus in idiomatibus diversis ejusdem linguæ; nam idioma est proprietas alicujus linguæ distincta ab alia; ut Picardicum, et Gallicum, et Provinciale, et omnia idiomata a finibus Apuliæ usque ad fines Hispaniæ. Nam lingua Latina est in his omnibus una et eadem, secundum substantiam, sed variata secundum idiomata diversa." In the next page he speaks of the Greek knowledge of Robert Grosseteste.

Giraldus, one may fairly say, noticed several of the points of likeness among all the Aryan languages of which he had any chance of coming across, and the British element in him gave him a wider field of observation than most of his contemporaries. There are two passages on this subject in the Itinerarium Kambriæ. In the former (i. 8, p. 75, Dimock), he had just told a wonderful story about a boy who had learned the language of the Elves, which was very like Greek. He goes on to remark the analogies between Greek and Bret-Welsh, and his legendary explanation of them is at least not worse than the theory which explained the likeness between Sanscrit and Greek by the Indian expedition of Alexander.

"Erant autem verba .... Græco idiomati valde conformia.

Cum enim aquam requirebant, dicebant *Ydor ydorum;* quod Latine sonat, aquam offer. *Ydor* enim aqua eorum lingua, sicut et Graeca, dicebatur: unde et vasa aquatica *Ydriæ* dicuntur: et *Duur* lingua Britannica similiter aqua dicitur. Item salem requirentes dicebant, *Halgein ydorum;* id est, salem affer. *Hal* vero Græce sal dicitur, et *haleyn* Britannice. Lingua namque Britannica, propter diutinam quam Britones, qui tunc Trojani, et postea Britones a Bruto eorum duce sunt vocati, post Trojæ excidium moram in Græcia fuerant, in multis Græco idiomati conformis invenitur."

He then goes on to remark the interchange between the initial *s* and the aspirate. "Hic autem mihi notabile videtur, quod in uno verbo tot linguas convenire non invenio, sicut in isto. *Hal* enim Græce, *Halein* Britannice, *Halein* similiter Hibernice; *Halgein*, *g* interposita, lingua prædicta. Item *sal* Latine,—quia, ut ait Priscianus, in quibusdam dictionibus pro aspiratione ponitur *s;* ut *Hal* Græce, *sal* Latine; *hemi, semi; hepta, septem,—Sel* Gallice, mutatione *a* vocalis in *e*, a Latino; additione *t* literæ, *salt* Anglice, *sout* Teutonice. Habetis ergo septem linguas, vel octo, in hac una dictione plurimum concordantes." "Teutonice" here must mean some form of the Low-Dutch.

In the other passage (i. 15, p. 194, Dimock) he notices other likenesses between Bret-Welsh and Latin and Greek, several of the numerals being among his instances.

"Notandum etiam, quod verba linguæ Britannicæ omnia fere vel Græco conveniunt vel Latino. Græci Ydor aquam vocant, Britones Duur; salem Hal, Britones Halein; Mis, Tis pro ego et tu, Britones autem Mi, Ti; Onoma, Enou Penta, Deca, Pimp, Dec. Item Latini frenum dicunt, et tripodem, gladium, et loricam; Britones froin, trebeth, cledhif, et lhuric; unico unig, cane can, belua beleu."

I do not undertake to vouch for Giraldus' Bret-Welsh,

but Mr. Dimock gives the British words in their modern shape. He says that he does not understand where Giraldus found his *mis* and *tis* as Greek for *ego* and *tu*. I conceive that what Giraldus had got hold of was the modern plurals μεῖς and σεῖς. We must remember that in those centuries, setting aside men of exceptional learning like Roger Bacon, a man who wanted to pick up a few words of Greek would have more chance of getting them from an Italian sailor than from any scholar of Paris or new-born Oxford.

(2) Page 300.—I have collected a few passages of the way in which Addison speaks of these matters. The name "Gothic," glorious to us in one way from the memory of Ulfilas and Theodoric, and no less glorious in another way from its application, however strange, to the national architecture of England, Germany, and France, is with Addison always a word of contempt. In No. 63 the "heathen temple consecrated to the God of Dulness" is described as "a monstrous fabric built after the gothic manner, and covered with innumerable devices in that barbarous kind of sculpture." He goes in and sees "the deity of the place dressed in the habit of a monk." In No. 70 he has something to say about "the Gothic manner in writing," which, it seems, "pleases only such as have formed to themselves a wrong artificial taste upon little fanciful authors and writers of epigram." It is by a sort of Nemesis that we are told in the same paper that Homer wrote his poems, "in order to establish among the Greeks an union which was so necessary for their safety" in times when their "collection of many governments" "gave the Persian Emperor, who was their common enemy, many advantages over them by their mutual jealousies and animosities." It is however in this paper that he first calls attention to the real power of Chevy Chase, though in the

next paper (74), when he speaks of it, he winds up his criticisms with saying: "If this song had been written in the Gothic manner, which is the delight of all our little wits whether writers or readers, it would not have hit the taste of so many ages." One would be curious to know what epithet Addison would have given to the "manner" of the songs of Brunanburh and Maldon. In No. 98, not unfittingly following a paper about "Pharamond King of the Gauls"—who in another paper (480) has courtiers with French names—we find some strange kind of head-dress spoken of as a "Gothic building." To be sure in No. 329 Sir Roger is, one degree more respectfully, compared to "the figure of an old Gothic king."

Two graver passages are worth referring to, one (No. 415) where Addison compares the Pantheon at Rome with a "Gothic cathedral" and says "how little" any one "in proportion, is affected with the inside of the mediæval building, though it be five times larger than the other; which can arise from nothing else but the greatness of the manner in the one, and the meanness in the other." So, in No. 201, he takes upon himself to explain the origin of ecclesiastical vestments and ceremonies, which he accounts for in this fashion:—

"A Gothic bishop, perhaps, thought it proper to repeat such a form in such particular shoes or slippers; another fancied it would be very decent if such a part of public devotions was performed with a mitre on his head, and a crosier in his hand. To this a brother Vandal, as wise as the others, adds an antic dress, which he conceived would allude very aptly to such and such mysteries, till by degrees the whole office has degenerated into an empty show."

Did Addison really fancy Ulfilas sitting down to devise a particular kind of shoe?

(3) Page 301.—"It is not long ago that one of them, [English travellers] half unconsciously becoming the mouthpiece of a Russo-Scandinavian theory of history, talked with an odd air of spontaneous contempt of 'that mushroom nation the Lithuanians.' This is like talking of 'those parvenu families the Courtenays and the Derings;' and it is a singularly unfortunate hit, because every other word of the Lithuanian's speech happens to be a genuine and remarkable voucher of the very hoariest Aryan antiquity, sometimes pre-Homeric, and even pre-Vedic. One is almost tempted to wish the writer up to his neck in a Lithuanian swamp, banished to the Lithuanian backwoods to keep company with the last living verb in -mi, the last old-world bison, and perhaps the last patriot." Selected Writings of Viscount Strangford, i. 6.

(4) Page 307.—I take my parable from the opening sentence of Saxo Grammaticus; "Dan et Angul, a quibus Danorum cœpit origo, patre Humblo procreati, non solum conditores gentis nostræ, verum etiam rectores fuere." He goes on to tell how Angul gave his name to a province, and how his descendants afterwards passed into Britain, while Dan staid at home. His wife, it may be noticed, was "Grytha, summæ inter Theutones dignitatis matrona."

A West-Saxon may perhaps kick at this genealogy, but it ought to pass for orthodox in Yorkshire and Lincolnshire.

(5) Page 312.—See Hist. of Fed. Government, i. 404, 451.

(6) Page 312.—See Plutarch, Philopoimên, 21.

(7) Page 313.—See Hist. of Fed. Government, i. 226.

(8) Page 314.—While the language of Polybios is Attic so far as the forms of the words are concerned, the Arcadian and Eleian inscriptions in Boeckh (i. 705 et seqq.) have all more or less of a Doric tinge, and in some the digamma is kept on till a wonderfully late time. Thus in the inscription numbered 1520, one so late as to contain the name of Lucius Mummius, we find the name ϝασστύοχος written in very ancient letters, and Mr. Warren (Greek Federal Coinage, 45) quotes ϜΑLEIΩΝ as the legend on the coins of the city which in high-polite Attic was called Ἦλις, but which seems, even in the second century B.C., to have still called itself ϝᾶλις.

(9) Page 316.—The first stage of this struggle was between the Greek colonists and the Carthaginians, the second between the Eastern Emperors and the Saracens. In each case both the contending parties were swallowed up by the lords of the neighbouring part of Italy, in the first case by the Romans, in the second by the Normans.

(10) Page 316.—See Knight's Normans in Sicily, 244, 334.

(11) Page 316.—On the conquest of Marseilles by Charles of Anjou and the fearful vengeance taken on the defenders of the commonwealth, see the narrative of William of Nangis in D'Achery, Spicilegium, iii. 40.

(12) Page 317.—On the history of the Commonwealth of Cherson see Finlay, Byzantine Empire, i. 415. He refers to the fragment published by Hase in his notes to Leo the Deacon, p. 503. But it is well to give the description in full, because I do not see where Mr. Finlay found the words

"cherish the institutions of Hellas," though I do not doubt that they are borne out by the facts. The exact words of the Byzantine writer are: *οἱ δὲ, εἴτε ὡς μηδέποτε βασιλικῆς εὐνοίας ἀπολελαυκότες, μηδ' Ἑλληνικωτέρων τρόπων ἐπιμελούμενοι, αὐτονόμων δὲ μάλιστα ἔργων ἀντιποιούμενοι, εἴτε ὅμοροι ὄντες πρὸς τὸν κατὰ τὰ βόρεια τοῦ Ἴστρου βασιλεύοντα, μετὰ τοῦ στρατῷ ἰσχύειν πολλῷ καὶ δυνάμει μάχης ἐπαίρεσθαι, ἤθεσί τε τοῖς ἐκεῖ τὰ παρὰ σφῶν αὐτῶν οὐκ ἀποδιαφέροντες, ἐκείνων καὶ σπείσασθαι καὶ παραδώσειν σφᾶς ξυνέθεντο.* This is at the time of the submission of the city to the Russian Wladimir. The anonymous writer speaks of course from a purely Byzantine point of view. But it is odd to find him using the word Ἑλληνικός at all, as in those days the word Ἕλλην and its derivatives commonly meant *pagan*, as opposed to Christian. There is an example in page 464 of the same volume.

(13) Page 318.—On the exact position of Philip and Alexander with regard to Greece, I have said what I have to say in the Essay on Alexander in the Second Series of Historical Essays. But I will here quote the words of Bishop Thirlwall, v. 479. "The honour of a seat in the Amphictyonic council, though conferred on the king, reflected upon his people; it was equivalent to an act of naturalisation, which wiped off the stain of its semi-barbarian origin: the Macedonians might henceforward be considered as Greeks."

(14) Page 318.—See Strabo, v. 112; Appian, Mithr. 114. There is something strange in the look of the forms Γαλλόγραικοι and Γαλλογραικία.

(15) Page 319.—Some one may ask why I speak of "monumental stones" in a city of brickwork like Ravenna. It is

because the great brick churches of Ravenna, even those which were built or finished after the Byzantine reconquest, were built too early to have any Greek inscriptions. In Justinian's time Latin was still, at all events at Ravenna, the speech of the Roman Empire. The Greek inscriptions, including the epitaph of the Armenian Isaac at Saint Vital and those which are collected in a room in the Archbishop's palace, belong to a later period of the Exarchate. But both at Torcello and at Saint Mark's the Greek legend MP ΘΥ, if nothing else, is clear enough in the mosaics of the apses.

(16) Page 320.—See the passage of William of Poitiers which I have quoted and commented upon at vol. iv. p. 86 of the History of the Norman Conquest.

(17) Page 320.—I do not presume to go into the theology of the matter, but I conceive that historically the insertion of the "Filioque" in the Nicene Creed is to be looked on like any other interpolation in any other document.

(18) Page 323.—The epitaph of Nævius, written by himself and preserved by Aulus Gellius, i. 24,

> "Mortales immortales flere si foret fas,
> Flerent Divæ Camenæ Nævium poetam;
> Itaque, postquam est Orcino traditus thesauro
> Obliti sunt Romæ loquier Latinâ linguâ"

must be compared with the fragment of Ennius preserved by Cicero, De Claris Oratoribus, 18,

> "Quos olim Fauni vatesque canebant,
> Cum neque Musarum scopulos quisquam superarat,
> Nec dicti studiosus erat . . ."

The Roman Camenæ and the Greek Musæ are here carefully distinguished and opposed. On the revival of the real Latin literature with the Christian poets, see Mr. J. M. Neale in the History of Roman Literature in the Encyclopædia Metropolitana, 214. "It is a curious thing that, in rejecting the foreign laws in which Latin had so long gloried, the Christian poets were in fact merely reviving, in an inspired form, the early melodies of republican Rome;—the *rhythmical* ballads which were the delight of the men that warred with the Samnites, and the Volscians, and Hannibal."

(19) Page 324.—The Saturnian line of Nævius,

"Fato Metelli Romæ fiunt consules,"

and the answer to it,

"Dabunt malum Metelli Nævio poetæ,"

have surely much more in common with mediæval than with classical metres (See the song in honour of the Emperor Frederick in note 82 on Lecture IV.). The great poem on the battle of Lewes, the manifesto of the Liberal party in the thirteenth century, will be found in the Political Songs of England, published by the Camden Society, p. 72.

(20) Page 324.—See Livy, i. 26.

(21) Page 326.—I have somewhere seen these words put into the mouth of Queen Christina of Sweden.

(22) Page 329.—Compare Horace, Odes, iii. 3, 11; Virgil, Georg. i. 24–36; Lucan, i. 45–59. We are commonly called on to believe that the flattery of Lucan was sarcastic; but see Merivale, vi. 99.

(23) Page 329.—The visit of Athanaric to Constantinople is recorded by Ammianus (xxvii. 5) and Zôsimos (iv. 34), but it is only in Jornandes (28) that we find this remarkable speech put into his mouth: "Regiam urbem ingressus est, miransque, 'En,' inquit, 'cerno quod sæpe incredulus audiebam, famam videlicet tantæ urbis,' et, huc illuc oculos volvens, nunc situm urbis commeatumque navium, nunc mœnia clara prospectans, miratur, populosque diversarum gentium, quasi fonte in uno e diversis partibus scaturiente unda, sic quoque militem ordinatum aspiciens: 'Deus,' inquit, 'sine dubio terrenus est Imperator, et quisquis adversus eum manum moverit, ipse sui sanguinis reus exsistit.'"

(24) Page 329.—Orosius, at the very end of his work, records this famous declaration of Ataulf: "Nam ego quoque ipsi virum quendam Narbonensem, illustris sub Theodosio militiæ, etiam religiosum, prudentem, et gravem, apud Bethleem oppidum Palæstinæ beatissimo Hieronymo præsbytero referentem audivi se familiarissimum Atthaulfo apud Narbonum fuisse, ac de eo sæpe sub testificatione didicisse quod ille, quum esset animo, viribus, ingenioque nimius referre solitus esset se in primis ardenter inhiasse ut, obliterato Romano nomine, Romanum omne solum Gothorum imperium et faceret et vocaret, essetque, ut, vulgariter loquar, Gothia quod Romania fuisset, fieret nunc Atthaulfus quod quondam Cæsar Augustus. At ubi multa experientia probavisset neque Gothos ullo modo parere legibus posse propter effrenatam barbariam, neque reipublicæ interdici leges oportere, sine quibus respublica non est respublica, elegisse se saltem ut gloriam sibi de restituendo in integrum augendoque Romano nomine Gothorum viribus quæreret, habereturque apud posteros Romanæ restitutionis auctor, postquam esse non poterat inmutator."

(25) Page 329.—See Gibbon, c. lxv. (xli. 21, Milman).

(26) Page 331.—See the account of the repulse of Alaric from the walls of Athens by the appearance of Athênê and Achilleus, Zôsimos, v. 6. ἐπιὼν Ἀλάριχος πανστρατιᾷ τῇ πόλει τὸ μὲν τεῖχος ἑώρα περινοστοῦσαν τὴν πρόμαχον Ἀθηνᾶν, ὡς ἔστιν αὐτὴν ὁρᾶν ἐν τοῖς ἀγάλμασιν, ὡπλισμένην καὶ οἷον τοῖς ἐπιοῦσιν ἐνίστασθαι μέλλουσαν, τοῖς δὲ τείχεσι προεστῶτα τὸν Ἀχιλλέα τὸν ἥρω τοιοῦτον οἷον αὐτὸν τοῖς Τρωσὶν ἔδειξεν Ὅμηρος, ὅτε κατ' ὀργὴν τῷ θανάτῳ τοῦ Πατρόκλου τιμωρῶν ἐπολέμει. ταύτην ὁ Ἀλάριχος τὴν ὄψιν οὐκ ἐνεγκὼν πάσης μὲν ἀπέστη κατὰ τῆς πόλεως ἐγχειρήσεως, ἐπεκηρυκεύετο δέ.

(27) Page 331.—See Plutarch, Dêmêtrios, 10, for the title of Καταιβάτης given to Dêmêtrios at Athens, and the altar dedicated to him under that name, and, still more, the account of the flatteries offered to him given by Dêmocharês and the ithyphallics of Douris of Samos, in Athênaios, vi. 62, 63.

(28) Page 332.—Most of the Bulgarian Kings bear Hebrew names, as Simeon, Gabriel, and, above all, Samuel, whose power it was the great exploit of the Emperor Basil to break down.

(29) Page 332.—For the whole scene see Finlay, Byzantine Empire, i. 452.

(30) Page 334.—For the dealings of Hugh the Great with King Lewis from-beyond-Sea, see Norman Conquest, i. 217–220.

(31) Page 334.—See Gibbon, c. lxv. 12, 8, Milman.

(32) Page 335.—See Creasy, History of the Ottoman Turks, i. 241.

(33) Page 336.—In an Inaugural Address delivered to the University of Saint Andrews, March 19th, 1869, by James Anthony Froude, M.A., Rector of the University (London, Longmans and Co., 1869), the writer says (page 17) that "a young man going to Oxford learns the same things which were taught there two centuries ago." In page 18, he speaks of "the old Latin and Greek which the schools must keep to while the Universities confine their honours to these," and in page 28 he says:

"The training of clergymen is, if anything, the special object of Oxford teaching. All arrangements are made with a view to it. The heads of Colleges, the resident Fellows, Tutors, Professors, are, with rare exceptions, ecclesiastics themselves." See Saturday Review, April 3rd, 1869.

The year before the Right Honourable Robert Lowe made a speech in Lancashire in the same romantic vein.

"Speak to any man who has gone through the ordinary routine of education in a public school or university, or to any man of sense, and is he of opinion that he sees things through the medium of prejudice, or is he satisfied when he leaves those places of education that he is fairly equipped and armed for the combat of life? . . . . It is because that, at a time when there really was nothing to learn and nothing to know, a number of foundations were made for the purpose of teaching Latin and Greek, and these foundations exist up to the present day, and attract to them a number of scholars to the public schools. All manner of knowledge, science, language, and literature have come into existence since then, but these foundations, like their original deeds, have remained perfectly immovable." See Sat. Rev. February 8, 1868.

Again, at a dinner given by the Institution of Civil Engineers in April 1871, Mr. Lowe, according to the Times, said:

"My own education, and I had the happiness of receiving it at one of our public schools and Universities, was directed mainly to learning something of the literature and the language of a people who have long since passed away,—people who knew very little of nature, very little of the world in which they lived, very little, indeed, of anything except the squabbles and quarrels in which they engaged with one another, and which they carried on upon a scale the most minute. (A laugh.) When I think of the celebrated battle of Marathon and all our schoolboy enthusiasm about the 192 persons who perished on that occasion on the side of the victorious (a laugh), and compare it with the grand drama which has been enacted in another part of Europe within the last seven or eight months, I cannot help feeling how small were the matters to which our early attention was directed. Why, a good colliery accident, under the auspices of these professional gentlemen whom I see around me, would throw one of these great events of ancient times completely into the shade. (A laugh.)" See Sat. Rev. April 29, 1871.

I suppose that things like these may be safely said in the University of Saint Andrews, at the Institution of Civil Engineers, or at some Institution at Liverpool. But it would be curious to see what would happen, if Mr. Froude or Mr. Lowe were to venture to repeat them in the presence of any Oxford man who has taken his degree or has lived in the University within the last twenty years, or—as they exclude mathematics, no less than modern history and natural science—in the presence of any Cambridge man of any standing.

(34) Page 336.—I have been myself striving for years to bring about the foundation of a reasonable School of History at Oxford, instead of the absurd system by which certain periods of History are yoked to questions about the Objective and the Unconditioned, while other periods were till lately yoked to professional Law, and now stand apart from the periods which are still kept in bondage. Ten thousand statutes may be made, but all will be useless till Thucydides, Tacitus, Eginhard, the Chronicles, and Clarendon are taken up in a single school. In the like sort, there should be a School of Philology in which English and German should be taken up in their natural relations to Greek and Latin. While I have been striving in vain at Oxford, a real School of History seems likely to arise at Cambridge, and that largely, I would hope, through the labours of Mr. A. W. Ward.

# INDEX.

## B.



## C.

## D.

## G.

## J.



## K.

## L.

## M.

## N.

## O.



## P.

## R.

## T.

## U.

## Z.



THE END.

LONDON: PRINTED BY WILLIAM CLOWES AND SONS, STAMFORD STREET AND CHARING CROSS.

www.ingramcontent.com/pod-product-compliance
Lightning Source LLC
LaVergne TN
LVHW021304110826
845150LV00003B/474